HELL FOR LEATHER

Ronnie Bellew and Dermot Crowe

HELL FOR LEATHER

A Journey Through Hurling in 100 Games

HACHETTE
BOOKS
IRELAND

First published in 2014 by Hachette Books Ireland

Photograph Acknowledgements

The authors and publisher would like to thank the following for allowing the use of their photographs: GAA Library and Archive • Irish Photo Archive • National Library of Ireland • Irish Examiner • Waterford County Museum • Nicholas Furlong • Sportsfile • Inpho

Every effort has been made to contact all copyright holders. If any images used in this book have been reproduced without permission, we would like to rectify this in future editions and encourage owners of copyright material used but not acknowledged to contact us.

A CIP catalogue record for this title is available from the British Library.

ISBN: 978 14447 8991 1

Typeset in Century Schoolbook by Bookends Publishing Services, Dublin
Printed by Clays Ltd, St Ives plc

Hachette Books Ireland policy is to use papers that are natural, renewable and recyclable products and made from wood grown in sustainable forests. The logging and manufacturing processes are expected to conform to the environmental regulations of the country of origin.

Hachette Books Ireland
8 Castlecourt Centre, Castleknock, Dublin 15, Ireland

A division of Hachette UK Ltd
338 Euston Road, London NW1 3BH

www.hachette.ie

Contents

Introduction

This journey begins with the story of a man who walked many miles to play in the first All-Ireland hurling final watched by an estimated crowd of a few thousand who were separated from the action by nothing more than a chalk line around the perimeter of a field in Birr. It ends with arguably the finest tactician the game has ever known and one of the most celebrated hurlers of them all celebrating their 10th All-Ireland success in 16 seasons after a replay viewed by over 82,000 spectators and millions more on television and online across the globe.

The contrasting experiences of John (Jack) Lowry in April 1888, and Brian Cody and Henry Shefflin in September 2014 reflect how a sport that hovered near extinction in the decades after the Great Famine was revived to become a wonder of the modern sporting world. This book doesn't claim to be a history of hurling, nor is it a conventional compendium of classic games. Instead, we have used the framework of 100 games spanning 126 years to give a broad flavour of how hurling has evolved from the fragile beginnings of the 1880s – when two scores were enough to decide the first All-Ireland – through to this year's drawn All-Ireland final when 54 scores couldn't separate the teams after what was hailed as possibly the greatest game ever.

Hell for Leather revisits the games that saw Tipperary, Cork and Kilkenny become 'the big three', and also traces the emergence of Wexford, Limerick, Laois, Clare, Dublin, Galway, Waterford and Offaly as contenders. It highlights the matches that made legends of the great players and analyses how the swashbuckling hurling of old has given way to a tactically nuanced game that, when played at its best, straddles sport and art. And it also considers the more inglorious and controversial aspects of hurling, the nitty-gritty, the eccentric and the sometimes downright curious character of the game.

In truth, though, a work of this nature can only deal in a fleeting way with events and personalities that deserve deeper consideration and more scholarly analysis. The Kilkenny team – and their trainer Danny O'Connell – that won seven All-Irelands between 1904 and 1913 did much to reinvent hurling in that era, and would make a fascinating study. A biography is surely long overdue on the life of the Jim 'Tough' Barry, the opera-loving tailor who, as a trainer, had a hand in every Cork senior All-Ireland victory from 1926 to 1966. The 1930s – from Kilkenny and Cork playing three games to decide the 1931 championship to the same two counties playing out an eerie classic on the day the Second World War was declared – was truly the beginning of modern hurling and again merits an in-depth modern analysis.

Hurling has been well served, though, by its historians, writers and journalists, especially from the 1940s, and we drew on some of their writing in our own attempt to give a new twist to some old tales. They are too countless to mention, but it would be remiss not to acknowledge the debt we owe writers such as Brendan Fullam, Tom Ryall (Kilkenny), Seamus King, Tim Horgan (Cork) and Paul Rouse, as well as the influence of the departed denizens of the press box, including John D. Hickey of the *Irish Independent* and the doyen of them all the late Paddy Downey of *The Irish Times*. We hope this book will lead some readers back to these writers' chronicles and, in turn, maybe prompt new work on some of the territory we have travelled here. It's been a long journey and we have done enough talking – it's time to throw in the ball.

Ronnie Bellew and Dermot Crowe
October 2014

1. Easter Rising

1887 ALL-IRELAND FINAL (Hoare's Field, 1 April 1888)

Tipperary 1–1 (and one forfeit point) Galway 0–0

Old men have forgotten the miseries of the Famine and had their youth renewed by the sights and sounds that were evoked by the thrilling music of the camán, the well-directed stroke of the cul baire, or the swift stride of the Gaelic forward in his pursuit of the ball to victory.
Michael Davitt[1]

J OHN LOWRY MUST have been a very vexed man by the evening of Easter Sunday 1888. Not alone had his team lost the All-Ireland hurling final but, depending on which account you read, he had either been taken off or sent off in the first half – all this after apparently walking 20 miles to play against Tipperary in Birr. The Galway side, a combination from the Meelick and Killimor districts, had travelled to Birr by a 'brake' – a horse-drawn coach that could carry 25 passengers – but Lowry from Killimor had rendezvoused at the wrong crossroads and the team journeyed without him. Undeterred, he set off on foot. One version of the story has him walking alone;[2] another relates that he was accompanied by a second Galway player who had also missed the coach.[3] The different accounts of John (Jack) Lowry's day illustrate how elusive many of the details about the first All-Ireland final are. For that reason, some speculation is required when narrating the events before and during the milestone match in the mission to revive hurling.

Fixing the first All-Ireland hurling final for Easter Sunday, 1

April 1888, would have helped ensure a large attendance, but it's tempting to speculate that choosing that date was also a symbolic gesture by the GAA. The association may have swept the country 'like a prairie fire' after its foundation on 1 November 1884, but it was in turmoil for much of 1887 when the conflict between physical-force and ballot-box nationalist factions created a split that threatened to unravel the remarkable achievements of the previous two years. The intervention of the GAA's formidable patrons, Archbishop Croke and Michael Davitt, in early 1888 helped broker a temporary solution and also cleared the way for Tipperary and Galway to play the 1887 hurling final. After the bitterness of the previous year, Easter Sunday, with its message of resurrection and rebirth, was an apt date for the reconciled GAA's first inter-county championship final.

Despite the boardroom conflicts, the GAA had continued to function at local level during 1887 and while its athletics meetings drew the biggest crowds and generated the most publicity for the association, the year also saw the inauguration of the inter-county championships. Twelve counties were drawn to play each other in both hurling and football: Wicklow v. Clare, Wexford v. Galway, Dublin v. Tipperary, Cork v. Kilkenny, Waterford v. Louth and Kilkenny v. Meath. The ferment behind the scenes was reflected in the stop–start progress of the hurling championship which, because of objections and walkovers as well as internal disputes in Limerick and Cork, was eventually contested by just five teams.

Tipperary (Thurles) reached the final with 1–7 to 0–2 and 4–7 to 0–0 victories over Clare (Smith O'Brien's) and Kilkenny (Tullaroan). On the other side of the draw, Galway (Meelick) defeated Wexford (Castlebridge) by 2–8 to 0–1 in the semi-final at Elm Park in Mount Merrion, Dublin in July 1887. The game didn't lack physicality with one report stating there was 'a good deal of heated temper on both sides. The conduct of the Wexford men was severely censured by most of those present.'

The Dublin weekly *Sport* newspaper correspondent described the play as 'fast and fierce, intensely exciting, full of furious charges and stubborn repulses. Though the camán had been rusting for the past couple of years among the Bold Shelmaliers, the opposing captain paid them a high tribute by saying that in all their matches in their own county they never met tougher opponents than the Wexford men.' On hearing the result, Lord French, the owner of Elm Park, directed his steward to donate £3 to the Galway team's expenses and £2 to the Galway player – John Lowry again – who had lost his front teeth from a blow of a hurl to the face.[4]

The GAA's infighting during the autumn of 1887 gave Lowry and his team-mates plenty of time to recover before the decider against Tipperary. It was an appropriate pairing for the inaugural final as few counties had clung as doggedly to the traditional summer form of hurling in the decades after the Great Famine as Tipperary and Galway.

On Easter Monday 1884, Michael Cusack had taken his Dublin Metropolitan hurlers to Ballinasloe to play Killimor and while Cusack withdrew his players in protest at the 'rough tactics' of the Galway men, the meeting was an important landmark in the early standardising of rules for hurling. Eight months later, the first hurling game under the GAA's auspices is reputed to have been played in Galway on 6 January 1885 when teams from Killimor and Ballinakill clashed for a 'plate of 10 guineas at Tynagh'.[5]

A year later, representative teams from North Tipperary and South Galway had played a match, billed as 'the championship of Ireland', in the Phoenix Park on 9 February 1886. Organised by Michael Cusack, this was the first major hurling game played in Dublin for 74 years and drew a sizeable attendance – when the park rangers had been persuaded by Cusack to open the gates, which had been locked amid warnings that a large crowd was approaching, armed with 'clubs [hurls] and battering rams [goalposts]'[6] intent on attacking the Lord Lieutenant's residence.

Cusack himself refereed the game, which was won by Tipperary, and he described it as 'a fine specimen of vigorous hurling ...

which gave a great stimulus [to the game] in Dublin'. The Dublin *Sport* correspondent was impressed with the occasion and the fine physique of the players, but bemoaned the absence of 'science' in the hurling style which he labelled 'crude and primitive'. Cusack dismissed that critique as being typical of what one would expect from 'the haters and traducers of our race'.

'Primitive' was a provocative choice of word, but the *Sport* correspondent's observation about the absence of science rings true. Compared to the modern inter-county game, the 21-a-side hurling played in the early years of the GAA was a rough diamond. The rudiments are similar, but there are vast differences between then and now in everything from team formations and playing equipment to the size of the scoring area and basic rules of the game.

Pitches – up to 196 x 140 yards – were larger; the hurls were longer with a much narrower bas and the sliotars far heavier. The scoring area in 1888 was similar to that still used by Australian Rules, the main difference being the GAA's addition of a crossbar. Under the early rules, the goalposts were set 21 feet apart with the crossbar 10 and a half feet high. 'Points posts' were provided seven yards each side of the goalposts and any shot that passed over the crossbar or between these posts counted as a point. Forfeit points were also awarded if a team played the ball over its own end line. The 1888 Rules of Hurling prohibited players from carrying the ball in the hand or lifting the ball off the ground; players could carry the ball on the hurl and were allowed catch a ball in play off the ground or from the air. Wrestling between two players while play continued elsewhere on the field was permitted until 1887.

The science and rules of hurling were refined over the following decade but, in 1888, tactics were still largely non-existent. In the early years, 'the most rousing spectacle in many games was provided by the tearaway downfield charge of fiery forwards and burly midfield men sweeping the ball and their opponents before them, often to initiate goalmouth struggles that were simply awe-inspiring,' wrote the GAA historian Seamus Ó Ceallaigh.[7] This hair-raising tactic seems to have been pioneered by Cusack himself. The formation of his Metropolitan hurling team was: goalkeeper, eight backs, six 'centres' (midfielders) and six forwards. The centres and forwards were coached to attack in the form of a wedge, with the wingmen circling and holding possession of the ball until it was driven over the enemy lines. The task of actually scoring fell to the speedy and skilful 'whips' – the equivalent of modern wing or corner-forwards – who kept their distance from the rolling mêlées and mauls, awaiting the breaking ball and the opportunity of an unhindered shot on goal. Judging by the scorelines, these opportunities were rare and just two scores (and one forfeit point) were enough to decide the 1887 final when the rules still dictated that a goal was worth more than any number of points.

Galway, though, might have claimed the first All-Ireland without pucking a ball and one account maintains they were actually awarded the title.[8] They had arrived in Birr at the appointed hour, but with no sign of the opposition and rumours that Tipperary weren't travelling, they adjourned to Cunningham's Hotel for refreshments which may have included something stronger than tea.

Tipp's tardiness was down to a row with county board officials over outstanding travelling expenses. The upshot was that seven Thurles town players, including team captain Denis Maher, were left behind on the platform at Thurles railway station. Maher was replaced as captain by Jim Stapleton, another Thurles player. On arriving in Birr, Stapleton led his men to Cunningham's Hotel where, after a parley, Captain James Lynam, Galway's non-playing captain, agreed to play the game.

Captain Lynam had received his officer's commission during the American Civil War and when the players 'had dressed themselves in Gaelic costume' – Galway in white jerseys with green stripes, Tipp in green – he marshalled the teams in military fashion, 'ordered them to fall into line and marched them down the town to the field'. Hoare's Field, close to the present-day St Brendan's Park, was the venue and the attendance was estimated at 5,000.

'Special trains carried crowds of people from Tipperary, Queen's County [Laois] and King's County [Offaly] to Birr, and East Galway seemed to have turned out to a man to escort the Meelick hurlers to the scene of strife,' reported the *Freeman's Journal*.

The ball was thrown in at 3 p.m. and after the early exchanges saw play 'whizzing up and down the field, now threatening one goal and now another', one of the Tipperary 'whips' scored a point in the 11th minute. Six minutes later, according to the *Freeman's Journal*, a Galway player – identified in some accounts as John Lowry[9] – 'had to be put out for tripping. From 15 past to half-time, the play was simply fierce and when Thurles whips were carrying the ball towards Galway posts, the Galway hurler who had been put out for foul play rushed in and struck the ball to one of his colleagues.' The referee, Patrick White, a Toomevara man resident in Birr, threatened to award the game to Tipperary if there were any more incursions.

Most of the annals agree on the identity of the player who scored Tipperary's winning goal. That honour fell to Tommy Healy from Coolcroo who struck the decisive score after receiving a pass from Jim Stapleton. The *Midland Tribune* reporter summed up the second half and winning goal as follows:

> The game was renewed with increased energy and some wonderful feats in manly powers were exhibited on both sides. The playing of Messrs Ryan and Stapleton (Thurles) and Larkin and Cosgrove (Meelick) was much admired. One of the Tipp men, Healy, by means of a dexterous left-hander, sent the ball flying from the middle of the field thus scoring a goal for Thurles.

Tipperary never looked back. The county's tally of All-Ireland titles had already increased to six by the turn of the century; in contrast, Galway didn't appear in another All-Ireland final until 1923. Many of the players who played in Birr were involved in the Land War campaign which was exceptionally bitter in southeast Galway. The Meelick captain, Pat Madden, was evicted from his home six months after the All-Ireland final and local lore relates that on the morning of the eviction, he gave the hurl he'd played with in Birr to the local postman for safekeeping.[10] A century or so later, Pat Madden's hurl found a final resting place, fittingly enough in the GAA Museum in Thurles where it sits alongside other mementos of the first All-Ireland final and the elusive men who made hurling history.

TIPPERARY (Thurles selection): J. Stapleton (capt), T. Burke, N. Murphy, P. Leahy, J. Dunne, A. Maher, M. Maher, N. Bowe, J. Mockler, T. Stapleton, J. Dwyer, T. Carroll, M. Carroll, T. Maher, D. Ryan, J. Ryan, J. Leamy, T. Healy, T. Dwyer, N. Lambe, M. McNamara.

GALWAY: P. Madden (capt), P. Cullen, M. Mannion, J. Colohan, J. Scally, W. Madden, T. Hanley, J. Kelly, P. Mannion, J. Connolly, J. Cosgrove, A. Cosgrove (Meelick); J. Lowry, J. Callinan, P. Haverty, T. Foley, O. Griffin, P. Larkin, J. Manning, C. Melody, J. Sanders (Killimor).

Referee: P. White (Offaly)

Attendance: 5,000

2. Building a Dynasty

1890 ALL-IRELAND FINAL (Clonturk Park, 16 November)

Cork (Aghabullogue) 1–6 Wexford (Castlebridge) 2–2

---

*Corkmen were hurling and winning All-Irelands before the GAA was even
formed. In 1882 my grandfather, Tommy Leahy from Blackrock, was captain
when Cork Nationals won the All-Ireland Hurling Challenge Cup. For many
years, the cup, a pretty large one, was in a public house in Douglas and the
names of the 21 players were engraved on it with 'Tommy Leahy' as captain.*
Pearse Leahy, Lord Mayor of Cork, 1969[1]

THERE IS NO mention in any of the GAA annals of the
1882 All-Ireland Hurling Challenge Cup, but Mayor Leahy
was correct in his assertion about the pre-GAA tradition of
hurling in Cork city and environs.

In 1876, a notable series of games were played between
Carrigaline and hurlers from the St Finbarr's parish and Blackrock
districts of the city. After defeating Carrigaline, the Barrs defeated
Blackrock in a fiery decider and the club date their official founding
to that year, while Blackrock Hurling Club was officially formed
in 1883. The Rockies and the Barrs went on to form – along with
Glen Rovers – Cork hurling's 'big three', but it was Aghabullogue,
a country club situated 15 miles north of the city in the district of
Muskerry, that won Cork's first hurling All-Ireland.

Homecomings for All-Ireland-winning Cork teams tend to be
raucous, mass celebrations of the Rebels' pre-eminent position in the
hurling world, but there was no victory reception for the wounded
warriors who returned to the Lee in mid-November 1890.

Not many people in the city were aware that the All-Ireland final had even taken place. Most interest centred on the Bostock and Bailey circus on the Western Road and in *Randolph the Reckless* which was playing to large crowds in the Opera House.[2]

If it had been a city side returning in triumph, the reaction would surely have been different, but Aghabullogue were what today would be described as an unfashionable club, and the indifference towards their achievement may also be connected with the split in Cork GAA during 1889 and 1890 when there were three separate 'county boards' operating in the county.

Nationally, the GAA had again been riven by division, as a fresh conflict about alleged IRB–Fenian infiltration of the association's executive led to a clerical boycott in some parts of the country and the subsequent disaffiliation of hundreds of clubs. The divisions in Cork were further complicated in 1889 when the county board president, Fr O'Connor resigned and a number of clubs, including St Finbarr's and Blackrock, formed the 'O'Connor Board' in support. This board – supported by another disaffected group in north Cork – organised its own hurling championship in 1889, with St Finbarr's defeating Blackrock in the final.

Aghabullogue were one of the few senior hurling clubs to remain loyal to the official Cork county board and easily won the official 1890 county championship before defeating Kilmoyley of Kerry 2–0 to 0–1 in the Munster final, one of just four games played in the 1890 All-Ireland championship. Wexford (Castlebridge) and Laois were the only two counties to field teams in Leinster, and Castlebridge won by 2–9 to 0–3 to qualify for the All-Ireland final at Clonturk Park in Drumcondra on 16 November. Played in front of an estimated 1,000 spectators, the game was described as 'very rough' by the *Freeman's Journal*.

The Castlebridgemen played a reckless game with the result that several of the Aghabullogue players were knocked out of action. The Cork men played in their bare feet and appear to have been the better team. They were faster and more skilful hurlers. In the first half, they scored 1–3 against one point. In the second half, the game became rougher and with the permission of the referee, the Aghabullogue captain Dan Lane withdrew his team from the field with the score at 1–6 to 2–2. On the recommendation of the referee [John Sheehy, Kerry], the Central Council awarded the match to Cork.

Cork hurling historian Tim Horgan wrote:

Shortly after the restart, the Castlebridge men began to tackle dangerously and instil terror into players and spectators alike. Two goals came of their efforts and it looked as though Aghabullogue would go down in the face of this tough approach. But Wexford went a step too far. After several players had suffered minor bruises, a Cork forward was downed openly as he broke past the Castlebridge defenders and, while he lay groaning on the ground, a second Cork man was struck. At this, a Wexford umpire ran on to the pitch and told the referee that the men were shamming, but on examining both players, the referee immediately abandoned the match. 'I can't allow this exhibition of savagery to continue,' he said.[3]

It's claimed that eight Cork men were injured, four requiring medical attention, and while the All-Ireland final ended in a disputed fashion, there was no doubting the value of Aghabullogue's victory. They had been one of the premier teams in Cork for several years. They had beaten Killenaule by 14 points when a group of Tipperary clubs 'invaded' Cork for a famous tournament played in August 1886; the following year they defeated St Finbarr's in another tournament final and 'for several years after 1890, Aghabullogue maintained a first-class team', wrote John T. Power, an early Cork hurling historian.[4]

He based his history of the first decades in Cork hurling on conversations with old-timers who could remember battles back into the 1870s, and his chapter on Aghabullogue gives character and colour to men who would otherwise remain ghostly figures in the story of hurling. Team captain Dan Lane, for example, was 'swift and courageous, a mighty hard man to pass with a ball. He always advocated what was to become a first principle in Cork hurling – pulling on the ball.' Vice-captain Jeremiah Henchion was a 'midfield man of great strength and daring [and] had sweeping pucks of surpassing length. In Clonturk Park, Wexford had three men marking him. Henchion was a worthy champion. Tom Twomey, the village schoolmaster was perhaps the outstanding ball-player of the lot. His beautiful overhead play was of a kind seldom seen in the old days. Tom Good too was a splendid hurler. He had that delightful trick of sweeping up the field with the ball hopping on his hurley brought to a fine art. Tom played little hurling after his match with Wexford as he soon afterwards left the country for Australia, where he died some years later.'

Many of his team-mates joined him in exile.

One after another they went to America, England and Australia; few of them ever saw home again. The turn of the century marked the end of the parish as a force in Cork hurling. Still, Aghabullogue had its day and won a proud position among the grand old pioneers of the GAA as well as that highest of all honours, a place among the hurling champions.

CORK (Aghabullogue): D. Lane (capt), D. Drew, M. Horgan, T. Good, J. Lenihan, T. Kelleher, J. Henchion, D. Linehan, D. Horgan, D. Looney, J. Buckley, T. Twomey, P. Buckley, J. O'Reilly, J. O'Sullivan, J. Kelleher, D. O'Sullivan, P. O'Riordan, T. O'Connor, P. O'Brien, E. O'Reilly.

WEXFORD (Castlebridge): Nick Daly (capt), E. Leacy, L. Leacy, T. Devereaux, O. Daly, J. Murphy, W. Neville, J. Murphy, P. McDonald, J. Rossiter, W. Furlong, J. O'Leary, W. Doran, G. Sinnott, P. Furlong, P. Devereaux, W. Fortune, G. Browne, M. Browne, J. Fogarty, W. O'Leary.

Referee: J. Sheehy (Kerry)

Attendance: 2,000

Alone it stands: Kerry's hurling All-Ireland

The 1891 All-Ireland championship was resolved in just five games with Ballyduff emerging victorious to claim Kerry's sole All-Ireland hurling title. In Munster, they were 2–7 to 0–3 winners over Blackrock, who led Cork to two All-Ireland titles in 1893 and 1894. The Kerry men lost by a point to Limerick in the Munster final but successfully appealed the result and then won the re-fixture by 2–4 to 0–1.

Awaiting them in the All-Ireland final were Crossbeg from Wexford who had defeated Dublin in the only fixture played in Leinster. Played at Clonturk Park, Drumcondra, on 28 February 1892, the teams were level at 1–1 apiece approaching the final whistle. Wexford were awarded a free and the ball was sailing true and high for a point when the referee Patrick Tobin of Dublin blew for full-time, insisting that time was up before the ball had reached the posts.

Half an hour of extra-time was played with Kerry, playing in their bare feet, winning by 2–3 to 1–5. By all accounts, it was stirring stuff with the *Kerry Sentinel* describing the hurling as 'muscular' and the teams as 'fast, wiry and long-winded … strong and scientific'. Local legend relates that a grand total of six Kerry supporters travelled to Dublin for the game.

The team was captained by John Mahony who died just short of his 80th birthday in 1944. His obituary in *The Kerryman* stated that 'it was a never failing source of regret to him that whilst football was brought to the peak of perfection it has reached in the county, hurling was utterly neglected and relegated to the background'.

3. The First Invincibles

1895 ALL-IRELAND FINAL (Jones's Road, 15 March 1896)

Tipperary (Tubberadora) 6–8 Kilkenny (Tullaroan) 0–1

Ably led by the strong and fearless Mikey Maher, the style of the Tipperary hurlers was fast, free and open, and their positional work perfect. In every unit, there was sting and dash; in every line there was ability and method. With such a gallant combination, it looks as if Tipperary is going to make some history in the ancient pastime.

Newspaper account, quoted by Philip Fogarty[1]

THIS WAS AN auspicious day for the GAA and Tipperary as an estimated 8,000 spectators paid in to the City and Municipal Sports Grounds on Jones's Road to watch the first All-Ireland finals played at what is now Croke Park. Arravale Rovers defeated Pierce O'Mahonys (Meath) by 0–4 to 0–3 to win the football title and Tubberadora routed Tullaroan to complete the Tipp double. Tullaroan were game opponents until half-time when they trailed by 1–6 to 1–0, but they were overwhelmed after the break. Pat Riordan of Drombane is credited with scoring all of Tubberadora's six goals and eight points which would make him the record scorer in any All-Ireland final, but match reports and statistics back then weren't the forensic affairs of today and Riordan's record has never been officially acknowledged.

The *Freeman's Journal* reported that 'there is not much to be said about the hurling match and for an All-Ireland championship, the display was a very poor one. This may be accounted for by the very weak team Tullaroan placed on the field and by the very unsuitable ground Jones's Road is for hurling. The Tubberadora men proved themselves masters of the situation early in the match, a lengthy description of which is impossible with such a score.'

Tubberadora built on the 1895 victory to become hurling's first invincibles. They won three All-Ireland titles in four years and never lost a championship game. They scored 71 goals and 108 points in 14 championship appearances and conceded just 17–46. If it hadn't been for a training-ground injury and subsequent withdrawal of the team from the 1897 Tipperary championship, they would surely have won hurling's first four-in-a-row. These achievements are all the more phenomenal when you consider that the spine of the team came from one townland in the northern end of what is now Boherlahan-Dualla parish. 'You look for the centre of their greatness and you find no town, no village there – just a townland of a mere dozen houses crossed from north to south by the Cashel–Thurles road, lying a mile from Boherlahan village and three miles from Holycross. Eight players who won no less than 28 All-Ireland medals came from five houses on this road,' wrote the late Raymond Smith.[2]

This group of players created a new mystique around Tipperary hurling. They were innovators who raised the game to new standards. In that sense, they were a vital link in the making of hurling as we know it today. 'Hurling was now settling down to a game of speed, skill with discipline and self-control,' wrote the renowned GAA writer P.D. Mehigan (Carbery) about this period. 'Hurlers togged out well, wore studded hurling shoes and kept their camáns clear of dangerous hoops. The corner had been turned.'[3]

For a few years in the early 1890s, it had looked as though hurling and the GAA would never turn the corner. The split in the Irish Home Rule Party in 1891 following the revelation of Charles Stewart Parnell's affair with Kitty O'Shea almost destroyed the association. The GAA executive remained loyal to Parnell, but the Home Rule Party split created divisions that saw hundreds of clubs divide and disband. These divisions also coincided with an economic recession which had led to renewed emigration.

It's little wonder then that the hurling championships of the early 1890s were low-key affairs contested by a handful of counties. Cork selections (Redmonds and Blackrock twice) completed a three-in-a-row between 1892 and 1894, but just three counties competed in the 1892 and 1893 championships, while only five fulfilled fixtures in 1894.

The GAA, however, experienced a steady resurgence in the middle years of the decade. Tipperary reorganised itself as a hurling power and Boherlahan-Dualla must have been teeming with hurlers because three teams from the district entered the 1895 county championship. Two of the three, Tubberadora and Suir View Rangers, met in the county final, with Tubberadora winning in extra-time after their captain Mikey Maher had inspired an equalising surge during the second half.

Any telling of the Tubberadora story centres around Maher, who won five All-Ireland medals and is the only Tipperary player to have captained three All-Ireland-winning teams. He appears to have been a force of nature on the field and a shrewd and charismatic general off it. P.D. Mehigan described him as 'a thundering man, 6 foot 2 and 15 stone hard trained', and added: 'Of the 100 All-Ireland captains I have seen, for inspired leadership and dynamic force in a crisis, I'll give the palm to Big Mikey of Tubberadora.'

Even though Tubberadora rampaged to victory in three All-Ireland finals, Big Mikey and his men had to negotiate several crises and close encounters in Munster. In the 1896 Munster final against Ballyhea of Cork, Tubberadora were 1–3 to 0–0 down, but they rallied and the Cork team walked off the field with 20 minutes left. Tipperary were awarded the title, but Ballyhea launched a successful objection. Neither side could agree on a neutral venue so, for the first and only time, a Munster hurling final was played outside the province. Jones's Road hosted the unique contest in January 1898 – Tubberadora swatting the Cork side aside by 7–9 to 2–3. Three months later, they ran in 8–14 in the All-Ireland final against Dublin Commercials (0–4).

Tubberadora withdrew from the 1897 championship after one of their players broke his leg in training. The injury caused such upset in their ranks that they sought and received permission from the board to withdraw. They returned to action the following year and the 1898 Munster final is considered the first classic in that competition. Tubberadora were back to their best in sweeping all before them in Tipperary while Blackrock retained some of the side who had won back-to-back All-Irelands for Cork earlier in the decade. As usual with fixtures in this era, the championship was behind schedule and the game was fixed for Dungarvan on 17 October 1899.

> Accompanied by the Cashel band, the Tubberadora team left Thurles to win back for Tipperary the prestige lost in 1897. The excursion train was crowded and broke down outside Kilmeaden. After a delay of two hours the train moved off, the hurlers stripped on the way and after this unwelcome experience made the bravest show of their career.[4]

Blackrock led by 2–2 to 0–0 at half-time, but barnstorming finishes were a Tubberadora trademark. Canon Philip Fogarty, the first Tipperary hurling historian, described what happened:

> Then there was the Tipperary finish and those were the days in which it was awaited and dreaded. It came as expected. A few attempts to take the Cork stronghold failed by inches; they were just a preliminary to the final rally which was a massed relentless drive that tore through stubborn enemy ranks and sent the green flag waving – Tubberdora! Tipperary 3–0, Cork 2–3.[5]

The replay at Kilmallock attracted a record crowd, but there was no logistical mishap on this occasion to knock the Tipperary champions off their stride and they won by 1–13 to 1–2.

The 1898 All-Ireland final, played at Jones's Road in March 1900, was a rematch of the 1895 final against the admirably persistent Kilkenny, represented this time by a Three Castles-led combination. It was 3–5 to 2–5 at half-time before goals from Denis

Walsh turned the game for Tubberadora who were assisted by Tim Condon, Jim O'Keefe and Dick O'Keefe from Horse and Jockey. It was the highest scoring hurling final – 7–13 to 3–10 – to date. The openness and marked skill of the play, commented on in the match reports, was evidence of how rule changes were beginning to refine and speed up the game.

Shortly after the 1898 victory, the leading citizens of Cashel honoured their country cousins with an official reception and set of silver watches. 'We recognised in you the ablest and most scientific exponents of our national game,' declared the official address. 'We admired your splendid discipline, your manly bearing, your good fellowship ... We hoped and prayed that Ireland might learn from you what can be done at home when we stand together as you did under the banner of temperance and mutual esteem.'[6]

While Tubberadora disbanded as a club in 1900, its spirit lived on. When Tipperary ended an eight-year wait for a title in 1916, the team was captained by Johnny Leahy of Tubberadora and included his younger brother Paddy, as well as Denis Walsh who had won the first of his five All-Ireland medals in 1895. Paddy Leahy went on to become one of the godfathers of Tipperary hurling, and was involved in eight Tipperary All-Ireland victories between 1949 and 1965. Michael Maher, a nephew of Big Mikey, played in the last five of those Tipperary victories between 1958 and 1965.

Big Mikey himself moved away from Tubberadora in 1918 after acquiring a farm in Gleneffy in County Limerick.

When he died in 1947, many of [his friends from Boherlahan] travelled there to help carry his giant frame to its last resting place in Tipperary's St Michael's Cemetery. To his neighbours at Gleneffy, he had been a big, soft-spoken, kindly man who worked hard and was a well-liked neighbour. But to the men of his native place, who knew him in his prime, he was Cu Chulainn and Napoleon and Matt the Thresher. He was Big Mikey and there would never be his like again.[7]

TIPPERARY (Tubberadora): M. Maher (capt), E. Maher, Phil Byrne,
W. Kerwick, John Maher, D. Walsh, J. Walsh, P. Maher, T. Flanagan, J. Flanagan,
P. Riordan, J. Gleeson, F. Moriarty, J. Connolly, J. Maher, E. Brennan,
W. Devane.

KILKENNY (Tullaroan): M. Dalton, P. Maher, J. Lalor, E. Teehan, E. Dunne,
P. Egan, P. Ryan, M. Coogan, M. Meagher, J. Walsh, W. Walsh, J. Dunne,
P. Malone, J. Grace (capt), J. Doheny, T. Grace, J. Doheny.

Referee: J.J. Kenny (Dublin)

Attendance: 8,000

Tipp's difficulty is Limerick's opportunity

Tubberadora's absence from the 1897 All-Ireland championship
offered a reprieve to the teams they had smitten in the previous
two years. Limerick – a Kilfinane selection backed up by players
from Cappamore, Ballingarry, Caherline and Croom – had
an easy victory – 4–9 to 1–6 – over Cork in the Munster final.
Kilkenny (Tullaroan) were equally clear victors in Leinster,
defeating Dublin 6–13 to 1–4 in the semi-final replay and
receiving a walkover from Wexford in the final.

The final was played in Tipperary on 20 November 1898 with
Limerick, captained by Denis Grimes, overturning a 2–4 to 1–1
half-time deficit to win by 3–4 to 2–4. The team's vice-captain
was Sean Óg Hanley who was rated by the old-time hurling
writers as one of the finest full-backs ever to play the game. He
emigrated to England and played on the losing London teams in
the 1900 and 1903 finals.

4. Exiles in Excelsis

1901 ALL-IRELAND FINAL (Jones's Road, 2 August 1903)

London (Emmets) 1–5 Cork (Redmonds) 0–4

The victory of the London-Irish has aroused many strange feelings; and while none will be ungracious or ungenerous enough to begrudge them their well-deserved honours, many Gaels will have a strange misgiving regarding the fact that the hurling champions are the selected best of the English province of the GAA.

Sport (8 August 1903)

O LIVER CROMWELL WATCHED a game of hurling on May Day 1654 in Hyde Park, London, but alas it wasn't hurling as we know it. The game the great bogeyman of Irish history viewed was Cornish hurling which involves throwing and passing a silver ball; elements of wrestling were also central to the game-plan. 'On this day there was the hurling of a great ball by 50 Cornish gentlemen on the one side and 50 on the other; one party playing in red caps and the other in white,' reported the *London Moderate Intelligencer* in May 1654. 'There was present his Highness the Lord Protector [Cromwell], many of his privy council and divers eminent gentlemen to whose view was presented great agility of body and most neat and exquisite wrestling ... The ball they played for was silver and designed for the party that won the goal.'

It's been speculated that the 50 players opposing the 'Cornish gentlemen' were Irish. It's certainly a possibility because there are records of 'proper' hurling matches between Irish and Cornish selections in this period when stick and ball games such as bando (bandy) were played in Cornwall and Wales. There are several songs and stories in Wexford folk tradition about teams from the county travelling across the water to play hurling games in Cornwall. One story has William of Orange watching such a contest and exclaiming come on or up the 'yellowbellies' to salute the valour of the Wexfordmen who wore yellow sashes around their waists to distinguish themselves from their Cornish opponents.[1] Another version of this story set a few decades later recounts how the Wexford men, while physically slighter than their opponents, played like men possessed after being given a pre-match nip of whiskey by their manager, the hurling-mad Squire Caesar Colclough of Tintern Hall.[2]

The stories about the origin of the 'Yellowbellies' nickname aren't just quaint historical puzzles or curiosities, they also illustrate the richness of hurling lore from the 17th to late 18th centuries, when Irishmen brought their game with them to England and beyond. There are stories of the Wild Geese playing hurling in Paris in the mid-18th century, watched on one occasion by Louis XV who was so impressed by the play of Thomas O'Gorman of Clare that he commissioned him an officer in the French army.[3] There is a detailed account of Irishmen regularly playing organised hurling in fields at the back of the British Museum in London in the late 18th century[4] an era when hurling matches were also played in New York City.[5]

Hurling was flourishing in London by the end of the 19th century when thousands of Irishmen emigrated to work on construction projects in the then largest city in the world. In 1900, England was admitted as a province of the GAA leading to restructured All-Ireland finals with the winners of the 'home' final playing London for ultimate honours. By 1902, London had assembled a formidable team of Munster exiles, including: Sean Óg Hanley, Limerick's 1897 All-Ireland captain; the Horgan brothers, Dan and Michael, who had won an All-Ireland with Cork in 1891; and the athlete Jack Coughlan from Tulla.

Despite this, London were complete underdogs when they played Tipperary in the 1900 All-Ireland final (played in October 1902). After close shaves against Cork and Kilkenny, Tipperary had steamrolled Galway by 6–13 to 1–5 in the home final and were expected to make equally quick work of the exiles who had arrived at the North Wall at 2 a.m. on the morning of the game following a rough crossing.

The passage from Holyhead, however, seemed to have little effect on London who led by five points with three minutes remaining of a game described by the *Freeman's Journal* as 'the best, the closest and the fastest we have ever seen in an All-Ireland final'. The Tipperary team included Mikey Maher from Tubberadora and he is credited with leading Tipperary's ferocious winning rally. 'At three minutes to go, a Londoner committed a foul and this gave Tipperary a free which they made good use of and in a twinkling the green flag went up for a goal,' reported the *Freeman's Journal*. 'Half a minute later, they came on with one of their headlong charges and smashing down the London defence made another major.' The two 'majors' gave Tipperary a fortunate 2–5 to 0–6 victory.

The exiles made amends a year later when they lined out at Jones's Road against Cork for the 1901 decider. Eight Cork men faced their native county with the remainder of the London team comprising four players from Clare, three from Limerick and one apiece from Tipperary and Kerry – the Kerry man being Ned Barrett from Ballyduff, who went on to win Olympic medals in wrestling and tug-of-war for Great Britain at the 1908 London Olympics.

Cork had beaten Galway by 7–12 to 1–3 in the semi-final and Wexford by 2–8 to 0–6 in a stormy home final. Cork, however, may have been fatally complacent about the London challenge. The game was played in a downpour which was also offered as an excuse for the Rebels' shock defeat with some reports suggesting they were ill-shod for the conditions. 'The weather militated against such a test as the popular mind would wish and certainly the Cork team had every reason to feel dissatisfied with the conditions prevailing on Sunday,' reported the Dublin weekly *Sport*. 'They were such – a sodden ground, incessant rain and a greasy ball – as to utterly spoil the combination of and play of Cork teams, who with a dry sod and an active ball, can develop a game which, at its best, few can beat. The London team, on the other hand, adapted themselves well to the conditions and seemed perfectly at home in the wet. While Cork missed running balls frequently, failed repeatedly to secure that favourite "drop puck" and "doubling stroke", London missed but rarely and by times, though fielding badly, showed excellent passing tactics which led up to a few of their scores.'

The woe was compounded for a party of Cork supporters who set out but never arrived for the final after their train was trapped behind a slow-moving British troop train from Limerick Junction to Dublin.

> The supporters arrived just in time to hear that the game was over and that London had won. The fact that eight of the London-Irishmen were Cork men by birth was no consolation at all. If anything, it made defeat even harder to bear.[6]

The Rebels exacted severe revenge on the Londoners a year later when Cork was en fête for the opening of the city's new Athletic Grounds, which hosted the 1902 All-Ireland final in September 1904. Apart from Jamesy Kelleher and the other Dungourney stars, such as Jimmy Ronayne, the Cork combination included two of the famed Coughlans and Steva Riordan from Blackrock as well as Billy O'Neill (Sarsfields), an all-round sportsman who played rugby for Cork Constitution and later competed in marathons. Cork led by 3–5 to 0–0 at half-time and added five more points in the second half as London failed to raise a flag.

Cork retained the title the following year with an 8–9 to 0–9 drubbing of Kilkenny in the home final followed by another lashing (3–16 to 1–1) to London in the final proper. Andy 'Dooric' Buckley is credited with scoring 7–4 of the tally for a Blackrock–Dungourney–Sarsfields–Redmonds–St Finbarr's combination that P.D. Mehigan (Carbery) rated as 'perhaps the finest side of skilled sticksmen yet seen in the GAA'.[7]

LONDON: D. Horgan, M. Horgan, J. Lynch, C. Crowley, J. Barry, J. O'Brien, Jer Kelliher, T. Barry (all Cork); J. Coughlan (capt), P. King, J. King, J. O'Brien (all Clare); J. O'Connell, J. Fitzgerald, T. Doody (all Limerick); M. McMahon (Tipperary), E. Barrett (Kerry).

CORK: P. Cantillon (capt), J. Ronayne, J. Leonard, D. McGrath, J. Kelleher, T. Hallahan, J. O'Neill, D. O'Keeffe, T. Powell, M. O'Reilly, J. Barrett, W. Sheehan, P. Sullivan, J. O'Leary, D. Daly, C. Young, J. Delea.

Referee: J. McCarthy (Kilkenny)

Hurler and horseman: Jamesy Kelleher (1878–1943)

Decades after he finished playing, Jamesy Kelleher of Dungourney was an automatic selection on teams of the all-time great hurlers, usually at centre-back or in the full-back line. Standing five foot eight and of light build, what he lacked in bulk he more than compensated for with 'brains, skill, stamina and ash-craft in abundance. I saw him play in 26 major matches and he never left the field without being the outstanding hurler of the hour,' wrote Carbery, who played against Kelleher in the 1902 final and alongside him in the 1905 decider against Kilkenny.

Kelleher played in seven All-Ireland finals, but Kilkenny thwarted the three-in-a-row bid in 1905 and haunted Cork like a bad dream for the next decade. Kelleher played on until 1914 by which time he was playing in the forwards, 'increasing in craft as he slackened in speed'.

In his prime, he moulded and trained his native Dungourney 'to such perfection that hurling men rated them with Blackrock of 1931 and Tubberadora of the 1890s as the greatest individual team of hurlers Ireland had ever seen'. The Cork chronicler John T. Power asserted that Kelleher was a key figure in taking hurling to a new plane of excellence.

His art with the camán was closely studied. His cleverness in rounding an opponent, in clipping the ball on to his hurley, his beautiful groundwork, all appeared in the hurling of Tipperary men and especially that of Kilkenny men.[8]

Even had he never lifted a hurley, Kelleher would have been a hero in east Cork for the gaisc he achieved in 1900 when he entered and won a prestigious steeplechase horse race at Rathcormac at a time when it was an 'unheard of thing for a farmer to ride against the "gentlemen" of the country – let alone beat them. In that gruelling six-miler, he didn't win only a horse race. He won a kind of freedom for his people … Jamesy Kelleher came into the tongues of the working men who knew him like Dan O'Connell once did and Parnell.'

5. Expert Wielders of the Camán

1904 ALL-IRELAND FINAL (Deerpark Estate, 24 June 1906)

Kilkenny (Tullaroan) 1–9 Cork (St Finbarr's) 1–8

*In a field at the borough boundary two teams of hurlers – consisting of about
30 men – were endeavouring to win superiority at the old game. There were
no spectators – a fact which proves conclusively what little hold the GAA has
taken in Kilkenny … The hurling of both teams was, we believe, the worst and
most spiritless ever witnessed on an Irish hillside. In the centre of the field of
play, there were at times during the contest a half dozen of the hurlers lying
with their faces on the ground, resting themselves. It would break the heart of
a Moycarkey or Galway Gael to witness such a contemptible perversion of the
grand old dashing game of hurling.*
Celtic Times (16 April 1887)

IN THE SECOND half of the 19th century, Kilkenny was cricket
country, a county in thrall to the bat and ball rather than the
hurley and sliotar. While the arrival of the GAA hastened the
decline of cricket in other counties, such as Tipperary where it
had previously flourished, it took decades for Kilkenny to be fully
evangelised and converted to the national game. There were 50
cricket teams in the county in 1896 and despite Kilkenny's rise as
a hurling power during the 1900s, there were still 20 active clubs
in 1930. It wasn't until the 1950s that cricket – with the exception
of Mount Juliet, the lone-surviving club in the county – finally
surrendered to hurling.

Why did cricket thrive and endure for so long in Kilkenny when
the GAA's cultural nationalism – which branded those who played
the 'west British' game as 'anti-Irish' – succeeded in more or less

wiping out the game in neighbouring counties and other strongholds
such as Westmeath? Michael O'Dwyer, the author of *The History of
Cricket in Kilkenny: The Forgotten Game*, writes that 'cricket was
never classed as a "foreign" game in County Kilkenny as it had been
in other counties such as Tipperary. The reason is probably because
it did not originate from the playing of cricket by the British army.'
Rather than being a 'garrison game', cricket in Kilkenny was played
by men 'from a wide range of backgrounds and from most sections
of society. In rural areas especially, local farmers provided cricket
pitches and farm labourers were prominent members of many teams
… Cricket was played throughout the county and drew support
from all classes.'[1]

The parish of Tullaroan provides a good example of the sporting
ecumenism that prevailed in Kilkenny from the 1880s to the early
1900s. Tullaroan was the first GAA club founded in Kilkenny and
quickly became the dominant hurling force in the county, but it also
continued to field cricket teams. One of the star players was Henry
J. Meagher who was present at the GAA's founding in Hayes's Hotel.
His son Lory became one of the all-time Kilkenny greats and three
more sons – Frank, Willie and Henry – also played for Kilkenny.
The Graces, another prominent Tullaroan hurling family, were also
enthusiastic cricketers. It wasn't until 1902 and the introduction of
the GAA's ban on its members playing 'foreign games' that cricket
began to decline in Tullaroan.

The victory of a Tullaroan-led Kilkenny selection in the 1904
All-Ireland final also widened the appeal of hurling in the county.
If ever an All-Ireland was earned by sheer persistence, it was the
1904 title. Over the previous two decades, Tullaroan and Kilkenny
combinations had suffered some terrible defeats in championship
deciders. These included 6–8 to 0–2 against Cork (Blackrock) in
1893; 6–8 to 1–0 against Tipperary (Tubberadora) in 1895 and 8–9 to
0–8 against Cork (Blackrock) in the 1903 final played in July 1905.
Against that, an all-Tullaroan Kilkenny team had run Limerick
(Kilfinane) to three points in the 1897 final and a Threecastles-led

combination had gone toe-to-toe for long spells against all-conquering Tubberadora in 1898.

The story of Kilkenny hurling in this period revolves around Mooncoin and Tullaroan, the latter an area which had a strong pre-GAA hurling tradition. Tullaroan's official history refers to pre-GAA matches between the parish and neighbouring Kilmanagh that were 'long, sustained, gruelling tests which invariably lasted all day and were a great test of strength and endurance'.[2] This tradition stood to Tullaroan between 1887 and 1900 when they were unbeaten in Kilkenny and won five county titles, adding another four in 1901, 1902, 1904 and 1905.

Tullaroan's near monopoly on the Kilkenny championship inevitably stirred up grievances. There were claims that the county's dismal record in All-Ireland finals was mostly due to players from other clubs being overlooked for selection. For the 1904 championship, though, Kilkenny selected a truly representative team which survived a 2–8 to 1–7 semi-final fright from Galway to reach the decider against a Cork side chasing an All-Ireland three-in-a-row. Kilkenny's victory in the final was a sensation. After their 25-point beating in the 1903 final, they had been written off in most quarters, not least by *Sport* whose correspondent's preview claimed 'the Kilkenny men seem to think they can win Leinster championships on any form while they look upon the All-Ireland final as a hopeless task'.

A pivotal encounter in hurling history, the 1904 final was played on 24 June 1906 at Maurice Davin's Deerpark Estate outside Carrick-on-Suir. 'About 4,000 spectators watched the game and were fairly surprised at the brilliant play of the Kilkenny men during the opening stages. They combined splendidly. On the other hand, the Cork men missed many rather good opportunities,' reported the *Freeman's Journal*. 'The second period was full of excitement, particularly when Cork shot the goal which put them on an equal footing. Then each team took the lead in turn and feeling was at fever pitch when, with five minutes to go, the sides were once more level at one goal eight points each. In that five minutes, Kilkenny scored the point which left them champions of Ireland.'

Kilkenny had led 1–5 to 0–5 at half-time, the goal scored by Dick Doyle from Mooncoin. Team captain Jer Doheny, who had played on five losing All-Ireland final teams, scored the opening point and Pat Fielding (Mooncoin) and Dick Brennan, from the city club Erin's Own, each scored three points. The hero of the hour, though, was another Tullaroan veteran, Pat 'Fox' Maher – a famed full-back who had switched to goals when Jack Rochford claimed the Number 3 jersey. Nominated as Man of the Match by Maurice Davin, Fox was presented with a miniature silver hurl by Davin and 'carried shoulder high to the dressing room by Kilkenny supporters. He had done more than anyone else to fashion the victory.'

The Fox retired after the 1904 final and became an accomplished coach. A comrade said of him in 1933:

Fox Maher was the man who first made it possible for Kilkenny to win All-Ireland honours. As regards the technique and progress of the game, he taught everyone – Tullaroan, Mooncoin and Erin's Own – every team since his time. He was the father of hurling ... He started with a few boys and, year after year, supplied the Kilkenny All-Ireland selection with first-class material.[3]

An *Irish Independent* tribute after his death stated that 'all Ireland was shocked around Christmas-time at the news of his death, for all Ireland loved Fox Maher [who] was on a hurling plane of his own'.

Tall, square, well built, a hurler to his fingertips, [he was] a grand natural striker off either hand, he never dallied in possession. He could hold up the most formidable group of attackers with his wide shoulders, bony hips and bold courage. He could drive ground balls a whole field's length. And he could stop a flying ball dead on the line. Down Kilkenny's way, Fox Maher was a personality of a hurler for all to copy, a stylist for all to study. Quiet and unobtrusive, he was the drollest of company. He had his romance too, for he loved with a 'Gael's' intensive faithfulness, though for him it meant exile. He travelled far and wide but returned to his old home in Tullaroan to teach the boys by word and example. He never missed a match.

The 1904 victory heralded a decade of success which has never been surpassed, not even by Brian Cody's 21st-century black-and-amber juggernaut. Kilkenny won seven All-Ireland titles in 10 years and the Kilkenny hurling historian Tom Ryall argued that they 'might well have won 11 All-Irelands in-a-row' (1904–1914) but for internal rowing which sabotaged their chances in 1906, 1908, 1910 and 1914. Four players – 'Drug' Walsh, Dick Doyle, Sim Walton and Jack Rochford – won seven All-Ireland medals each. Drug Walsh became the only Kilkenny man to captain three All-Ireland-winning sides; Dick Doyle (with seven) and his brothers Eddie (with six) and Mick (with five) won 18 All-Ireland medals between them – surely a record that will never be bettered.

These men didn't just bring glory to Kilkenny and establish the county as one of the 'big three'; they became some of the game's first household names and extended hurling's appeal beyond its traditional borders. Their clashes with Cork and Tipperary drew record crowds to new venues such as Fraher's Field in Dungarvan and the expanding Jones's Road. During a decade when the fundamentals of hurling were refined, Kilkenny's craft and artistry embellished and elevated the game.

KILKENNY: P. Maher (goal), J. Hoyne, J. Rochford, P. Lanigan, D. Grace, D. Walsh, E. Doyle, P. Fielding (0–3), J. Lalor, P. Saunders, D. Stapleton, M. Lalor, S. Walton, J. Anthony, J. Doheny (capt) (0–1), D. Brennan (0–3), D. Doyle (1–1).

CORK: D. Linehan, J. Desmond, J. Kelleher, W. Sheehan, M. O'Leary, J. Harrington, J. Kelly, J. Ronayne, W. Maloney, P. O'Sullivan, B. Hennessy, T. Coughlan, S. Coughlan, D. O'Keeffe, D. Sheehan, D. Harrington, D. McGrath.

Referee: M.F. Crowe (Limerick)

6. Tom Semple's Hurling Machine

1906 MUNSTER FINAL (Tipperary Town, 18 August 1907)

Tipperary (Thurles Blues) 3–4 Cork (Dungourney) 0–9

Our record in the championships is not what we should like to see it, but I make a prophecy for 1906 – we fear or dread nothing and an All-Ireland is coming to Tipperary.

Tipperary County Chairman Denis O'Keeffe

TIPPERARY'S HURLING FRATERNITY was getting restless by the beginning of 1906. Five years had passed without an All-Ireland or Munster title as Blackrock, Dungourney and St Finbarr's-led Cork selections ruled in Munster. To the east, Kilkenny – long-time whipping boys for Tipp teams – had made the All-Ireland breakthrough. Even London had won an All-Ireland since Tipp's last title in 1900, but cometh Tipperary's hour of need, cometh Tom Semple and his Thurles Blues.

A native of Drombane who had moved to Thurles as a teenager to work with the Great Southern & Western Railway Company, Semple was a Tipperary regular by 1900, but it was only on assuming the county captaincy in 1906 that his talents were given full expression. The first indication of the gathering Tipperary revival came early that year when an all-Tipperary selection – made up of players from Two-Mile-Borris, Thurles, Moycarkey, Ballytarsna and Ballymackey – represented Munster in the Inter-Provincial Shield final against Leinster. The game was played at Maurice

Davin's estate in Carrick-on-Suir where Leinster, backboned by 13 Kilkenny players, led by 3–9 to 0–1 with 15 minutes to go before Semple led what the Tipperary hurling historian Canon Fogarty described as 'the bravest finish ever made by the old masters in their long career of determined and desperate hurling'.

> Hurricane assaults started and tore the enemy defence in ribbons. Gradually the Tipps ascended from the byway to the highway and the bookies calling six to four Kilkenny suddenly stopped. Three minutes to go, it was 3–9 to 4–6. One minute to go, Tipperary sent wide by inches. At the whistle, the whole audience rose to the occasion and cheered the heroes who treated them to the greatest sensation up to then in the annals of the native pastime.[1]

The 'Tipps' retained the momentum in the replay, leading by 4–7 to 2–2 at half-time and while Leinster resumed with 'a big intensive push to retrieve their fallen fortunes ... there was nothing doing against a bunch of men, cool, grim and resolute. Once again, the veteran captain [Semple] had reason to be proud of the fighting blood of his brave hurlers who brought to bay the pick of a province.'

After overcoming Moycarkey in the replayed Tipperary county final, Thurles Blues were unstoppable as they crushed Limerick (Caherline) and Clare en route to the Munster final against Cork. Played at Tipperary town in August 1907, the showdown between Cork's veterans and Semple's tyros attracted a record attendance and was the first in a trilogy of games that helped mythologise the Cork–Tipperary rivalry. Canon Fogarty reports that 'during the interval, Leeside faces were long but their hearts were undismayed. The battle resumed, both sides showing top form with energy seemingly stored for the big occasion. Cheers and compliments were showered on the Tipps; they were the real thing; too well trained, too well coached to be brushed aside or lightly overthrown. When the final whistle went, Semple's vow was fulfilled; he had changed the line of succession and his men had written the first epic event in their history.'[2]

Galway were pulverised 7–14 to 0–2 in the All-Ireland semi-final, but a Dublin team packed with 11 Tipperary men provided spirited opposition in the 1906 final played in Kilkenny in October 1907. The city team led 2–7 to 1–7 at half-time, before a typical second-half surge saw Tipperary run out 3–16 to 3–8 winners. It completed a double for Semple who, a few weeks earlier, had won the National Long Puck title with a 96-yard drive of a sliotar weighing nine ounces (more than twice the weight of the modern championship ball).

So, what sort of hurler and man was Tom Semple? Even allowing for the heroic tone and purple prose of hurling writing from this era, he appears to have been a man of exceptional physique, hurling talent and temperament. P.D. Mehigan (Carbery) described Semple as a 'six-foot-three lath of a man, handsome as a Greek god; brown hair, a clump of close curls; limbs like a thoroughbred; all life and nervous movement ... Great long strides Semple had, and such a sweep of ash. Grounder of 90 yards off either hand; lightning lifts and soaring pucks goalwards; fierce and fearless at hurling; kind and gentle as a maid at festive board. Such was Tom Semple, prince of hurlers.'

Canon Fogarty was equally in awe:

> From his first appearance to the date of his retirement, he was akin in feeling with Matt the Thresher, enthusiastic as the winter tempest on our heather-clad hill, and [with] an innate genius for leadership.

His leadership qualities are repeatedly referenced in the profiles and tributes. A team captain in this era was also the de facto manager, trainer and role model for his players and Semple excelled in these tasks.

> He immediately commanded respect and the wonderful effect of his example and enthusiasm inspired the players around him with the burning desire for victory.[3]

Semple also had a modern approach to training, combining hurling drills with physical training – focused on walking, skipping and sessions at a punch-ball – to build endurance and sharpen the reflexes.

It was Tipperary's good fortune that an exceptional Thurles team emerged in 1906 when he was 27 and at the peak of his powers. As Raymond Smith, himself a Thurles man, wrote:

Tom Semple set out to put Thurles and Tipperary back on the Everest heights. And the players emerged to realise this ambition – Jack Mooney and Jack Mockler, a powerful midfield partnership; James O'Brien, known as 'The Hawk' because of the quickness of his eye and the speed of his reactions between the posts; Tom Kerwick and Martin O'Brien, two top-class defenders who when the mood caught them could completely suppress an opposing attack and still supply their own; Paddy Brolan and Hughie Shelly, forwards of rare skill and talent – Shelly noted for his brilliant burst of speed and Brolan for his first-time hitting.[4]

Decades later, they were acclaimed by Paddy Leahy, whose playing and coaching career with Tipperary spanned 50 years, as 'the most perfect machine that ever graced a hurling field'.

TIPPERARY (Thurles Blues selection): T. Semple (capt), J. O'Brien, J. Hayes, T. Allen, T. Kerwick, T. Condon, P. Burke, T. Gleeson, J. O'Keeffe, P. Maher, J. Burke, J. Mooney, J. Mockler, H. Shelly, T. Gleeson, M. Gleeson, P.J. Riordan.

CORK (St Finbarr's selection): C. Young, W. Hennessy, D. O'Leary, C. Nolan, W. Sheehan, J. Harrington, D. Sheehan, J. Beckett, J. Kelleher, J. Ronayne, W. Mackessy, D. Buckley, D. O'Keeffe, M. O'Shea, D. Keating, J.H. Deasy, J.N. Deasy.

7. More Satisfaction Than a Thousand Years in America

1907 ALL-IRELAND FINAL (Dungarvan, 21 June 1908)

Kilkenny 3–12 Cork 4–8

In such a tremendous struggle, the almost entire absence of any exhibitions of ill-temper among the hurlers was truly marvellous. Hurling as played by these premier teams is truly a national game to be proud of, a national heritage, a national glory. On both sides, seemingly impossible feats were performed with the ball. The only feat I did not see performed was that one of young Cuchulain of striking the ball back and forth, beating it on the way and keeping it in the air for an indefinite period.

Fr James Dollard, *Sport* **(June 1908)**

I N THE EARLY years of the 20th century, some Kilkenny players believed that victory would follow if a Kilkenny priest threw in the sliotar to start a game.[1] The belief may be connected with the 1904 All-Ireland final when Fr Andy Doyle from Mooncoin, a brother of the famous hurling brothers, had travelled home from Minnesota for the game. He set the ball rolling and Kilkenny duly won their first All-Ireland hurling title. This faith in mediated divine assistance probably gathered more converts a few years later when another Kilkenny priest – Fr James Dollard, also from Mooncoin – threw in the ball for the 1907 All-Ireland final and Kilkenny again defeated Cork by a point.

Often described as 'the poet-priest', Fr Dollard spent his adult life ministering in Canada, but in his imagination, he never left Ireland. A poet of the Celtic Twilight school, he was also an ardent hurling man. Bliss must it have been then for him to be home on vacation and present in Dungarvan in June 1907 for what observers agreed was the greatest hurling final yet: 'Hurling reached its peak that great day,' declared Carbery decades later.

Writing for the Dublin weekly *Sport*, Fr Dollard enthused 'about the beauties of the improved game of hurling, the stamina and skill and self-control of the teams … The swiftness of the game took one's breath away.' He concluded with a plea to would-be emigrants:

> If the young men of Ireland could only be made see that one grand day like that in Dungarvan gives pure enjoyment and more genuine satisfaction than a thousand years of America or other foreign lands, they would know how privileged they are, and would choose the better part of staying in the old country working for her weal; living and dying within the four walls of her holy hills.

An estimated 15,000 spectators – a record for a hurling final – had packed Dan Fraher's venue for the fourth instalment in three years of the Kilkenny–Cork rivalry which exploded to life in this decade. Cork had a score to settle having been denied the 1905 title in the boardroom. A St Finbarr's selection had 'won' the final (played in April 1907) against Kilkenny by 5–10 to 3–13, but Kilkenny then lodged an objection against Cork's goalkeeper 'Sonny Jim' McCarthy on the grounds that he was a British army reservist. Cork counter-objected against Kilkenny's Matt Gargan on the grounds that he had played for Waterford earlier in the year. In the end, Central Council had ordered a replay that Kilkenny won 7–7 to 2–9.

'Kilkenny won the second game fairly easily, possibly because the Cork men could not muster enough enthusiasm to fight again for a title they had won on the playing field and lost in the council room,' Tim Horgan wrote in *Cork's Hurling Story*. 'Had the opposition been weaker, they might have made a go of the replay, but the Kilkenny hurlers of 1905 were anything but weak [so] it was not a great surprise to find them beating a demoralised Cork side by a high margin in Dungarvan.'

A Kilkenny chronicler, the late Joe Cody, provides a different take in *The Stripy Men*. Cork started at 'a frantic pace' and were 2–3 to 0–0 ahead in the first half as 'Kilkenny were really struggling and only herculean defence from goalkeeper Ned Teehan and full-back Jack Rochford kept their slim hopes alive'. Kilkenny fought back with two goals from Jimmy 'the Wren' Kelly, but Cork still led by 2–7 to 2–2 early in the second half before the champions cut loose, Kelly finishing with 5–2.

'The Wren' Kelly was to the fore again in the 1907 final, scoring a first-minute goal, but Kilkenny soon came under constant Cork pressure and Jack Kelleher bagged three first-half goals to give his team a 4–2 to 2–4 interval lead with Kilkenny rallying well before half-time. Neither side could establish a clear advantage in the second half. A third goal from Kelly gave Kilkenny the lead for the first time, but Jamesy Kelleher levelled the game with a point from a 50 three minutes from time.

> Jack Anthony, however, earned undying fame when he scored what proved to be the winning point. Twice, Cork almost snatched a goal in the closing minutes, but [goalkeeper, John] Power and [full-back] Rochford saved in the nick of time. It was a glorious All-Ireland triumph.[2]

Glorious for Kilkenny, but the source of much frustration for the Dungourney-powered Cork team who had enough possession and chances to avenge Cork's 1905 defeat.

The recriminations began on the Tuesday night after the game. *Sport* reported the Cork county board chairman M. O'Riordan as claiming 'the onus of the defeat rested on the Dungourney team. He would like it to go forward that the county board were in no way responsible for the picking of the team.'

Just one Dungourney player was selected when a Blackrock-dominated Cork side and Kilkenny clashed in the 1912 All-Ireland final, but the pattern remained the same – Kilkenny winning by a point after withstanding sustained Cork pressure. It wasn't quite a hoodoo, but Cork had to wait until 1926 before finally slaying their eastern nemesis.

KILKENNY: J. Power, J. Keoghan, J. Rochford, P. Lanigan, D. Grace, D. Walsh (capt), E. Doyle (0–1), D. Doherty, M. Gargan (0–1), D. Kennedy (0–2), D. Stapleton, T. Kenny, S. Walton (0–2), J. Anthony (0–3), M. Doyle, J. Kelly (3–2), D. Doyle (0–1).

CORK: W. Parfrey, J. Desmond, Jamesy Kelleher (0–1, 50) J. Beckett, J. O'Shea, G. Buckley, J. Ronayne, T. Lynch (0–1), D. O'Keeffe, P. Leahy, T. Coughlan (0–1), B. Hennessy (1–1), S. Riordan, B. O'Neill (0–2), Jack Kelleher (3–2), D. Kidney.

Referee: M.F. Crowe (Limerick)

Attendance: 15,000

A selection dispute between Mooncoin and Tullaroan may well have sabotaged Kilkenny's hopes of completing a three-in-a-row by winning the delayed 1906 All-Ireland championship. Mooncoin, as county champions, picked the team and selected their goalkeeper Jim Dunphy ahead of Tullaroan's Ned Teehan. Tullaroan reacted by withdrawing their players from the squad before the Leinster final where Kilkenny were well beaten by Dublin, 1–14 to 0–5.[3]

8. Raging Fires, Dying Flames

1909 ALL-IRELAND FINAL (Cork Athletic Grounds, 12 December)

Kilkenny (Mooncoin) 4–6 Tipperary (Thurles) 0–12

Great interest was evinced in the contest, and although in the depths of winter, thousands poured into the Leeside city to witness one of the greatest games ever played for the All-Ireland crown.
Phil O'Neill ('Sliabh Ruadh')[1]

O N 26 DECEMBER 1908, Jack Johnson became the first black heavyweight champion of the world when he defeated Canada's Tommy Burns after 14 rounds in front of 20,000 spectators in Sydney. The aftershock from this seismic sporting event reverberated around the world and Dublin's *Sport* newspaper featured lengthy analysis of the fight in its first edition of 1909. Under the heading 'How Johnson Beat Burns', the writer noted that:

> Johnson in action appears like a gigantic human hinge. In delivering a blow, the whole upper part of the body moves easily forward from the hips, impelled by the great back muscles and weighted by the massive shining trunk. The blow delivered, back goes the giant hinge, the hands already in position for offence or defence.

The same edition carried a report on another sporting heavyweight – Tipperary's hurling talisman Tom Semple who had been honoured with a testimonial presentation in Thurles over Christmas. The financial testimonial was 'subscribed to by Gaels the world over' and was made to him 'as practical recognition of his invaluable services to the GAA in Tipperary'. Semple modestly insisted that 'he had done nothing but what every Tipperary man with a love for his county and the national pastime should have done'.

1909 was a bittersweet year for Tom Semple and his Thurles Blues and Tipperary teams. It was the year when they won an All-Ireland and defeated their greatest rivals Dungourney in the last serious joust between the teams, but it was also the year when they surrendered their All-Ireland title to Kilkenny in a landmark final played in Cork two weeks before Christmas. The 1909 championship was in ways hurling's equivalent of a 'unification' bout to decide the team of the decade. Cork had dominated the early 1900s; Tipperary and Kilkenny had alternately claimed the high ground in the middle years, and the 1909 Munster and All-Ireland finals were the decisive knockout matches.

First, though, the 1908 All-Ireland championship had to be completed and as usual it was well behind schedule with the Connacht and Leinster championships for that year only finishing in January and March 1909 – Galway and Dublin claiming the titles. Dublin received a walkover in the Leinster final from All-Ireland champions Kilkenny who were embroiled in a dispute with the authorities about the possession of the Railway Inter-Provincial Shield. Tipperary had received a walkover from Kerry in the 1908 Munster final after defeating Dungourney in the semi-final played before a huge crowd at Fermoy. A late score from Bill Harris (Horse and Jockey) secured the 2–11 to 3–7 victory for Tipp who had lost the 1907 instalment between the teams by 1–6 to 1–4 when Jamesy Kelleher had saved Semple's drive for victory from a close-in free.

By the time they met in the 1909 Munster final, Tipp were, once again, All-Ireland champions. Dublin had forced a draw in the 1908 final played at Jones's Road on 25 April 1909 with the future War of Independence leader Harry Boland scoring one of the late equalising points. The replay was played two months later in Athy with Tipp turning on the style in the second half to win by 3–15 to 1–5.

The close-run games, however, were accumulating with an ominous frequency for Semple's men. Next up were Clare in the Munster semi-final played in humid conditions in Limerick. Tipperary won by 4–10 to 2–9 against opponents who surprised most observers with their pluck and skill.

The Munster final versus Cork (Dungourney) was played in Dungarvan on 20 August. 'This is a game indeed that might rank with the contests of the Fianna,' was the bold summing-up of the *Kilkenny Journal*'s correspondent, 'Vigilant' (Seamus Upton). It was a day when Tipperary made a stirring second-half comeback after Cork (Dungourney) supporters had dispatched carrier pigeons southwards at half-time with news of victory. The Cork cockiness is puzzling because they only led by 1–6 to 1–2 at the break after playing with the breeze. The sight of the departing pigeon post only served to galvanise Tipperary, but Cork's confidence looked justified when they scored a second goal to go seven up before Semple was felled in an all-out rally.

'Seven points in front! And Semple down – it looked a foregone conclusion now,' wrote Raymond Smith. 'But having received attention, Semple resumed, like a gladiator rising from the dust of the Coliseum. The Thurles effort turned from a dying flame into a raging fire. Cork's resistance was slowly but surely overcome by the power of the Thurles attacks. Mick O'Dwyer, covered in blood, Tom Gleeson, Hughie Shelly, Martin O'Brien, Joe McLoughney and the Burkes were acclaimed for their performances.'[2]

Canon Fogarty's account of the game was equally fervent. He described the crowd as being in a 'fever heat' as the Tipp revival commenced.

Roofs of sheds collapsed in the pandemonium as hurricanes of applause greeted their unparalleled courage, obstinacy and endurance. The Cork forwards were completely blotted out but the team as a whole held out to the bitter end, unwilling to yield but unable to rise.[3]

Two months later, Semple's men were again taken to the wire, this time in the All-Ireland semi-final at Jones's Road against a Galway side they had overwhelmed by 5–15 to 1–0 the previous February in the 1908 semi-final. This time round, Tipperary just about held out to win by 6–7 to 5–7.

While Tipperary were slogging it out in the delayed 1908 All-Ireland series and the far more demanding 1909 campaign, a well-rested Kilkenny side – selected by county champions Mooncoin – sauntered into the All-Ireland final with crushing victories over Laois in the Leinster final (5–16 to 2–7) and Derry (3–17 to 0–3) in the All-Ireland semi-final on 14 November.

Their relative freshness was a telling factor in the final on 12 December when Kilkenny arrived at the Cork Athletic Grounds with a depleted squad after Piltown withdrew their players – Jack Anthony, Jack Butler and John T. Power – in protest at alleged rough treatment from Mooncoin in the county semi-final.[4]

Whatever dissension there was in the Kilkenny camp was quickly forgotten as Tipperary were outfought and out-smarted all over the pitch in front of an estimated 11,000 spectators. Two goals from Bill Hennebry and the prolific Jimmy Kelly gave Kilkenny a 3–4 to 0–3 half-time lead. Even though Canon Fogarty lamented that all the Blues' 'old fire and dash was missing' on 'soft and boggy ground', Semple roused his team for one last stand. They scored four points in a four-minute spell after the break and reduced the gap to three before a Sim Walton point and third goal from Hennebry finally broke their spirit in the fading winter light.

'It was wonderful to see how accurate Kilkenny were under the troublesome conditions; they showed a command over the leather that one rarely sees on such a sod,' wrote P.D. Mehigan (Carbery) in the *Cork Sportsman*. '[But] the grand effort of Tipperary was to my mind the most striking feature – it was really wonderful to see the recovery they made. At one time, it looked as though they would mow down Kilkenny like grass before a scythe. But in combination and scoring ability they were far behind.'

It was Tipperary's first defeat in nine All-Ireland finals and also the first time their all-out assaults and rallies had failed to yield a goal in a final. Tom Semple played on for three more years, but his Thurles Blues 'hurling machine' went into decline. For Kilkenny, 1909 was another milestone victory. Infighting again scuppered their campaign in 1910, but in the following three seasons they took hurling to new heights with a sequence of victories that wouldn't be bettered for three decades.

KILKENNY: J. Dunphy, J. Keoghan, J. Rochford, P. Lanigan, D. Kennedy, D. Walsh (capt), E. Doyle, J. Delahunty, D. Doherty, M. Gargan, J. Ryan, M. Shortall, S. Walton, D. Doyle, B. Hennebry, J. Kelly, M. Doyle. Subs: D. Grace for D. Doherty (inj., HT), T. McCormack.

TIPPERARY: J. O'Brien, M. O'Brien, T. Kerwick, T. Gleeson, J. Hackett, J. McLoughney, P. Fitzgerald, T. Semple (capt), J. Mooney, J. Mockler, B. Mockler, P. Burke, J. Murphy, P. Brolan H. Shelly, A. Carew, J. Fitzgerald.

Referee: M.F. Crowe (Limerick)

Attendance: 11,000

9. After the Goal Rush

1910 ALL-IRELAND FINAL (Jones's Road, 20 November)

Wexford (Castlebridge) 7–0 Limerick (Castleconnell) 6–2

When the final whistle went, the Wexford following broke in on the ground and chaired every one of the Wexford team to their dressing room … At least 6,000 people gathered in one solid mass to do honour to the new champions.
Sport (26 November 1910)

THE NEW DECADE began with the most significant changes to the playing guidelines since the 1892 reduction of teams from 21-a-side to 17-a-side. The ungainly hybrid combination of soccer-style goalposts and Australian Rules-style side-posts for points was replaced by goalposts as we know them today. Other changes included extending the 50 to 70 yards and the creation of a 45 foot x 15 foot parallelogram in front of goal for both codes. This zone facilitated a new 'square ball' type rule that disallowed a goal if the scoring forward was adjudged to be inside the parallelogram before the ball. These changes were well received by players and supporters, but the interpretation of the 'square ball' rule cost Limerick dearly in the 1910 final.

The records for the 1910 championship present an odd picture to the modern eye. Having brought the All-Ireland hurling championships up to date in 1909, the GAA's administrators seemed determined to maintain order even if it meant nominating teams to play in All-Ireland championship fixtures before the provincial championships had been concluded.

This explains why Limerick and Wexford reached the 1910 final without playing semi-finals. Instead, the semis were won by Dublin who defeated Glasgow by 6–6 to 5–1 on 2 October, six weeks after Cork had walloped Galway in Tuam in the first semi. To make it even more confusing, Kilkenny had defeated London in the All-Ireland quarter-final in September. But Kilkenny – yet again troubled by infighting – were then beaten by Dublin in the Leinster championship and the Dubs advanced to the All-Ireland semi-final pending the Leinster final, where they were beaten by Wexford.

It was a similar story in Munster where Cork had been nominated to play in the All-Ireland semi-final pending the Munster final where they were beaten 5–1 to 4–2 by Limerick, who had already beaten Tipperary. Limerick's Munster final victory was 'most unexpected and came as a big surprise to all followers of hurling. Cork were cocksure of victory, and Willie Mackessey, one of the Cork players, stated afterwards: "We left the All-Ireland fall off our hurleys."'[1]

Led by John 'Tyler' Mackey, the Limerick team of this period was much admired, but two Munster titles in 1910 and 1911 were a poor return for the efforts of Mackey and players such as Egon Clancy, Tom Hayes, Con Scanlon, Paddy Vaughan, Sean Carroll and Mick Fehilly, who arguably should have won back-to-back All-Irelands in these years. Wexford had also been a coming team for several seasons and had actually beaten Kilkenny 1–8 to 0–10 in the 1908 Leinster semi-final; the reigning All-Ireland champions objected, however, and the result was overturned by the Leinster Council on the grounds that Wexford's Sim Donoghue had been sent off in a junior football curtain-raiser between the counties prior to the hurling clash. To add injury to objection, Kilkenny then withdrew from the championship because of a dispute with the Leinster Council over the Railway Shield, which meant Dublin were awarded that year's provincial title.

When the 1910 fixtures' knots were eventually unravelled, Wexford v. Limerick was a liberating final pairing after the dominance of Cork, Kilkenny and Tipperary who had won all but four of the 22 finals up to that point. *Sport* reported that 'the attendance was enormous, the largest that has yet been recorded for a hurling final [at Jones's Road]. Consequently the gate receipts – £288 – was a record.' The *Irish Independent* declared it 'a dashing, inspiriting game and all concerned, victors and vanquished, deserve the highest credit for their conduct throughout such a trying ordeal'.

Both teams were fixated on goals. Team captain Richard Doyle scored three in the first half for Wexford – the first coming in the opening minute, the second after a 'picturesque criss-cross movement' and the third after a 'gigantic goal puck by [Sean] Kennedy'. Limerick kept in touch with scores from Mangan, Mackey and John Madden, but Wexford led by 6–0 to 3–2 at half-time and Doyle scored his fourth goal early in the second half to push them further ahead.

It was the Leinster champions' final score before Limerick launched a scorching comeback. They pinned Wexford back in their own half and despite some disallowed goals, they had closed the gap to one point with seven minutes to play. 'The excitement among the spectators was intense. Limerick were attacking and it looked as though their heroic work would be crowned with success, but in Kennedy the Wexford full-back they met a stonewall,' reported the *Irish Independent*. 'He beat them off time and again ... and Wexford retired victors of their first All-Ireland hurling championship.'

Glory at last for Wexford, but there was a postscript in the boardroom. The referee M.F. Crowe, a Limerick man who had refereed many finals, came under fire from his own countymen who launched an objection a few days after the final. While Wexford had a goal and a point disallowed, Limerick 'lost' 3–1 in scores, mainly it seems because of the match officials' interpretation of the new rule about forwards being in the parallelogram before the ball. Limerick seemed to have a strong case, but Central Council dismissed the appeal because the objection papers hadn't been lodged in accordance with procedures.

Wexford were no strangers themselves to controversy and bad luck in All-Ireland finals, going back to 1890 when Cork had walked off the field in protest at the rough play of a Castlebridge selection. The following year, a Crossbeg selection lost to Ballyduff of Kerry in extra-time after being denied the winning point in normal time when the referee blew the final whistle as the ball was on its way over the bar. Wexford teams were also well beaten in the 1899 and 1901 home finals, so 1910 was overdue reward for those who had persevered with hurling in a county where it had struggled to lay down solid roots.

There is a documented hurling tradition in Wexford going back to at least the 17th and 18th centuries, but hurling had a fragmented existence in the county from 1884 until well into the 20th century. The county championship 'was only sporadically contested until 1910. Perhaps this was due in part to the alternative appeal of cricket which was still hugely popular with those who liked their games to feature timber and ball,' wrote David Medcalf in *Purple and Gold: A Photographic Record of Gaelic Games in Wexford*. 'The Wexford GAA county board did not exactly approve of this non-Irish pastime, but they could do little to counter it for a long time. Besides, they had plenty to do in keeping some sort of control over the startling expression of interest in football. By 1887, they claimed to have around 400 "branches" though it is unclear as to exactly how many of these were actually capable of fielding a team. What is certain is that many of the original strongholds of football are now almost entirely in the thrall of hurling.'

The 1910 All-Ireland victory helped stabilise hurling in the county. It also made heroes of players such as the captain Dick Doyle, whose son Pat recalled that part of the team's training involved a four-mile run through Castlebridge, Kilcorral and Mullinagore. On evenings when the team was training, 'blessed candles were lit by the households and placed in the windows. It was a form of prayer, a symbol, a display of solidarity, an expression of support.'[2] He also recalled his father saying that the two stylists on the team were Davy Kavanagh and Bill McHugh.

And while Castlebridge (now the Shelmaliers club) supplied most of the team, two outsiders from New Ross and Kilkenny made telling contributions. Full-back Sean Kennedy from New Ross is credited with holding the Wexford defence together against Limerick's onslaughts in 1910. He went on to captain the county to three All-Ireland football titles between 1915 and 1917 – missing out on the four-in-a-row in 1918 because of injury. 'He was something of a national idol in the period,' wrote Raymond Smith, who quoted Limerick's John Madden as saying of Kennedy that 'no more powerful or impressive player ever graced the playing fields of Ireland'.[3] Another 'outsider' and dual star was Paddy Mackey. Originally from Rosbercon in Kilkenny, he had been recruited by Kennedy to play for New Ross.

It was 45 years before another generation of Wexford hurlers matched the achievements and reputation of Doyle, Kennedy, Mackey and the rest of the 1910 brigade. Limerick were denied by more boardroom ructions in 1911, but their deliverance was closer at hand.

WEXFORD (Castlebridge selection with players from Screen, New Ross and Oulart): R. Doyle (capt), D. Kavanagh, M. Cummins, A. Kehoe, W. McHugh, J. Shortle, P Mackey, S. Donohue, P. Corcoran, M. Neville, M. Parker, J. Mythen, T. Fortune, S. Kennedy, W. Devereux, F. Fortune, P. Roche.

LIMERICK: J. Bourke, M. Mangan, M. Feely, T. Mangan, C. Scanlon, M. Harrington, E. Clancy, E. Treacy, T. O'Brien, T. Hayes, J. Madden, P. Flaherty, J. Mackey (capt), M. Danaher, J. Carroll, D. Conway, M. Sweeney.

Referee: M.F. Crowe (Limerick)

Attendance: 12,000

10. The Toomevara Greyhounds

1913 ALL-IRELAND FINAL (Jones's Road, 2 November)

Kilkenny (Mooncoin) 2–4 Tipperary (Toomevara) 1–2

Never in their whole lives had they witnessed a contest of such boundless excellence as that between Kilkenny and Tipperary. For it was a battle of brave men – the bravest hurlers in the land – a battle of champions in the art of hurling which set spectators wild with enthusiasm, with joy, with hope.
***Sport** (8 November 1913)*

O N AND OFF the pitch, 1913 was a crucial year for the GAA. A new attendance record was created when an estimated 32,000 spectators filled Jones's Road on 29 June for the Croke Cup football final replay between the powerhouses of the era, Louth and Kerry. Both teams had gone into 'collective training' for the replay – Louth hiring a soccer coach and Kerry recruiting athletics and gymnastics experts. The athletic approach prevailed with Kerry winning 2–4 to 0–5.

The financial windfall from the Louth–Kerry games enabled the GAA to buy Jones's Road from Frank Dineen later in 1913, at which point the ground was renamed Croke Memorial Park. The new regulations reducing player numbers to 15-a-side and obliging teams to wear distinctive county colours added to the sense of progress and vibrancy. Compared to the claustrophobia of the 21-a-side era, the reduced team numbers 'made the games more strenuous and enlivening to an extent previously unimagined'.[1]

And an apparently unstoppable new hurling force had emerged from Tipperary. Patrick 'Wedger' Meagher's Toomevara

Greyhounds swept all before them when winning the Croke Cup hurling tournament, humbling All-Ireland champions Kilkenny by 5–4 to 1–1 in the final played at Dungarvan on 1 June.

> The Tipperary supporters who were almost delirious with joy in that second half began singing 'It's a Long Way to Tipperary' and the sound of thousands of voices echoing across the ground in the super-charged atmosphere acted as a further spur to Wedger Meagher and his men … Toomevara were the team of the moment and few could see them beaten.[2]

This impression was confirmed in the Munster final where Tipperary defeated Cork by 8–1 to 5–3 on 21 September. The bedrock of the team was four Toomevara men: goalkeeper Jack 'Skinny' O'Meara and the full-back line of Wedger, Frank McGrath and Stephen Hackett. Two more greyhounds, Jack Harty and Ned Gilmartin, also anchored midfield. Thurles Blues' Paddy Brolan and Hughie Shelly provided experience in the forward line led from Number 11 by Jimmy Murphy whose Horse and Jockey club-mate Bob Mockler was another experienced operator. Wedger's crew predictably crushed Connacht champions Roscommon 10–0 to 0–1 in the All-Ireland semi-final on 19 October; Galway were hockeyed 11–2 to 0–2 by Tipperary in the junior semi-final curtain-raiser at Jones's Road.

Roscommon had beaten Galway 3–4 to 3–2 to win their first and only Connacht title and the Tipp–Roscommon semi-final (10–1 to 0–1) was one of several curious fixtures that year, particularly on the Leinster side of the championship. While Tipperary were lording it in Munster, Kilkenny were taking a scenic route to the All-Ireland final. As the Leinster championship was behind schedule, the reigning champions were nominated for the All-Ireland quarter-final against Glasgow who were defeated 10–6 to 5–2 in the Scottish capital. The All-Ireland semi-final versus Lancashire (Liverpool-Irish) was played on 2 August in Liverpool with Kilkenny winning 4–4 to 1–4. Another curio is that on the same date 'a great hurling match was played at Cardiff between the Cardiff teams and Merthyr [who] won by 13 points to 12. The gate went to the fund in aid of Mr William Ludwig, the well-known Irish tenor.'[3]

After running in 14 goals on their cross-channel jaunts, Kilkenny were held scoreless by Dublin in the first half of the Leinster final and needed a late point from John James Brennan to scrape a 1–0 to 0–3 draw. Suitably chastened, they routed the Dubs 7–5 to 2–1 in the replay to qualify for a seventh All-Ireland final in a decade. 'The Dublin team were simply bewildered by the play of Kilkenny and some members of the Dublin team admitted very graphically indeed that Kilkenny did not allow them to play at all,' reported *Sport*.

The growing grip of the GAA on the public imagination was reflected by expanded coverage in *Sport* which ran an extensive preview for the final including pithy player profiles. John Keoghan was described as 'ambidextrous in his striking and the perfection of his play is a treat to witness'; Pierce Grace 'holds the appointment of Assistant Medical Director to the Kilkenny District Asylum – he is almost as prominent at football and he has what few men can boast of having, All-Ireland medals for both'; as for John T. Power, 'Kilkenny were hard set to find a goalkeeper to fill the place of P. [Fox] Maher when they decided to try young Power who has proved himself a dependable custodian'; Matt Gargan 'plays at midfield and has as many goals and points to his credit from his long shots as any man in Ireland'; James Kelly 'is tremendously fast and knows the play of the brothers Doyle to a nicety. Amongst his admirers he is spoken of as the Kilkenny scoring machine.' The Tipperary profiles were less detailed, but invariably included descriptions such as 'accurate' and 'very fast'.

Tipperary's speed and relative youth made them favourites to finish off the ageing Kilkenny monolith in the final. Kilkenny, mindful of the Croke Cup humiliation in June, had gone into collective training for the final and were a different proposition when it mattered most. Jimmy Kelly scored an early goal for the challengers, but Matt Gargan responded in kind for Kilkenny as the game settled into a tight battle with defences on top. Points from Mick Doyle and Sim Walton helped Kilkenny to a 1–4 to 1–1 half-time lead; the champions' strength and craft told in the second half, played in a downpour, when they adopted a short passing game to cope with the greasy ball. The breakthrough score was an opportunistic Sim Walton goal in the 48th minute. While Tipperary had plenty of possession, Kilkenny dug in for a rearguard action with Paddy Grace outstanding at midfield, Jack Rochford 'herculean' at full-back and John T. Power unbeatable in goal.

For the third time in three years, Dick 'Drug' Walsh lifted the Great Southern & Western Railway Silver Cup for Kilkenny. That November day was the zenith and beginning of the end for Drug Walsh, Sim Walton, John T. Power, Matt Gargan, 'The Wren' Kelly, the Doyle brothers, Jack Rochford and company. Even at this distance, it's clear they were a team of exceptional personalities who moulded style and steel to create the unyielding Kilkenny brand of hurling.

KILKENNY: J.T. Power, J. Keoghan, J. Rochford, J. Lennon, D. Kennedy, D. Walsh (capt), D. Grace, J. J. Brennan, M. Gargan, P. Grace, S. Walton, D. Hoherty, D. Doyle, J. Kelly, M. Doyle.

TIPPERARY: J. O'Meara, P. Meagher (capt), F. McGrath, S. Hackett, B. Mockler, J. Raleigh, T. Gleeson, N. Gilmartin, J. Harty, N. Cawley, J. Murphy, P. Brolan, H. Shelly, E. O'Keefe, B. Kelly.

Referee: M.F. Crowe (Limerick)

A controversial three-in-a-row

Some hurling people question the validity of Kilkenny's three-in-a-row between 1911 and 1913, arguing the 1911 title was won in the boardroom rather than on the field of play. The 1911 final between Kilkenny and Limerick was fixed for the Cork Athletic Grounds on 18 February 1912 but 'the day came terribly wet, the pitch was a quagmire, and it was utterly impossible to carry out the fixture. The match was postponed, although the Limerick team appeared on the pitch, and, as a sequel to this gesture, claimed the match.'[4]

Central Council re-fixed the final for Thurles on 21 April, but Limerick declared that they would play 'in Cork or nowhere' and were duly suspended with Kilkenny awarded the title. Tipperary were nominated to represent Munster in a 'substitute final' to recoup some expenses for the GAA. Played in July at Dungarvan, Kilkenny won a 'strenuous contest' by 3–3 to 2–1.

There were no doubts about Kilkenny's 1912 title when they defeated Cork (Blackrock) 2–1 to 1–3 at Jones's Road in front of a crowd estimated at 20,000. The *Irish Independent* reported that 30 special trains were 'run into Dublin' for the final and the 'crowd was a very cosmopolitan one including very many clergy, doctors, lawyers, professors and members of public bodies'. Overcrowding in the cheap seats caused stoppages in play during the first half when Cork were well on top, leading 1–2 to 0–1 at half-time despite what the *Independent* described as 'execrable shooting'. Jimmy 'The Wren' Kelly scored Kilkenny's first goal five minutes after half-time and the decisive score came in the 43rd minute. Matt Gargan shot from out the field and Cork custodian Andy Fitzgerald 'with every manifestation of confusion and dejection let the ball slip past him for as fluky a goal as was ever scored at Jones's Road'.

11. To the Banner Born

1914 ALL-IRELAND FINAL (Croke Park, 18 October)

Clare 5–1 Laois 1–0

Early in the contest it was quite apparent that the Clare men would prove more than a match for the Leinster champions who were outclassed, especially in the finer aspects of the game.
Irish Independent (19 October 1914)

THE WINE FLOWED freely in Wynn's Hotel on Abbey Street as Clare celebrated the county's first All-Ireland hurling title. The cup was filled and many toasts were raised during the banquet hosted by Willie Redmond, the long-time Home Rule MP for East Clare who had led the Banner men out on to Croke Park earlier that day.[1] A hero of the Land War campaigns of the 1880s, Redmond had later promoted the GAA in Clare and was involved in the team's preparations for the 1914 final.

It's poignant to read about the Wynn's Hotel banquet and then consider Redmond's fate. Believing that fighting for a common cause in Europe would help unite Irishmen north and south, Redmond, even though he was 53, led by example and was commissioned a captain in the Royal Irish Regiment in 1915. He was killed in action at the Battle of Messines on 7 June 1917.

The duration and horrors of the First World War would have been unimaginable in the autumn of 1914 as Clare savoured a long-overdue All-Ireland title. One Munster title in 1889 and Croke Cup victories in 1897 and 1908 were a paltry return for three decades of endeavour. Tulla had represented Clare in the

1889 All-Ireland final against Kickhams of Dublin at Inchicore on
3 November. Playing in their bare feet didn't help the Clare players'
cause as they went down 5–1 to 1–6 on a ground where sawdust had
to be spread on some sections of the pitch. 'Though beaten by such a
big score, the Clare men are really skilled hurlers, but their staying
power and discipline were inferior to the Dubliners,' reported *Sport*.

Eight years later, Tulla – along with players from Feakle,
Broadford, O'Callaghan's Mills and Bodyke – ambushed Tipperary
(Tubberadora) and then crushed Wexford 6–16 to 0–2 in the Croke
Cup final. After pushing a powerful Cork team very close in the
1901 Munster final, Clare regressed and were beaten by Kerry in
the 1907 and 1908 championships although a successful 1908 Croke
Cup campaign hinted at the coming revival.

The balance of hurling power within the county had shifted from
Ogonelloe, Tulla and Kilnamona to clubs including O'Callaghan's
Mills, Newmarket, Quin and Ennis Dalcassians; these four supplied
the players for the 1914 campaign which began with big wins over
Kerry and Limerick before the Munster final showdown against
Cork at Thurles on 20 September. Cork led 1–1 to 1–0 at half-time,
but Clare's fitness told as they battled to a 3–2 to 3–1 victory. The
referee, Tom Semple, commented that 'it was as hard-fought a
Munster final as I have ever seen'. Conveniently for Clare, Munster
nominees Cork had already beaten Galway in the All-Ireland semi-
final a few weeks previously.

Scenting the long-awaited All-Ireland title, Clare went into
collective training in Lisdoonvarna with Jim O'Hehir, father of the
commentator Michael, overseeing the drills which included 10-mile
dawn marches.[2] O'Hehir had four basic tenets for his men: don't
drink, don't smoke, don't overeat and don't lose sleep.[3]

Facing Clare were the other sensation of the season, Leinster
champions Laois, or Leix as the county was then known. Laois had
won their first provincial title the hard way, seeing off Wexford and
Dublin before stunning All-Ireland champions Kilkenny 3–2 to 2–4
in the Leinster final played at Kilkenny.

Like Clare, Laois went into seclusion before the All-Ireland final. A typewritten page of advice on drills for their players included headings such as 'Fighting for Possession' which instructed players to pair off, chase and fight for the ball 'somewhat like two dogs for a hare. There is no practice better suited to give endurance and grip on a ball than this.' On striking, players were instructed that 'quickness and vim at end of strike tends to give more distance than mere strength'. For frees, four or five men were required to take 30 pucks apiece from the 70 and other points with 'a record to be kept of the surest scorer'. And in another note on striking and general tactics, the instructions emphasised that 'ground play must be practised. Clare men too fast and determined for fancy work.'[4]

That staccato closing message was prescient. The Clare men, playing in white jerseys with a green sash, quickly proved the superior force in the final attended by 15,000 spectators at Croke Park. Laois were simply overwhelmed as goals from Jim Clancy and Jim Guerin steered Clare to a 3–1 to 0–0 half-time lead. Laois captain John Carroll scored an early second-half goal, but that was his team's only score as goalkeeper Pa 'Fowler' McInerney, Amby Power, Jack Shalloo and Joe Power took a grip at the back and midfield while Clancy and Guerin added more scores, the latter completing a hat-trick.

Apart from being meticulously prepared, the 1914 Clare team were noted as being unusually tall and well built. The forwards included 17-year-old Brendan Considine from St Flannan's who chipped in with a point; decades later he described his team-mates as a 'fine body of men'.

Most of them were six foot or over. Many of them were highly skilled in the art of doubling on the ball. The captain of the team was Amby Power and at six foot four, he was the team's giant. The Dodger – that was my brother Willie – played a wonderful game in the final. He had strength and courage beyond the ordinary. Martin Maloney, who was better known as 'Handsome', was a beautiful player and a lovely striker of the ball. Tom McGrath from O'Callaghan's Mills was a fine full-forward. He had great drive and speed. Bob Doherty of Newmarket always played with determination and distinction and he later hurled with Dublin.[5]

Frank Dineen felt that Laois, who played in black-and-amber jerseys, had left their best hurling behind them in training.

I know that prior to the match they were putting in a lot of hard training and that some of their players had reduced very much in weight ... [they] were certainly many goals and points behind the form that defeated last year's All-Ireland champions.

Laois's day would come in 1915, while Clare fell away as quickly as they had appeared. The turbulent times took their toll with John Fox enlisting in the British army. Several of his team-mates including Ned Grace, Fowler McInerney, Brendan Considine and Seamus 'Sham' Spellissey 'distinguished themselves as volunteers' during the War of Independence.[6] Fowler McInenery and Brendan Considine were among a number of Clare men who later won All-Ireland medals playing for Dublin. Fowler answered his county's call again for the 1932 championship campaign, the closest Clare would come to winning a second All-Ireland title until Ger Loughnane's stormtroopers shook hurling to its core in 1995.

CLARE: P. McInenery; J. Fox, J. Shalloo, N. Grace; M. Maloney, A. Power (capt), M. Flanagan; J. Power, S. Spellissey; B. Doherty, W. Considine, J. Guerin; B. Considine, T. McGrath, J. Clancy; Subs: J. Rogers for S. Spellissey, P. Moloney for J. Fox.

LAOIS: Jack Carroll (capt), R. O'Keeffe, Jim Carroll, W. Lenihan, J. Jones, T. Hyland, R. Reilly (goal), T. Higgins, P. Goulding, J. Daly, E.P. McEvoy, F. Killeen, T. Jones, J. Hiney, T. Finlay.

Referee: J. Lalor (Kilkenny)

Attendance: 11,000

12. Wild With Delight

1915 ALL-IRELAND FINAL (Croke Park, 23 October)
Laois 6–2 Cork 4–1

Cork was confronted with the biggest and most amazing surprise that has ever been effected in the Gaelic athletic arena. There was no luck in it and beyond all possible shadow of doubt the better team won.
'Vigilant' (Seamus Upton), *Kilkenny Journal* **(October 1915)**

STRADBALLY HALL IN County Laois is the palatial setting for the annual Electric Picnic festival but, in the early 18th century it seems to have hosted a different type of entertainment – gentry-sponsored hurling contests. The then lord of the manor, Dudley Cosby, was, according to his son's memoirs, 'a fine tennis player, a most extraordinary fine hurler … and practised [them] very much when he was young and able'.[1] Sir Dudley aside, however, references to hurling in Laois in the pre-GAA era are scarce, although the speedy revival of the game there after 1884 would indicate a lengthy tradition, especially in districts bordering Tipperary and Kilkenny. Rathdowney, for example, ran Mooncoin to a goal in the unfinished 1888 All-Ireland championship, but for many years that was as good as it got for Laois. Hidings usually ensued when the county competed in the Leinster senior championship with Kilkenny, the tormentors in chief until Laois finally shouted stop in 1914 – beating the three-in-a-row All-Ireland champions by a point in the Leinster final played in Kilkenny.

Despite a heavy defeat to Clare in the subsequent All-Ireland final, Laois quickly bounced back. Reinvigorated by an infusion of players from the new county champions Ballygeehan, they bamboozled Kilkenny in the first half of the 1915 Leinster semi-final played at Tullamore. It was 3–1 to 0–0 at half-time before Kilkenny launched a counter-offensive to lead by two points, 2–6 to 3–1, approaching full-time. Imagine the consternation then when Laois were awarded a last-minute free, after an altercation between Jack Rochford and Jim Hiney, and the ball was worked to 18-year-old Tom Finlay for the winning goal. A 3–2 to 0–5 victory over Dublin in the Leinster final qualified Laois for another All-Ireland final where they faced Cork.

Seventeen 'special' trains brought thousands of spectators to Dublin for the final, boosting the attendance to approximately 14,000. Few neutrals or experts gave Laois any hope. Cork arrived in Croke Park with eight of the team that had lost by a point to Kilkenny in the 1912 final, and they had every reason to be confident after a Munster campaign that had mixed the sublime with the grisly.

The Rebels' 4–0 to 3–1 win over Tipp in the Munster quarter-final was hailed by Vigilant as 'a masterly exhibition of the greatest game ever devised for the recreation of mankind'. The semi-final between Cork and Limerick, though, was an exhibition of a different kind. The 0–0 to 0–0 half-time score says it all about a game described as 'one of the hardest finals ever played for the Munster title'.[2]

> Interest in the match was widespread and partisan feeling was at fever pitch. There was a crowd of 20,000 present. Much open betting was indulged in which was mainly responsible for an unhappy and untimely ending to what was a dour and determined clash. In the first period, no score was recorded at either side which showed the closeness of the struggle. The Cork men asserted themselves well in the second half and looked likely winners when the match was abruptly terminated owing to two opposing players coming into handgrips.

In an era when GAA reporters generally tended to whitewash the dark side of hurling, the *Irish Independent* described 'a disgraceful scene' and reported that 'several people were injured. Order was restored after 10 minutes, but some people remained on the ground and the match was declared off.' Cork, who had led by two goals before the premature end, were subsequently awarded the game and they were back in the free-scoring groove when they defeated Clare 8–2 to 2–1 in the Munster final. The consensus was that all they had to do was turn up against Laois to end 12 frustrating years without a title.

Laois had other ideas. Mindful of the over-zealous training that may have undermined their chances the previous year, they drafted in Dick 'Drug' Walsh as an advisor. One of the Laois players, Bob O'Keeffe, who later became the GAA general secretary, was a native of Mooncoin, Walsh's club, and it's likely he helped persuade Drug across the border to assist Laois. The 'Drug' nickname raises eyebrows these days, but it had innocent origins in Dick's mispronunciation of 'dragoon' in 'The Clare Dragoons' ballad he had learned in school. The Kilkenny captain in three of his seven All-Ireland finals, Drug oversaw a training regime that included playing challenge matches against Kilkenny in the lead-up to the final. On the weekend of the game, 'the panel and mentors went up to Dublin by train on the Saturday night and stayed in a hotel on Gardiner Street. There was close surveillance on all the players so that nothing amiss would be done by them or to them.'[3]

The attention to detail looked in vain when Cork led by three goals to one point after 20 minutes. But as heavy rain fell, Laois, wearing black-and-amber hooped jerseys, bestirred themselves. John and Joe Phelan from Ballygeehan scored goals and Tom Finlay added a point to leave it Cork 3–0 Laois 2–2 at half-time. Then the heavens opened.

As the rain lashed down, the floodgates opened for Laois. Jim Hiney put them ahead with a goal five minutes after the break and when he added a second 'the Leix following went wild with delight … There was never a greater outburst of cheering heard at Jones's Road than the Leix following gave at that record,' reported the *Irish*

Independent. In a scenario similar to the 1901 final when they had played London in a deluge, Cork were rattled and unable to respond. With Bob O'Keeffe holding the Laois defence firm, Jack Finlay outstanding at midfield, his brother Tom giving an exhibition and Joe Phelan a constant threat in the forwards, the underdogs took control – finishing the game in style with goals from John Carroll and Jim Hiney.

> Some of the team travelled home on the Sunday [while] a section of the team that remained in Dublin until Monday evening received a very cordial reception on their arrival by the 5.20 train at Abbeyleix. John [Jack] Finlay the captain on alighting from the train was borne shoulder high through the town. Abbeyleix Pipers Band and about 70 cars took part in the triumphal procession.[4]

A century later, Laois are still awaiting a second hurling homecoming and a team to build on the legacy of the 1915 hurlers from Ballygeehan, Kilcotton, Rathdowney, Abbeyleix and Rapla.

LAOIS: J. Finlay (capt), P. Ryan (goal), J. Walsh, Joe Phelan, John Phelan, T. Finlay, J. Hiney, J. Daly, E.P. McEvoy, John Carroll, Joseph Carroll, B. O'Keefe, James Carroll, J. Dunphy, P. Campion.

CORK: B. Murphy, W. Walsh, S. Óg Murphy, J. Ramsell, L. O'Flaherty, J. Murphy, C. Sheehan, W. Fitzgerald, T. Nagle, M. Byrne, J. Hyde, T. O'Riordan, P. O'Halloran, F. Buckley, J. Kennedy.

Referee: W. Walsh (Waterford)

Attendance: 14,000

13. 1916

1916 ALL-IRELAND FINAL (Croke Park, 17 January 1917)
Tipperary 5–4 Kilkenny 3–2

The ideals of the founders of the GAA were carried to their logical conclusion.
'Sliabh Ruadh' (Phil O'Neill)[1]

THE STORY GOES that at the end of the 1916 All-Ireland hurling final, the Kilkenny captain Sim Walton shook hands with his Tipperary counterpart Johnny Leahy and remarked, 'we were the better hurlers', to which Leahy replied, 'we were the better men'. It was a friendly, throwaway exchange, but over time was reinvented as a terrace taunt – 'Kilkenny for the hurlers; Tipp for the men' – which would rankle with Kilkenny for many decades.

The 1916 final wasn't played until January 1917, but after the events of the previous seven months that was a minor detail for all concerned. The day before the 1916 Rising on Easter Monday, 24 April, the GAA's Annual Congress had convened in City Hall on Dame Street – no more than a short puck away from Dublin Castle, the centre of British administration in Ireland. There was little business of note as congress 'got through the agenda at unprecedented speed – this would indicate that the majority of those present were aware that sterner work was waiting'.[2]

Most delegates had arrived in Dublin the previous day to pay their respects to Frank Dineen, the former GAA president and secretary, who had died suddenly on Good Friday at his desk in the offices of *Sport* where he was Gaelic games editor. When the official congress business was finished on Sunday, delegates retired for private discussions. It's not known if these discussions included consideration of the Easter Rising. But given that the association's president, Alderman James Nowlan, was a lifelong member of the Irish Republican Brotherhood (IRB) and an elected Sinn Féin representative, it's most unlikely he and his inner circle were unaware of the rebellion plans.

The official GAA position was that while it was a non-political, non-sectarian sporting organisation, its members were free to join any political movement of their choosing. In 1914, however, in a rare slip from the official line, Alderman Nowlan had urged GAA members to join the Volunteers and 'learn to shoot straight'.[3] By 1916, there were GAA men shooting straight for the British army as well as the thousands who opposed the war and drilled at home with the Irish Volunteers in anticipation of a rebellion or conflict with Edward Carson's Ulster Volunteers. The GAA's position was further complicated when you consider that some members of Central Council were staunch supporters of John Redmond's Home Rule Party while others were non-political.

In any case, hundreds of GAA players and officials were arrested during the British crackdown a week after the Rising. Among them were Michael Collins, Harry Boland, Austin Stack and Alderman Nowlan, who was arrested when he arrived in Kilkenny on 1 May. Also arrested the same night was Willie Walsh, the leading hurling referee of the era, a prominent administrator in Waterford and another IRB man. With no transport out of the city, Nowlan and Walsh had spent Easter Week in Dublin, staying in a Kilkenny family's home in Phibsboro.[4]

Alderman Nowlan was detained in Wakefield Prison before being released in June, but most of the GAA members arrested were held at Frongoch Internment Camp in Wales where they quickly organised football competitions. Kerry, led by Dick Fitzgerald, defeated Louth by a point in one noted joust. Hurling, though, was prohibited in the camp which made thoughtful and ruthless revolutionaries of many young men who had entered it as raw idealists. 'John Bull made an awful blunder when he put us all together there,' said William Mullins from Tralee Mitchells many years later.[5]

After the Rising, the GAA suspended all fixtures, but action resumed as internees returned later in the summer. The first big hurling game was played on 23 July when Tipperary, wearing black rosettes on their jerseys in honour of the Easter Rising martyrs, defeated Cork in a tournament game at Limerick.

The same teams met in the Munster final played in terrible conditions at Dungarvan on 1 October with Tipperary winning by 5–0 to 0–2. Wedger Meagher and his Toomevara Greyhounds of 1913 were absent, smarting from a row with the county board, so it was county champions Boherlahan who backboned Tipperary for the 1916 All-Ireland championship campaign. This began with a 4–2 to 0–1 first-round victory in Fermoy over Kerry. Limerick provided much sterner opposition, but were defeated 4–4 to 2–4 in the Munster semi. Galway, who had needed a replay to defeat Roscommon in the Connacht final, didn't resume for the second half of the All-Ireland semi-final in Athlone after going in 8–1 to 0–0 in arrears.

On the other side of the draw, Kilkenny regained the Leinster title with an 11–3 to 2–2 pummelling of Wexford, who had knocked out All-Ireland champions Laois in the semis. 'After five minutes, it was evident that Kilkenny were masters of the situation,' reported *Sport*, adding that the Kilkenny 'display made nonsense of the many rumours circulating about their domestic differences'. Those 'domestic differences' – rows and objections involving the leading clubs – were blamed by the diehards for the unexpected defeats to Laois in 1914 and 1915, and had prompted letters to the *Kilkenny Journal* that summer appealing for unity. Mick Kennedy of Tullaroan scored 6–1 against Wexford which still stands as an individual scoring record for a Leinster final.

The Kilkenny v. Tipperary All-Ireland final was fixed for 3 December in Croke Park, but was declared off when a row between the GAA and British government over a new entertainment tax on games and sporting events prompted the pro-government railway companies to withdraw the provision of special trains for the final. The final was re-fixed for 21 January 1921 when 'the day was cold, the pitch sodden and lack of trains resulted in a reduced attendance; those who came, some 5,000 or more, were rewarded by seeing one of the greatest finals for years'.[6]

The ball was thrown in at noon and 'from start to finish a very hot pace was maintained and the hurling exhibited by both teams was reminiscent of the old-time dash and skill which has made [the] finalists famous', reported the *Irish Independent*. Tipperary led by 1–2 to 0–1 at half-time, but Kilkenny took control on the restart. Captained by Sim Walton, they had opened up a five-point lead before the game turned on the dismissals of Dick Grace and Tipperary's Tommy Shanahan who would claim in later years that he had been selected with the express purpose of getting Grace sent off.[7]

Grace's sending off seemed to unhinge the momentum of a Kilkenny team who had overcome the pre-match blow of last-minute defections by some big names including the Doyles of Mooncoin, Jack Rochford and Paddy Donohue from Dicksboro. The sending off had 'a most demoralising effect on the Kilkenny team', noted the *Irish Independent*. Walton was switched to the backs with 'the result that a couple of chances went a-begging which this brilliant player would have undoubtedly placed to account if he had been operating in his own position'. Jimmy Murphy scored a Tipperary goal just after the sendings off, but Kilkenny still led by two points with 10 minutes remaining, before Tipperary launched an old-school, all-out assault on the Kilkenny goal which was 'subjected to a terrific bombardment'. With captain Johnny Leahy pulling the strings, Hugh Shelly – one of Tom Semple's 1908 Thurles Blues – scored the two goals that broke the Kilkenny challenge.

Tipperary's whirlwind finish drew many comparisons with the Tubberadora teams of the 1895–1898 era, and there were

Tubberadora fingerprints all over this stirring triumph which wasn't surprising as Boherlahan had taken Tubberadora into the fold when that townland's side broke up in the early 1900s. The 1916 team was coached by Mikey Maher while 39-year-old Denis Walsh, another link with the old days, came out of retirement for the game. The Tipp lineout included Jer Collisson from Moneygall who became the first north Tipperary hurler to win an All-Ireland medal and it was also the first final in which Tipperary wore the blue-and-gold colours.

TIPPERARY: J. Leahy (capt), T. Dwan, J. Doherty, W. Dwyer, T. Shanahan, J. Power, J. Fitzpatrick, J. Collisson, P. Leahy, H. Shelly, J. Murphy, R. Walsh, D. Walsh.

KILKENNY: S. Walton (capt), J. Kerwick, J. Walsh, T. Hanrahan, J. Ryan, D. Kennedy, J. Holohan, D. Grace, J. Whelan, P. Clohessy, J. Byrne, W. Finn, R. Tobin, M. Kennedy, P. Walsh.

Referee: Willie Walsh (Waterford)

Attendance: 5,000

14. Scaling the Summit

1918 ALL-IRELAND FINAL (Croke Park, 26 January 1919)
Limerick 9–5 Wexford 1–3

The match was too one-sided to be interesting, but the really splendid display of Limerick held the attention of the spectators – some 10,000 in number – from beginning to end.
Sport **(1 February 1917)**

O NE OF THE starkest patterns in hurling history is how long even an established county with a firm tradition and playing base can remain absent from the pinnacle while the 'big three' harvest titles at such a rate that, for them, a decade without an All-Ireland constitutes a grave crisis. Until Clare's 2013 victory, the other previous winners of the senior hurling title – apart from the big three – were all looking at lengthy gaps to their last title which now range from 16 years for Offaly to 55 for Waterford and close on a century for Laois.

Limerick's 41 years and counting is probably the most puzzling of the lot. The county's woes are the subject of Henry Martin's unsparing analysis, *Unlimited Heartbreak*, which takes the 1940s as a starting point. Limerick won five All-Ireland titles between 1918 and 1940 and could, maybe should, have pushed on from there to form a 'big four' with Kilkenny, Cork and Tipp. Go far enough back, though, and you will find that Limerick's current predicament is mirrored by the county's experiences between 1887 and 1918.

Led by Sean Óg Hanley – who was rated by the old-timers as an all-time great – Limerick (Kilfinane) did win an All-Ireland in

1897, swooping for the title in a year when all results have to be measured against Tubberadora's absence. But that victory aside, controversy, self-sabotage and near misses were frequently the order of the day, especially between 1910 and 1916. Limerick possibly could have won two All-Ireland titles in those years if it hadn't been for some dubious refereeing decisions (1910) and their own stubborn shenanigans (1911). In 1912, they played Cork in 'one of the toughest and most terrible tussles ever waged' in the province.[1] There were only two scores after half-time in this semi-final and the second was a late Cork goal to steal a 2–2 to 1–3 victory. The 1915 semi between Cork and Limerick was another infamous encounter – the game abandoned after a mass brawl and pitch invasion. In 1916, there was very little between Limerick and the eventual All-Ireland champions, Tipperary. Most counties would have buckled under these setbacks, but Limerick persevered and their luck eventually turned in 1918, one of the most difficult years in the GAA's history.

Desperate for manpower on the western front, the British unsuccessfully attempted to introduce conscription in Ireland. Conscription crisis aside, 'Gaelic games took second place to political and military-style activities [while] curtailment of trains hampered the arrangements for big games'.[2] And when the championships began in May, the GAA was hit with another hammer blow – a Dublin Castle edict declaring illegal all public gatherings that didn't have a British army permit. The GAA responded by organising 'Gaelic Sunday', a display of mass defiance that has few equals anywhere in the sporting world. Staring down the government, the GAA instructed all county boards to organise games, without permits, on 4 August. It's estimated that over 1,500 games were played with some sources estimating 100,000 people turning out in support.

Only in Dublin was any attempt made to prevent Gaelic games; there the entry to Croke Park was barred by armed police with troops in attendance – who found themselves treated to the unusual spectacle of a camogie match on the road outside.[3]

The championships resumed in July when Limerick and Tipperary clashed at the Markets Field in a Munster semi-final that was the decisive game of the year. It ended 5–3 apiece the first day and Limerick reportedly went into collective training at Foynes for the replay – the regime under trainer Jim Dalton including hikes of Knockpatrick Hill. The hard slog paid off when Limerick edged the replay 3–0 to 2–2 and then destroyed Clare by 11–3 to 1–2 in the Munster final. Factor in the four goals against Waterford in the Munster quarter and Limerick had scored 23 goals en route to the All-Ireland final against Wexford – Bob McConkey, Paddy Barry and Willie Gleeson the chief marksmen in the blitz. Wexford were no slouches either, running in 10 goals to Offaly's six in the Leinster semi before ambushing All-Ireland champions Dublin by 2–3 to 1–3 in the provincial final.

1918 took another terrible turn when, as the First World War approached its end, the Spanish flu started to sweep the globe, eventually claiming more lives than the war itself. The flu's impact was so severe in Wexford that the county had to withdraw from the All-Ireland hurling final fixed for November, but Limerick – back in Foynes for training – declined the offer of a walkover and the game was refixed for 26 January 1919. Picked by a county board committee, Limerick were a 'proper' county team with players drawn from a number of clubs, including Young Irelands, Claughaun, Pallas, Boher, Cappamore and county champions Newcastlewest.

In the lingo of the day, they 'were trained to the ounce' and, judging from the player profiles in the local papers, the team had added some athleticism and 'science' to the 'brawn and bravery' Limerick approach of old. They were captained from centre-back by Willie Hough and he was flanked by Jack Keane and Dinny Lanigan to form a formidable half-back line nicknamed the 'Hindenburg

Line' after the German defensive stronghold during the war. It was the springboard for another tearaway Limerick display in the final. The *Sport* correspondent was impressed:

> It was immaterial to the Limerick men how the ball came their way, whether on the ground or in the air, as they never failed to get on to it. Another feature of their play was their overhead passing which at times completely non-plussed their opponents.

As for poor Wexford, they were 'too bad to be true. Seldom indeed in an important match have we seen such missing … their hitting was short and lacked direction.' It was 5–4 to 1–2 at half-time and McConkey, Barry and Gleeson piled on more misery in the second half, with Gleeson completing a hat-trick. The most graphic summing up of the day was a newspaper sketch depicting Limerick goalkeeper Mick Murphy flapping his arms about himself to keep warm.

LIMERICK: M. Murphy; M. Rochford, P. Kennedy, P. McInerney; J. Keane, W. Hough, D. Lanigan; D. Troy, J. Humphreys; D. Ryan, W. Gleeson, W. Ryan; T. McGrath, B. McConkey, P. Barry.

WEXFORD: M. Cummins (capt), M. Stafford, C. Hyland, D. Kavanagh, P. Roche, L. Leary, J. Fortune, R. Walsh, N. Leary, J. Synnott, J. Fogarty, M. Neville, M. Murphy, P. Fagan, R. Lambert.

Referee: W. Walsh (Waterford)

Attendance: 20,000

15. Blood and Bandages

1919 MUNSTER FINAL (Markets Field, 24 August)
Cork 3–5 Limerick 1–6

The Cork team gave a wonderful display of hurling ... In my opinion, they are the finest combination that ever played in Croke Park.
Michael Collins (September 1919)[1]

DO THEIR CRIMSON-RED jerseys give Cork hurlers a psychological advantage over opponents donning more muted tones? The answer is yes, according to academic studies which claim that sportspeople may be subconsciously intimidated by opponents kitted out in red[2] while in contests where athletes are evenly matched, those wearing red were more likely to win.[3] The success of Manchester United, Liverpool, Arsenal, Bayern Munich, Munster rugby, Ferrari in Formula One and Tiger Woods are cited as evidence by supporters of the theories. However, Cork ended up playing in their famed and feared 'blood and bandages' colours by dint of a historical quirk rather than design. In early 1919, the crown forces raided Cork county board's offices and made off with the blue-and-saffron jerseys, emblazoned with an outsized 'C' in Gaelic lettering, which had been Cork's uniform since the GAA made official county strips obligatory in 1913. No replacement 'C' jerseys were readily available and Cork officials borrowed some kit from the Fr O'Leary Temperance Association hurling team which had amalgamated with St Finbarr's.

More maroon than red, the Fr O'Leary jerseys were first worn by Cork in their 1919 Munster quarter-final victory over Waterford and were retained for the semi-final against Tipperary on 29 June at the Athletic Grounds in Cork where the *Examiner* reported that 'spectators were provided with a scientific exhibition of the code' and it 'was only in the closing stages that Cork assumed control', winning by 2–4 to 2–3.

> In the front division and also in some portions of their midfield department, Cork were weak but the backs were reliable. Some changes will be needed in the team if success over Limerick is to be secured.

Known as the 'big four', the Cork county board selection committee largely kept faith with a team led by Jimmy 'Major' Kennedy, a prolific goal scorer from county champions Carrigtwohill. In contrast to previous years, when the county champions called the shots and often provided the bulk of the county team, this Cork side drew players from seven clubs in addition to Major Kennedy and his Carrigtwohill team-mates – goalkeeper Ned Grey and the versatile John O'Keeffe. Blackrock's Sean Óg Murphy at full-back and Connie Sheehan (Redmonds) at Number 6 led the defence and Tim Nagle, the blacksmith from Killavullen, was a formidable figure in midfield. O'Keefe, Con Lucy (Collegians), John Barry Murphy (Cloughduv) and Kennedy had nailed down places in the supposedly weak forward division where 19-year-old Paddy 'Balty' Aherne was drafted in at Number 11 for the Munster final against All-Ireland champions Limerick at the Markets Field on 24 August.

There was immense interest, hype even, in the game. *Sport* had begun its countdown in the 2 August edition telling readers that 'the skill and resources of Cork hurling cannot be depreciated and a Munster championship is long due around Shandon way ... so the prospects of a Fiannaic contest are assured'. Two weeks later, the paper reported that 'Cork are pretty sanguine of lowering the colours of the champions. Both teams have undergone a special preparation for the match and Cork will complete their training tomorrow with a match at Queenstown Junction when the

Probables oppose the famous Blackrock combination.' The *Cork Weekly Examiner* correspondent stated he didn't 'remember a Munster final in which there has been such widespread interest manifested. There is not the smallest doubt that the attendance will break all previous records.' That it did. It's estimated that at least 20,000 spectators travelled to Limerick for the game with the *Cork Examiner* reporting 'every conceivable mode of conveyance was requisitioned regardless of expense or personal inconvenience'. The mass manoeuvre involved legions of bicycles, pony and traps and the few motorised vehicles available while many others walked long distances to see the match.

The throw-in was delayed because of an overflow of spectators into the pitch, but referee Willie Walsh got the game underway at 4.15 and the hurling in the early stages was of a 'most strenuous order, man marking was giving little opportunity for open play'. The breakthrough score came late in the half when 'Major' Kennedy rushed a goal to leave Cork leading 1–3 to 0–3 at half-time. Limerick scored a 'sensational' goal on the restart, but a goal from free-taker J.J. Hassett steadied Cork, and as the game opened up 'from end to end the ball travelled with lightning like rapidity'. The deciding score came when Hassett landed a 70 in the square, the Cork forwards piled in and Kennedy 'rushed the leather to the net for a goal of a very meritorious nature and at a very critical time'. Limerick launched some 'desperate onslaughts', but could only manage a point in reply.

The same venue hosted the All-Ireland semi-final on 7 September when Kennedy and Hassett were again Cork's chief scorers in a 3–8 to 0–1 victory over Galway. Awaiting Cork in the final were Dublin who had sleepwalked their through an 8–8 to 5–4 victory over Meath in the Leinster semi-final before defeating Kilkenny by 1–5 to 1–2 in a provincial final described by *Sport* 'as a battle of giants from beginning to end ... there was not a single weak spot in either combination'. Not for the first or last time, Clare's Tommy Daly in goal was the difference for Dublin and he 'effected some marvellous saves' in the final 10 minutes when Dick Grace led Kilkenny's charge for a winner.

Not even Daly could stop Major Kennedy and his team-mates in the All-Ireland final played in front of 27,000 spectators on 21 September. Sixteen years of frustration, not to mention three All-Ireland final defeats by one point to Kilkenny, were swept away. The *Examiner* reported that Cork had 'played the first half with a masterly resourcefulness which never left the issue clouded'. Cork led by 4–2 to 1–1 at half-time and Major Kennedy, Con Lucy and John Barry Murphy scored two goals apiece while Hassett chipped in with three points as the Dubs were overwhelmed by 6–4 to 2–4. The contributions of Sean Murphy, Connie Sheehan, Tim Nagle, John Barry Murphy and young Balty Aherne were also acclaimed by the *Examiner*.

A week later, 32,000 people paid in to Croke Park to watch Kildare defeat Galway in the football final. The two finals contributed to a record year's gate receipts for the GAA which for a few months during 1919 regained its pre-1915 momentum to the extent that 'a whole series of improvements to Croke Park, to accommodate even bigger crowds, were decided on by the central council'.[4] These ambitious plans had to be shelved, though, as the GAA found itself consumed by the national struggle and terror of the next two years.

CORK: E. Grey; P. O'Halloran, S. Óg Murphy, F. Kelleher; M. Murphy, C. Sheehan; D. Ring; J.J. Hassett; T. Nagle; J. O'Keeffe; P. Aherne, J. Barry Murphy; R. O'Gorman, C. Lucey, J. Kennedy.

LIMERICK: M. Murphy; J. Rochford, P. Kennedy, D. Lanigan; J. Keane, W. Hough, W. Ryan; D. Ryan, J. Humphrey; P. McGrath, W. Gleeson, P. Barry; R. McConkey, J. Griffin, P. McInerney.

Referee: Willie Walsh (Waterford)

Attendance: 20,000

16. Hurricane Hurling

1922 ALL-IRELAND FINAL (Croke Park, 9 September 1923)
Kilkenny 4–2 Tipperary 2–6

The spectators lining the pitch were on their feet now and the pressmen were shut out, but the exciting game proceeded – hats and sticks were thrown promiscuously into the air when Kilkenny smashed through the winning goal.

The Irish Times (10 September 1923)

THERE WAS INTENSE pressure on Kilkenny approaching the delayed 1922 All-Ireland final. In the decade since the county's last title, they had been beaten twice by Laois, were sucker-punched by Tipperary in the 1916 decider and then lost five times on the bounce to Dublin. Dick Grace from Tullaroan was the only playing link with the 1904–1913 era as a young squad went into collective training under mentors that included six-time All-Ireland medallist Paddy 'Icy' Lanigan and seven-times medallist Jack Rochford. Collective training usually involved a military-style approach to physical preparation in quiet surroundings, but some unlikely benefactors gave an unconventional twist to Kilkenny's countdown.

While the team was training, the Earl of Ormonde invited them to visit the Picture Gallery in Kilkenny Castle. Senator Countess Dowager Desert allowed the players to spend hours in the gardens at Talbot's Inch and the C.Y.M.S. placed the billiards tables and premises at their disposal. The team appreciated these gestures and took advantage of all the facilities.[1]

As Kilkenny fine-tuned body and soul by the Nore, the Tipperary team, drawn from Boherlahan, Toomevara and Moycarkey-Borris were recovering from a thunderous Munster final replay against Limerick. It had been 2–2 apiece the first day, and the press reports paint a hair-raising picture of the replay won 4–2 to 1–4 by Tipperary on 12 August at the Markets Field. 'The contest will rank as the most Homeric encounter in the annals of the game. Its pace was terrific and the casualty list abnormal,' was one summing up. Not to be outdone, *Sport*'s correspondent wrote that:

> If you were to put two strong, swift, eager hurlers with camáns and 'slitter' on the threshing floor of a farm, you would have something like the breast-to-breast, stroke upon stroke, which took place in the Markets Field on Sunday last. 'Hurricane hurling' one report described it while another compared it to an 'ancient battle' where every man was pitted against an opponent whose undoing was his vital purpose. It was grim and fierce and dangerous work and necessarily casualties were heavy; but to the eternal honour of the teams, it was clean and chivalric.

Twenty-seven special trains, from as far away as Belfast, Sligo and Galway, were laid on to bring supporters to Dublin on 9 September for the showdown between Tipp's warriors and Kilkenny's emerging stylists. The Waterford 'special' was packed by the time it reached Attanagh and Abbeyleix stations. These stations, although geographically in Laois, were the connections for some Kilkenny supporters who, stranded on the platforms, missed out on what *Sport* adjudged 'a great game, perhaps as great as any ever seen'.

The *Irish Times* correspondent rated it as a game 'which will be ranked as perhaps the best played in the hurling code of modern times'. From the off, the 26,119 spectators were treated to 'alternate scoring, clean hard hitting, with clashing splintering ash wielded by the greatest experts in the land; electric movement from goal to goal; frequent blade to blade duels for possession; quickly changing fortunes – yet for all, a struggle fought out to the end with splendid, though relentless spirit'. The first-half scoring, though, was low with a Dick Grace goal from a 21 cancelling out three Tipp points from John Cleary and J.J. Hayes. Martin 'Roundy' Lalor and Hayes swapped points to leave it 1–1 to 0–4 at the break.

Tipperary resumed as though determined to kill off the challengers with one sustained charge. 'For fully 10 minutes, the intensity of Tipperary's attack brought the huge crowd of stand seaters to their feet. It was immense,' gasped the *Irish Times*' man. 'Yet Kilkenny backs fought back doggedly; half a score of players were grouped together and a forest of hurlers stormed the Leinster goal. When a respite came with the ball out of play, the attackers and defenders seemed too weary to hold their camáns.'[2] Tipp's pressure eventually yielded a goal from Boherlahan's Paddy Power and another point from Hayes to push them four ahead.

Kilkenny held their nerve and their 'speedy, accurate hitting, particularly [in] overhead passages' opened up the play. John Roberts scored a fine point before they engineered a 'rushed' goal which is credited to Mattie Power although Paddy O'Donoghue, Roberts and Dick Tobin were also involved after Dick Grace had floated in a 70 with 10 or so minutes remaining. The title, however, looked to be heading south when Bill Dwan raced through to finish a long drive from Johnny Leahy past Kilkenny keeper Mark McDonald.

Kilkenny exploded to life again with three minutes left. A goal from Paddy O'Donoghue levelled the match before Dick Tobin, from Clomanto near Urlingford, flashed the winning goal past Jack 'Skinny' O'Meara, the famed Toomevara keeper who had missed the 1916 final, and lost out in the 1913 and 1917 finals to Kilkenny and Dublin respectively. Bill Dwan scored a final Tipperary point, but Kilkenny held out for a victory the likes of which wouldn't be seen again in an All-Ireland hurling final until Offaly's 'five-minute miracle' in 1994. The new champions were captained by Mooncoin's Wattie Dunphy from centre-back. He was the first Kilkenny man to lift the MacCarthy Cup and his brother Eddie led the forwards from

Number 11 (two more Dunphy brothers, Joe and William, would later play for the county). The result was also notable for being Kilkenny's last championship victory over Tipperary until 1967.

The thrilling quality of the Kilkenny–Tipperary clash confirmed the observation in *Sport*'s preview that 'it is a strange and gratifying fact that the national pastime has emerged from the ordeal through which we have just passed with unimpaired vitality and growing popularity'. It was the third and best of the five All-Ireland hurling finals played at Croke Park between May 1922 and December 1924 as the GAA made up for lost time and embraced the sort of future not even Michael Cusack could have imagined for the national pastime.

KILKENNY: M. McDonald; J. Tobin, J. Holahan, P. Glendon; T. Carroll, W. Dunphy (capt), D. Grace (1–0, f); P. Aylward, B. Kenny; M. Lalor, E. Dunphy, P. O'Donoghue (1–0); D. Tobin (1–0), J. Roberts (0–1), M. Power (1–0).

TIPPERARY: J. O'Meara; S. Hackett, A. O'Donnell, J. Power; J. Leahy (capt), P. Browne, T. Dwan; J. Cleary, J.J. Hayes (0–4, 2fs); B. Dwan (1–1), J. Fitzpatrick, P. Power (1–0); J. Darcy, M. Kennedy, P. Spillane.

Referee: Pat Dunphy (Laois)

Attendance: 26,119

17. Into the West

1923 ALL-IRELAND FINAL (Croke Park, 14 September 1924)
Galway 7–3 Limerick 4–5

For the first time in the history of the GAA, Galway undertook to give their team serious preparation for the All-Ireland final and the material ably responded to the test.
Connacht Tribun, (20 September 1924)

THE SCENARIO IS familiar. Underdogs Galway tear out of the blocks in an All-Ireland semi-final and dismantle the opposition who, on this occasion, don't even manage a single score in the first half. The date is 18 May 1924, and Galway have just knocked Kilkenny, the defending All-Ireland champions, out of the championship. Even allowing for the champions' lethargy and Galway's improving form, it was still a sensational result – the first of the semi-final thunderbolts that would in time become a Galway speciality. Unlike most of those later ambushes, this one was followed by an equally convincing performance in the All-Ireland final. Galway started and finished the stronger against Limerick to win a first All-Ireland title, becoming the 11th county to enter the hurling roll of honour.

Why it took so long to win that first title is as puzzling as the county's current woes, and shows that it's not today or yesterday that Galway hurlers became exasperating underachievers. When the GAA was founded in 1884, Galway had a hurling tradition to match if not surpass that of all its rivals bar Tipperary and, at a push, Cork. But after losing the first All-Ireland hurling final to Tipperary, Galway's fortunes nosedived while other counties built dynasties. Galway didn't compete in the championship again until 1897 and it was 1900 before they next won a game, defeating Antrim in the All-Ireland semi-final before being beaten 6–13 to 1–5 by Tipperary in the home final.

That sort of hiding became the norm rather than the exception. Some of the semi-final capitulations included a 10–13 to 0–0 against Cork in 1902 and a 27-point beating from Tipperary in 1908. It was 8–1 to 0–0 against Limerick in 1911 and 6–6 to 0–0 in 1914 against Cork who were nominated to represent Munster although Clare, in turn, beat Cork in the southern decider. Roscommon defeated Galway in the 1913 Connacht semi-final and the most bizarre entry in the litany is the 10–1 to 4–1 defeat to Mayo (Castlebar) in the 1909 Connacht final, played shortly after Galway had run Tipperary to a goal in the 1909 All-Ireland semi-final! Little wonder then that the *Connacht Tribune* report on the 1923 All-Ireland victory lamented that 'for 36 years [Galway] had participated in the [All-Ireland] semi-final without a thought of winning, depending on some unforeseen act of providence or ill-luck to their opponents to put up a good fight'.

They put up a good fight in 1904 when Kilkenny needed a late burst of scores to win by four points in a semi-final played before an estimated 10,000 crowd in Athlone. Tom Semple's Tipperary machine barely held out, 6–7 to 5–7, in the 1909 All-Ireland semi-final. 'We have always maintained and we have told the Galway hurlers that they could hurl with any team in Ireland if they could only get rid of that nervousness that grips them when they go to play outside Connaught,' was the *Sport* verdict.

Those 1904 and 1909 semis, along with a Croke Cup success in 1907, proved that the hurling talent was there, so how then to account for Galway's woeful overall championship record? The Land War and emigration undoubtedly took a toll in the 1890s and 1900s, but these factors weren't unique to Galway. Although isolated in Connacht, they were still exposed to top-class opposition in competitions such as the Croke Cup and they surely could have learned something about the evolving nature of post-1884 hurling from their near neighbours Tipperary. A more likely explanation is that the Galway championship was seen as an end in itself by the dominant clubs such as Ardrahan, Peterwell, Kilconeiron and Craughwell.

Galway eventually put the pieces together in the early 1920s. A powerful new club side from Tynagh was one catalyst; another was the influence of Tom Kenny, the IRB activist, long-time GAA administrator and blacksmith from Craughwell. He ensured that Galway picked a proper county team and embraced the collective training approach that had helped Limerick, Clare and Laois win titles in the previous decade.

The 1923 championship campaign began with a 13–8 to 0–1 victory over Roscommon in the Connacht final. The delayed Munster championship meant that the 1923 All-Ireland series wasn't resolved until 1924. Galway went into full-time training for two weeks before the All-Ireland semi-final against Kilkenny played at Croke Park on 24 May in 'brilliant sunshine which taxed the players heavily', according to the *Irish Independent*. The champions were held scoreless in the first half while the challengers ran up 3–2 by half-time. There was no let-up and Leonard McGrath, Ignatius Harney and Bernie Gibbs were the main scorers as Galway rattled in 5–4 to Kilkenny's two goals.

Two months earlier, Limerick had defeated Tipperary by six points in the Munster final and coasted to a 7–4 to 0–1 semi-final win over Ulster champions Donegal on 27 April. 'It was the first visit of a Donegal team to Dublin and the Ulster representatives relied to a large extent on members of the Civic Guard stationed in their county,' reported the *Irish Independent*. 'Though outclassed on the play, they fought stubbornly to the end.' The final was fixed for 24 June, but Limerick refused to play as a protest against the continued detention by the state of Republican prisoners from the Civil War. They were disqualified from the championship, but Galway wouldn't accept a walkover and when the prisoner issue was resolved in July, the path was cleared for the counties to meet at Croke Park on 14 September.

The previous month, three players from Galway – John 'Junior' Mahony, Mick Dervan and Bernie Gibbs – and five from Limerick – Willie Ryan, Dave Murnane, Garrett Howard, Willie Gleeson and Jimmy Humphries – had played together on the Irish team that won the international hurling event at the inaugural Tailteann Games in Croke Park. Junior Mahony, the dashing goalkeeper from Ardrahan, did much to thwart Limerick's comeback in the second half of the All-Ireland final.

Two goals – attributed in some accounts to Leonard McGrath, in others to Mick Kenny and McGrath – gave Galway an early advantage. Limerick, reportedly taken aback by Galway's pace and physicality, clawed their way back. Willie Gleeson and Dinny Lanigan scored goals to push them ahead but Andy Kelly bustled the Limerick keeper over the line just before half-time to level it at 3–0 to 2–3. Mick Gill from Ballindereen took command of the game for Galway after the break, lobbing high balls into the Limerick goalmouth where Gibbs, Dick Morrissey and McGrath goaled to give Galway a commanding lead. Limerick rallied but 'Mahony was as safe as a stone wall, bringing down successive shots from McConkey, Neville and Gleeson ... the Galway keeper saved the game at this critical stage', wrote Pat'O (P.D. Mehigan) in *The Irish Times*.

'The vigour and dash of the westerners' had 'thrown Limerick off their game' enthused the *Connacht Tribune*. The 'masterly' Mick Gill was hailed as 'clearly the most effective player on the field' and the *Tribune* also emphasised the role of collective training in Galway's victory.

The team spent several weeks before the All-Ireland final at the Rockfield House estate near Athenry preparing under manager Tom Kenny and trainer Jack Berry from Gort. The Rockfield regime began at 6 a.m. with a cold bath followed by a dose of health salts and an hour's exercise before breakfast. Hurling drills and training took the squad up to dinner at 1 p.m. followed by some rest and an afternoon running session on a nearby railway line. The players unwound by playing handball and cards in the evening before lights out at 10 p.m.

Fortune didn't smile for too long on Galway. After proving their worth by defeating Tipperary 3–1 to 2–3 in the 1924 All-Ireland semi-final on 27 November, they faced Dublin in the All-Ireland final on 15 December. Lining out at midfield for Dublin was September's hero Mick Gill. He was a Dublin-based garda and a new rule, applicable for the 1924 championships, meant that players had to declare for the county in which they were resident. The game was level at half-time, but Dublin went on to win by 5–3 to 2–6, Gill giving another masterclass from midfield for a powerful Dublin side that included Tommy Daly from Clare, Bob Mockler from Tipperary, Garrett Howard from Limerick and Tom Finlay from Laois. Mick Gill later stated:

> I will without hesitation say that if I had been playing for Galway in the 1924 final, I honestly think that they would have beaten Dublin. And by keeping together, they would have won through in 1925 and 1926.[1]

As it was, only four of the 1923 team played in the 13-point defeat to Tipperary in the 1925 final. The most prolific forwards – McGrath from Mullagh and Gibbs from Gort – had emigrated and apart from Gill's change of allegiance, Galway were also without the defensive axis of Jim Power and Mick Kenny. The good times were over and it was 57 years before they returned.

GALWAY: J. Mahony; M. Dervan, J. Power, T. Fleming; N. Gilmartin, M. Kenny (capt), S. Garvey; M. Gill, J. Morris; I. Harney, D. Morrissey, M. King; L. McGrath, A. Kelly, B. Gibbs.

LIMERICK: P. McInerney (capt), J. Hanley, D. Murnane, W. Hough, D. Lanigan, W. Gleeson, J. Humphries, M. Neville, J.J. Kinnane, J. Keane, T. McGrath, M. Cross, R. McConkey, J. O'Grady, M. Fitzgibbon; Subs: S. Shanny for J.J. Kinnane, J. O'Shea for R. McConkey.

Referee: P. Kennifick (Cork)

Attendance: 15,000

18. Changing of the Guard

1926 MUNSTER FINAL REPLAY (Semple Stadium, 3 October)
Cork 3–6 Tipperary 2–4

The year was a vintage one in GAA annals. The sun of success beamed benignly from every quarter.
Phil O'Neill, *Twenty Years of the GAA*

1926 WAS A year of new beginnings for the GAA, a year when the calendar and character of hurling as we know it began to take shape. The first National Hurling League, which had begun the previous November, was concluded in May – with Cork defeating Dublin for the inaugural title. In August, 2RN, as the national radio station was then known, relayed the first live outside broadcast of a sports event anywhere in Europe when it covered the Kilkenny v. Galway hurling semi-final in Croke Park. There were also record attendances for the Munster and All-Ireland hurling finals. In another landmark, Tipperary, the 1925 All-Ireland champions, embarked on a coast-to-coast tour of the United States, the first hurling team to tour the States since the 1888 'Invasion'.

Tipperary travelled on the invitation of the Gaels of Chicago, led by P.J. Cahill of Holycross, and the seven-week tour took in games in New York, Boston, Buffalo, Chicago and San Francisco. The excitement of Jazz Age America and the acclaim of their exiled countrymen must have been all the sweeter reward for veteran team captain Johnny Leahy and his players when you consider the sequence of killer defeats Tipperary had experienced in the decade bookended by their 1916 and 1925 All-Ireland victories. They had been defeated narrowly by the subsequent champions Limerick and Cork in 1918 and 1919, hit for two late goals by Kilkenny in 1922 and had been one-point losers to resurgent Galway in the 1924 semi-final. Complacency was their undoing in the 1917 final when Dublin selected seven students from the Collegians club. 'We thought we were going to wallop the schoolboys but 'twas they who taught us our lessons,' was Leahy's appraisal of that one.[1]

But after beating Cork by two points in the Munster semi, the rest of the 1925 campaign was a lap of honour for a Tipp team which included Martin Kennedy, a young full-forward already well on his way to becoming a blue-and-gold legend. Waterford were taken by 17 points in the Munster final, Antrim were hit for a dozen goals in the All-Ireland semi and, after a good start, Galway folded by 13 points in the final.

A member of the Tipp party, Thomas Kenny from Youghalarra, later published a detailed tour diary which covered everything from the day-to-day adventures of the party to the nature of hurling in the States and the impact of prohibition. The diary includes a letter sent to each player a few months before the tour from the Tipperary county board emphasising that on them rested not alone 'the honour of gallant Tipperary ... but the honour of Ireland'. They were urged to 'train consistently and earnestly' so that 'when the final whistle sounds, Tipperary's victory will be broadcasted to the world, and the waiting Gaels at home will smile and say: "Good old Tipperary; we sent the right men"'. The selected players were also instructed to bring with them: '4 good Hurleys, 1 pair Hurling Boots, 1 spare Suit Clothes, 1 small Hand Bag, 1 Attaché Case.'[2]

The Tipperary party sailed from Cobh and their first game against Offaly, the champions of New York, was played at the Polo Grounds on 30 May and set the tone for the rest of the tour – the Irish champions coasting to an 11–4 to 2–2 victory. They swept the exiles before them in the remaining six games – Martin Kennedy scoring a total 27 goals, including seven in one match. Thomas Kenny noted that 'a lot of bitterness seems to exist' between the Irishmen who organised themselves along county lines in their new country.

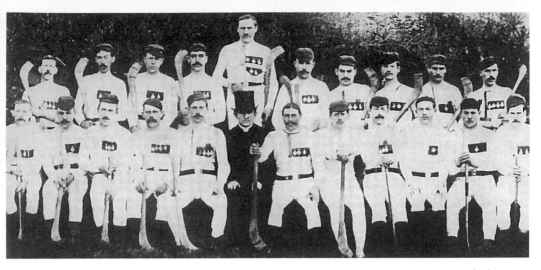

The 1890 Aghabullogue team that won Cork's first All-Ireland hurling title. Back (l-r): J. Buckley, D. Linehan, D. Looney, D. Drew, D. Lane (capt), J. Henchion, J. O'Connor, T. Twomey, M. Horgan, P. Buckley. Front: P. O'Riordan, J. O'Reilly, T. Kelleher, D. O'Sullivan, T. Good, Rev. A. O'Sullivan, D. Horgan, E. O'Reilly, J. Linehan, J. Kelleher, J. O'Sullivan, O. O'Riordan

The London team that shocked Cork to win the 1901 All-Ireland title. Also pictured are the team's mentors and the match referee J. McCarthy. Back: W. Douglas (Secretary) P. King (Clare) J. O'Connell (Cork) T. Daly (Limerick) T. Redmond (Wexford) D. Horgan (Cork) J. McCarthy (Referee) L. O'Toole J. Shine (Galway). Middle: J. Tobin (Treasurer) J. Lynch (Cork) J. King (Clare) N. Barret (Kerry) C. Crowley (Cork) J. Fitzgerald (Limerick) M. McMahon (Tipperary) M. O'Brien Liam McCarthy (President). Front: M. Horgan (Cork) J. Barry (Cork) J. O'Brien (Cork) J.G. Coughlan Capt (Clare) J. Kellagher (Cork) T. Barry (Cork) J. O'Brien (Clare)

The 1904 Kilkenny team that won the county's first All-Ireland title, defeating Cork 1-9 to 1-8 in Carrick on Suir. Back: Dick Brennan, Dick 'Drug' Walsh, Eddie Doyle, Paddy 'Icy' Lanigan, J.J. Brennan, Martin Lalor, Jack Hoyne. Seated: Jim Dunne, Sim Walton, Pat Fielding, Dan Stapleton, Jer Doheny (capt), Jim Lalor, Jack Rochford, Pat 'Fox' Maher. Front: Dick Doyle, Pat Saunders.

The 1907 All-Ireland final was rated as the best played up to then and saw Kilkenny edge out Cork 3-12 to 4-8 in Dungarvan. Back: Jack Keoghan, Jack Rochford, Tom Kenny, Dan Stapleton, Danny O'Connell (Trainer/Manager), Paddy 'Icy' Lanigan, John T Power, Dick Brennan, Sim Walton. Middle: Eddie Doyle, Dick Doherty, Mick Doyle, Father James Dollard (Mooncoin), Dick 'Drug' Walsh, Jimmy 'The Wren' Kelly, Dick Doyle, Dan Kennedy. Front: Matt Gargan, Jack Anthony.

The team captains, Tipperary's Patrick 'Wedger' Meagher (left) and Cork's Barry Murphy, shake hands before the 1913 Munster final which was won by Meagher's team who were nicknamed 'the Toomevara Greyhounds'.

The Clare team weren't short of mentors when they won the county's first All-Ireland title in 1914, defeating Laois by 5-1 to 1-0 in the final. Back (players only): Thomas McGrath, John Fox, Rob Doherty, Michael Flanagan, Jim Clancy, Joe Power. Seated: Jim Guerin, Pat 'Fowler' McInerney, Willie 'Dodger' Considine, Amby Power, Martin 'Handsome' Moloney, Ed Grace, John Shalloo. Front: Brendan Considine, James 'Sham' Spellissy.

Laois ambushed Cork in the 1915 final to win the county's only All-Ireland senior hurling title. Back (players only): Joe Carroll, J. Deegan, J. Loughman, P. Ryan, J. Dunphy, J. Phelan, P. Campion. Seated: J. Phelan, T. Finlay, J. Walsh, J. Finlay (capt), B. O'Keeffe, E. McEvoy, Jim Carroll. Front: J. Hiney, J. Daly, Jack Carroll.

Cork wore the famed red jerseys for the first time in 1919 after the county's official saffron-and-blue colours were seized by Crown Forces. Back: S. McCarthy, M. Byrne, N. Grey, J. Barry Murphy, T. Irwin, S. Óg Murphy, D. O'Gorman, C. Sheehan, J. Lynch, D. Ring, J.J. Walsh. Seated: T. Nagle, P O'Halloran, J O'Keefe, Rev. Fr. Fitzgerald, J. 'Major' Kennedy (capt), I. Murphy, J.B. Murphy, J. Hassett. Front: F. Barry, C. Lucey, F. Kelleher, M. Murphy, P. Healy, E. Coughlan.

The Dublin hurlers are interested onlookers as Michael Collins shakes hands with GAA President Alderman Jim Nowlan (Kilkenny) at the 1921 Leinster final in Croke Park on 11 September, 1921. Dublin defeated Kilkenny 4-4 to 1-5, but were beaten by Limerick in the All-Ireland final. On the left is Harry Boland, another War of Independence hero and former Dublin hurler.

The Dublin team that defeated Galway in the 1924 All-Ireland final (played 14 December) included Mick Gill who had helped his native Galway win the 1923 final two months previously. Back (including mentors and officials): E. Fleming, P. Donnelly, R. Doherty, J. Bannon, T. Kelly, P. Kenefick, J. Ryan. Middle: R. McCowen, M. Dromgoole, P. Kavanagh, M. Darcy, P. Aylward, J. Walsh, M. Holland, J. Conroy, R. Mockler, A. Harty, J O'Neill. Front: T. Finlay, T. Barry, T. Wall (capt), P.J. Walsh (Dublin County Board President), D. O'Neill, W. Small, G. Howard, M. Gill. Seated: W. Banim, T. Daly.

Lory Meagher poses for posterity with the Liam MacCarthy. The Tullaroan midfield wizard captained Kilkenny to a 2-5 to 2-4 victory in the 1935 All-Ireland final.

Cork completed hurling's first All-Ireland four-in-a-row when they defeated Dublin 2-13 to 1-2 in the 1944 final. Back: Billy Walsh (Cork County Board Chairman), John Quirke, Con Murphy, Alan Lotty, Willie Murphy, Joe Kelly, Tom Mulcahy, Paddy O'Donovan, Batt Thornhill, Jim 'Tough' Barry (trainer). Front: Jim Young, Jack Lynch, Sean Condon, Jim Morrisson, Con Cottrell, Christy Ring, Din Joe Buckley.

On their return, it was back to the hard grind of Munster championship hurling for the 'Tipperary Terrors' as they had been labelled by one San Franciscan newspaper. They played Limerick in Dungarvan on 22 August, scoring two late goals to win 6–5 to 4–6 in a game refereed by Paddy O'Keefe, or Pádraig Ó Chaoimh as he was better known in later years when he became general secretary of the GAA.

O'Keefe was then secretary of the Cork county board which took criticism for what the *Cork Examiner* labelled a 'fiasco' at the Cork Athletic Grounds in September when the Munster final between Cork and Tipp had to be abandoned after 20 minutes with Tipp leading by 1–2 to 0–0. The stewarding was inadequate for the estimated 25,000–30,000 crowd and crushing in the sideline seats and standing areas forced thousands of spectators onto the pitch. The re-fixture was played in Thurles and was acclaimed by the *Examiner* as 'one of the most brilliant, stirring and exacting exhibitions of the code that has been witnessed in the country for many years'. Two goals from Michael 'Gah' Aherne helped Cork to a 2–3 to 1–0 half-time lead, but Gah was sent off shortly before the break along with Tipp's Martin Mockler. Thurles erupted when Martin Kennedy scored a goal to give Tipp the lead in the final minutes, but Paddy 'Balty' Aherne, brother of Gah, scored a late equalising goal.

The capacity was increased still further for the replay on 4 October attended by an estimated 30,000–35,000 crowd who witnessed Cork win by 3–6 to 2–4 in a game that marked a significant changing of the guard in hurling.

Meanwhile, on 29 August the journalist P.D. Mehigan had provided the commentary for 2RN's coverage of the Kilkenny v. Galway All-Ireland semi-final. He would prove himself as talented with a microphone as a pen as he relayed the report of a thrilling game in which John Roberts scored five goals for Kilkenny who won by 6–2 to 5–1. It was a notable reversal of the previous year's semi-final when Galway had beaten Kilkenny 9–4 to 6–0 – a setback Kilkenny historian Tom Ryall partly blamed on the selectors' decision to recall 43-year-old goalkeeper John T. Power of Piltown. Earlier in the 1926 campaign, Kilkenny had defeated Dublin by 4–8 to 5–4 in a classic Leinster semi-final attended by over 12,000 spectators at New Ross.

A record attendance of 26,829 for the All-Ireland final on 24 October might well have been larger if it hadn't been for the falls of snow, hail and rain overnight and on the morning of the game. The sun eventually broke through and the first half was a tight affair with Lory Meagher, Dick Grace and Wattie Dunphy prominent for Kilkenny and Eudie Coughlan and Balty Aherne scoring the goals that gave Cork a 2–1 to 2–0 lead. That was as good as it got for Kilkenny as Cork, playing with the wind, cut loose after half-time – Balty Aherne completing a hat-trick as Cork ended a painful losing streak against Kilkenny dating back to 1904. Final score: Cork 4–6, Kilkenny 2–0.

It was the first of the three All-Irelands and two National League titles won in a six-year spell by the first Cork team managed by Jim 'Tough' Barry – the opera-loving tailor, former champion boxer and Old IRA man. Fittingly enough, the last big hurling engagement of the year was the Cork county final when St Finbarr's staged an audacious comeback to defeat Blackrock, who had supplied 10 of Cork's All-Ireland-winning team, by 6–2 to 5–4. The Rockies led 3–3 to 1–1 at half-time and were 5–4 to 2–2 ahead before the Barrs scored four goals in the last six minutes to claim the title.

CORK: J. Coughlan; M. Murphy, S. Murphy, E. O'Connell; D.B. Murphy, M. Murphy, J. O'Regan; E. Coughlan, J. Hurley; W. Higgins, P. Aherne, P. O'Sullivan; Dr J. Kearney, D. Aherne, M. Aherne.

TIPPERARY: M. Kennedy; S. Hackett, J. Leahy, M. Mockler; J. Gleeson, A. O'Donnell, S. Kenny; P. Collison, M. Darcy; P. Leahy, P. Cahill, P. Dwyer; M. Leahy, J.J. Callanan, Martin Kennedy.

Referee: P. McCullagh (Wexford)

Attendance: 30,000

19. Up the 'Dubs'

1927 ALL-IRELAND FINAL (Croke Park, 4 September)
Dublin 4–8 Cork 1–3

[Cork were] outpaced and outplayed by probably the best 15 men who have ever contested a championship final. This 15 representing Dublin in 1927 are the best I have seen.

The Irish Times (5 September 1927)

DUBLIN OCCUPIES A curious position in the hurling world. It has six All-Ireland senior hurling titles to its credit yet only one native Dubliner – Jim Byrne in 1938 – has won an All-Ireland hurling medal. There are 216 clubs affiliated to Dublin county board, a sizeable number of them dual entities, yet Dublin hurlers still struggle for support compared to the footballers.

The historian Paul Rouse has made a convincing argument, however, that without the initial support of native Dubliners, Michael Cusack's mission to revive hurling might never have got off the ground,[1] but by the 1900s football was the Gaelic game of choice in the capital. The hurlers were the first to win an All-Ireland title in 1889, but Dublin footballers had won 11 of their 24 All-Irelands by 1908. And while there was plenty of hurling played in the city, Dubliners' ambivalence towards the game increased in the 1910s when 'culchies', especially those working in the bar trade, began to dominate hurling in the city. The exclusion of native Dubs from their own county team peaked in the 1920s and 1930s when legions of countrymen migrated Liffeyside to join the guards, army or civil service.

The upshot was that not one Dubliner played on the 1927 team which P.D. Mehigan, who had witnessed over 30 All-Ireland hurling finals, rated as the finest to that point. Nine members of the Garda Club and three army men lined out on a team which was more or less a 1920s equivalent of the All Stars – from the great Dr Tommy Daly in goal and his countyman Pa 'Fowler' McInerney at full-back, through to Jimmy 'Builder' Walsh of Kilkenny at Number 7, the midfield maestro Mick Gill of Galway and Garrett Howard of Limerick on the wing. Tom Barry of Tipperary, Ned Fahy of Clare and Mattie Power of Kilkenny were prolific scorers in a forward line led by Dinny O'Neill of Laois.

Tommy Daly was the sole link with the 1917 student-powered Dublin team; he was also the only survivor from the 1920 team that had beaten Cork in the final. That team was captained by Bob Mockler of Tipperary who together with his Faughs club-mate Tommy Moore, had persuaded Joe Phelan of Laois to fall in with Dublin a few weeks before the final. Decades later in an interview with John D. Hickey of the *Irish Independent*, Moore recalled how he and Mockler had plotted the coup during an evening stroll through the city.

'What do you think of our chances?' asked Bob. 'It's going to be tough,' said I [Moore], 'but there's one man that can win it for us if we can get him and that's Joe Phelan of Laois who is studying medicine in the college.' We did get around him and although he only had three weeks to train, Phelan really got down to it and turned out on the day of the final like a greyhound. We were determined to win that match and the one thing that worried me was how Joe Phelan would stand up to Frank Kelleher [Cork full-back]. Well, I was not long wondering. The very first ball that dropped down between them Phelan burst the back of the net with it and we were never troubled after that.[2]

Phelan scored a hat-trick in Dublin's 4–9 to 4–6 victory.

A native of Ballyragget in Kilkenny, Moore was the quintessential countryman who made good in the capital through his hurling contacts. In 1924, he acquired Nagle's bar on Cathedral Street and renamed it the Gaelic Bar and, for many years, it was a halting point for All-Ireland-winning teams and the MacCarthy Cup. He died in 1973 and he is remembered by the Tommy Moore Cup his Faughs clubmen presented the following year to the GAA for the fledgling All-Ireland club hurling championship. Recalling the 1917 final between Dublin and Tipperary which had started at noon, Moore, a barman or 'curate' as they were then known, said that at the final whistle he and a few others had 'made a dash for the dressing room, tore into our clothes and away helter skelter to our jobs. I had eaten my breakfast at 8.30 that morning and all I had between that and 7 o'clock was a glass of water. These were tough times, tough games and tough men that played in them.'[3]

Tom Barry, Mattie Power and full-forward Ned Fahy of Clare were the most prolific scorers for Dublin during the 1927 campaign which began with an easy win over Wexford in the Leinster semi-final before Kilkenny were humbled 7–7 to 4–6 in the Leinster final. Dublin had led 7–4 to 1–2 at half-time; Builder Walsh and Mattie Power were two of the most prominent players in the crushing of their native county.

Dublin–Kilkenny was one of the keenest rivalries of this decade. They had played out a classic Leinster semi-final in 1926 at New Ross where Lory Meagher contributed 2–1 from midfield towards his side's 4–8 to 5–4 victory.

If Dublin had looked hot in the 1927 Leinster campaign, Cork initially looked unbeatable in Munster – following up a nine-goal rout of Kerry with a 2–13 to 2–3 defeat of Limerick in the semi. Clare pushed them hard in the final, losing by 5–3 to 3–4, but Eudie Coughlan, Dinny Barry Murphy, Jim O'Regan, Jim Hurley and the Ahernes resumed normal service by wiping out Galway by 5–6 to 0–2 in the All-Ireland semi-final.

Cork were firm favourites to retain their title but it was quickly apparent they were in trouble. 'From the moment when [Builder] Walsh scored that first long point to the final whistle, Cork never looked like retaining their championship,' wrote Pat'O in *The Irish*

Times. 'They were struggling yet struggling like champions.' Dublin led 2–3 to 0–1 at half-time, Mattie Power and Tom Barry scoring the goals.

The *Irish Independent* reported that:

Dublin played with fine combination and lasted better than the ex-champions who made a great rally midway through the second half, but failed to sustain the effort. The forwards were always well held by the Dublin backs. Cork had one goal disallowed – it was a score made direct from a touch puck[4] – but against this Dublin should, with luck, have increased their winning margin. Barry, Fahy and Power, the Dublin forwards, were a great force and the first-named, though knocked out twice, was an efficient marksman with frees. In the Dublin goal, Dr Daly, who was appearing for the fourth time in a final on the successful side, covered himself in glory, some of his saves being electrifying.

Reading between the lines, it appears that some old scores were also settled when the game had long been sorted. There were 'a few heated incidents which should be foreign to any form of sport', commented the *Irish Independent*, adding that referee Dinny Lanigan of Limerick 'had a betimes difficult task'. The journalist and GAA historian Seamus Ó Ceallaigh called it 'the tough as teak All-Ireland ... the most hard hitting game I remember on All-Ireland final day'.[5]

DUBLIN: T. Daly (Clare); J. Bannon (Tipperary), P. McInerney (Clare), J. Phelan (Laois); N. Tobin (Laois), M. Hayes (Limerick), J. Walsh (Kilkenny); M. Gill (Galway), J. Gleeson (Clare); T. O'Rourke (Clare), D. O'Neill (Laois), G. Howard (Limerick); T. Barry (Tipperary), N. Fahy (Clare), M. Power (Kilkenny).

CORK: J. Burke; Maurice Murphy, D. Barry Murphy, S. Óg Murphy; Michael Murphy, E. O'Connell, J. O'Regan; W. Higgins, P. Daly; J. Hurley, E. Coughlan, M. Leahy, P. Aherne, P. Delea, M. Aherne.

Referee: D. Lanigan (Limerick)

Attendance: 23,824

20. Rebels Halted

1930 MUNSTER SEMI-FINAL (Gaelic Grounds, 6 July)
Clare 6–6 Cork 5–6

Clare had exerted themselves more than ever before in fielding 15 of the strongest possible nature. Timely [reminders] were sent out calling to the aid of the Banner County those non-resident players who could be called upon to do battle in sterling terms.

Cork Examiner (7 July 1930)

EUDIE COUGHLAN WAS born to be a hurler. Other clans have amassed more All-Ireland medals, but none can match the Coughlans' achievement of supplying Cork with seven All-Ireland winners over two generations. Eudie's father Pat ('Parson') led the way during Cork's first three-in-a-row between 1892 and 1894 while on his mother's side, two of his uncles – William and Mick Dorney – played for Cork during the 1900s. The Coughlans and Dorneys were among the dozen or so families who made Blackrock a celebrated hurling village during the early decades of the GAA.

> To see the native Blackrock men was a revelation. They never caught a ball with hand after a lift; they never dallied with a ball. Their swing was long but crisp and graceful. They drew on 'lightning' balls off left and right, showing a command of ash that was astonishing. Hurling was in their blood – the Coughlans, Dorneys, O'Learys, Flahertys, Buckleys, Kidneys, Fitzgeralds, O'Riordans, Cotters, Deleas, Scannells, Murphys ...[1]

Eudie Coughlan was considered the finest of them all. Unlike the previous generation of Coughlans, who had generally played at the back, Eudie was a tough, athletic, high-scoring stylist whose legacy ensured he was chosen at Number 10 on the Cork hurling team of the century. He was one of 10 Blackrock men who had played on Cork's 1926 All-Ireland-winning team and they were still the dominant club in the county by 1930 when Cork were gunning for three-in-a-row.

Cork had responded to the 1927 All-Ireland defeat to Dublin by winning back-to-back titles. Galway were routed by 6–13 to 1–0 in the 1928 final which was marred by an early incident in which Galway's most influential player Mick King broke his leg. The previous month, King had captivated the Croke Park crowds with his display from midfield for Ireland against the United States in the Tailteann Games hurling final. Jim Power, a veteran of Galway's 1923 victory, 'was so upset by what happened to Mick King that when the final whistle sounded he threw down his hurley in disgust and never played county hurling again'.[2] 'Remember Mick King' was Galway's rallying cry when they faced Cork in the 1929 final, but the Munster champions were runaway winners again, 4–9 to 1–3, in front of just 15,000 spectators.

By the summer of 1930, Cork were also league champions and were fancied to become the first team to win five-in-a-row in Munster. The first obstacle was Clare in the Gaelic Grounds on 6 July. The Banner had flagged badly after their 1914 All-Ireland victory and were rocked by a 1926 Munster championship defeat to Kerry. They recovered to run Cork to five points in the 1927 Munster final and defeated Tipperary by three goals in the 1928 semi before losing to Cork in a replay.

By 1930, the GAA rules on residency had changed, meaning players domiciled in Dublin, for example, could play for their native counties if they signed a non-residents' declaration. This cleared the way for Tommy Daly, regarded as the greatest goalkeeper of this era, to resume duty for Clare for the first time since 1915 when he had played in the losing All-Ireland junior final against Laois. In the intervening years, he had won four All-Ireland medals with

Dublin and was routinely singled out in dispatches for his startling saves, his clearances and ability to side-step the full-on charges of two or three forwards. Also resuming service in the saffron and blue was Tom O'Rourke who had won an All-Ireland with Dublin in 1927.

The Gaelic Grounds was packed an hour before throw-in for a game the *Cork Examiner* reported was 'as thrilling an exhibition as the most ardent Gael could wish to witness'. Clare led by 3–5 to 3–4 at half-time and the *Clare Champion* reported the tension and excitement of the closing exchanges as 'indescribable'. Tom O'Rourke had scored a goal to put Clare ahead after half-time, but Jim Hurley, Eudie Coughlan and Paddy 'Balty' Aherne led a Cork rally and a goal from Willie Clancy – no relation to the piper – gave them the lead minutes from time. The identity of the man who scored Clare's decisive goal is unclear, the *Examiner* reporting that 'Clare whipped down the green and did the unexpected in registering another major'. And just when 'it seemed Cork's chance had come again Dr Daly ran out to intercept and clear'. Dr Daly is also credited with making a 'point blank save from Balty Aherne when he denied the Cork man a certain goal from close range'.[3]

A goalkeeper was also the hero of the hour in the Munster final three weeks later at the Cork Athletic Grounds, but this time it was Tipperary's Tommy O'Meara. The *Examiner* reported that the Toomevara man's 'wonderful netkeeping was to a very material extent responsible for the success' of his team. Apart from O'Meara's vigilance, Clare never seemed to get to grips with a pacey Tipp team. The ever-green Martin Kennedy, J.J. Callinan – back from a lengthy spell with Dublin – and Tom Leahy were Tipp's main scorers while midfielder Phil Cahill is credited with 'initiating the move away from ground hurling to the more spectacular catching and striking from the hand'.[4]

Mick King, following two years in recuperation, was back for Galway in the All-Ireland semi-final played at Birr where Tipp pulled away in the final quarter to win by 6–8 to 2–4. The final against Dublin was a much tighter affair, Tipp eventually outpacing a side captained by Kilkenny's Builder Walsh and featuring five Tipperary men in their line-up. The Munster champions led by a point at half-time and ran out 2–7 to 1–3 winners.

The 1930 defeat could have signalled the end for a Cork side who were the team of the 1920s, but they decided to give it one more year. With Eudie Coughlan as captain, they returned to win perhaps the most storied All-Ireland of them all – the 1931 trilogy against Kilkenny. Tommy Daly and Clare would also have one more unbelievable day in the sun.

CLARE: T. Daly, T. Mullane, J.J. Guinnane, J. Higgins, A. Neylan, J. Gleeson, J.J. Doyle, T. O'Rourke, L. Blake, M. White, J. Holohan, M. O'Rourke, M. Falvey, T. Considine (capt), T. Burnell.

CORK: P. Delea; M. Madden, E O'Connell, P. Collins; D.B. Murphy J. O'Regan, T. Barry; J. Hurley, M. O'Connell; E. Coughlan, P. Aherne, J. Barry; P. O'Grady, M. Aherne, W. Clancy.

Referee: Willie Walsh (Waterford)

Attendance: 25,000

21. 1931

1931 ALL-IRELAND FINAL, SECOND REPLAY (Croke Park, 1 November)
Cork 5–8 Kilkenny 3–4

We are living in an unparalleled hurling epoch.
Irish Press (12 October 1931)

TIME WAS ALMOST up in the 1931 All-Ireland final when Cork captain Eudie Coughlan slipped in possession within striking distance of the Kilkenny goal. The most reliable newspaper account says 'the sands were running out' when Coughlan executed the equalising score from a desperate position – 'he picked up a ball while lying prone and hurled it on his knees high above the posts'.[1] Coughlan's point saved Cork and led to two replays that are credited with being the making of hurling as a sport with an appeal far beyond its narrow playing base. The trilogy that concluded on 1 November broke attendance and gate-receipt records and created new levels of media and public interest.

There is an almost classical symmetry to the plot of the 1931 saga. Coughlan's equaliser – the response to a Lory Meagher point – was a decisive twist matched by the inspired Meagher playing through injury for most of the second game. In the third game, there was the pathos of Meagher rendered helpless on the sideline as Coughlan, 'playing undoubtedly the game of his career', drove Cork on. 'I can still see him [Meagher] in my mind's eye as I saw him then, in his best suit, hunched and bowed on the touchline seat, white-knuckled hands clasped tightly on a hurley, tears rolling down his cheeks because he could not answer his county's urgent call,' wrote the journalist and novelist Padraig Puirseal, a Kilkenny man.[2]

There was no shortage of other characters, incidents and black comedy but, in Coughlan and Meagher, the 1931 final had dual protagonists who personified much about their teams. Blackrock and Tullaroan, their respective clubs, were the most powerful hurling dynasties of the time, and both men were scions of families steeped in the game. Coughlan had been a 19-year-old sub when Cork had won the 1919 All-Ireland; by 1931, he was the leader of hardened and canny men who faced mostly youthful, inexperienced opponents whose leader Meagher was a late-blossoming genius. Meagher didn't have the aura of Christy Ring or Mick Mackey, but few hurlers have matched him for finesse and intelligence. 'I have not seen the equal of his artistry or watched a more supreme stylist,' wrote Puirseal, adding that Meagher had a 'remarkable sense of position and anticipation that gave the spectator the illusion that he could attract the ball to wherever he happened to be'.

While Coughlan and Meagher were the main characters, there would have been no trilogy in Croke Park without a stoppage-time point from Cork midfielder Jim Hurley that had forced a 4–0 to 1–9 draw in the Munster final against Waterford on 16 August. The Déise had 'surprised all by their scientific hurling and grim fighting spirit', reported the *Cork Examiner*, but Cork won the replay two weeks later by 5–4 to 2–1. In the Leinster final at Nowlan Park on 2 August, Kilkenny were pushed hard by Laois and required a late surge to eke out a 4–7 to 4–2 victory.

Matty Power, who had hurled with Dublin during the 1920s, was the only survivor from the 1922 All-Ireland-winning team to line out against Cork on 6 September. Meagher, full-back Peter O'Reilly and half-back Eddie Doyle had played in the losing 1926 final against Cork. Centre-back Podge Byrne had made his debut in 1927. What Kilkenny lacked in experience they compensated for in potential. Two defensive newcomers, Paddy Phelan and Paddy

Larkin, would in time become black-and-amber legends. County champions Mooncoin supplied a promising centre-forward Dick Morrissey while Martin White from Tullaroan and Dan Dunne were the other main scorers in a campaign that had seen Kilkenny defeat Galway 7–2 to 3–1 in the All-Ireland semi-final.

Cork started the 1931 final with 12 All-Ireland medallists. Eugene 'Marie' O'Connell, Dinny Barry Murphy and Jim Regan were the bedrock of the defence, while Mick O'Connell and Jim Hurley were a powerful midfield duo. The Aherne brothers, Mick 'Gah' and Paddy 'Balty', Pat Delea, and newcomers Willie Clancy and 'Hawker' O'Grady formed the forward sextet with Coughlan, who operated from Number 10.

The merits of both sides were considered in detail by a new national newspaper, the *Irish Press*, launched the day before the final. It was auspicious timing for all concerned. From the off, the new title's sports pages raised the bar for its competitors. It ran a full-page preview for the All-Ireland hurling final with cut-out photos of all 30 starting players. Expert analysis was provided by Willie Hough who had captained Limerick to the 1918 title – he predicted that 'the match will perhaps be the greatest hurling final ever played at the national stadium'.

In his preview, the *Irish Times* correspondent Pat'O noted that Cork, Kilkenny and Tipperary had won 30 of the 45 All-Irelands contested since 1887. He contrasted the 'purely scientific ball-playing' of previous Kilkenny–Cork finals as setting them apart from 'the daredevil, rushing tactics of Tipperary, Galway, Limerick and Clare … It's clear that deep in Kilkenny and Cork hurling there is a subtle something' which other counties hadn't captured. 'Spectators will mark it tomorrow,' he wrote, predicting that 'the teams will be level around the third quarter. The last quarter may be hectic … I believe Cork's weight and experience will prevail.'

He was as right as makes no difference. 'Hurling such as was seen yesterday at Croke Park defies graphic description,' was the *Irish Press*' verdict on the 1–6 to 1–6 draw.

The marking and striking was exceptionally keen and accurate ... The Kilkenny captain Lory Meagher was once more an outstanding figure on his side and his Cork vis-à-vis Hurley was equally brilliant. Regan, until his knee gave out, was as prominent as usual and Mattie Power was always a menace to the Cork defence. Individual mention beyond these would be invidious for there were no really weak points and few balls went loose in this splendid final.

Gah Aherne's goal shortly before half-time gave Cork a 1–3 to 0–2 interval lead, but Kilkenny rallied with a Dan Dunne goal and a succession of points from Meagher. His last was a free struck from 70 or so yards and looked like the winner until Coughlan's equaliser. The one sombre note from the game was an injury to Dick Morrissey who never hurled again after damaging his back so badly that he spent several years on crutches. His Mooncoin club-mate Jack Duggan replaced him for the replay on 11 October, which was played before a record 33,124 attendance in ideal conditions. It would prove the best of the three games.

The front page of the following Monday's *Irish Press* carried a photo of Eudie Coughlan on bended knee kissing the Archbishop of Cashel Dr Harty's episcopal ring. Lory Meagher wasn't standing on ceremony, with the match report noting 'as the ball left the hand of his Lordship Dr Harty, it was pounced on by Meagher'. It was a statement of intent as Kilkenny started the faster and they led until a 'rasping' goal from Coughlan steadied Cork. Paddy Delea then added a second to leave Cork 2–4 to 1–3 in front at half-time. A point from Meagher and a goal from Paddy 'Skipper' Walsh in the 43rd minute drew Kilkenny level. There was no separating the teams in the closing 10 minutes – it ended 2–6 apiece. 'Extra time was thought of but it would have been cruel and impracticable,' reported the *Press*. 'A joint championship was suggested and it would have been a graceful solution. The [Central] Council has decided on a third meeting on 1 November in the same arena.' Central Council had to meet again to rule, by 10 votes to five, against awarding a joint championship. There were even suggestions of awarding the players half a medal each![3] Central Council would later present all the players involved in the three matches with a gold watch to reward their efforts.

Meagher's absence for the 1 November game because of the injury sustained from a crunching third-man tackle five minutes into the replay was a body blow to Kilkenny. He had played on to great effect in that game, but the damage became apparent later: 'I hurled for 55 minutes with three broken ribs and hardly knew it,' he told John D. Hickey in an *Irish Independent* interview years later. 'The mishap happened under the Hogan Stand when I got possession of the ball and as soon as I did a second Cork man came up to tackle me, charged me and I went down.'

Apart from Meagher and Dick Morrissey, Kilkenny were also missing Paddy Larkin and Martin White for the final game on 1 November when Cork lined out with the same 15 who had started on 6 September. That in itself says much about Cork's resilience and toughness. Kilkenny, though, showed their grit in a game 'played at terrific speed – even faster than the two games already played. [It was] always ahead of the earlier games in fierceness and rigour – nothing [and] nobody was spared and yet not once was Willie Walsh called upon to intervene.' Gah Aherne and Paddy Delea scored two first-half goals to push Cork 2–5 to 1–2 ahead at half-time. Mattie Power scored the Kilkenny goal and when Dan Dunne scored a second, Kilkenny briefly rallied, 'Power playing heroically to retrieve the situation'.

But Cork and Coughlan would not be stopped. 'If there was a hero on the scene yesterday, it was Eudie Coughlan, not because he captained the victorious side but because of his individual play,' reported the *Irish Press*. 'He was tireless, daring and elusive.' Cork scored three late goals from Willie Clancy, Gah Aherne and Paddy Delea to settle the issue 5–8 to 3–4 in the dying light of All Souls Day.

P.D. Mehigan, in *The Irish Times*, provided the keenest analysis of the trilogy. 'The sod was definitely slower, the light was dull, the men were keyed up to a higher pitch. The September and October games were attractive, spectacular exhibitions of the born hurlers' art. Yesterday's was a fight to the finish,' he wrote, maintaining that Cork would have won even if Meagher – 'the biggest and most inspiring figure in the October replay' – had been available. '[Cork] were the steady, war-worn championship fighters who played themselves out to the bitter end while Kilkenny played in flashes.' They were, he concluded, 'worn down by sheer determination and by that will to win which makes champions'.

Coughlan never hurled again for Cork, his retirement hastened by the Cork board taking the selection of the 1932 county team away from his beloved 'Rockies' who had completed a three-in-a-row in 1931.

Every generation creates its own epics and the second game of the 1931 trilogy was rated by hurling judges who had seen dozens of finals, and would see many more, as the greatest. And while 1931 was the end for Eudie Coughlan and his Cork team, it was only the beginning for Lory Meagher and Kilkenny.

CORK: J. Coughlan; M. Madden, E. O'Connell, P. Collins; D. Barry Murphy, J. Regan, T. Barry; J. Hurley, M. O'Connell; E. Coughlan, M. Aherne, P. O'Grady; P. Delea, P. Aherne, W. Clancy.

KILKENNY: J. Dermody; P. Phelan, P. O'Reilly, D. Treacy; T. Carroll, P. Byrne, E. Doyle; E. Byrne, T. Leahy; J. Duggan, J. Leahy, M. Power; D. Dunne, M. Larkin, P. Walsh.

Referee: Willie Walsh (Waterford)

Attendance: 31,135

22. Raging Tull

1932 ALL-IRELAND SEMI-FINAL (Gaelic Grounds, 16 August)
Clare 9–4 Galway 4–14

And when Tull let drive he did not pat the ball. It went 'Zipp' and believe me I am rather thankful that Mahoney was not in direct range of the shots; otherwise there might have been a funeral.
Irish Press (15 August 1932)

THERE HAD NEVER been an All-Ireland semi-final like this freakish wonder of a game. One team watched on more or less mesmerised as their opponents conjured up a huge lead, yet by the final whistle the mesmerised had worked their own magic.

Galway led by 4–7 to 2–0 at half-time and then extended their lead with two quick points after the break. They were still winning 4–14 to 4–2 with 12 minutes left when Tull Considine and his team-mates snapped out of their spell and scored 5–2 to win the match. Christened Turlough Owen Considine, the nickname 'Tull' has a tough, derring-do ring to it that's appropriate for a man whose rampaging form in the summer of 1932 almost won a second All-Ireland title for his county.

Two weeks before the Galway game, the Ennis Dalcassian player had scored two late goals to break Cork in the Munster final at Thurles. Clare were well primed after pushing Cork to a replay in 1928 and halting their All-Ireland three-in-a-row ambitions in 1930. Eighteen years after winning an All-Ireland in 1914, Pa 'Fowler' McInerney was back in the Clare colours, having spent most of his career playing with Dublin, alongside Tommy Daly, another returned exile. The attack was spearheaded by Tull who had been playing for Clare since 1918.

Facing them was a much changed Cork side from the 15 who had triumphed in the second All-Ireland replay the previous November. The most notable absentee was Eudie Coughlan and the rejigged Rebels were overrun in the first half – Clare's 'smashing tactics made the play of the Cork team appear puerile', reported the *Irish Press*. Clare won by 5–4 to 4–1 and 'Tull Considine gave a brilliant performance worthy of a man who might not unfairly be called the wellspring of Clare hurling', the *Press* report continued.

Like Clare, Galway had also been reassembling their forces. Mick King had resumed action in 1930 following a lengthy recuperation from injury, and Mick Gill had also declared again for his native county after winning two All-Irelands with Dublin.

The semi-final in Limerick on 14 August was just the second championship showdown between Clare and Galway since the GAA's foundation and drew an estimated 20,000 spectators. J.N.S. in the *Irish Press* reported that the 'Galway forwards, with that mastermind Mick King engineering most raids, went through the Clare defence like a cyclone through wheat'. King scored 2–3 of Galway's 4–7 first-half tally. The only interruption to the procession was a Considine goal after 10 minutes while Jim Mullane added Clare's second just before the break.

When Galway notched the first two points of the second half, many supporters made for home. A Mick O'Rourke goal barely raised a murmur, neither did his second. Tull scored another to cut the lead to 12 points with 15 minutes left. Galway, though, were still playing well when a long-range shot from out the wing by Tull beat 'Junior' Mahoney in the Galway goal. Then a Jimmy Houlihan sideline cut sailed to the Galway net and 'Clare went all out for victory' after Mick King scored Galway's final point. 'Like Galway in the first half, [Clare] started helping themselves to goals just as easy as a gangster taking candy from a schoolgirl. The Galway defence began to crack up with a vengeance,' reported the *Connacht Tribune*.

Tull goaled to give them the lead in the 59th minute and a point from Holohan and the last of Tull's green flags completed the

21-point turnaround. The bewilderment of Galway supporters was summed by the *Tribune*'s report:

> On the return journey, we discussed what had happened and we did not know, don't know yet. It was a great day – nine hours in a train, two hours in a mudhole and all for the pleasure of seeing our boys who could have won licked to a frizzle.

The unfortunate Galway goalkeeper, Junior Mahoney, outstanding in the 1923 final, was predictably enough scapegoated by some. The *Irish Press* reporter came to Mahoney's defence, saying that while he was lax for a few goals he was also poorly protected:

> Tull Considine was left all on his lonesome to pick up passes and hit the ball with such ferocity he made us all think he intensely disliked the look of the thing … there was no one to pester the Clare attackers; they were permitted to go as they pleased.

Clare defender John Joe 'Goggles' Doyle, who had been switched onto King in the first half, attributed Clare's revival to a desire to salvage some honour. 'We went out steeled with the determination that even if we could not save it, we would at least go down with colours flying,' Doyle said years later in an interview with Raymond Smith.[1] The same writer quoted Tull Considine as saying that 'for 50 minutes we had been hypnotised by the magic of this perfect Galway machine [when] I was fortunate to get through for two goals in two minutes'.

Tull scored just one goal in the All-Ireland final against Kilkenny, but the timing was vital as it brought Clare back into contention after they had been hit by three goals in the six minutes after half-time. A record attendance of over 34,000 had seen a tense first half end with Kilkenny 0–3 to 0–2 ahead, Tommy Daly's brilliance helping to keep them at bay. His stops included a spectacular one-handed save from a Meagher 'cannonball' that 'brought down the house'. But not even Daly could halt the Kilkenny blitz after half-time when Dan Dunne scored a goal and Martin White added two more with overhead connections on sideline cuts dropped in towards the square by Meagher. Many teams would have folded, but the Considine goal and a second from Tom Burnell closed the gap to two points with two minutes remaining.

Tull then had a chance to win the All-Ireland. J.N.S. of the *Irish Press* reported:

> Yes Tull's got it ... he's sidestepped Paddy O'Reilly ... but alas for Clare, Tull Considine, Ireland's far-famed marksman has lashed the air, clean missed the ball and Dermody [Kilkenny's goalkeeper] not 15 yards away.'

Tull saw it differently, maintaining he was pushed in the back as he prepared to strike.[2] Kilkenny saw it differently again:

> It looked all over for Kilkenny. Then out of nowhere came Podge Byrne and his tackle put Considine off and his shot went wide. It was a save in a million and probably won the All-Ireland for Kilkenny.[3]

From the puckout, Mattie Power, who had played with Tommy Daly on the 1927 Dublin All-Ireland winning team, shot a point – final score 3–3 to 2–3.

After nine years without an All-Ireland, Kilkenny's homecoming was wild, as Martin White recalled seven decades later:

> The place was mobbed. It was estimated there was nearly 10,000 people in Kilkenny that night. They walked, came in ass and carts and on bicycles to welcome us home. As we got off the train, one by one we were raised up on the shoulders of the supporters ... I don't know if it was the same people carried us all the way, but our feet didn't touch the ground until we landed at the Town Hall. It was absolutely great.[4]

CLARE: T. Daly; J. Higgins, P. McInerney, J.J. Doyle; J. Houlihan, J. Hogan, L. Blake; J. Gleeson, M. Falvey; T. McInerney, J. Mullane, M. Connery; M. Rourke, T. Considine, T. Burnell.

GALWAY: J. Mahoney, J. Kelly, W. Donnelly, F. Shiel, P. Clarke, M. Finn, W. Keane, W. Hannify, M. Gill, I. Harney, M. King, G. O'Reilly, R. Donoghue, C. Griffin, J. Deely.

23. 'Disgusting and Un-Gaelic Scenes'

1933 MUNSTER FINAL (Cork Athletic Grounds, 6 August)

Limerick 3–7 Waterford 1–2

(game abandoned and awarded to Limerick)

We are not going to stand silent when the reputation of our association and what it stands for is besmirched by any patronising interloper who is on the hunt for journalistic sensations.

Camán **(12 August 1933)**

B Y THE 1930s, the long-established GAA approach towards dealing with hurling indiscipline and violence was to behave as though it didn't exist. Most national newspaper GAA reporters toed the line and didn't comment on dangerous play or the 'taking out' of star players – even in the full glare of an All-Ireland final. Riotous behaviour among spectators was reported, but the code of silence about what happened on the field was such that sendings-off were glossed over and the specifics were rarely detailed.

There was uproar in official GAA circles, then, when the *Irish Press* had the temerity to publish what to modern eyes appears a relatively restrained account of the on- and off-the-field mayhem at the 1933 Munster final between Limerick and Waterford. Since its launch in 1931, the *Press* had devoted considerable space to GAA coverage. The strongly republican paper could hardly be accused of being an 'enemy of the Gael', but that's what it was labelled after its coverage of the 1933 Munster final.

It was Waterford's first time to reach a Munster final and,

ominously, 'the weather was rather too sultry for a strenuous game like hurling and one of the biggest crowds ever seen in Cork sweltered in abnormal conditions'.[1] What should have been a celebration of the Déise's arrival on the big stage degenerated instead into a mean-spirited match with a riotous aftermath. Limerick led by 11 points with eight or so minutes remaining when the referee P. Fitzgerald of Kerry abandoned the game following a pitch invasion by Waterford supporters. The *Irish Press* reported that the invasion followed a sustained bust-up between the players.

> It happened thus – Chris O'Brien had a minute before banged through Limerick's last score which really assured them of victory when he was felled by a blow of a hurley. Almost immediately Dave Clohessy of Limerick, who was a target all through for rough handling, was also set upon.
>
> In a twinkling, many of the players on both sides joined in a pitched battle with upraised hurleys swinging dangerously at one another. In a minute, a big portion of the spectators, obviously Waterford to judge by a flag they carried, invaded the playing area. Rowdyism and general fighting followed.

It had been 'a final of wild scenes', continued the report, as 'right from the start Waterford adopted vigorous and a deal of unfair tactics' against superior opposition.

The *Irish Independent* had a different slant, one more sympathetic towards Waterford:

> Shortly after Limerick had scored their third goal, a Waterford player was so severely injured that a doctor had to be called for. As he was struck, other players lifted their camáns, not in play but in fight and rival supporters rushed in from the sidelines. Jim Ware the Waterford goalkeeper was carried off on a stretcher with head injuries. Gardaí and stewards were unable to clear the field.

The match had been 'rather rough and each team was blameworthy', it added.

Waterford had beaten Tipperary by 5–5 to 5–2 in a Munster semi-final replay on 25 June, a result the *Irish Press* had headlined the 'Surprise of the Century'. Ten thousand spectators had witnessed 'a rare feast of spirited, full-blooded, tip top hurling' at Davin Park in Carrick-on-Suir where former world champion athlete Pat Davin threw in the ball.

After toppling the might of Tipperary, expectations were immense in Waterford ahead of the Munster final, but it was their misfortune that just as they were emerging, Limerick had also struck on a combination of hurlers who would raze all before them for much of the mid-1930s. After losing the 1932–1933 league final to Kilkenny, Limerick had beaten Clare by 19 points and Cork by six en route to the Munster final with their tearaway centre-forward Mick Mackey leading the charge.

In the Munster final, Mackey was sent off 10 minutes into the second half. 'Up to then, he had shown excellent restraint' and had been the standout player scoring 2–1, reported the *Irish Press*.

Besides making most of Limerick's scores, he played a grand game. He was as elusive as an eel and on the ball like a shot each time. He suffered an unkind and undeserved fate in being sent off.

The GAA's official weekly paper *Camán* ('The Organ of Irish Ireland' as it also called itself) was outraged by the *Irish Press* coverage. 'We have no desire to hide any detail about the conduct of our games, but we certainly do resent being made a cock-shot for competition in sensation mongering [between rival newspapers],' it stated in a front-page editorial the following week.

Camán's own hurling analyst, however, didn't spare the ash in his report. 'Tempers were getting frayed and ugly incidents were frequently occurring,' he wrote of the second half. 'The racket started at the far end and, in a few minutes, as disgusting and as un-Gaelic a scene as ever I witnessed took place. In the city by the Suir, whose people were worked up to the highest pitch of interest and enthusiasm, the result will prove a terrible drawback to the progress of the game.'

The Waterford players stuck together, however, and within five years were Munster champions. Limerick came up just short in the 1933 All-Ireland final against the reigning champions Kilkenny who had seen off Galway by 5–10 to 3–8 in a classic semi-final in Birr. Kilkenny's biggest scare, though, was in the Leinster final where they had beaten Dublin by 7–5 to 5–5 at Wexford Park. 'Glorious Rally Averts a Bombshell Result' was the *Irish Press* headline on a report which related that it was 'the most sensational, exciting and eventful hurling struggle witnessed for years and Kilkenny came within an ace of being beaten'. The champions had trailed by 5–4 to 2–1 at half-time, but within eight minutes of the restart, they had scored 2–2 and they reeled in the Dubs who had run themselves into the ground in the first half.

The All-Ireland final was a tense affair, with the Kilkenny defence led by Paddy Phelan masterful in holding off the threat of Mick and John Mackey, Dave Clohessy and the two Ryans at midfield for Limerick. Johnny Dunne's 50th-minute goal was the game-changer in a match 'of the highest quality which kept 50,000 people on tiptoes to the end', reported Pat'O in *The Irish Times*.

Noting that 'Limerick were more fleet of foot, Kilkenny more deft or wrist', he added that 'after the goal, Limerick challenged in most determined fashion. The Ryans and Mackeys swept down the field like an avalanche and Kilkenny's steady backs put in the hardest minutes of the hour but held their posts safe to the end. Steadier attackers would have got Limerick scores and the shrewder attackers won.' Prescient as ever, he concluded that while 'Limerick lacked the necessary finesse, [it] will come with experience. The Garryowen men will be a big force in the jubilee year of 1934.'

LIMERICK: P. Scanlon; E. Gregan, T. McCarthy, M. Fitzgibbon; M. Cross, P. Clohessy, G. Howard; T. Ryan, M. Ryan; J. Mackey, M. Mackey, J. Roche; D. Clohessy, P. Ryan, C. O'Brien.

WATERFORD: J. Ware; J. Ryan, C. Ware, J. Fanning; R. Power, J. Ware, C. Ryan; P. Browne, T. Greaney; N. Fardy, D. Wyse, J. Butler; M. Wyse, L. Byrne, N. Condon.

Referee: P. Fitzgerald (Kerry)

24. Jubilee Jitters

1934 ALL-IRELAND FINAL REPLAY (Croke Park, 30 September)
Limerick 5–2 Dublin 2–6

Are we following sound lines in catering for speed and dainty ball play as contrasted with the dare-devil pluck of sweeping, dashing, fearless men of might and brawn which took our hearts and breaths away in those brave days when our association was young?

P.D. Mehigan, *Camán* (27 January 1934)

THE MORE HURLING changes, the more the debate about the state of the game remains the same. In 1934 – the golden jubilee of the GAA's foundation – P.D. Mehigan, the elder statesman of hurling writing, was concerned that tactical and other innovations were stripping the game of its core skills, manliness and helter-skelter thrills. Writing in the GAA's official paper *Camán*, he posed some questions about the game that would echo repeatedly in subsequent decades. They are still echoing today.

> From being the rushing, impulsive, sweep-all-before-you game of the 1880s, we have evolved that magnificent exhibition of skill and beauty which Cork, Kilkenny and Limerick have shown us at Croke Park in the immediate past. Discipline, speed, science are the orders of the day. Have we overstepped the mark? Are we catering for a diminutive race of men? Are the magnificent six-foot giants, wide shouldered and of surpassing power being elbowed out in the recent evolution of the game?

A noted player who had played in All-Ireland finals for London and Cork, Mehigan abhorred the preference for lifting the ball into the hand over first-time ground and aerial pulling. The sliotar was too light, he argued, and he also believed hurleys should be heavier and narrower in the bas to restore the art of 'hurling shoulder to shoulder, blade to blade'.

He provided an instructive perspective by mentioning that decades earlier he had been one of the prime movers behind successful motions at congress to reduce team numbers to 15 and standardise the goalposts and scoring area as it is today. Back then, old-timers such as Dan Fraher of Waterford had warned Mehigan and other Young Turks that their innovations would 'kill hurling'. 'He called on us in the name of the old heroes and martyrs to desist; to stick with the heavy ball and the rushing scores and the mighty men,' recalled Mehigan in his *Camán* essay. 'And by the Hounds of Finn, I'm wondering today was that Prince of Gaeldom – Dan Fraher of Dungarvan – right?'

Mehigan reflected the concerns felt by many hurling men of his generation. Jamesy Kelleher, the great Cork player of the 1900s, went so far as to dismiss the men of the 1930s as 'hair-oil hurlers'![1] The Cork author John P. Power, writing in 1941, quoted a possibly fictitious old-timer who resented 'the intrusion of modern conveniences into an old, almost sacred game. He knew that the improvements were for the best, but he hated them. He saw the swift, spruce, shower-bathed, well-trained figure with a grim, serious face and a number on his back. He saw the "hard man" of the old days, cap over one eye, endangering a blood vessel in his effort to beat an opponent so that people might not guess he had been on a "booze" the night before. He saw the laughing face, the careless way he was togged out. He saw the punishment the poor fellow could take. And the devil-may-care madness of the latter, he wanted more than the grim accuracy of the former.'[2]

However, Limerick, the team who dominated this jubilee year, seemed to have struck on the right combination of 'devil-may-care' attitude and 'scientific' but robust hurling to reassure the old-timers that the game's heritage was safe. Mick Mackey's men, though, looked in trouble at half-time in the Munster final against

Waterford on 22 July at the Cork Athletic Grounds, the scene of such pandemonium the previous year. This time round, both the players and spectators behaved themselves and Waterford trailed by just three points after playing against the strong breeze and sun. 'In every department, Waterford were the equal of the champions and it was only the grand defensive play of Limerick that held the team together,' reported the *Irish Press*.

In the second half, Limerick recovered their 'dash and vim of the previous year ... the Mackey brothers were the dynamic force in this second-half rally, John in particular playing a raking type of game that spelled danger to the Waterford goal every time he got loose, though Mick was the more prolific scorer. Dave Clohessy proved a great success at full-forward ... Paddy Scanlon received a number of ovations for his coolness in the Limerick goal, some of his saves being brilliance personified.' The Mackeys' efforts, Clohessy's two goals and Scanlon's saves saw the champions through by 4–8 to 2–5.

Limerick struggled again in the All-Ireland semi-final against Galway but finished strongly to win 4–4 to 2–4 in Roscrea. Facing them in the All-Ireland were Dublin who had dethroned All-Ireland champions Kilkenny after a replay. Kilkenny had departed Ireland in early June for a six-week tour of America and they looked a weary and beaten team when they trailed 2–7 to 1–2 with five minutes remaining in the Leinster final at Portlaoise on 12 August. Not for the first time, Lory Meagher, Mattie Power and their team-mates conjured up a remarkable comeback, one that saw Kilkenny bag three quick goals and take the lead. Dublin needed a Tommy Treacy point from a free at the death to force a draw. That defiant stand seemed to drain Kilkenny, though, and they were held scoreless in the first half of the replay a week later, Dublin leading by 3–3 and going on to win 3–5 to 2–2.

There were no national papers published between the end of July and October 1934 because of an ITGWU strike, but *Camán*, by then retitled *An Gaedhael* in a joint-venture with Conradh na

Gaeilge, stepped into the bearna baoil by substantially upping its coverage.

The final on 2 September was a tense draw, Limerick 2–7 Dublin 3–4, and the *Camán* correspondent Lámh Dearg declared:

> Candour above all things is required in hurling criticism. We have had laudation in excelsis with disastrous results; we have developed a super-sensitiveness more in keeping with a community of film stars given to hysteria.

He found fault with Paddy Scanlon's goalkeeping and while the Mackeys 'played more of the ball than any two men on the field … with them I also find fault now and then. They are artistic and alert, full of speed and strength but I often ask myself if they don't overdo the fancy stuff? Weaving figure eight with the ball oscillating between your toe and tip of the hurley looks beautiful but is it always effective?'

Limerick had led by five points with eight minutes remaining before 'a partial collapse' allowed Dublin to salvage a draw. The Dublin goalkeeper Chris Forde was 'the talk of Ireland' for his performance in the drawn game, but he didn't make it to half-time in the replay on 30 September after 'a collision with four Limerick forwards'. Dublin still led by three points heading into the final quarter when the Limerick mentors, including their guest trainer Jim 'Tough' Barry, took advantage of a break in play to get their men to change tack. Led by the 1921 All-Ireland veteran Garrett Howard, they began to play a more controlled game. The Dublin backs were unhinged by an avalanche of hanging balls into the square with Mick Mackey helping to rush one goal and Dave Clohessy scoring the clincher, his fourth goal of the day.

'The long whistle was the signal for a demonstration the like of which was never witnessed in Croke Park before' as thousands joined in the singing of 'Hurrah, hurrah, hurrah for Garryowen', reported the *Limerick Leader*. The homecoming on Monday night saw 15,000–20,000 people gather for a 'monster procession' in the city. The approach of the team train 'was heralded by the discharge of numerous fog signals and sky rockets' and the players paraded the city 'preceded by a cavalcade of horsemen, the riders being decorated with the colours of the team. Tar barrels and bonfires blazed.'

LIMERICK: P. Scanlon; N. Gregan, T. McCarthy, M. Kennedy; M. Cross, P. Clohessy; G. Howard; T. Ryan, M. Ryan; J. Mackey, M. Mackey, J. Roche; J. O'Connell, D. Clohessy, M. Close.

DUBLIN: C. Forde; A. Murphy, J. Bannon, T. Teehan; J.A. Walsh, D. Canniffe, P. Roche; N. Wade, M. Daniels; S. Hegarty, T. Treacy, S. Muldowney; C. Boland, D. O'Neill, J. O'Connell.

Referee: S. Jordan (Galway)

Attendance: 30,250

25. Grit and Élan

1935 ALL-IRELAND FINAL (Croke Park, 1 September)
Kilkenny 2–5 Limerick 2–4

The veterans of 1933 have rocked the Gaelic world to its foundations ...
Tradition has been upheld, nay enriched, a thousandfold and the children of
Clann na nGaedheal worship at the shrine of Kilkenny – the nation's greatest
hurlers.

Kilkenny People (September 1935)

O NE OF THE most eerie scenes ever to unfold on a hurling field occurred during the second half of the 1935 Munster semi-final between Cork and Limerick in Thurles. Mick Ryan of Limerick and Cork's Tommy Kelly pulled on a high ball and, in the clash, Kelly was struck on the forehead and knocked unconscious. The word spread through the crowd that Kelly was dead. So concerned were the medics that a priest was summoned to administer the Last Rites. As he did so, players and officials knelt on the pitch and joined the crowd in reciting a decade of the Rosary. The Cork man was stretchered off and taken to hospital in Thurles and the game resumed. He woke from a coma the following night and made a full recovery, resuming his career with Blackrock and Cork. Tony Herbert, a Limerick player, recalled meeting him years later: 'The man who was with me said: "There's Tommy Kelly, the fella who died and came back to life on the field in Thurles."'[1]

The game ended in a 3–12 to 2–3 defeat for Cork who were outrun and outfoxed from the first to final whistles. A crowd of 30,000-plus paid gate receipts of more than £2,000 – a record for a venue outside Croke Park – and saw Mick Mackey deliver what was rated the best performance of his career to that point. Attacking the Cork defence down the centre with his distinctive crowd-pleasing solo-runs, Mackey was the conductor of an unstoppable Limerick forward line. 'The match was a personal triumph for Mick Mackey of Limerick who gave one of the most brilliant and spectacular individual displays of hurling ever seen,' reported the *Irish Independent*.

'Limerick from the outset were the superior team,' reported the *Irish Press*. 'They combined in machine-like movements that caught the Cork defence napping early on and were two goals up in the first five minutes.'

Jackie O'Connell scored the early goals and the sending off of centre-back Paddy Clohessy did little to disrupt Limerick's momentum in a game where the classy Dinny Barry Murphy, one of five survivors from the 1931 All-Ireland-winning team, offered most resistance for Cork.

Reading between the lines of the match reports, which only mentioned Tommy Kelly's injury in passing and without any detail on the extraordinary scene that followed, there appear to have been several flashpoints and bustups. Hard and tight or fast and open, it made little difference to Limerick. 'By their display yesterday, they must be marked as the team of the century,' said the *Press*. 'With only 14 men in the second half, they were still the masters and will be hot favourites to retain the All-Ireland title.'

This looked even more likely when Limerick routed Tipperary by 5–5 to 1–4 in the Munster final on 11 August. The challengers put it up to the champions for 40 minutes and only trailed by 2–2 to 1–2 at half-time with Paddy Scanlon a busy man in the Limerick goal, but their resistance faded in the final 20 minutes.

The consensus before the All-Ireland final was that the defending champions were nigh unbeatable. They hadn't lost a game since the 1933 All-Ireland final defeat to Kilkenny and the 31-match unbeaten run had reaped two Munster titles, one All-Ireland and two league titles along with a host of secondary tournament victories. They scored 33–43 during their 1934–1935 league title win and conceded an average of roughly 2–4 in those eight games. In contrast, Kilkenny were deemed to be an ageing and spent force, depending on players such as Lory Meagher, Mattie Power, Peter Reilly, Podge Byrne, Eddie Byrne and Martin White, some of whom had been hurling for the county since the early 1920s. A low-key campaign where they coasted past Offaly and Laois in Leinster and Galway in the All-Ireland semi-final appeared inadequate preparation for taking on Mackey's machine.

A hard rain fell on Dublin from early morning on 1 September, and while it's too simplistic to say the weather won or lost the All-Ireland title for either side, observers agreed that the conditions inhibited Limerick's exuberant style and played to the timeless Kilkenny attributes of guile and economy. Instead of being eclipsed by Mick Mackey, 35-year-old Lory Meagher, Kilkenny's captain for the game, dictated proceedings in front of a record crowd of 46,591 braving the 'blinding downpour' that enveloped Croke Park.

'If ever he taught a sliotar to obey his every wish it was on that September Sunday,' wrote Meagher's fellow county man Padraig Puirséal.[2] 'He guided that sodden ball over the rain-drenched sod wherever he willed. His amazing ball control under such conditions foiled Limerick time and again around midfield while his shrewd and accurate passes to his forwards forged the second-half winning scores despite all Mick Mackey's herculean efforts to cancel them out.'

Kilkenny led by 1–3 to 1–2 at the break after adapting to the conditions by keeping the ball moving on the ground. They 'hurled with rare élan, [as] facing a strong breeze and rain they manfully beat back raid after raid by the Shannonsiders', reported the *Irish Press*. In contrast, Limerick's 'front line did not appear to relish the conditions and it was here the penchant to dally with the ball was most apparent'. Dallying was fatal against a Kilkenny defence where the veterans Peter O'Reilly, the Byrnes, Paddy Larkin and in particular Paddy Phelan were 'like hawks ready to pounce on any chance to lash hard and fast to safety'.

The scoring was equally sparse in the second half when Meagher and his midfield partner Tommy Leahy again held sway. Martin White scored Kilkenny's second goal in the 49th minute after Meagher had landed a sideline cut in his paw. As in 1933, Limerick stormed back and a Paddy McMahon goal reduced the gap to a point. A draw seemed likely when they were awarded a close-in free with time up. Team captain Timmy 'Good Boy' Ryan stood over the shot and the referee Tommy Daly of Clare indicated that there was only time for a direct score. Ryan never got to take the free as he was brushed aside by Mick Mackey whose shot was saved and cleared by the three men on the Kilkenny line. Ryan always maintained that Mackey had miscued his shot after failing to lift the ball with sufficient traction to tap over the saving point. 'What really annoyed me was that I knew we would beat them in the replay.'[3] Mackey never publicly shared his thoughts on the miss, but many Limerick supporters of that era went to their graves convinced he had shot for goal and victory. The story went that when he was told to tap it over the bar, he had replied, 'What use is a draw?'

KILKENNY: J. O'Connell; P. Larkin, P. O'Reilly, P. Blanchfield; P. Phelan, P. Byrne, T. Leahy; L. Meagher (0–1), E. Byrne; J. Walsh (0–2), J. Duggan (1–0), M. White (1–0); J. Dunne, L. Byrne (0–1), M. Power (0–1).

LIMERICK: P. Scanlon; N. Gregan, T. McCarthy, M. Kennedy; M. Cross (0–1, f), P. Clohessy, G. Howard; T. Ryan, M. Ryan; J. Mackey, M. Mackey (0–3, 1f), J. Roche; J. O'Connell, P. McMahon (2–0), J. Close.

Referee: Dr Tommy Daly (Clare)

Attendance: 46,591

26. The Ahane Colossus

1936 MUNSTER FINAL (Thurles, 1 August)
Limerick 8–5 Tipperary 4–6

What was it that Mick had? Something we all know in our hearts, but find difficult to articulate. His dynamism, the sheer force of his personality, his leadership, courage, spirit of abandonment. All these and something more. Someone described it last night as 'the old Duchas'.
Fr Liam O'Kelly[1]

MICK MACKEY'S INTER-COUNTY career began with him being called in from the crowd to tog out for Limerick in a league game against Kilkenny in November 1930 and ended with an appearance as a sub in a 1947 Munster championship game against Tipperary. In the intervening years, he became hurling's first superstar, celebrated as the game's 'laughing cavalier', 'the playboy of the southern world'. His favoured position was centre-forward and while he was a skilful ground hurler and adept overhead striker, it was his electrifying solo-runs, goal-scoring and devil-may-care persona that endeared him to the crowds.

He is credited by some chroniclers with inventing the solo-run. Others maintain his father John 'Tyler' Mackey, another one-off who was presented with a gift of £100 by the Gaels of Limerick on his retirement, pioneered the tactic during his 16-year inter-county career that ended in 1917. Standing about five foot 11 inches and weighing 13 stone, by all accounts Mick Mackey possessed unusual natural strength to match an innate sporting talent that would have made him formidable in any code. He treated Gaelic football as a secondary entertainment, but on one of his rare appearances for the county footballers, he scored 2–5 off the Kerry legend Paddy 'Bawn' Brosnan in a 1945 Munster championship game.[2]

For close to 15 years, Mackey was an ever-present for club, county and province. Apart from the league and championship fixtures with Limerick, there were near annual appearances in the Munster colours and a relentless schedule of games with his club, Ahane. Ranked as one of the greatest club teams, Ahane twice won seven-in-a-rows of Limerick titles – 1933–1939 and 1943–1949, and there was a football five-in-a-row (1935–1939). There were also many tournament and challenge games for club and county and all the time Mackey was a marked man, taking more punishment than he dispensed, though he was able to look after himself. He had to be, to survive in the era of the third-man tackle, frontal charge, and routine first-time pulling on the ball – without regard for head, arm, leg or any other body part in the firing line.

There is very little visual footage of Mackey in his prime, so the most compelling evidence about his hurling style is the testimony of his team-mates and writers such as P.D. Mehigan and Padraig Puirseal who, between them, were able to compare and contrast players from the 1900s through to the 1970s.

Mackey's club and county team-mate Jackie Power used to go at it 'hammer and tongs' with Mackey at county training and remembered him as a 'beautiful ball player, both left and right, he was strong as a lion and of course he perfected the solo-run. If Mick Mackey was playing today, the rules would suit his style of play down to the ground. He often showed his body, on say Tuesday after a game and he would be black and blue. It was a case of stop him at all costs ... You will hear a lot of hurling critics confirming other players for their scientific play, but Mackey was something special – he had great physique as well as skill and mobility, and daring spirit.'[3]

Another Limerick team-mate, Dr Dick Stokes, remembered that it was Mackey's sheer physical presence that drove his genius. Stokes maintained that 'nobody hurled like him. He was a very strong, well-built man ... and could use it and could think as well as everything else. He was able to throw fellows out of his way in a very purposeful way. In other words, it was always where the ball was ... it was always constructive ... He was unique in that respect. He could go up the middle. He never had to go up the sideline or anything like that.'[4]

Alluding to Mackey's fondness for playing to the crowd and joshing opponents, Padraig Puirseal wrote that Mackey 'was the laughing cavalier of the hurling fields, a man to whom every game, big or small, brought an equal amount of immense personal enjoyment and an intense sense of personal challenge'.

Like many others, Puirseal felt Mackey reached his peak in the 1936 Munster final when he laid waste to Tipperary in Thurles and 'utterly dominated the scene [and] silenced even the faithful Tipperary fans with an amazing total of five goals and three points, although there were times when it seemed he was being chased by half the opposing 15'.[5]

The performance of Mackey and Limerick is all the more impressive given that they weren't long back from a tour of America where Mackey had picked up a knee injury. Limerick came up with the idea of bandaging up his good knee as a ruse against Tipp in the Munster final.

Limerick's stateside itinerary had included two games against a New York selection. The first joust drew over 40,000 spectators to Yankee Stadium and American sports journalist Dan Parker, writing for the *New York Daily Mirror*, was impressed by our national pastime.

Hurling combines the best features of baseball, a heavyweight elimination tournament, hockey, a battle royal, golf and football. It is no game for a fellow with a dash of lavender in his make-up. It takes a strong physique to stand up under an hour of hurling for the pace is swift as well as gruelling. It is little wonder that the Irish have no plagiarists in hurling. They invented the game and though they haven't copyrighted it, no other race has attempted to play it. I supposed the explanation is that no other race is constituted temperamentally like the Irish.

It's a shame Dan Parker never got to see the 'pure drop' of championship hurling as personified by Mackey and Limerick during 1936 when Mackey, aged 25 and captain, was a force of nature conducting a team of many talents. There were few if any weak links from the gifted Paddy Scanlon in goal through to the classy Jackie Power at corner-forward. The half-back line of Mick Cross, Paddy Clohessy and Garrett Howard was the sturdy heart of the team with Howard a veteran of the 1921 All-Ireland-winning team. At midfield were the Ryan brothers – Mick and Timmy 'Good Boy', famed for his stamina and overhead striking. The forwards included Bob McConkey, who had captained the 1921 team, Mackey's brother John – rated by some as the better stickman – and Paddy McMahon, a native of Kildimo in west Limerick, who had been 'signed' by Ahane. McMahon was known as 'the man to rock the net' which says it all about his goal-scoring touch.

The Munster final was over after 15 minutes when Limerick led 3–1 to 0–0, Mackey having scored two goals and McMahon the third. Tipp tried to rally, but it was showboat time for Limerick, and Mackey relished sewing it into his near neighbours. His third green flag was described by the *Irish Press* as 'a peach of a goal' after a team effort involving several passes. It was 5–3 to 2–0 at half-time and in the second half 'Mackey raced clean through for his fourth goal' and for the fifth 'crashed his way through a bunch of players to slap a pass from Cross to the net'.

The main photo on the sports pages of the *Press* two weeks after the Munster final showed hardy-looking gangs of Galway and Limerick supporters squaring up to each other with a garda standing between the two main protagonists. Ructions erupted in the second half of the All-Ireland semi-final at Roscrea. Galway had led 2–3 to 0–7, but 'Limerick exploded out of the blocks' in the second half, scoring 2–2 in three and a half minutes to reach the 'fairway to victory'. The row started after Mackey made an 'unstoppable burst, breaking through all opposition for a goal' that made it 4–9 to 2–4. The Galway team then walked off the pitch in protest at the referee's failure to take action after one of their men had been 'badly hurt', reported the *Press*.

The sense that Limerick were unstoppable was confirmed in the All-Ireland final where they emphatically reversed the 1935 defeat – wiping out Kilkenny by 5–6 to 1–5. 'Youth and physique allied to vastly improved hurling skill triumphed in Croke Park in front of a record attendance,' reported Pat'O in *The Irish Times*.

> They are the first team to lay the American ghost – Tipperary, Kerry, Kilkenny, Galway, Mayo, Cavan, all have failed to hold their titles on return from American tours. Limerick seemed to have thrived on Dr Atlantic. That they should prove Kilkenny's masters in pure ball playing art was a surprise to all the critics ... In the open as well as the close, overhead as well as on the sod, the Munster men were superior.

Mackey slalomed past four Kilkenny defenders for the final Limerick goal. It brought the curtain down on the perfect season for the Ahane man. Later in life, when asked about his own hurling style by Val Dorgan, Christy Ring's biographer, Mackey said, 'I suppose I was a cool class of customer. It was good crack ... Maybe Ring didn't get the same fun out of it.'[6]

LIMERICK: P. Scanlon; P. O'Carroll, T. McCarthy, M. Kennedy; M. Cross, P. Clohessy, G. Howard; M. Ryan, T. Ryan; J. Mackey, M. Mackey (capt), J. Roche; D. Clohessy, P. McMahon, J. Close.

TIPPERARY: J. Flanagan; D. O'Gorman, D. McLoughlin, J. Lanigan (capt); J. Ryan, J. Maher, W. Wall; J. Cooney, P. Purcell; J. Coffey, T. Treacy, M. Bourke; W. O'Donnell, J Heaney, J. Devaney.

Referee: Jim Regan (Cork)

27. 'A Master Leathering'

1937 ALL-IRELAND FINAL (Killarney, 5 September)
Tipperary 3–11 Kilkenny 0–3

Tipperary simply walked away with the game from start to finish; in a word it was so disappointing that fully 5,000 of the 50,000 present had left the field long before the finish.

P.D. Mehigan, *The Irish Times* (6 September 1937)

ELL HATH NO fury like Tipperary hurling scorned. There were claims that Mick Mackey had taunted a section of the home supporters after scoring 5–3 in the 1936 Munster final at Thurles. If he did, it must have been galling beyond belief for the legions of Tipperary people reared on the glories of Big Mikey Maher, Tom Semple, Wedger Meagher and Johnny Leahy. It was bad enough that Limerick had reinvented themselves as the most invincible hurling team since Tubberadora and Tipp in the 1890s; now they were strutting their superiority in the home of hurling itself. Something had to be done. By the summer of 1937 – the 50th anniversary of their first All-Ireland title – Tipperary had assembled a young team whose mission was to halt Mackey and Limerick's bid for an unprecedented five-in-a-row of Munster titles.

Waterford had very nearly done the job for them in the Munster semi-final, played at Clonmel on 4 July. Limerick had trailed by two points with time up but the referee, Jerry O'Keefe from Clonmel, played an estimated five minutes of 'lost time' and blew the final whistle after Dave Clohessy had scored the goal that gave Limerick a 3–4 to 3–2 win.

Waterford had been the better side throughout. They went ahead in the final quarter, but 'Paddy Scanlon in the Limerick goal brought off three marvellous saves in rapid succession to hold the game for the champions', reported the *Irish Independent*. The challengers' 20-year-old centre-back John Keane had shackled Mick Mackey and was the 'hero of the day' according to the *Irish Press*.

Time caught up with Limerick in the Munster final at the Cork Athletic Grounds on 27 July. No other team in hurling history had played as they did during the mid-1930s. It's an oft-quoted statistic that they played 65 competitive games between October 1933 and April 1938, winning 58, drawing four and losing three. The Mackeys and the other Ahane players were also unbeatable for long stretches in both hurling and football. Then there was Railway Cup duty, the 1936 tour to America, and the wear and tear of normal life outside of hurling which, for many of the team, meant hard physical graft.

Little wonder that Limerick were vulnerable when they faced Tipperary in Cork. They were defeated 6–3 to 4–3 in a game that the *Irish Independent* described as 'a triumph for youth and the brilliant form of the winners dumbfounded even their own supporters'. Full-forward Denis 'Bunny' Murphy scored two quick goals in the second half to finish off Limerick, reported the *Independent*, adding that 'Mackey was magnificent in defeat'.

The years were also telling on Kilkenny who needed three late goals from Martin White to prevent the 'shock of the century' against Westmeath in the Leinster final. The 1937 campaign was the first and only time Westmeath reached the provincial senior final. They had won an All-Ireland junior title in 1936; and on promotion to the senior ranks they defeated Meath, Offaly and Laois to earn a crack at the champions. They did themselves proud in the final, producing a 'top-notch display against Kilkenny who were winning their 26th Leinster title', reported the *Independent*. Kilkenny led by two goals at half-time, 'but they were fully extended in the closing moiety and Westmeath fighting, with a grit and spirit that would have done credit to any county, went into the lead for the first time within the final quarter' before White snuffed out the unthinkable.

Kilkenny just about scraped home by 0–8 to 0–6 against Galway in the All-Ireland semi-final at Birr. Under the heading 'Two Men Saved Kilkenny', the *Irish Press* reported that:

> Jimmy O'Connell has often been described as one of Ireland's best goalkeepers, but on yesterday's display the Dicksboro hurler must rank as the best to ever stand between sticks in a championship. With a magic touch, he snapped balls shot at him from every angle ... his coolness was amazing in the face of a barrage that all but found the Noreside net a dozen times in the first 20 minutes. Paddy Phelan [also] rallied the Black and Amber forces [by] playing as he has seldom played before.

A builders' strike delayed the opening of the new Cusack Stand and the All-Ireland hurling final was fixed for Killarney. A small group of Kilkenny supporters cycled the 120 or so miles to Kerry. Nineteen-year-old Dick Walshe from Tullaroan was among them. Recalling the journey, he said that, on the Saturday, they cycled to the Kerry border before finding a bed for the night and then set off again at four in the morning for Fitzgerald Stadium, but were crestfallen when they faced for home that evening:

> Tipp gave us a master leathering. We only scored three points. We were in great gusto going but I needn't tell you, to come home bet ... we came home a different way. We went through Tipp and they all recognised us and they were shouting. Some of them were decent enough and asked us in for tea. No matter what you saw, and what anyone says, there is no one more decent than Tipperary people.[1]

In his *Irish Times* match report, P.D. Mehigan declared it was the most one-sided All-Ireland final of the 36 he had seen.

> The wide field found weak spots in [Kilkenny's] speed and their ageing hurlers were beaten in every race to a ball by fleet footed Tipperary

men who were not only more nimble, but had far more ball control. Kilkenny were disjointed and inaccurate.

Tipperary led by 2–8 to 0–2 at half-time and toyed with their opponents in the second half when not even Lory Meagher's introduction as a sub could halt the blue-and-gold procession. It was Meagher's last game in the black and amber and he was joined in retirement by several team-mates, including Eddie and Podge Byrne, Martin White, Tommy Leahy and Mattie Power.

Kilkenny were back in a final within two years, but 1937 was a one-off rather than a landmark for Tipperary. Their attempts to retain the title were undone by the boardroom farce that was the 'Cooney affair' of 1938.

TIPPERARY: T. Butler; D. O'Gorman, G. Cornally, J. Lanigan (capt); J. Ryan, J. Maher, W. Wall; J. Cooney (0–2), J. Gleeson; J. Coffey (1–3), T. Treacy (0–1), T. Doyle (0–2); W. O'Donnell, D. Murphy (2–1), P. Ryan (0–1); Subs: D. Mackey (0–1) for J. Gleeson, T. Kennedy for W. Wall.

KILKENNY: J.J. O'Connell; P. Larkin, P. Byrne, P. Blanchfield; E. Byrne, W. Burke, P. Phelan (0–1); T. Leahy, V. Madigan; J. Morrissey (0–1), J. Duggan (capt), P. Obbins; L. Duggan, M. White, M. Power; Sub: L. Meagher (0–1) for T. Leahy.

Referee: J. Flaherty (Offaly)

Attendance: 44,000

28. Up the Déise

1938 MUNSTER FINAL (Cork Athletic Grounds, 31 July)
Waterford 3–5 Clare 2–5

Waterford needn't feel downhearted – Kilkenny had four thrashings before they won through.
***Irish Press* (5 September 1938)**

THE DÉISE OF Waterford are one of hurling's most distinct tribes. Spend a few hours among them at a championship game in Munster or Croke Park and you come away with a sense of a people apart – a people with a proudly separatist identity that finds its rawest expression at hurling matches against their very noisy and upwardly mobile neighbours Cork, Tipperary and Kilkenny. There are different theories about where the Déise came from; a medieval tale called the 'The Expulsion of the Déisi' claims they were a tribe who lived in south Meath until the eighth century when they had one row too many with the High King at Tara who then demanded their complete submission and higher taxes. The Déise refused, declaring they would prefer starvation and death to slavery. Expelled from the Royal County, they wandered homeless for many years until a sympathetic Munster king granted them territory in what is now modern Waterford.

Maybe it was a remnant of that defiant spirit that kept the Déise going for the 50 or more years after 1884 when they were the lost tribe of Munster hurling, even though there was a notable tradition of the game in the city. 'In the springtime of 1848, the silver-tongued orator of Young Ireland, the renowned Thomas Francis Meagher, made eloquent overtures to the young men of his native city to revive hurling ... and the historic hill of Ballybricken soon shook to the powerful tramp of marching men,' wrote the old-school GAA historian Seamus Ó Ceallaigh. The revival petered out following the Young Irelanders' doomed rebellion of 1848. Another band of Waterford Fenians made a second attempt to reintroduce the game in 1866 when the 'greatest and one of the very last games in the old tradition was played at a spot called Knockhouse ... 21 men from the roads and streets opposed 21 stalwarts from Kilmacthomas in an epic contest of skill and sinew'.[1]

Despite this heritage, Gaelic football was the stronger sport in Waterford after the GAA's founding, and it was 1902 before a hurling championship was organised in the county. Waterford didn't emerge as a serious hurling force until the late 1920s when the county's minors won the 1929 All-Ireland title. The senior team lost to Cork by nine points in the 1929 Munster final and two years later, they had one hand on the Munster Cup before Jim Hurley's stoppage-time point rescued a 1–9 to 4–0 draw for Cork who then won the replay by 10 points. The riotous shenanigans of the Waterford supporters led to the abandonment of the 1933 Munster final against Limerick, but the county got back on track by winning the 1934 All-Ireland junior title.

The lost tribe still had a distance to travel, but they found a new chieftain in John Keane who was 17 when he played full-back on the 1934 junior team. From Barrack Street in the city, Keane learned his hurling at Mount Sion CBS where a Brother Malone from Limerick laid the foundations for the powerful Mount Sion GAA club which became one of the new powerhouses of hurling in the county alongside another city club, Erin's Own. Keane made his senior debut in 1935 and his performance against Mick Mackey in the 1937 Munster semi-final was the spark for a renewed tilt at the Munster crown in 1938. Decades later, Pat Fanning, former GAA president and Waterford hurler, recalled:

In 1937, he was only just out of his teens when he had that extraordinary game against Mackey [who] was at his zenith. Keane was magnificent in his youth, a magnificent figure of a man, strong, well built, a head of fair hair set on his shoulders, a massive body and with plenty of speed. He outmatched Mackey that day. That was the beginning. It was that bred the belief that they could come [good].[2]

Youthful All-Ireland champions Tipperary were strong favourites to retain their Munster title in 1938 until they were derailed by a shocking example of spiteful GAA bureaucracy. Jimmy Cooney, one of the outstanding players in 1937, was spied at a rugby international in February and, under Rule 27 – 'the Ban', prohibiting GAA members from playing or attending 'foreign games' – he was suspended for three months by the Leinster Council. Cooney, who lived in Dublin, was reinstated in time for the championship, but Croke Park then nobbled him on absurd technicalities relating to the declaration papers a non-resident player had to sign each year if he wanted to play for his native county. Tipperary defied HQ by playing Cooney against Clare in the Munster championship even though the Banner had warned Tipp they would object. Tipp won the match by 3–10 to 2–3 and Clare objected on the basis that Cooney was 'illegal'. Their objection was upheld and Tipperary were expelled from the championship. Jimmy Cooney was in good company as the Gaelic revivalist Douglas Hyde was delisted as a patron of the GAA in 1939 after attending a soccer international in his capacity as President of Ireland.

Clare got their comeuppance in the Munster final when Waterford were favourites after a historic championship victory against Cork. Over 16,000 people had attended the semi-final clash in Dungarvan where the home team had won by 5–2 to 1–3. The players were 'shouldered from the ground as thousands of Waterford supporters gave vent to feelings of delight at their side's smashing win', reported the *Munster Express*. 'The best player on view was Tom Greaney whose midfield work was faultless and he was ably assisted by

[S.] Feeney, Moylan and John Keane. Locky Byrne was an elusive opportunist and a deadly marksman.'

It was a substitute, Jackie Butler, who nabbed the winning goal against Clare in a tight final on 31 July in Cork which ended with Waterford under siege after they had led by five points early in the second half. The *Irish Press* reported:

> It looked as though Waterford had gone to pieces. Chaos had replaced method and the fire had gone out of their play. It was left to a substitute J. Butler to turn the tide ... when all seemed lost, he went off on an electric dash that left a trail of Clare defenders in his wake to crash home the goal that gave Waterford the lead and restored their spirit.
>
> The last three minutes were fought out in the Waterford goalmouth ... the blue and gold swept down relentlessly on the Waterford posts only to be met with an unwavering resistance ... it was to a gallant defence that they owed the honours. [Charlie] Ware, Keane, [Jimmy] Mountain and [Johnny] Fanning were the rocks upon which Clare's hopes were dashed ... they were real champions in a crisis and saved the day.

With Cork, Limerick and Tipperary gone and Kilkenny falling in Leinster, the prospect of a 'soft' All-Ireland made the Waterford v. Galway semi-final a high-stakes game. The Déise won by 4–8 to 3–1 after a hard battle in 'broiling conditions and on a heavy sod' in Ennis where the *Press* reported that 'John Keane was the big man of Waterford's triumph.'

Keane had another brilliant game in the All-Ireland final, but overtraining could well have contributed to Waterford's 2–5 to 1–6 loss to an experienced Dublin team appearing in their second final in five years. A former Kerry footballer, Paul Russell – a garda sergeant based in Dungarvan – had overseen the team's preparations and he 'initiated a training regime that was more suited to marathon running' than honing the speed on which Waterford's light forwards depended.[3] Combine heavy legs with Croke Park nerves and

Waterford did well to get as close as they did in their first final appearance.

Keane was named Man of the Match by the *Irish Press* which reported on its front page that:

> The actual match was not outstanding, but the unique atmosphere of an All-Ireland final was present. It was more than a game; it was a national occasion. Sections of the crowd were still singing 'Faith of our Fathers' when Padraig Mac Con Midhe, President of the GAA, escorted the Most Rev. Dr Kinane Bishop of Waterford on the field to throw the ball in.

WATERFORD: M. Curley; C. Curley, C. Ware, J. Fanning; W. Walsh, J. Keane, J. Mountain; C. Moylan (0–2), S. Feeney (0–2); W. Barron, T. Greaney (0–1), D. Wyse; J. Halpin (1–0), L. Byrne (1–0), D. Good; Sub: J. Butler (1–0).

CLARE: O. O'Callaghan; M. Hayes, T. Loughnane, P. McGrath; L. Blake, C. Flanagan, S. Harrington; J. Mullane, M.P. Loughnane; M. Murphy (0–2), M. Hennessey (1–1), S. Guinnane (0–2); P. Loughnane (1–0), C. Flynn, J.J. Quane.

Referee: J. O'Regan (Cork)

29. Thunder and Lightning

1939 ALL-IRELAND FINAL (Croke Park, 3 September)
Kilkenny 2–7 Cork 3–3

Radio sets were turned off, war news ignored and houses deserted as thousands thronged the streets ... fireworks soared to the sky contrasting with the intense darkness all round ... crowds danced in the streets to the music of pipers who scarcely had room to play. The players were carried shoulder high through the streets from the railway station, the dimmed headlights of motor cars lighting the way.
***Irish Press* (5 September 1939)**

THERE HAD BEEN a feverish, unreal atmosphere around the city and Croke Park all day on 3 September following that morning's declaration of war on Germany by Britain and France. The sense of foreboding was heightened when the last quarter of the game was played out in a deluge that gave way to a crescendo of thunder and lightning. The conditions 'struck terror into the hearts of many spectators and at least one Cork player'.[1] It got so bad that the Kilkenny minors, who had lost their final by nine points to Cork, were brought into the Cusack Stand dressing rooms to say the Rosary.[2] Undaunted on the Kilkenny sidelines, though, was Matty Power – 'nipper and nephew of the famous Matty of many a Noreside All-Ireland triumph'.

'Young Power had listened to Kilkenny stars of other days tell how they rubbed their hands with resin if the weather was wet to give them a grip on their hurleys,' reported 'Green Flag' in the *Irish Press* two days after the game. 'Just to be certain the resin would not be forgotten, he bought a couple of packets and, when the rain started to fall in bucketfuls at Croke Park, he waited for his chance, until a player went down injured. Then like a greyhound from a leash, he raced on to the pitch and from Noreman to Noreman he sped, shaking powdered resin on their hands. Cork had turned on the pressure at this stage, but the Kilkenny men with a firm grip on their hurleys were able to stand up to the barrage. The Cork men's hurleys made slippery by the rain flew from their hands while the Kilkenny men held theirs firmly. It is by little things like this an All-Ireland is won when two teams are evenly matched,' added the reporter who had button-holed the nipper Power for the inside story after the game.

Even if the story exaggerates the importance of a handful of resin, it says a lot about the role of tradition in hurling – an important part of which is built around the seamless, almost unthinking transmission of knowledge and the ability to react decisively in a crisis. There hadn't been much of a hurling tradition, though, in Carrickshock until the 1900s when a Tullaroan man took up a job in the district, bringing the hurling gospel with him to what had previously been mainly a footballing part of Kilkenny. The Carrickshock men progressed from junior to county senior champions between 1928 and 1931 with Jimmy Walsh captaining Kilkenny in 1932 and leading the county again in 1939. His club-mate and midfield partner Jimmy Kelly scored the winning point in the last minute of the 1939 final. 'Kilkenny had the last swing of fortune's pendulum,' wrote P.D. Mehigan in his *Irish Times* match report.

> [Paddy] Phelan dropped a free within scoring range; [Terry] Leahy and Kelly were on it in a twinkling and the ball sailed over the bar for the winning point just as the referee was looking at his watch for full time.

Goalkeeper Jimmy O'Connell, full-back Paddy Larkin, corner-back Peter Blanchfield, and the great Paddy Phelan at Number 7 and Walsh at midfield all had All-Ireland-winning experience, but the rest of the team were barely out of their teens. Eight of the 1935 All-Ireland minor-winning team had been drafted in to the squad, and

22-year-old Terry Leahy was the oldest of the starting six forwards. In the pre-match previews, wing-forward Jimmy Gargan's vital statistics listed him as being five foot eight tall and weighing 10 stone.

Despite their callow attacking line-up, Kilkenny had been confident of victory. 'Old students of Kilkenny hurling who have watched the team in training – men like Dan O'Connell, Lorenzo Meagher … Dick Grace – are very much impressed by their speed, earnestness and skill. Kilkenny's front line of attack – Phelan, O'Brien, Langton and Mulcahy – all juniors or minors of last year – are so elusive I think they will register heavily for Kilkenny,' predicted P.D. Mehigan in his All-Ireland final preview.

Twenty-year-old Phelan from Tullaroan registered the heaviest, scoring two first-half goals to give Kilkenny a 2–4 to 1–1 half-time lead, the second goal coming from 'an overhead backhanded flick'.[3] The first score of the second half was a Terry Leahy point, but then the Cork rally started. Jack Lynch scored a goal before the heavens opened. A second goal from the first-half goal scorer Ted O'Sullivan closed the gap further 'as players slipped on the surface and hurls left the grasp of numbed hands'.

A Jimmy Phelan point steadied Kilkenny, but the Rebels were jubilant two minutes from time when Willie Campbell struck a 70 all the way to the net for the equalising goal before Phelan, Leahy and Kelly combined for the last-gasp point to inflict a cruel defeat on Cork. They had also lost by the minimum to Kilkenny in the 1904, 1909 and 1913 finals. The 'usual point' was how Jack Lynch referred to the defeat, rueing a chance that slipped from his grasp in the final minute: 'I missed an open goal when it would have been easier to score than miss.'[4]

Lynch and the rest of his young Cork team-mates could still take a lot from the year. In what's rated a vintage Munster final, they had proved their mettle against Limerick, winning by 4–3 to 3–4 in front of 40,986 spectators in Thurles, an attendance that broke the previous record by over 10,000.

The *Irish Press* reported that 'right from the start Cork hurled with a wonderful confidence and it was only [Paddy] Scanlon's brilliant net minding that kept the scoreboard at level chalks after the half hour'. Limerick played with the breeze in the second half but Cork met 'every crafty move of the Shannonsiders with hard-hitting methods that gave the Limerick machine very little chance to function. Mick Mackey tried every one of his old tricks but they were of no avail as John Quirke stuck like a leech to the Limerick skipper.'

That portentous first Sunday in September, though, belonged to Kilkenny. Among those watching in Croke Park was the Belfast-born poet Louis MacNeice who wrote:

> I spent Saturday drinking in a bar with the Dublin literati; they hardly mentioned the war but debated the correct versions of Dublin street-songs ... To Croke Park next day to watch the All-Ireland hurling final ... A huge crowd of Gaelic Leaguers, all wearing the fáinne, one-minded partisans. Talk about escapism, I thought ...[5]

Seventeen-year-old Nickey Rackard was on the terraces wearing a black and amber paper hat. Somewhere in the crowd too was the artist Tony O'Malley. Afterwards, he and his travelling companion 'embarked on an eerie journey north, scoured dark Dundalk for a pub and celebrated victory by guttering candlelight, "contented Kilkenny hurling men although the shadow of a world war hung about us everywhere"'.[6]

KILKENNY: J. O'Connell; P. Grace, P. Larkin, P. Blanchfield; B. Hinks, B. Burke, P. Phelan; J. Kelly (0–1), J. Walsh (capt); J. Langton (0–3, 1f), T. Leahy (0-1), J. Gargan; J. Mulcahy, S. O'Brien (0–1), J. Phelan (2–1); Subs: Bobby Branigan for J. Gargan (inj. HT).

CORK: J. Buttimer; A. Lotty, B. Thornhill, B. Murohy; W. Campbell (1–0), J. Quirke, J. Young; J. Barrett, J. Lynch (capt) (1–2, 1f); C. Buckley, B. Dineen, W. Tabb; J. Ryng, T. O'Sullivan (1–1), M. Brennan.

Referee: Jim Flaherty (Offaly)

Attendance: 40,000

30. Hell for Leather

1940 MUNSTER FINAL REPLAY (Semple Stadium, 4 August)
Limerick 3–3 Cork 2–4

---

*The supporters were firing sticks, stones and coats at Scanlon in the goals ...
and he was blocking balls while it was going on.*
Limerick hurler, Tony Herbert[1]

THE LIMERICK GOALKEEPER Paddy Scanlon had, by his own admission, taken plenty of liquid on board before the 1940 Munster final against Cork. He worked in a timber merchant's in Galway and had been unable to get to Limerick on Saturday night. At 7 a.m. on Sunday, he set out on his motorcycle from Galway to catch the train from Limerick to Thurles. He was parched by the time he reached Gort and 'after spotting a light in one of his watering holes, he was admitted and had two quick pints of the black stuff'. Onwards he sped, to Ennis where he had two or three more and he slaked his thirst with another swift pint in Limerick before boarding the train for Thurles. This is the story as it was related by Scanlon to Fr E. de Faoite, the parish priest of Ahane from 1945 to 1955.[2]

When asked by Fr de Faoite how he had played after that amount of drink, Scanlon replied:

> I played the game of my life. Every time when play was near my goal, I looked up and saw three or four hurling balls coming at me. I just pulled at one of them or caught it in my hand and cleared my lines. Surely to God, I had to hit or catch one of them.

Fr de Faoite concluded by stating: 'Such was Paddy Scanlon – in my estimation the greatest goalkeeper I ever saw play.'

Few would have disputed his judgement after Scanlon's form during the summer of 1940. Along with the Mackeys, Paddy Clohessy, Tim Ryan, Jackie Power and Paddy McMahon, and newer players, such as Mick Kennedy and Dick Stokes, he helped propel a supposedly waning Limerick team to what was arguably the most notable of all their victories in this era. Scanlon was outstanding in the closing stages of the Munster quarter-final in Killarney when Waterford staged a terrific rally to close a five-point gap and earn a draw. The replay in Clonmel was a similar battle with Limerick just about shading it, 3–5 to 3–3.

After the thunderous 1939 Munster final, there was massive interest ahead of the Limerick–Cork rematch in Thurles on 26 July 1940, when Cork fielded 13 of the 1939 side and two newcomers from Glen Rovers – Din Joe Buckley and 20-year-old Christy Ring.

It's unclear from Fr de Faoite's account whether or not it was the drawn game or the replay that was preceded by Scanlon's stout-fuelled motorcycle dash to Limerick. By all accounts the Ahane man, who had been a constant in the Limerick goal since 1932, was equally brilliant in both games; he also sparked a pitch invasion and riot in the replay.

The drawn game is one of the 'epics' that make up the official Munster hurling canon. 'There was a spate of wonderful hurling and a glorious abandon about the clash of man and ash in a hundred brilliant passages that drove a packed Thurles enclosure into ecstasies,' declared the *Irish Press* about a match where a closing crescendo of Cork scores forced a 4–3 to 3–6 draw. Limerick had led at half-time and two goals from Paddy McMahon pushed them seven clear before Jack Lynch, Bill Campbell and John Quirke struck for Cork's equalising scores. The *Irish Press* had special mention for the Limerick goalkeeper:

One of Scanlon's saves will be spoken about for many a day as he stopped a rat-tat fusillade peppered at him from three different angles in as many seconds.

The half-time score in the replay – Cork 0–3, Limerick 0–0 – tells its own story. Jackie Power, another of the Ahane greats, played one of the matches of his life in the second half. Roaming wide for possession and drawing the Cork defence, he set up McMahon for two goals in a minute and when Dick Stokes added a third, Limerick were seven ahead. After sustained Cork pressure, Jack Lynch and Ted O'Sullivan finally got the better of Scanlon with goals to cut the deficit to one. Chaos ensued when Scanlon struck Cork forward Micka Brennan in the mistaken belief that Brennan was approaching goal with the intention of taking him out of the game.[3] Fists and hurls swung after Brennan, who was bleeding from a head wound, was taken off. That prompted an invasion of Cork supporters from the Killinan End behind the Limerick goal.

The day after the game, the *Irish Independent* reported in its news pages that:

> Excitement was at fever pitch with Cork attacking when P. Scanlon in the Limerick goal brought off several fine saves. Immediately there was violent striking with hurleys around the Limerick goal and one of the Cork forwards M. Brennan was carried off and a substitute brought on.

After play resumed, 'a section of the spectators encroached on the pitch around and in front of the Limerick goal. Blows were exchanged and efforts by the gardaí to restore order and clear the pitch were ineffective ... play had to be suspended owing to spectators still being in possession. It was nearly 10 minutes before gardaí and stewards succeeded in clearing the pitch.'

Limerick forward Tony Herbert claimed that 'three or four thousand Cork supporters rushed the field' when the referee Dan Ryan, a football man from Kerry, 'who knew nothing about hurling lost control of the game. Paddy Leahy of Tipperary who was doing umpire for him got a belt of a fist and the hat flew off him. Leahy followed the man who hit him and nailed him before giving him an awful beating.'[4]

Two more minutes of actual hurling were played and Limerick

held out and, as expected, proved too strong for Galway in the semi-final. They looked in serious trouble when Kilkenny controlled the first 10 minutes of the All-Ireland final but a goal from Jackie Power steadied them even though Kilkenny still led 1–4 to 1–2 at half-time. Limerick's experience and strength told in the second half. Mick Mackey's influence increased after he was switched to midfield in the second half, but the day belonged to Jackie Power.

'Jackie Power of Ahane playing all over the field was the man of the hour – he led up to every vital Limerick score,' *The Irish Times* reported. 'Limerick's massed power of shoulder, lung and limb wore down Kilkenny's hurling artistry.' Limerick won by 3–7 to 1–7 to claim a third title in seven seasons. The county's minors also won an All-Ireland the same day, defeating Antrim by 6–4 to 2–4, but rather than building on the success, Limerick went into freefall for several seasons. A family tragedy and infighting among the Limerick clubs meant the Mackeys didn't play in 1941; Paddy Clohessy was also absent when Cork inflicted a shocking 8–10 to 3–2 defeat in the delayed Munster championship. It was a nightmare game for 35-year-old Paddy Scanlon and his team-mate Tommy Cooke recalled: 'They brought him down from Galway on the Saturday and kept him in Limerick overnight, and wouldn't give him a drink. He went up to Cork in cold blood.'[5] He never hurled for Limerick again.

LIMERICK: P. Scanlon; J. McCarthy, M. Hickey, M. Kennedy; T. Cooke, P. Clohessy, P. Cregan; T. Ryan, J. Mackey (0–1); J. Power, M. Mackey (capt) (0–2, f), R. Stokes (1–0); T. Herbert, P. McMahon (2–0), J. Roche; Sub: E. Chawke for T. Herbert (inj).

CORK: J. Buttimer; W. Murphy, E. Thornhill, A. Lotty; W. Campbell, D.J. Buckley, G. Barrett; C. Buckley, J. Lynch (capt) (1–1); C. Ring (0–1), J. Quirke (0–2), J. Young; D. Moylan, T. O'Sullivan (1–0), M. Brennan; Subs: J. Ryng for Moylan, C. Tobin for M. Brennan.

Referee: Dan Ryan (Kerry)

31. 'A First-Class Sporting Sensation'

1943 ALL-IRELAND SEMI-FINAL (Corrigan Park, 1 August)

Antrim 3–3 Kilkenny 1–6

Antrim beating Kilkenny was unheard of. Jack Mulcahy was there and they were asking him, 'What the hell happened ye at all?' 'An awful bad oul field,' says Jack Mulcahy, 'there were rushes in it.' And Pat Clohosey says, 'Will you tell me, were the two of ye hurling in the one field?' Pat Clohosey didn't take codology.

Dick Walshe[1]

BLAMING THE STATE of the pitch is about the feeblest of excuses a defeated team can proffer, but the Corrigan Park ground in west Belfast appears to have given Antrim teams a decided edge during the 1940s. Kilkenny weren't the only southern team to come a cropper at the venue that had a poor and undulating playing surface. Antrim won an All-Ireland senior camogie three-in-a-row between 1945 and 1947 and a scholarly review of Ulster camogie in this era states that 'a major factor' in Antrim's winning run of the 1940s 'was the playing of so many of the semi-finals at Corrigan Park. There the sizeable partisan crowd as well as the dubious state of the pitch were possibly worth several points advantage to Antrim in each game.'[2]

The first southern senior hurling team to crack at Corrigan Park were Galway hurlers in the 1943 quarter-final. The westerners led by two points close to full-time, but a sideline cut from Noel Campbell whizzed under the bar to give the home team a 7–0 to 6–2 victory, which was described as a 'bombshell result' by the southern papers. Full-forward Danny McAllister from Glenariff scored four goals and Sammy Mulholland from Loughgiel scored two.

Mulholland and John Butler from Ballycastle played on the Antrim minor team that had beaten Laois by a point in the 1940 All-Ireland minor semi-final before performing respectably enough when they lost the final to Limerick by 6–4 to 2–4. That minor team was built around hurlers produced by CBS schools in Belfast along with the pick of the young hurlers from the Glens where a form of hurling, probably closer to shinty than the southern summer iomáin, had been played for centuries before the GAA's arrival.

At senior level, though, there had been little hint of an Antrim revival. They had competed in the junior championship during the 1930s and were only admitted to the 1943 Liam MacCarthy race when the junior grade was suspended because of war-time travel restrictions.

On the same day that Antrim beat Galway, Kilkenny regained the Leinster title with a six-point win over Dublin who had humiliated them by 4–8 to 1–4 in the 1942 Leinster final at Nowlan Park. That defeat ranks alongside the 1937 collapse against Tipperary as one of the darkest days in Kilkenny's history.

Having avenged themselves against the Dubs, Kilkenny departed for Belfast on Friday, 30 July, in confident mood. The travelling party included nine of the team that had won the 1939 'Thunder and Lightning' All-Ireland final – what could possibly go wrong?

There's no record of how the visitors passed the Saturday in Belfast, but on Sunday the momentum was with Antrim from the first minute when Danny McAllister goaled. 'That Antrim should outplay these acknowledged masters of the art of hurling is a first-class sporting sensation,' reported the *Irish News*. 'Kilkenny had no excuse to offer. The Antrim victory was no fluke – it was clear cut and decisive ... [they] were the better craftsmen and tacticians.'

The home team's midfield pairing of Jacky Bateson and Campbell from the Mitchel's Club in Belfast, played 'magnificent hurling' to eclipse Carrickshock's Jimmy Walsh and Jimmy Kelly. Another man called Jimmy Walsh, the Antrim captain playing at centre-back, shackled the great Jimmy Langton whose 'wizardry was rarely in evidence'. Beside Walsh on the left wing was Pat McKeown from Creggan who though 'without polish, took the polish off the opposition – his headlong dashing tackles, despite serious risk, frequently prevented Kilkenny from scoring'. Another hero was goalkeeper John Hurl from Creggan, reported the *Irish News*.

The dual player Kevin Armstrong was the pick of the Antrim forwards after the high-scoring Danny McAllister had to retire injured at half-time upon 'meeting a ruthless opponent in Paddy Larkin who merited the referee's attention'. Antrim led by 2–2 to 1–3 at the break and pushed further clear when Armstrong scored a point and Mulholland added another. Kilkenny rallied with three points in the final quarter, but they could find no way past Hurl, and Antrim held out for the greatest shock in hurling history.

The *Irish Independent* reported that Antrim were an evenly balanced team who 'had excelled in speed and quick and effective striking'. They had been the 'masters in ball control while turning spoiling tactics to good account'.

Antrim's aspirations were crushed by Cork in the All-Ireland final played on 5 September before 48,843 spectators. The team captains exchanged gifts of tea and butter – scarce war-time commodities – before the throw-in, but that's where the Munster champions' generosity ended. The step up in class and the occasion got to the Ulstermen against a side completing a three-in-a-row of All-Ireland titles. Cork led by 3–11 to 0–2 at half-time and won by 5–16 to 0–4.

Antrim were so traumatised by the defeat they were almost beaten by Monaghan in the following year's Ulster final and humbled 6–12 to 3–1 by Dublin in that year's All-Ireland semi at Corrigan Park. There was one more glorious day in Corrigan Park in 1945 when the Antrim players led Ulster to a Railway Cup semi-final victory over Leinster, but that was a lone high point for Ulster hurling for many decades. 'To my mind, the greatest blow to hurling in Antrim and Ulster was the demolition of Antrim by Cork in the 1943 final ... had Antrim been left with a bit of pride they might have come back,' wrote Maurice Hayes, a hurling man from Down who helped mastermind that county's football revolution in the 1960s.[3]

One ironic upshot of the 1943 All-Ireland final defeat was the redevelopment of Corrigan Park. The Antrim county board concluded that if its hurlers were to compete consistently with the southern teams, they needed to train and play on a sward to match Thurles or Croke Park. To this end, they raised the then incredible sum of £100,000 to build Casement Park, a new stadium in west Belfast which opened in 1953.

The spirit of the men who kept the GAA alive in Belfast and Antrim was recalled by Kevin Armstrong in an interview with Brendan Fullam for *Giants of the Ash*. For Armstrong, this spirit was personified by F.J. McCarragher, a county board official. During 'the troubled times, he left his home near Corrigan Park and travelled by bicycle to Dublin to attend the convention [GAA Congress]. He returned to Belfast, dodging Black and Tan forces on the way, to bring news of the convention to his colleagues in Antrim.' His odyssey seemed to strike a special chord with Cavan officials who many years later told Armstrong: 'We still have no one to beat your man on the bike.'

ANTRIM: J. Hurl; J. Currie, K. Murphy, W. Graham; J. Butler, J. Walsh, P. McKeown; J. Bateson, N. Campbell; P. McGarry, D. McKillop, J. Mullan; K. Armstrong, D. McAllister, S. Mulholland.

KILKENNY: J. Gilmartin; P. Grace, P. Larkin, P. Blanchfield; E. Fitzpatrick, J. Phelan, R. Hinks; J. Walsh, J. Kelly; T. Walsh, J. Langton, M. Heffernan; J. Mulcahy, T. O'Brien, T. Murphy.

Referee: Dr J.J. Stuart (Dublin)

32. Solo Brothers

1944 MUNSTER FINAL REPLAY (Semple Stadium, 30 July)
Cork 4–6 Limerick 3–6

As grand a solo-run as ever Mick Mackey essayed in his greatest moment was accomplished by Christy Ring ... it was one of those goals that a man gets in a lifetime and it came at the right minute when a score was worth a king's ransom.
Irish Press (2 August 1944)

IT WAS A tale of two solo-runs. Limerick were leading the All-Ireland champions of the previous three years by five points with about 15 minutes left when Mick Mackey embarked on one of his headlong bursts and crashed the ball to the Cork net. The goal, though, was disallowed for a foul on the Limerick skipper before he struck the ball, and the let-off sparked a floundering Cork team to life. With Jack Lynch leading the way from midfield, they hurled up a storm in the final 10 minutes to level the game as full-time approached. What happened next was arguably the beginning of the legend of Christy Ring. As 'Green Flag' reported in the *Irish Press*:

> The crowd was getting ready to watch extra time played when Christy Ring away out on the Cork right wing trapped a rolling ball, lifted it on to his hurley and tapped it for 30 yards before letting fly at the Limerick goal. A dozen players pulled on the ball which [goalkeeper] Malone made an effort to stop, but it slipped to the net and victory was with the champions.

The *Cork Examiner* match report noted that Cork corner-forward Joe Kelly provided a crucial assist when 'he raced in and parried

Malone's hurley to allow the ball find the net amidst rising cheers from jubilant Cork supporters'. Whatever about Kelly's assist – and apart from the athleticism and technique required to execute the score – it was Ring's chutzpah in going for goal when a point might have sufficed for victory that marked him out as possessing the stuff of which Cork heroes are made. 'It was the effort of an athlete who would not accept defeat. An effort the like of which for sheer dramatic intensity occurs only once perhaps in a lifetime ... Christy Ring is the hero of Cork's record-breaking hurling champions and, in my book anyway, the hurler of 1944,' wrote John P. Power.[1] The ultimate imprimatur came from Jimmy 'Major' Kennedy, captain of the 1919 All-Ireland-winning Cork team, when he declared Ring was 'the greatest hurler Cork has produced since Jamesy Kelleher, the Lord have mercy on him'.[2]

Kelleher, a revered figure for Cork hurling people, had died in 1943 so there was a sense of the baton being passed on, as Ring transformed himself from being a very good player on a great team to a great player who in later years led some very good teams to All-Ireland honours. The accepted hurling wisdom is that the 1944 Munster replay was also the day that the baton of being hurling's supreme maestro was assumed by Ring from Mackey, although on the overall run of play over the two games, it appears that Mackey was by far the more influential player. At 32, he was still the rampaging force of old. He scored two goals in the drawn game as Limerick rallied from nine points down.

The *Press* reported that the first game had 'scintillated and sparkled from the opening clash to the final whistle'; the replay was 'a game that poets could rave about' and such was Mackey's first-half performance that he was 'again the idol of the Limerick crowd'. The idol didn't disappoint in the second half either and apart from his disallowed goal, he almost saved the game for Limerick at the death when, after Ring's wonder goal, he 'knocked the lime off the upright in a bid for the goal that would have again levelled up. When he appeared after the game with his little two-year-old son dressed in the Limerick colours, he was given a great ovation as a tribute from all on his great display.'

But it was Ring and Cork who marched on to complete the first hurling four-in-a-row, though they only just scraped through the All-Ireland semi-final against Galway in Ennis by 1–10 to 3–3. Sean Condon's accuracy from frees – he scored seven points – and some last-ditch defending saved Cork on a day when they started without Jack Lynch and John Quirke.

In Leinster, there was a significant shock when Wexford beat Kilkenny for the first time in 38 years, scoring a 6–4 to 4–6 semi-final victory in New Ross. One of Wexford's stars was 22-year-old Nickey Rackard playing at midfield. Dublin, however, won the Leinster decider 4–7 to 3–3 before crushing Antrim by 6–12 to 3–1 in an All-Ireland semi-final played in front of a record crowd at Corrigan Park in Belfast.

Dublin took a hiding themselves when, after a promising opening 10 minutes, they folded to Cork in a final for the third time in four years. The champions led by 0–8 to 0–2 at half-time and the second half was a lap of honour. 'Once they opened their shoulders there was no stopping them,' reported Pat'O in *The Irish Times*. 'Cork's instinctive hurling, their pace and their smooth combination and understanding in attack quickly made the game safe for the champions.' Goalkeeper Tom Mulcahy and corner-forward Joe Kelly were 'hailed as Cork's heroes of the 1944 win'.[3] The *Irish Press* described Kelly, who later ministered as a priest in New Zealand, as 'the darling of the Cork supporters ... [he] danced his way through a bewildered Dublin defence'.

Bill Murphy, Batt Thornhill, Allan Lotty, Con Cottrell, Jack Lynch, Christy Ring, Jim Young, John Quirke and Paddy O'Donovan were the nine players who featured in all four of Cork's 1941–1944 All-Ireland final victories. The drive for a five-in-a-row, however, was derailed by Tipperary and, while Cork regrouped in style the following year, Ring would know more losing than winning days during a seven-year spell when Munster hurling attained new levels of fame and ferocity.

CORK: T. Mulcahy; B. Murphy, B. Thornhill, C. Murphy; D.J. Buckley, A. Lotty, J. Young; C. Cottrell, J. Lynch (0–2); C. Ring (1–0), P. Healy, S. Condon (capt) (0–2); J. Quirke (0–2), J. Morrisson (2–0), J. Kelly (1–1); Sub: Paddy O'Donovan.

LIMERICK: D. Malone; J. Cooney, M. Kennedy, P. Cregan; P. O'Shea, J. Power, T. Cregan; T. Ryan, P. McCarthy; S. Herbert, R. Stokes, P. Fitzgerald; M. Mackey (capt), J. Mackey, J. Clohessy.

Referee: Willie O'Donnell (Tipperary)

'The Great Bicycle Final'

It would make an interesting reality TV fitness challenge if a group of modern GAA supporters were asked to re-enact the type of journeys undertaken on foot and bicycle by their diehard counterparts from the 1930s, 1940s and 1950s.

The hurling peloton phenomenon peaked in the 1940s when war-time restrictions meant a curtailment of train services and petrol rations were conserved for those motor vehicles making essential journeys. The hurling final was an essential journey for the estimated 18,000 attendance at the 1944 Munster final replay, which became known as 'the Great Bicycle Final' because of the number of people who pedalled their way to Thurles.

The spirit of the day was summed up in this newspaper report:

> I myself met a man and his young sons at Thurles who had cycled from Cork ... On the way to Thurles, the chain of the 15-year-old boy's cycle broke. His two companions made sugan ropes in a field, tied his bike to their own and towed him the rest of the way to Thurles.

Those who walked to the match included 65-year-old Peter Ryan who tramped the 40 miles from Lisnagry in County Limerick. There were reports of people breaking their journey by overnighting in hay sheds en route while some hurling pilgrims are said to have slept in Liberty Square the night before the match.

33. The Pride of Knocknagow

1945 MUNSTER SEMI-FINAL (Semple Stadium, 1 July)
Tipperary 2–13 Cork 3–2

Johnny Leahy lived for the game and the glory of Tipperary. It seemed that his one great purpose in life – as player first and later as county secretary and chief mentor – was the defeat of Cork.
Raymond Smith[1]

THE TERM 'BURNOUT' wasn't coined until the 1970s, but that was effectively the diagnosis in Cork after the four-in-a-row champions surrendered their Munster and All-Ireland crowns to Tipperary in the provincial semi-final. 'The edge wears in any metal of high quality,' explained Carbery after his county's 2–13 to 3–2 exit. 'Cork's skill and keenness was as dull as a scythe that has mowed heavy and prolific hay for four consecutive seasons.'

Such was the sense of liberation in Thurles that team captain John Maher was carried shoulder high from the field of battle. The jubilation was understandable after seven lean and controversial years that included a 4–15 to 4–1 beating from Cork in the 1942 Munster final played at the Athletic Grounds by the Lee. In 1945, though, there was a sense of something stirring at last for Tipperary when they defeated a strong Waterford side by 3–6 to 0–3 in the Munster quarter-final.

The 'chief mentor' Johnny Leahy, Tipp's captain for the 1916 and 1925 All-Ireland victories, was confident about the team's chances and 'followers flocked in by bike, trap, outside car, float, dray or shank's mare,' reported the *Irish Press*. 'They made no secret of their confidence in John Maher and his men from Thurles, Moycarkey,

Boherlahan, Cashel, Clonoulty and Carrick. Cork followers were not as numerous as usual. Many of them, we were told, were waiting for the final.'

They were left waiting as the champions were in trouble from the off; they 'were far from the Cork we saw last year, the backs being shaky and hesitant, while the forwards could do nothing right,' added the *Irish Press*. They were held scoreless for the first 15 minutes as Tipperary went six ahead against a strong breeze. Two Cork goals against the run of play levelled the game at 1–4 to 2–1 by half-time, but Tipp cut loose in the second half, outscoring the champions by 1–9 to 1–1.

Tommy Doyle of Thurles was the chief scorer and Man of the Match. Tony Brennan, who had won a minor All-Ireland alongside Tommy Doyle in 1933 and had played for Galway while stationed there with the army, was another influential forward. So too was Mutt Ryan from Moycarkey – his brothers Johnny and Paddy ('Sweeper') also featured at different stages of the 1945 campaign. Lieutenant Harry Goldsboro and Tom Wall, older brother of Tony, had overrun the Cork midfield, but the engine room of the team was the half-back line of Jim Devitt, John Maher and Tommy Purcell. Devitt, from Cashel, weighed less than 10 stone but compensated with fine stickwork and anticipation, while 24-year-old Tommy Purcell from Moycarkey had the distinction of holding Christy Ring scoreless. Purcell was one of the younger players on a seasoned team led by 37-year-old John Maher who had won All-Ireland medals in 1930 and 1937.

From farming stock in Killinan just outside Thurles, Maher had enjoyed some hectic jousts with Mick Mackey in his day: 'He was a tough, bony divil – you would know if you got past him all right,' was Mackey's description of Maher.[2] The two ageing sluggers acquitted themselves honourably when they clashed again in the 1945 Munster final on 14 July in Thurles before 25,000 spectators. Mackey had turned 33 two days earlier, but he was still a lethal force. The previous month he had scored 2–5 off Paddy Bawn Brosnan in Limerick's defeat to Kerry in the Munster football championship.[3]

He was in fine fettle again in Thurles where Limerick led by 0–5 to 1–1 at half-time in another Munster grueller with the *Irish Press* reporting that 'the hurling was hard with men standing shoulder to shoulder and pulling first time in the air or on the ground with an abandon that was almost reckless'. After Tipperary took control early in the second half, 'Limerick looked all set for a recovery when Mick Mackey with one of his old dare-devil solo-runs spread-eagled the Tipperary defence for a goal [but] Mutt Ryan swept through for the goal that set his county on the rocky road to Dublin'. Ryan scored 1–3 as Tipperary won by 4–3 to 2–6 in what was Timmy 'Good Boy' Ryan's farewell match for Limerick.

On the same day, Kilkenny regained the Leinster title, crushing Dublin by 5–12 to 3–4 at Croke Park. 'It was a grand display by a young team with a leavening of experience and possibly heralds another golden age of Kilkenny hurling, but so poor was the Dublin side that one would be tempted to wait and see the black and amber against stronger opposition,' reported the *Irish Independent*. The paper highlighted the 'individual genius' of Jimmy Langton who had scored 25 points in Kilkenny's three wins in Leinster – a notable strike rate at a time when teams' points tallies were usually in single figures per game.

Langton had an off day in the All-Ireland semi-final against Galway in Birr on 28 July, but he still struck the winning scores as Kilkenny edged it 5–3 to 2–11 on another day of misery and what might have been for the westerners. Galway led by 2–9 to 2–1 at half-time and while they were 'playing with dash and determination', the *Irish Independent* reported they 'just lacked the cleverness around goal that might readily have altered the result'. They still led by a point approaching full-time, but Jimmy Langton equalised from a free and struck another placed ball over the bar in 'lost time' for the winner. To compound Galway's woes, their ace Josie Gallaher then narrowly missed a 50-yard free. The writer Breandán Ó hEithir was one of many Galway supporters who had cycled to Birr. 'Even in my dismay, I remember marvelling that his sleek, well-oiled hair showed not a strand out of place after an hour of furious hurling,' he wrote of Langton in *Over the Bar*. 'Only when we had left Birr, with Galway City an unimaginable distance away to the west, did dark depression descend, aided by the doleful conversation of our fellow travellers. For it was during this painful journey that I first heard of the curse that hung over the Galway hurling team like the black cloud that appears over Clonmel every market day since the day Fr Sheehy was hanged.[4]

Kilkenny's limitations were exposed in the All-Ireland final on 2 September where a record attendance of 69,459 watched Tipperary win by 5–8 to 3–6 in what the radio commentator Michael O'Hehir, moonlighting for the *Irish Independent*, described as 'a good game, but not a great one'. An estimated 5,000 supporters were locked out and inside 'every vantage point was seized by enthusiasts. The entire railway wall, a perilous seat at best, was packed; so too was the canal wall and some daring spirits were actually on top of the stands.' Kilkenny had been expected to run Tipperary off the pitch, but the reverse was true and the Munster champions led by 4–3 to 0–3 at half-time. Kilkenny rallied to cut the gap to two points, but the goalkeeper – 'little Jimmy Maher' from Boherlahan – was a hero for Tipperary as was the old warhorse John Maher who blotted out Langton's influence. Maher played on for one more year, but the 1945 campaign was the grand finale for a player who, in one tribute after his death, was described as 'eternally … the pride of Knocknagow'.[5]

TIPPERARY: James Maher; J. Ryan, G. Cornally, F. Coffey; J. Devitt, John Maher (capt), (0–2, 0–1 70), T. Purcell; T. Wall, H. Gouldsboro (0–1); M. Ryan (1–1), T. Brennan (0–2), T. Doyle (1–3); J. Delahunty, J. Dwyer (0–1), J. Coffey (0–2); Sub: T. Ryan (0–1).

CORK: T. Mulcahy; J. Neill, W. Murphy, J. Murphy; P. O'Donovan, D.J. Buckley, J. Young; C. Cottrell, J. Lynch (1–0); C. Ring, S. Condon (0–1), J. O'Brien; J. Quirke (1–1), P. Healy (1–0), J. Kelly.

Referee: Jim Roche (Limerick)

Attendance: 15,000

34. Ring on Fire

1946 ALL-IRELAND FINAL (Croke Park, 1 September)
Cork 7–5 Kilkenny 3–8

---

*I would go through a stone wall to get a 50–50 ball, I would stop at nothing
... all-round physical strength was my best weapon. I never did anything
like weightlifting or anything like that to develop this strength. I had it
automatically and I'd say it was in the mind. Seventy per cent of everything
is in the mind and it's mind that counts.*
Christy Ring[1]

THE PHOTOGRAPHS WE most commonly see of Christy Ring
are from the middle to later phases of his career. Balding and
stocky, he cuts a figure at odds with the modern ideal of the
buffed, athletic hurler, but all the testimony from his contemporaries
and biographers suggests that he possessed a power that can't be
acquired in a gym. His innate sporting ability and intelligence
aside, Ring himself believed his heft, allied to an unending pursuit
of technical perfection and thinking about the game, was vital in
establishing himself as hurling's supreme maestro.

His fighting weight from the late 1940s on was between 13 and
13½ stone – at this weight, and travelling at full speed, he felt he
could take on any player.[2] He played an estimated 1,200 games for
Cloyne, Glen Rovers, Cork and Munster, and, to the end, he retained
the physical presence to facilitate his artistry. 'What a fantastic,
incredible man he is,' wrote Paddy Downey of *The Irish Times* after
Ring's display for the Glen in a Munster club game against Mount
Sion in 1966. 'Forty-six years old and still hurling as if he were a
fiery youth of 20. He revealed his age only when the spurt to the ball

was more than 10 yards. Otherwise, he gave us the whole gamut of his enormous skill.'[3]

The maestro was a whippet when he first pulled on a Cork jersey as a senior in 1939 – 'When I started out I was only nine and a half stone weight and I had nothing to recommend me' was his own assessment[4] – but by the mid-1940s the slightly built, crop-haired Ring of the early years was filling out. The player statistics in the *Irish Press* preview of the 1946 All-Ireland final listed him as being five foot nine and 11 stone seven pounds – still some way off the warrior Ring, able to mix it with Tipperary's prototype 'Hell's Kitchen' defence. Val Dorgan, Ring's first biographer, wrote that Ring's game at this stage was all about speed and skill. Until the end of 1946, Ring's 'emerging genius included the sort of lightning pace and reflexes that kept him free of even the most legitimate challenge. If you impose this speed on total technical talent, you have the ultimate hurler.'[5]

Dorgan, who also played for Glen Rovers, divided his club-mate's career into five periods. These started with the 'honeymoon years', concluding in 1946 with Ring captaining his county to an All-Ireland title that did much to enhance the value of the four-in-a-row achievement. Cork had 'only' beaten weak Dublin teams in 1941, 1942 and 1944. Before lashing poor Antrim in the 1943 All-Ireland final, they had been fortunate to beat Waterford by two points in that year's Munster final campaign when John Keane, the heart and soul of the Waterford team, was carrying an injury. The absence of Tipperary and Kilkenny from the 1941 championship because of foot-and-mouth disease outbreaks was another question mark over the merit of the four-in-a-row. Tipperary actually defeated Cork in a rearranged Munster championship played after the 1941 All-Ireland final, but Cork avenged that defeat by 14 points in Thurles a year later. Until they faced down Kilkenny, however, there would still be doubters.

After trouncing Wexford in the 1946 Leinster semi-final, Kilkenny shaded the final against Dublin by 3–9 to 1–12 after an hour of 'hurling the likes of which would have thrilled the fairy hosts of

Banba at Croke Park' as Green Flag reported in the *Irish Press*. A week later, Cork humbled Limerick by 3–8 to 1–3 in the Munster final at Thurles. It was Mick Mackey's last game for Limerick, but the 'expected thrills were painfully absent – thousands had left the grounds 10 minutes before the end'. Ring scored five points and had a hand in two of the Cork goals to set up a semi-final with Galway played at Birr in 'wretched underfoot conditions'.

An attendance of 15,560, a record for the ground, braved a downpour, anticipating a possible Galway breakthrough, but Cork were never troubled. They led by five at half-time and 'it was over when Joe Kelly slapped home a grounder', reported the *Irish Press* on the 2–10 to 0–3 result. 'Outstanding was Christy Ring. Never flurried and always guiding rather than hitting the ball, he was grand to watch and it was his deadly accuracy from frees that put Galway on the downward path.'

Ring appeared to be struggling in the All-Ireland final before he struck for a goal which turned the game. Ring had 'seemed to have lost his touch with frees and his solo-runs were generally smothered by Jimmy Kelly or Shem Downey', reported the *Irish Press*. 'Then suddenly – like the sun bursting from behind a cloud – the Cork skipper started to sparkle.' He created a goal for Gerry O'Riordan and, two minutes before half-time, he went solo. The *Cork Examiner* reported the score in unusually lengthy detail, describing how Ring won possession 70 yards out before soloing goalwards, hopping the ball on the stick and dancing his way past three tackles to within five yards of goal.

> He deftly placed the ball with a neat flick out of Donegan's reach for one of the grandest goals he ever scored in his career. The crowd, which had cheered lustily as he made his run, now gave him a tremendous ovation, an ovation that came from friend and foe alike.

The *Irish Press* estimated that Ring was about 30 yards from goal before starting the solo, but whatever the distance, the goal put Cork 2–3 to 0–5 in front at half-time. Ring was on fire in the second half, driving Cork into the lead with a point and teeing up Mossie

O'Riordan for a goal. 'It was then we saw Christy Ring at his best, roaming from wing to wing and back to centrefield to rally his men,' reported the *Press*. At the captain's promptings, Cork found the scoring groove. The livewire Joe Kelly and two new additions to the team, Connie Murphy and Mossie O'Riordan, banged in four goals to break Kilkenny's resistance.

Fielding 11 players who saw action during the four-in-a-row, Cork had won a fifth title in six years after a championship season in which no team got closer to them than eight points. It was a special day too for Jack Lynch, winning his sixth successive All-Ireland medal having also starred for Cork footballers in their 1945 victory. A survivor from the 1939 team, Lynch was another Glen Rovers man who, apart from being a 'glutton for work', managed to be a stylish and exceptionally sporting hurler without ever backing down from the many hard men he encountered in Munster and beyond.

This time, though, it was Ring who was chaired off the field by supporters and team-mates. The *Irish Press* headline the Monday after the match ran with: 'Christy Ring – Man of the Match – Bewildering Display Puzzles Kilkenny.' Ring's display aside, though, it seems to have been a poor final for the record attendance of 64,415. P.D. Mehigan in *The Irish Times* reported that 'the quality of the striking for the goals saved the game from mediocrity for at times it was as meek as a league final', adding that on occasions the Kilkenny defence had been 'as open as a barn door'.

CORK: T. Mulcahy; B. Murphy (0–1), Con Murphy, D.J. Buckley; P. O'Donovan, A. Lotty, J. Young; J. Lynch (0–1), C. Cottrell; P. Healy, C. Ring (capt) (1–3), Connie Murphy (2–0); M. O'Riordan (2–0), G. O'Riordan (1–0), J. Kelly (1–0); Subs: S. O'Brien, D. Creedon, Bobby O'Regan, D. Beckett.

KILKENNY: S. Donegan; P. Grace, M. Burler, W. Walsh; J. Kelly, S. Downey, J. Mulcahy (capt); D. Kennedy, T. Leahy (2–0); J. Gargan, J. Langton (0–5), L. Reidy; T. Walton (0–2), P. O'Brien (1–0), S. O'Brien (0–1); Subs: T. Murphy for S. O'Brien, M. Kelly for M. Butler.

Referee: J. O'Flaherty (Offaly)

Attendance: 64,415

35. 'A Dazzling Sheen of Brilliancy'

1947 ALL-IRELAND FINAL (Croke Park, 7 September)
Kilkenny 0–14 Cork 2–7

It was an epic that followers of the camán waited and yearned for because until Sunday's game, the hurling finals during the forties lacked the classic, feverish and exciting touch.
***Irish Press** (8 September 1947)*

THE FIRST ALL-IRELAND final to be filmed in full for public viewing was the celebrated 1947 football decider between Cavan and Kerry at the Polo Grounds in New York, where a Gael Linn crew filmed the game for showing in cinemas at home.[1] It's a shame the Gael Linn cameras hadn't started rolling a week earlier as the 1947 hurling final quickly became enshrined in hurling gospel as the greatest ever.

You would almost need to reach for the smelling salts when reading the dizzying accounts of a game where Kilkenny essentially outsmarted Cork. They achieved this by double-marking Christy Ring and shooting for points from distance rather than getting involved in conventional man-to-man combat with a hardened set of Cork backs. But it was the thrilling final quarter when the lead changed hands several times and Terry Leahy pounced in 'lost time' for the winning point that had hurling men in ecstasy.

Seamus Ó Ceallaigh, a Kilkenny man who lived in Limerick for most of his life, was a prolific GAA writer who attended every hurling final between 1922 and 1981 and this was his verdict:

It was gripping, glorious and dazzling ... all the lustre and genius hurling has known was paraded before our admiring, if spellbound, eyes.

The *Irish Press* reported that the tension in the closing minutes had driven the crowd 'berserk with excitement ... every single phase of play had a dazzling sheen of brilliancy where men hurled as if possessed with the combined genius of past great players'.

The one dissenting voice was P.D. Mehigan, who had played for London in the 1902 hurling final and his native Cork in the 1905 decider. He could embellish and exaggerate with the best of them when writing as Carbery, but his *Irish Times* reports under the Pat'O by-line were the most measured of this period. Perhaps the sight of Cork being sucker-punched at the death coloured his opinion, but he declared 'it was a good game without being of the highest hurling quality ... Opening quietly enough there was a crowded session of dramatic changes of fortune packed into the closing 15 minutes.'

Just how good was it and how would it compare with, for example, the majestic 2013 Cork v. Clare double bill?

Without visual evidence, it's futile to argue the merits of a game from one era against another, but all the reports suggest the 1947 final was fast with the emphasis on speedy ground and overhead striking. Kilkenny adapted a strategic approach against Cork's more direct and traditional style. Played in near-perfect conditions after the hottest summer in 80 years, the scoring was tight with neither team able to open a decisive lead. The free count – 24 – was low. The combined tally of 20 wides indicates that there were plenty of scoring chances despite the low conversion rate. Most of all, in contrast to the previous six finals, which were mostly dull, one-sided contests, the intensity of this game appears to have steadily increased right up to the final, nerve-wracking minutes.

Kilkenny had led by 0–7 to 0–5 after the first 30 minutes during which Jimmy Langton was the most influential forward on the field. A big talking point at half-time was the challengers' success in curbing Christy Ring. The defence that P.D. Mehigan had accused of being as 'wide open as a barn door' in the 1946 final had been rebuilt. Pat 'Diamond' Hayden came in at full-back, Mark Marnell in the corner and Peter Prendergast at centre-back. The versatile Jimmy Kelly and Jack Mulcahy, who had played in the 1939 final at midfield and full-forward respectively, flanked Prendergast who stuck tight to Ring from the start of the game with Mulcahy sweeping across to assist. In the opening minutes, Ring had embarked on a threatening solo-run, but his shadow laid down a marker by giving chase, knocking the sliotar away from his stick and clearing.

'The two man marking of Christy rankled with many followers,' wrote Tim Horgan in his biography of Ring.[2] For his troubles, Prendergast was carried off injured five minutes into the second half and the Kilkenny historian Tom Ryall maintained that had the Thomastown man not 'been forced to retire, it's probable that Kilkenny would have won by a bigger margin'.[3]

Cork's livewire corner-forward Joe Kelly recalled that 'Prendergast followed Christy everywhere and it wasn't until [Ring] was switched to wing-forward that he broke loose and helped us make a recovery. Paddy Grace was doing much the same with me.'[4] Ring cut a sideline ball over the bar in the 43rd minute and Cork trailed by 0–9 to 0–7 entering the final quarter. The newspaper reports are vague on times for the next sequence of scores, but it appears that less than 10 minutes remained when Mossie O'Riordan scored Cork's first goal – flashing a Con Murphy cross past Kilkenny goalkeeper Jim Donegan who had made several fine saves in the first half. Cork led by two but it was quickly back to one when Tom Walton pointed. Terry Leahy then struck a point when on his knees to restore Kilkenny's lead. He added a free to make it 0–12 to 1–7.

Normal time was up when Cork corner-back Bill 'Long Puck' Murphy, who had been driving massive puckouts in behind Kilkenny's half-backs, lofted a free into the square. A flurry of hurls swung and another green flag was raised for Cork to put them a point ahead. Joe Kelly was credited with the goal but he later confirmed that it was Jack Lynch who got the last touch in the mêlée.[5]

Kilkenny attacked and Leahy slotted over the equaliser from a free at a tricky angle 30 yards from goal. From the puckout, a Cork attack broke down when Paddy Grace intercepted a ball that looked destined for Jack Lynch. Grace drove it back towards the Cork goal and Leahy snapped up a breaking ball to shoot the winner.

The *Cork Examiner* had no doubts about where the game had been won and lost:

> It would be difficult to overemphasise the part which Langton and Leahy played in their team's success. Seldom did a puck goalwards from either of them go wide of the posts.

The *Irish Press* viewed Kilkenny's pace as the telling factor against a great but ageing team:

> One vital fact stood out above all others and that was Kilkenny's speed. They were like hares speeding in and out through the Cork lines and all the time they eschewed the net, preferring to flick ball to hurley and shoot with amazing accuracy for points.

P.D. Mehigan's verdict was that 'Cork had lost their snap – pace and youth told'.

KILKENNY: J. Donegan; P. Grace, P. Hayden, M. Marnell; J. Kelly, P. Prendergast J. Mulcahy (0–1); D. Kennedy, J. Heffernan; T. Walton (0–1), T. Leahy (0–6, 4fs), J. Langton (0–3); S. Downey (0–2), B. Cahill, L Reidy (0–1); Subs: N. Kavanagh for P. Prendergast; P. O'Brien, N. O'Donnell, P. Lennon, T. Murphy, J. Egan.

CORK: T. Mulcahy; B. Murphy, Con Murphy (Valley Rovers), D.J. Buckley; P. O'Donovan, A. Lotty, J. Young; J. Lynch (1–2), C. Cottrell; S. Condon (0–4, 2fs), C. Ring (0–1), Con Murphy (Bride Rovers); M. O'Riordan (1–0), G. O'Riordan, J. Kelly; Subs: E.J. O'Sullivan, D. Creedon, M. Fouhy, J. Thornhill, W.J. Daly.

Referee: Phil Purcell (Tipperary)

Attendance: 61,510

36. 'The Greatest Man in Ireland'

1948 ALL-IRELAND FINAL (Croke Park, 5 September)
Waterford 6–7 Dublin 4–2

Praise is due to those counties which keep pegging away year after year in the face of seemingly hopeless odds. Admitted, it is a hard road that leads to the top in hurling [but] Waterford have charted the route for all aspirants.
Irish Press (7 September 1948)

COMPARED TO THE highs of the previous September, this All-Ireland final was a poor contest. 'The 1948 final will not go down in GAA history as one of its great games,' wrote Pat'O in *The Irish Times*. 'The big crowd saw more than a share of indifferent hurling, mainly on Dublin's part.' The *Irish Press* was equally underwhelmed, stating that it was 'overall a mediocre match – now and then we got flashes of the real stuff but these were never of long duration'. For Waterford supporters, the quality was a minor concern compared to the scale of the achievement. Sixty years after the first All-Ireland final was played, they became the 12th county to enter the senior roll of honour, and the county's minors made it a rare double by beating Kilkenny in their final. In the main event, John Keane, who had reinvented himself as an imperious centre-forward, scored 3–2. Midfielders Johnny O'Connor and Eddie Carew swept all before them, and Vin Baston at centre-back played a splendid game as the Munster champions made quick work of a young Dublin side lining out with six native sons.

The victorious teams returned home on Monday evening to 'the biggest spectacle Waterford has ever known', reported the *Irish Independent*, which estimated that 25,000 people marched across the city's main bridge led by six bands.

> The hillside at Sallybank, a few hundred yards from the town, and the top of the famous Mount Misery were set on fire and blazed a welcome to the teams.

No one, not even the most deluded of Déise diehards, had seen this coming. Waterford had been on the slide since 1943 when they had lost the Munster final against Cork by two points – one of the hardest games the four-in-a-row All-Ireland champions had experienced. Waterford didn't win a game in Munster for the next four campaigns. An 11-point beating from Cork in the 1947 Munster semi-final was the low point. It looked over for John Keane, Jim Ware and Christy Moylan – the last survivors from the 1938 Munster-title-winning team.

Infighting about the county team's selection committee added to the general pessimism ahead of the 1948 Munster championship. Waterford had a bye into the semi-final against Clare in Thurles on 23 May, and put their troubles to one side – they led by nine points with 10 minutes left before calamity struck. 'In a sudden burst of inspired play, Clare shattered the Waterford defence and scored two goals and two points and seemed in sight of at least a draw,' reported the *Irish Independent*. John Keane reacted by reorganising the team, going back to Number 6 himself, and this intervention combined with some vital clearances from Vin Baston saw them through by 4–8 to 5–3.

It was a similar story in the Munster final against Cork on 1 August in Thurles. This time, Waterford led by eight with 10 minutes left but, inevitably, back came Cork. The margin was down to five when Cork scored a goal in lost time and Willie John Daly pointed to cut the margin to one. Christy Ring was winding up to puck the equaliser when Waterford wing-back Mick Hayes got in a 'timely and well-judged shoulder' on the maestro just as he struck the ball.[1] It was enough to disrupt the trajectory of Ring's shot and even though the 'Waterford players and supporters watched helplessly and in horror as the ball rose in what seemed its unerring flight towards the posts ... it drifted to the right and missed by a whisker'.[2]

Waterford, for once, had caught a break in a tight game. Another hero on the day was goalkeeper Jim Ware, who was born in Cork but who had moved to Waterford as a boy. A brother of Charlie who had played in 1938, Jim had been hurling for the county since the late 1920s and was approaching 40 in 1948. Out the field, Johnny O'Connor got the better of Christy Ring. There was also a big shock in the minor final when a highly regarded Tipperary side were dismantled 3–6 to 0–3 by the Déise youths. After the nerve-jangling journey through Munster, Waterford enjoyed a decisive 3–7 to 1–6 victory over Galway in the All-Ireland semi at Croke Park.

Meanwhile, in Leinster, Laois probably surprised even themselves when they defeated the All-Ireland champions Kilkenny by 4–5 to 2–7 at Portlaoise. The euphoria was short-lived as they were routed 5–9 to 3–3 by Dublin in the Leinster final at Tullamore on 11 July where there were 'disgraceful scenes ... towards the end of the first half. With Dublin well on top, L. Donnelly scored a point from long range and was struck by a Laois player. A Dublin player intervened and when further blows were exchanged, a general mêlée involving players and spectators followed,' reported the *Irish Independent*.

In the build-up to the final, much was made of the six home-produced players on the Dublin side. They were the product of Dublin's first hurling revolution which had begun with the launch of a citywide Primary Schools and Colleges Hurling League in 1928. The natives were bolstered for the final by five Tipperary men including UCD student Jimmy Kennedy who would become an important player for his native county.

Kennedy was one of the few Dublin players to perform on All-Ireland day. The enthusiastic but raw Metropolitans never stood a chance against the likes of Jim Ware, Vin Baston, Moylan,

Hayes, O'Connor, Carew and Keane, as Waterford opened up a commanding 2–5 to 0–2 half-time lead. They also had to deal with Mick Hickey who had captained Waterford in the 1938 final. He hadn't played for the county since 1946 when he'd been suspended for six months after an incident in a club match, and his sudden recall for the final was big news. No one doubted the edge he would add to the team.

> Mick Hickey was known throughout the province as the hard man of Munster, a label that belied his slender physique – he was close to six feet but was only 10 stone nine pounds in weight. He was a fearsome competitor and his reputation went before him.[3]

Winning an All-Ireland medal in the twilight of their careers was as sweet as it was unexpected for Hickey, Ware, Moylan and, most of all, John Keane, who had driven on the county's teams since 1934. A player who had the measure of both Mackey and Ring, he was an automatic selection for decades at centre-back on many selections of all-time greats including the 2000 Team of the Millennium.

It's ironic then that he reached the summit playing at Number 11, but it was a switch he had been planning since 1943 when he'd convinced Vin Baston, who was an army officer based in Galway, to return to the Waterford side. Getting Baston back in the team was a masterstroke by the Déise general. In 1948, Baston manned centre-back with complete authority, freeing Keane to cajole and direct the forwards as well as scoring freely himself. 'He was gone past his zenith ... he was on a down curve, but he was still the great man. Of course his hurling brain stood to him, he was the master of tactics and he was the natural leader of men who responded to his urgings,' said Pat Fanning, the Waterford hurler of this era who later became GAA president.[4]

Fanning's assessment is from an interview he gave for David Smith's fine biography of Keane. Fanning also recalls a story from 1943 when Keane sustained a fractured ankle and associated tendon injuries in a workplace accident. He was told he wouldn't be able to hurl for months, but even though he could barely stand on the leg, he togged out to face Tipperary and played 'one of the best games of his career'.

Afterwards, his ankle was so badly swollen he couldn't make it as far as the dressing room. He lay on the grass while Pat Fanning cut the boot away to relieve the foot.

> When I removed his sock ... the ankle was unrecognisable as such. A crowd had gathered around John as he lay on the ground. I well remember the old Tipperary man who pushed his way through the throng of admirers to where John lay and, bending down and thrusting out his hand, he said that he 'wanted to shake the hand of John Keane the greatest man in Ireland'.[5]

WATERFORD: J. Ware, A. Fleming, J. Cusack, J. Goode, M. Hickey, V. Baston (0–1), M. Hayes, J. O'Connor, E Carew (0–1), K. O'Connor, J. Keane (3–2), C. Moylan (1–2), W. Galvin (1–1), E. Daly (1–0), T. Curran.

DUBLIN: K. Matthews, E. Dunphy, D. Walsh, S. Cronin, A. Herbert, J. Butler, P. Donnelly, M. Hassett, L. Donnelly, J. Kennedy (2–2), D. Cantwell, S. O'Callaghan (1–0), M. Williams, J. Prior, F. Cummins (1–0).

Referee: Con Murphy (Cork)

Attendance: 61,430

37. The Heat Is On

1949 MUNSTER QUARTER-FINAL REPLAY (Gaelic Grounds, 26 June)

Tipperary 2–8 Cork 1–9

The sun which blistered the Gaelic Grounds was not as hot as the tempers of the Cork and Tipperary teams ... I do not think any one of the players escaped unscathed in those hectic clashes.

Irish Independent (27 June 1949)

COUNTRY CUNNING AND a dash of water may have been the winning of this encounter which marked a significant shift in hurling's balance of power. Temperatures had hit the high 20s in the weeks leading up to the game and Mick Blake, a cross-country runner and Tipperary team masseur, brought a churn of spring water to Limerick along with his other linaments and potions. When the teams drew a second time – 1–5 apiece – it was decided to play extra-time despite the heatwave conditions and injuries on both sides. Paddy Leahy of Boherlahan, who had taken over from his brother Johnny as Tipp's chief mentor, ordered his men back to the dressing room. There, Mick Blake went to work – 'one by one the Tipperary players were doused in the blessedly cooling waters by Blake while their opponents lay baking in the hot sun'.[1]

In another stroke, Tipp kept Cork waiting for almost half an hour before charging back to the fray. 'Tipperary appeared a different team,' reported the *Irish Independent*. 'They looked for scores in the right way and got them and held off a series of Cork attacks before which most teams would have collapsed.' Martin Ryan scored the goal that eventually finished Cork and Jimmy Kennedy added a point to stem a last desperate charge from Ring and company. It was the beginning of a three-year unbeaten run in the championship which balanced up the record books and restored the traditional Tipperary swagger.

The drawn game, which had ended 3–10 each, and this match are celebrated in hurling folklore for Tommy Doyle's achievement in holding Christy Ring scoreless from play for 150 minutes although Ring did score one point from play while briefly unmarked by Doyle. Doyle's performance, though, was just one of several unusual factors behind Tipp's victory. Newcomers Tony Reddin in goal, a teenager called John Doyle at corner-back and UCD student Jimmy Kennedy proved their mettle in what appears to have been more of a pitched battle than a hurling match.

'From the word go, it was pull first and ask questions afterwards and as the game progressed we saw some regrettable incidents,' reported the *Irish Independent*. 'In the heat of battle, Tipperary always appeared to come out worse and they introduced no fewer than four substitutes, but I think the blame for the rough play can be equally apportioned [and] certain sections of the crowd were ever ready to invite trouble.'

Some spectators, it seems, were incensed by the dark deeds in the white heat, but they had to make do with fist-fighting among themselves after stewards had repelled attempted pitch invasions. The trouble began in the first minute when Tommy Doyle was wounded after a tussle with Ring under a high ball. A keen boxer and fitness fanatic from Thurles who was nicknamed 'the Rubber Man', Doyle was stitched up and sent back in on Ring. 'He was dizzy but came back and tapped Ring one back. It was give and take and none of them complained.'[2]

There was no score in the first 10 minutes, but points from Jack Lynch and Mossie O'Riordan put Cork 0–2 to 0–0 ahead before Jimmy Kennedy scored Tipperary's first point in the 25th minute. Gerry O'Riordan scored a goal to make it 1–2 to 0–2 at the break. Cork were well on top in general play after half time, but a critical incident was the referee and umpires' decision to disallow a Mossie O'Riordan 'goal'. His rocket of a shot had ricocheted back into play from some point on the goalposts. Cork maintained the ball rebounded from the wooden support at the back of the goal; Tony Reddin and John Doyle believed it had rebounded off a spot underneath the crossbar and hadn't crossed the white line. Ring's biographer Val Dorgan, after extensive enquiries, was inclined to side with the Tipp men.[3] In any case, Cork still led by a goal well into 'lost time' before Martin Ryan set up Jimmy Kennedy for the equalising goal as the crowds streamed out of the grounds.

Kennedy, a specialist free-taker and Dublin's outstanding player in the 1948 final, had declared for his native county in 1949. The story goes that on Easter Sunday, the deadline for inter-county transfers, the Tipperary county board secretary Phil Purcell travelled to Dublin, met Kennedy in Barry's Hotel and 'locked him in a room and wouldn't let him leave until he'd signed the transfer forms'.[4] Kennedy's return was one of a series of unlikely breaks that transformed Tipp's fortunes.

Another unwitting ally for Tipp was Galway goalkeeper Seanie Duggan whose consistent brilliance had prompted his understudy Tony Reddin to cross the border from Mullagh to Lorrha and declare for Tipp in 1948. Reddin blossomed to such an extent that he is generally regarded as the greatest goalkeeper in hurling history, and he did more than any player to thwart Ring and Cork in 1949 and subsequent years. The goal man's unconventional approach included a customised hurley that 'even by today's standards, looked more like a medieval instrument of war. It was almost twice as heavy as an average hurley and its narrow bas was encased in four evil-looking metal hoops. And unlike other hurleys, the top of the bas was just as thick as the bottom because Reddin didn't want it twisting in his hand when he attempted to save a well struck shot.'[5]

Tommy Doyle, who had won All-Irelands in 1937 and 1945 as a forward, had planned to retire before the 1949 championship but was persuaded otherwise when Tommy Purcell, who had held Ring in 1945, became fatally ill. Also in for the 1949 replay was John Doyle who had played county minor for the previous three years. Burly, fearless and an astute reader of a game, Doyle's strength and conditioning regime included ploughing in his bare feet. Backed by Mick 'the Rattler' Byrne, Tony Brennan and others, the novice soon declared 'Hell's Kitchen' open for business.

The newcomers were the making of a team that benefited from another very controversial refereeing decision in the Munster final. This time, Limerick's Jackie Power had an equalising goal disallowed at the death by the referee Con Murphy of Cork who instead blew for a free that was saved and cleared by the massed Tipperary defence. Tipperary won by 1–16 to 2–10 and Antrim were brushed aside by 6–18 to 1–4 in the All-Ireland semi-final. Poor Laois didn't fare much better in the All-Ireland final, taking a 3–11 to 0–3 beating when they froze in what was the county's first final appearance since 1915.

Laois had overrun Dublin by 6–6 to 3–7 in the Leinster semi-final where Paddy Rutchitzko, born in Ireland but of Polish extraction, was a favourite with the Laois following. Laois had other notable players in the veteran Harry Gray, Billy Bohane, Joe Styles, Paddy Lalor and goalkeeper Tommy Fitzpatrick who had starred in the Leinster final ambush of Kilkenny at Nowlan Park on 17 July. The *Irish Independent* reported that Laois led by 10 points at half-time before Kilkenny 'came to life with a vengeance' and whittled away at the lead. Laois held firm to win a first provincial title for 36 years by 3–8 to 3–6 after a late onslaught when 'almost the whole Kilkenny team with the exception of the goalkeeper and the full-back came downfield to lend a hand in attack'. Galway were defeated 4–6 to 3–5 in the All-Ireland semi-final, but the final was a 'sorry business for Laois' reported the *Irish Independent* which declared it 'one of the most disappointing All-Ireland finals ever seen at Croke Park'.

For Tipperary, though, there was the sense of a new era. The victory drew them level alongside Kilkenny on 14 All-Ireland titles and within two years they would, briefly, overtake Cork to become the top dogs of hurling once again.

TIPPERARY: T. Reddin; M. Byrne, A. Brennan, J. Doyle; J. Devitt, F. Coffey, T. Doyle; P. Stakelum, S. Kenny; M. Ryan (1–1), S. Bannon, J. Kennedy (1–6); J. Ryan, M. Maher (0–1), W. Carroll; Subs: P. Shanahan for D. Carroll, R. Stakelum for J. Devitt, P. Furlong for F. Coffey.

CORK: T. Mulcahy; B. Murphy (0–1), C. Murphy, J. Young; J. Hartnett (0–1), P. O'Donovan, A. Lotty; B. Murphy (0–1), S. Twomey; C. Ring, J. Lynch (0–3), W.J. Daly (0–1); M. O'Riordan (0–1), G. O'Riordan (1–1), P. Barry; Sub: G. Murphy for A. Lotty.

Referee: M. Quane (Clare)

38. Anarchy in the GAA

1950 MUNSTER FINAL (Fitzgerald Stadium, 23 July)
Tipperary 2–17 Cork 3–11

---

*The game was played in a fine sporting spirit and I wish to congratulate
both teams. Towards the end of the game, spectators encroached on the
field and I had difficulty in leaving. I wish to thank especially the captain of
the Cork team, Mr Christy Ring, for his help and support.*
Referee Willie O'Donoghue[1]

IT WAS ONE of the wildest and most anarchic fixtures the hurling
championship had witnessed, putting even the mayhem of the
1933 and 1940 Munster finals in the shade. More sinister events
have occurred in hurling, on and off the field, but for chaos and pure
devilment bordering on black farce, the 1950 Munster final is in a
class of its own.

Val Dorgan, Christy Ring's biographer, recalls cycling from Cork
to Killarney 'for that mid-century Munster final which threatened
to become a Middle Ages-style massacre with the Tipp team as
the victims … We sat on a wall to watch the most chaotic scenes I
have ever seen in a major sports fixture,' he wrote. 'Even before the
game, Cork followers seemed afflicted with some strange madness,
possibly induced by over-nighting in Killarney.'[2]

The sequence of extraordinary incidents included: the smashing
down of the stadium gates by thousands of locked-out supporters;
repeated pitch invasions by intoxicated Cork supporters; attacks on
Tipperary goalkeeper Tony Reddin, and a confrontation between
future Taoiseach Jack Lynch, Christy Ring and the Cork supporters.
There was also the tearing down of perimeter fencing, an attempted

uprooting of a goalpost and the need for the referee to be rescued
from the mob by Lynch and Ring when clerical intervention might
not have been enough. Finally, Tony Reddin had to be disguised in
a clerical hat and long coat after the match to ensure his safety.

If just one of those incidents occurred in a corresponding fixture
today, the media would be ablaze with outrage about the loss of
our national moral compass. But in the supposedly more innocent
Ireland of the 1950s, the media, GAA and civil authorities were
more sanguine about riotous behaviour at hurling matches and
effectively conspired to whitewash anything that might stain
individual or collective reputations.

The *Irish Independent* headlined its report: 'Tipperary Oust Cork
In Munster Final Thriller', and its correspondent, 'Moltoir', led off
by declaring:

> All the best traditions of Munster hurling were upheld at Killarney
> yesterday when a crowd of nearly 40,000 saw Tipperary take a further
> step towards the retention of the crown in as thrilling a provincial final
> as I have ever witnessed.

Moltoir did mention that 'it was a pity that the stewarding
arrangements broke down almost completely and it was fortunate
that the game ended on the quiet note that it did', before going on
to mention the 'bouts of fisticuffs' among spectators and denouncing
the 'deplorable' attempts to attack the referee.

The *Irish Press* ran a spectacular aerial photograph of a packed
Fitzgerald Stadium on its front page and estimated the crowd at
50,000, but there was no mention of the prevailing menace and
madness. The match report stated:

> ... the game ended amid amazing scenes as the crowd of almost
> 50,000 encroached further and further on to the pitch ... At the end
> of the match, the crowd surged onto the field and the referee, Mr W.
> O'Donoghue of Limerick, had to be escorted from the field by gardaí.
> There were periodic outbreaks of fighting among sections of the crowd

and Sean Kenny of Tipperary was attacked by one spectator during
the first half.

The backdrop to the game was the extra-time saga between the
sides in 1949 when Tipperary had prevailed by two points. Cork
supporters still felt aggrieved by a controversial disallowed 'goal'.
Tipperary goalkeeper Tony Reddin had also repeatedly thwarted
Cork – Christy Ring in particular – in the 1949 games and he was
singled out for special attention by some of the Rebel supporters
who travelled to Killarney in huge numbers for the 1950 renewal.

The official attendance was 39,818, but some sources estimate
an additional 20,000 gained admission by scaling walls and rushing
the gates. The overflow saw the sidelines packed with supporters
and fights had broken out before the teams emerged. A gang of Cork
diehards attempted to attack Tipp's hardman Sean Kenny before
the throw-in and, not for the first time that day, Jack Lynch calmed
the situation. A hefty early tackle on Ring prompted a brief pitch
invasion by Cork supporters, who repeatedly halted play with their
forays as the game wore on. They were only warming up.

Tipp led by 1–13 to 1–6 at half-time after playing some scorching
hurling with Jimmy Kennedy their chief marksmen – he finished
the game with 10 points. When Reddin and his full-back line
re-emerged for the second half, they were greeted by a wall of Cork
supporters who had positioned themselves behind the goal after
ripping up the perimeter fencing. Two wonder saves by Reddin from
Lynch and Ring saw even Lynch briefly lose the plot. He decided to
charge the Tipp keeper, but Reddin was alert to the manoeuvre, side-
stepped out of trouble and Lynch crashed off a goalpost into the net.
'Try that again, you f**ker, and there will be a by-election in Cork,'
was Reddin's famous parting shot as Lynch ran back out the field.

It looked dire for Cork when Tipp moved 2–17 to 2–9 ahead with
10 minutes left and the Cork supporters attempted to halt the game
by invading the pitch in their hundreds. 'Even Lynch and Ring were
having little joy talking sense into the maddened horde, the latter

receiving a punch which he returned with considerable interest,' John Harrington wrote in his biography of John Doyle.[3]

When the game resumed after a 15-minute stoppage, Reddin was pelted with 'stones, bottles and sods of earth' and events took an absurdist twist when one supporter threw a coat over the Tipp keeper's head as he attempted to clear a ball. Reddin upped the ante further after the Cork supporters had loosened one of the goalposts. With Cork staging a late rally and every puck vital, a long-distance effort looked to be heading over the bar before the Tipp goalkeeper tugged the loosened post towards him to ensure the shot went wide. An umpire bore the brunt of the crowd's fury and Reddin had to protect him from a hail of bottles.[4]

The full-time whistle – blown too early according to some versions of the story – signalled bedlam. Reddin sprinted to the centre of the pitch, pursued by a posse of Cork supporters. He was saved by a group of priests, but remained on the pitch for another two hours disguised in long coat and hat before it was deemed safe for him to tog in. The enraged supporters also turned on Willie O'Donoghue and just when it seemed that not even the priests' pleas would save the ref's skin, Ring intervened and the Cork posse backed down.

The storm eventually blew itself out even if isolated skirmishes between boozed-up supporters persisted late into the evening around Killarney.

Reflecting on the affair two days after the game, the *Irish Press* correspondent stated that 'crowd encroachments seem to have been the one blot on a great day at Killarney'.

TIPPERARY: T. Reddin; M. Byrne, T. Brennan, J. Doyle; S. Bannon (0–1), P. Stakelum, T. Doyle; P. Shanahan, S. Kenny; E. Ryan, M. Ryan (0–2), T. Ryan (0–2); P. Kenny (2–2), M. Maher, J. Kennedy (0–10).

CORK: T. Mulcahy; J. Thornhill, C. Murphy, G. O'Riordan; S. O'Brien, P. O'Donovan, J. Hartnett; S. Twomey, M. Fouhy (1–0); W.J. Daly (0–2), C. Ring (1–4), S. Conden (0–3); M. O'Riordan, J. Lynch (1–2), J.J. O'Brien.

Referee: W. O'Donoghue (Limerick)

Attendance: 45,000–50,000

39. Tipp Titans

1951 ALL-IRELAND FINAL (Croke Park, 2 September)
Tipperary 7–7 Wexford 3–9

Among the large assortment of vehicles that brought the Wexford people from Oulart Hill, Boulavogue and The Harrow were five hearses. They were on a large undertaking, but it was certainly not Tipperary's funeral.
Irish Press (3 September 1951)

T HE PRE-MATCH PARADE must have been a spine-tingling experience for the Wexford supporters who outnumbered the Tipperary following by four or five to one in a near record attendance at Croke Park. Appearing in their first All-Ireland final since 1918, Wexford, wearing the green of Leinster, marched behind two pikemen, a reminder to all of the county's valour and sacrifice during the 1798 Rebellion. One of the martyrs of 1798 was John Kelly from Killane, near Rathnure, a leader in the rebel attack on Wexford town. In the ballad 'Kelly the Boy from Killane', he is described as 'a giant with gold curling hair ... seven feet is his height with some inches to spare, he looks like a king in command'.

In 1951, Wexford were led by Nickey Rackard, another fair-haired giant from Killane. No man wins an All-Ireland single-handedly but in the opening stages, Rackard looked capable of ending Tipperary's three-in-a-row ambitions on his own. A few minutes after throw-in 'the Wexford forwards led by Rackard charged in like tigers and Reddin, ball and all, finished in the back of the net', reported the *Irish Independent*. Rackard had scored another goal and a point by the 15th minute and twice drew the best from Tony Reddin.

Tipp were being ransacked by the six foot three, 16 stone marauder, but some strategic thinking by their sideline general Paddy Leahy turned the tide. During a break in play, he instructed the corner-backs John Doyle and Mick 'the Rattler' Byrne to support Tony Brennan at full-back. 'Come in from the sides and give it to him [Rackard] as hard as ye can,' was the cry. Leahy's logic was that Rackard was so fixated on route one to goal that he wouldn't pass the ball. It was a risky tactic, but Leahy's intuition was sound. 'When Rackard won the next ball that came his way and turned to run at Brennan again, he was immediately crucified by a pincer attack from Doyle and Byrne that stopped him dead in his tracks,' explains John Harrington in his biography of John Doyle.

> Paddy Kehoe and Tim Flood were free either side of him ... but Leahy was right, Rackard didn't pass it.[1]

Shortly after Leahy's intervention, Tipperary scored their first goal and they added two more opportunistic strikes from Ned Ryan and Mick Ryan to lead by 3–6 to 2–6 at half-time even though Wexford had done most of the hurling. Their chances faded when Rackard drew a blank from two 21-yard frees in the 43rd and 44th minutes. Tipperary had gone four ahead after half-time with a Sonny Maher goal and the *Irish Independent*'s reporter John D. Hickey felt that Rackard should have taken his points from the close-in frees.

Hickey also lamented the 'weakness of Wexford goalkeeper Brennan in tipping out rather than killing the ball' which was a factor in giving Tim Ryan, Seamus Bannon and Mick Ryan simple finishes for the killer goals. 'Tipperary put in some really brainy and fiery hurling,' wrote Pat'O in *The Irish Times* of the scoring burst.

> Using crossing ground balls, they flashed home three goals in as many minutes and Wexford's defence all at once fell to pieces. Tipperary won the final in that brilliant 10-minute period when their six forwards were moving and weaving in one attacking machine of great potency.

There was much favourable comment afterwards on the sporting nature of the contest. 'There were a few fiery incidents, but the general tenor of the game was exemplified by Paddy Kenny being helped off the field by his opponent Wilkie Thorpe and both players shaking hands cordially as they parted on the sideline,' reported the *Independent*.

Kenny, aged 22 from Borrisoleigh, was rated as Man of the Match and Tipp were captained by another Borrisoleigh player, Jimmy Finn who was just 20 when he raised the Liam MacCarthy. Kenny, Finn and players such as 22-year-old midfielder Phil Shanahan, nicknamed the 'Gorgeous Gael', were products of an endless stream of Tipperary minor teams who had dominated Munster for two decades. The overall age profile of the team looked ominous for their rivals. John Doyle and centre-back Pat Stakelum were 21 and 24 respectively while centre-forward Mick Ryan from Roscrea was 26. Tommy Doyle and Tony Brennan were among the few players the wrong side of 30 on a team rated capable of putting four or even five All-Irelands back to back. Christy Ring and Cork would unhinge those grand ambitions as the baton changed again in 1952.

Much of the reverence and mythology about Munster hurling dates back to this glorious age when Limerick, Cork, Tipperary and Waterford won 19 All-Ireland titles between 1930 and 1954. Three of Leinster's six were won by Kilkenny in 1932, 1933 and 1935. The statistics underline how far the province's stock had fallen by the late 1940s and early 1950s when hurling in the east had become volatile and unpredictable.

The south, though, didn't have a monopoly on classic hurling. The 1950 Leinster final between Kilkenny and Wexford drew a record attendance of 36,494 to Nowlan Park where the home team won by 3–11 to 2–11. 'Leinster hurling final day had taken on a new significance as regards the quality of play,' wrote Kilkenny historian Tom Ryall.[2]

Kilkenny subsequently gave Tipperary plenty to think about in the All-Ireland final, before fading in the second half. It finished 1–9 to 1–8, but Kilkenny scored their goal with the last puck and six of their points were first-half frees scored by Jimmy Langton. Instead of building on that All-Ireland appearance, Kilkenny regressed and were beaten 5–10 to 3–7 by Laois in the 1951 Leinster semi-final at Portlaoise. It was Kilkenny's heaviest defeat to Laois and their third in four years against the 1949 Leinster champions. A few weeks earlier, Wexford had been fortunate to escape from Trim with a draw, after Meath had hurled up a storm. That was as tough as it got for Wexford, however, and after coasting through the replay, they eased past Dublin and Laois to claim a first Leinster title in 33 years.

The All-Ireland semi-final was a rematch of April's National League home final that Galway had won by 6–7 to 2–4. Wexford were a different, far more tenacious team in August and Nickey Rackard scored the third and decisive goal after 47 minutes in the 3–11 to 2–9 victory.

Wexford went into collective training at Bellefield, Enniscorthy, for the All-Ireland final and over £1,000 was raised for the training fund with everyone from long-departed exiles to schoolchildren contributing to the cause. Kilkenny ace Jimmy Langton, an All-Ireland winner in 1939 and 1947, visited the camp three times to drill the players on what to expect in Croke Park. 'We are not merely hopeful now; we are supremely confident,' declared Wexford county board secretary Tom Kehoe in Saturday's papers. But while the final proved a game too far for Nickey Rackard and his team-mates, their journey was only beginning.

Hurling didn't realise what was about to hit it.

TIPPERARY: A. Reddan, M. Byrne, A. Brennan, J. Doyle, J. Finn (capt), P. Stakelum, T. Doyle, P. Shanahan, J. Hough, N. Ryan (1–0), M. Ryan (1–0), T Ryan (2–0), P. Kenny (0–7, 2fs, 1 cut), S. Maher (1–0), S. Bannon (2–0); Sub: S. Kenny for P. Kenny.

WEXFORD: R. Brennan, M. Byrne, N. O'Donnell, M. O'Hanlon, S. Thorpe, R. Rackard, W. Rackard, E. Wheeler (0–1), J. Morrissey, Padge Kehoe (0–2), J. Cummins, T. Russell (0–3), T. Flood, N. Rackard (capt) (3–2), Paddy Kehoe (0–1).

Referee: Willie O'Donoghue (Limerick)

Attendance: 68,515

40. Ring the Merciless

1952 MUNSTER FINAL (Gaelic Grounds, 13 July)

Cork 1–11 Tipperary 2–6

A steward later stated that a gate at another part of the ground yielded to the crowd's shoulders so that as far as could be learned nobody was left in the unhappy position of not seeing the game.

Cork Examiner (14 July 1952)

I T WAS A different continent, but the same result for Christy Ring – there was no geographical cure for his Tipperary problem.

He had been invited by the Cork hurling team in New York to appear as a guest player in the New York championship against Tipperary in October 1951. Ring accepted and his schedule also included hurling exhibitions in Boston and Philadelphia. He scored a goal and a point in the New York final, but the familiar blue-and-gold roadblock soon appeared. An Irish-American newspaper reported there were 'spasmodic flashes of greatness [but] the blond, mercury-footed Corkonian who in Croke Park or Thurles is as hard to pin down as a ju-jitsu instructor was an easy prey for the half-nelsons and body tackles which he encountered in the confines of John 'Kerry' O'Donnell's Gaelic Park'.[1]

The previous July, however, he had defied the best Tipperary could throw at him in the Munster final played at Limerick. Connoisseurs rate his display that day as one of the greatest in the nearly 25 years he played for Cork. Tipperary won by two points – 2–11 to 2–9 – but 'it was of Ring the crowds were talking as they shuffled in their thousands back down the Ennis Road', recalled the Kilkenny writer Padraig Puirseal.[2]

Ring back in defence ... Ring up in attack ... Ring performing heroics in the last quarter as he cut down the Tipperary lead score by score ... Ring so narrowly foiled in his last death-or-glory bid for the winning score. That July day was, for me, the zenith of Christy Ring's hurling career.

Val Dorgan, Ring's biographer, went further, writing that it 'may have been the most complete hurling performance of all time [in terms] of technique, effectiveness, excitement, courage. If the game had permanence on film, then I would say, "Judge him on that one."'[3]

He added that he had 'never seen so much naked adulation from a sports crowd as Cork gave Ring that day'. Dorgan categorises the period between 1947 and 1954 as Ring's 'confrontation' phase, 'brutally exacting years when he proved himself not alone the best hurler, but indisputably a man'.

There's a perfectly framed *Cork Examiner* photograph taken after the 1952 Munster final that shows Ring the warrior king being acclaimed by his people for ending the three-year Tipperary tyranny. His forehead is wrapped in bloody bandages, there's what looks like dry blood on his face and even though he looks drawn and spent, there's a hint of serenity in the barely visible eyes.

With the counties tied on 16 All-Irelands apiece and Tipperary closing in on Cork's treasured four-in-a-row, 1952 was make or break for a new-look Cork team. Selector Sean Óg Murphy is said to have delivered an impassioned dressing-room speech asking them if they were going to be the first Cork side to lose to Tipperary for four years running. Spearheaded by Ring, Cork gave Sean Óg, a famed full-back during the 1920s, the answers he wanted.

The Dublin newspapers were on strike between 12 July and the eve of the All-Ireland final, but the *Examiner* soldiered on and its report paid due tribute to 'C. Ring, hero of so many Cork victories, [who] must again claim most of the credit. His second half display was second to none in his colourful career.'

In the first half, Ring had been repeatedly thwarted yet again by the super-human reactions of Reddin in the Tipperary goal. The champions led by 2–5 to 0–5 at half-time but, in the second half, Ring hurled in a frenzy. This time Tipp had no answers. Tommy Doyle had gone off injured after 12 minutes and Cork seized the momentum after one of the newcomers, Liam Dowling from Castlemartyr, finished the ball to the net following another solo-run from Ring. Tipp only scored one point in the second half as Cork cut loose to reclaim the Munster Cup.

The following month, over 25,000 supporters travelled to Ennis for the All-Ireland semi-final between Cork and Galway. It ended in another soul-destroying defeat for Galway whose supporters must have felt they were now being punished by the weather as well as the hurling Gods. The final score was 1–5 to 0–6 and the *Examiner* reported that:

> 11 minutes of lost time were played and during this period the Munster champions scored the two points which qualified them for the final … thus close did Cork come to suffering defeat and, on the run of play, Galway were deserving of a replay at least.

It was 0–2 apiece at half-time, but Galway had played against the elements and looked set for a first semi-final victory since 1929. But the stiff-breeze blew itself out before half-time. 'Had [it] continued, the westerners would likely have won,' reported the *Examiner*. The sides were level in the 58th minute, but 'in a spate of sallies, the spirit which tumbled Tipperary from the All-Ireland throne took possession and victory was theirs'.

Ring was marked for most of the game by Mickey Burke who went off with an arm injury 10 minutes from time. Some Galway players and supporters were convinced – wrongly – that Ring had deliberately struck Burke with the hurley. Josie Hartnett later explained that he had been the player who accidentally injured the Galwayman. The conviction that Ring was the culprit would have dire consequences for Galway a year later.

Dublin caused a big upset in the Leinster final, defeating

Waterford won the Liam MacCarthy for the first time in 1948, defeating Dublin in the final by 6-7 to 4-2. Back: M. Cullen (selector), M. Foley (selector), J. Keane, C. Ware (selector), E. Daly, J. Ware, K. O'Connor, M. Hayes, E. Carew, T. Curran, T. Lanagan (selector). Front: D. Goode (County Secretary), J. Goode, J. Cusack, A. Fleming, W. Galvin, J. O'Connor, V. Baston, C. Moylan.

Bloodied and bandaged, Christy Ring is acclaimed by the Cork crowd after the 1952 Munster final in Limerick where he inspired the Rebels to halt Tipperary's push for a Munster and All-Ireland four-in-a-row.

Christy Ring and Jim 'Tough' Barry with the Liam MacCarthy after Cork's 3-3 to 0-8 victory over Galway in the 1953 All-Ireland final, which became notorious for events on and off the field.

The 1954 Railway Cup final attracted a record attendance of 49,021 to Croke Park as Leinster defeated Munster in a low-scoring affair. Christy Ring (no 15), seen here waiting on a breaking ball, was a crowd favourite who helped popularise the competition. He won a record 18 inter-provincial medals.

Cork completed three-in-a-row by winning the 1954 All Ireland final against Wexford. They were captained by Christy Ring, who became the first hurler to win eight All-Ireland medals. Back: Jack Barrett (selector), Andy Scannell (county chairman), Dave Creedon, Gerry O'Riordan, John Lyons, Matt Fuohy, Gerard Murphy, Paddy 'Fox' Collins (selector), Jim 'Tough' Barry (trainer). Front: Eamonn Goulding, Willie John Daly, Tony O'Shaughnessy, Johnny Clifford, Josie Hartnett, Christy Ring (captain), Paddy Barry, Vincent Twomey, Willie Moore.

In 1956, Wexford completed back-to-back All-Ireland victories and denied Christy Ring a ninth All-Ireland medal. Back: Billy Rackard, Nick O'Donnell, Ned Wheeler, Jim Morrissey, Martin Codd, Nickey Rackard, Padge Kehoe, Bobby Rackard. Front: Tom Ryan, Mick Morrissey, Jim English (capt), Art Foley, Tim Flood, Tom Dixon, Seamus Hearne.

Wexford's Tom Dixon follows through after his side scores a point in the 1956 All-Ireland final against Cork. Vin Twomey is on his back, with Jim Brohan of Cork also pictured. Wexford's Tom Ryan is on the extreme right

Kilkenny shocked Wexford in the 1957 Leinster final and went on to win the All-Ireland. Kilkenny goalkeeper Ollie Walsh prepares to meet the sliotar; also pictured are John Maher of Kilkenny and Wexford's Tom Ryan, a native of Clara in Kilkenny.

Waterford won their second All-Ireland title by defeating Kilkenny 3-12 to 1-10 in a replay. Back: Freddie O'Brien, John Barron, Ned Power, Jackie Condon, Martin Og Morrissey, Joe Harney, Austin Flynn, Phil Grimes, Mick Lacey, Joe Coady. Front: Paudie Casey, Tom Cheasty, Larry Guinan, Mick Flannelly, Frankie Walsh, John Kiely, Tom Cunningham, Seamus Power, Michael O'Connor, Charlie Ware, Donal Whelan.

The Tipperary goal comes under intense Dublin pressure in the 1961 All-Ireland final, with (left to right) Kieran Carey, goalkeeper Donal O'Brien and Michael Maher defending. Dublin's narrow defeat was a missed opportunity to boost the game's popularity in the capital and led to many barren years until their Leinster Championship breakthrough in 2013.

The Tipperary squad that swept all before it 1964, culminating in a 5-13 to 2-8 All-Ireland final win over Kilkenny. Back: Tony Wall, Michael 'Babs' Keating, Mick Burns, Mick Maher, Mick Roche, Kieran Carey, John Doyle, Sean McLoughlin, Mick Lonergan, Liam Devaney, John O'Donoghue. Front: Pat Ryan, Peter O'Sullivan, Mick Murphy (captain), Jimmy Doyle, John 'Mackey' McKenna, Larry Kiely, Len Gaynor, Theo English.

Tipperary captain Jimmy Doyle holds the Liam MacCarthy aloft after the 2-16 to 0-10 victory over Wexford in the 1965 final.

Cork captain Gerald McCarthy and his team-mates celebrate the 3-9 to 1-10 victory over Kilkenny in the 1966 final.

The Cork team that 'mushroomed' from nowhere to win the 1966 All-Ireland. Back: Jack Barrett (mentor), Denis Murphy, Tom O'Donoghue, John O'Halloran, Tony Connolly, Peter Doolan, Mick Waters, Justin McCarthy, Paddy Fitzgerald, Donal Sheehan, John Bennett, Jim 'Tough' Barry (trainer). Front: Gerry O'Sullivan, Colm Sheehan, Paddy Barry, Charlie McCarthy, Gerald McCarthy (capt), Seanie Barry, Finbarr O'Neill, Ger O'Leary.

Jim Lynch shoots Kilkenny's first goal against Tipperary in the pivotal 1967 All-Ireland final where Kilkenny won a 16th senior title by 3-8 to 2-7. Since then they have won another 19 All-Irelands, compared to five for Tipperary and 10 for Cork in the same period.

Sean McLoughlin prepares to shoot in the 1968 All-Ireland final where Wexford defeated Tipperary by 5-8 to 3-12

Wexford by 7–2 to 3–8, and they approached the All-Ireland final on 7 September with the usual enthusiasm, but it ended with the customary, comprehensive Cork victory. The Dublin team included Lieutenant Con Murphy who had won an All-Ireland with Cork in 1946, Tony Herbert who had hurled with Limerick in 1941 and Phil Ryan who had captained Tipperary in the foot-and-mouth year of 1941.

One of the natives, Des 'Snitchy' Ferguson, was Dublin's top player in a game where they trailed by just 1–5 to 0–5 at half-time, but fell apart in the second half. Twenty-year-old Snitchy from St Vincent's marked Ring and the *Irish Press* reported that the 'Ferguson–Ring duels were the delight and highlight of the game. Ferguson stuck to him like a leech but Christy waited and watched his opportunity and inspired hurler that he is, got away for vital scores. One of these was a peach – a direct cut on a ball when he was on his knees to put it clean between the posts.'

Cork won pulling up, 2–14 to 0–7, and the *Press* lamented that the ball 'went around the posts and in front of them [Dublin] and even at the back … it is hard to put in words this spate of missed Dublin chances'.

CORK: D. Creedon, G. O'Riordan, J. Lyons, T. O' Shaughnessy, W.J. Daly, V. Twomey S. O'Brien (0–1), J. Twomey, G. Murphy (0–1), M. O'Riordan, J. Hartnett, C. Ring (0–5), P. Healy, L. Dowling (1–3), P. Barry (capt) (0–1).

TIPPERARY: T. Reddin; M. Byrne, A. Brennan, J. Doyle; J. Finn, P. Stakelum (0–2, 70s), T. Doyle; P. Shanahan, S. Bannon (1–0); N. Ryan, M. Ryan (0–1), T. Ryan; P. Kenny (1–2, 1 cut), M. Maher, J. Ryan; Subs: B. Mockler for T. Doyle (12 mins), G. Doyle (0–1) for B. Mockler.

Referee: J. Vaughan (Lismore)

41. 1953

1953 ALL-IRELAND FINAL (Croke Park, 6 September)
Cork 3–3 Galway 0–8

Many neutrals and even followers of Galway were disgusted by the attitude of certain large contingents of the crowd. A particular 'set' was made from the start on Cork's captain, Christy Ring.
Tom Higgins, *Cork Examiner* (7 September 1953)

[Christy Ring's] display on Sunday was not that of a sports hero and whether or not Burke's close marking annoyed him or bruised his ego, Cork's idol lost not a little of his gilt in the eyes of many neutral spectators.
Jarlath P. Burke, *Tuam Herald* (10 September 1953)

THE WRITER BREANDÁN Ó hEithir suggested that anyone curious about this infamous final – in particular the off-the-ball incident where Christy Ring neutralised his marker Mickey Burke – should travel to the National Film Archive in Dublin and study the film of the game. 'As the camera moves away from Ring and Burke to follow the play, the blow is recorded in the top right-hand corner of the screen.'[1] Alas, the film of the 1953 final has gone missing from the archive, so the forensic approach suggested by Ó hEithir is no longer an option.

Most of the match reports and other accounts, though, seem to agree on some aspects of a game that drew a record crowd to Croke Park on a perfect day for hurling. Cork were the better team and deserved to win the match. Their full-back line of Jerry O'Riordan, John Lyons and Tony O'Shaughnessy played masterfully in repelling the pressure when their team was being overrun at midfield. The ineptitude of the Galway forwards and mentors – especially their fixation on containing Ring – possibly cost them the title.

Christy Ring did strike his marker Burke in the second half when the momentum was with Galway but individual Galway players shamed themselves by later attacking and attempting to attack Ring. The first incident took place at the post-match reception in the Gresham Hotel when an unidentified Galway player attacked Ring on a flight of stairs, hitting him a box on the head which caused him to lose his footing. Both teams were staying in Barry's Hotel and the following morning an unspecified number of Galway players tried to get Ring at the breakfast table before fleeing when the Glen Rovers brigade rallied around their captain.

The upshot of these attacks was that as well as claiming the title, Cork won the subsequent war of words. What happened on the pitch in Croke Park became secondary to the assaults on Ring. The Cork county board and players took the high moral ground as the Galway county board made a ham-fisted effort to seek justice for Burke. The GAA authorities remained cravenly aloof from it all. 'The courage, fearlessness and devotion to truth and fair play which the GAA never displays on such occasions were also conspicuous by their absence in 1953,' wrote Ó hEithir.

Cork had been firm favourites to defeat Galway, but they were underdogs when they faced Tipperary in the 1953 Munster final at the Gaelic Grounds, but with Ring again on fire, Cork prevailed 3–10 to 1–11. He scored a goal in the first minute from a 25-yard free and finished with 1–8. 'Yearly he becomes even more of a prodigy,' reported the *Irish Independent*. Ring was the Cork captain in 1953, but there were doubts about his availability for the All-Ireland final as his mother had died on 8 August and it was 'only after much agonising and encouragement from his brothers and sisters [that] he rejoined the Cork team in training'.[2]

On 16 August, Galway defeated Kilkenny by a point – 3–5 to 1–10 – to end a decade of semi-final setbacks that included one-point defeats against Cork (1944) and Kilkenny (1945 and 1947). In

1950, All-Ireland champions Tipperary had won a hard-hitting All-Ireland semi-final played at Tuam by seven points. Tipperary were aggrieved by the punishment dished out to their gifted forward and freetaker Jimmy Kennedy, who had been reportedly 'cleaved' by a Galway defender with a reputation 'for losing the run of himself entirely when his dander was up'.[3]

There had been no cleaving in the 1952 semi-final at the Gaelic Grounds where Cork won by 1–5 to 0–6. The *Cork Examiner* reported that Galway were very unlucky not to have at least drawn a game where Cork scored the winning points in 'lost time'. 'Galway should have beaten us. They were the better team. We stole the match,' said Cork centre-forward Josie Hartnett.[4] He was involved in an incident late in the match when Mickey Burke, who had very effectively marked Ring, was sidelined with an arm injury. Galway were convinced Burke had been struck by Ring, but Hartnett had maintained: 'I hit him in the hand. It was a complete accident.'

There was nothing accidental about the Burke–Ring incident which occurred in the second half of the 1953 final at a time when Galway were making a potentially match-winning surge. They had trailed 2–1 to 0–3 at half-time after opting to play against the sun. Josie Hartnett scored Cork's first goal and the second came when a long-range shot from Ring beat Galway goalkeeper Seanie Duggan. But with Joe Salmon and Billy Duffy ruling midfield and Ring, according to the *Irish Press*, being 'hounded relentlessly' by Burke, Galway were far from finished.

Points from Josie Gallagher, Billy Duffy, John Molloy and Hubert Gordon levelled the match with approximately 15 minutes left. 'I think it was at a point when Joe Salmon went down to a wild swing at midfield that Mickey Burke was struck off the ball,' wrote Val Dorgan. 'I did not see the incident ... I cannot say if there was provocation but I think now on the evidence there can be no doubt Ring was the offender. He struck Burke with the fist and not his hurley as was generally believed at the time.'[5]

Breandán Ó hEithir disagreed:

Maurice Gorham, Director of Radio Éireann, was the only one I met who actually saw the blow delivered. He was on the Cusack Stand side and kept his eye on the pair when play moved away from them. He then saw Ring turn and give Burke a dig of his hurley in the jaw or mouth.[6]

While Burke was being treated, Ring switched to midfield where he was followed by Burke who played on in a daze when he should have been substituted. 'It was an ill-advised move in more ways than one; it upset the rhythm of Galway's play; the balance of the team, which had at last settled down, was upset,' maintained Ó hEithir. Ring put Cork ahead from a free conceded by Burke, but there were no more scores until late in the day when Willie John Daly put Cork two ahead. John Molloy made it a one-point match before Tommy O'Sullivan scored the winning goal in the ninth and last minute of 'lost' time.

The consensus afterwards was that it was their stonewall full-back line who had won the game for Cork. Willie John Daly and Josie Hartnett were also lauded for their attacking efforts. Given the infamy that now surrounds the game and the belief that it was one of the dirtiest finals ever played, there was a notable absence of comment in the Dublin papers on the Monday after the game. None of them mentioned the Ring–Burke altercation. The overall impression was of a tense, desperately fought and mediocre game rather than an x-rated slashing match. The Ó hEithir and Dorgan accounts both state that while the hurling was 'hard', there was nothing particularly shocking about it. In his *Irish Times* match report, P.D. Mehigan, a Cork man, wrote:

Galway played attractive as well as bold, constructive hurling … Ring got in some delightful ground shots, but Burke swayed and countered every thrust of Cork's greatest scoring medium. Two Galway men were often around Ring when the ball came his way and this gave room to Hartnett, Daly and Barry to drive home winners. Cork's backs once again won the game for their county. I have rarely watched a more tenacious, calculating and fearless lot.

A day later, Mehigan elaborated that the final was 'somewhat disappointing in hurling quality. There were passages of indifferent and rather crude hurling in both half hours and there were too many frees and stoppages for minor injuries. Wides were too frequent and there was a regrettable inclination on the part of a few to swing their hurleys at the wrong time and in the wrong direction.'

The Galway papers had no complaints. 'Situations vacant: wanted scoring forwards. Semi-permanent employment with bonus of All-Ireland hurling championship medal of 1954 guaranteed. Apply Galway county board,' scoffed John Bertie Donoghue in the *Connacht Tribune*'s match report. 'The story of Galway's forward failures is really the story of the game.'

In the *Tuam Herald*, Jarlath P. Burke did cite Ring for the blow on Burke, but the main thrust of his report was that 'Cork deserved to win this final: they finished the better team and their sideline strategists made the moves that ended Galway's bid'. It was 'the dismal failure of the forwards that shattered Galway's hopes'.

It was the lightning bolts from the *Cork Examiner*, though, that inflamed passions for weeks afterwards. Its assertion that it was 'one of the most unsporting finals ever witnessed in Croke Park' has become accepted wisdom about the game. 'It soon became apparent that every means was being used to subdue the Cork hurlers,' wrote Tom Higgins in his match report the Monday after the game. He highlighted the behaviour of a section of the Galway support, but didn't specify any specific offences against the Cork players:

> No one could find fault with Galway's 'policing' tactics were the rules of fair play followed. But far from it, the unruly element in the crowd continued their unsporting tactics and boohed Christy in the most unrelenting manner.

Jimmy Kennedy and the 1950 semi-final in Tuam was referenced as another example where the Galway crowd had taken a 'similar' set on a player. Higgins added that 'there will be many who must wish it will be at least another 24 years before Galway will again be seen in an All-Ireland final'. The *Connacht Tribune* reprinted the incendiary *Examiner* report, but there's no evidence that outraged Galwegians burned 'de paper' in Eyre Square.

After Cork had returned home on Monday, Andy Scannell, the Cork county secretary, highlighted the Galway players' attacks on Ring after the match. Combined with the *Examiner* report, his comments pushed Galway county board officials over the edge at the board's post All-Ireland meeting. Delegates proposed that Central Council should compensate Mickey Burke for his injuries while the Galway team trainer Padraig Fahy demanded that Burke's assailant be expelled from the GAA. Eventually, it was decided that a special gold medal would be struck to recognise Burke's 'courage, endurance and chivalry on the field'.

An official statement noted that 'while the Cork captain was telling the other guests at the [post All-Ireland] central council dinner of his desire to hand the MacCarthy Cup to Galway as Cork's successors, the Galway captain was having his broken teeth attended and eight stitches put in his lips at a Dublin hospital'.

As for the attacks on Ring, the board criticised two Galway players who 'regrettably took the law into their own hands and later retaliated'. It then veered into the absurd by claiming that the attacks on Ring were 'grossly exaggerated … the Cork captain suffered no injury as the steps where the incidents occurred were well carpeted ones'.

And as Val Dorgan drolly noted: 'Incredibly, under the GAA carpet, went the whole extraordinary affair.'

CORK: D. Creedon; G. O'Riordan, J. Lyons, T. O'Shaughnessy; M. Fouhy, V. Twomey, S. O'Brien; J. Twomey, G. Murphy; W.J. Daly (0–1), J. Hartnett (1–1), C. Ring (capt) (1–1, f); T. O'Sullivan (1–0), L. Dowling, P. Barry.

GALWAY: S. Duggan; C. Corless, B. O'Neill, J. Brophy; M. Burke (capt), J. Molloy (0–2, 0–1 70), E. Quinn; J. Salmon, B. Duffy (0–2); J. Duggan (0–1), H. Gordon (0–1), J. Killeen; M. McInerney (0–1), J. Gallagher (0–1, cut), P. Nolan; Subs: M.J. Flaherty for Nolan, P. Duggan for J. Duggan.

Referee: P. Connell (Offaly)

Attendance: 71,195

42. Alien Attack

1954 RAILWAY CUP FINAL (Croke Park, 17 March)
Leinster 0–9 Munster 0–5

---

*There is something wrong with them. I think the players are getting too
many honours, and the Railway Cup games are taking a secondary place
… It's the players' attitudes that are responsible for the fall in interest.*
Christy Ring[1]

I N 1954, DURING the golden age of the inter-provincials, a
record 49,021 turned up to see if Leinster could put a halt to a
Munster team on a formidable winning run. But before a ball
was struck, a row erupted between the GAA and Radio Éireann
over the broadcaster's plans to report from a soccer match during
the half-time interval in the hurling final. The association made no
secret of its horror at the prospect of the Gaelic ear being exposed to
the fortunes of an 'alien' game.

A fuss over a Railway Cup final's broadcasting rights is
unimaginable now at a time when the competition struggles for
survival. Back then, it was worth fighting for. In a letter, the GAA
accused Radio Éireann of 'a fundamental deviation by introducing
intermittent commentaries on an alien game into the Gaelic
programme'. As a result, no radio broadcast of the inter-provincial
hurling final was available to home or overseas listeners.

Those relying on the wireless to discover how Munster fared
in their quest for six-in-a-row were left disappointed. The hostile
exchanges between the GAA and Radio Éireann reflected the mood
of the times. Maurice Gorham, director of Radio Éireann, wrote:

I understand that the only condition on which your executive would withdraw this ban is if we cancelled the broadcast from Dalymount Park [a match between Irish League and Scottish League selections] which we had planned for this wavelength, and I can only say that we cannot let the Gaelic Athletic Association decide for us what sports we should, or should not, broadcast and at what time.

We must therefore cancel the overseas broadcast from Croke Park, although, as you will realise, this will be a great disappointment to Irish listeners overseas. I also understand from you that your executive will not permit us to broadcast a commentary on the hurling final on the Athlone wavelength if we use the free time at the interval to report on the match at Dalymount Park. If this is so, I am afraid we shall be left with no broadcast from Croke Park except that of the football match, a position that I very greatly regret.

The GAA was unrepentant:

For 27 years, it has been an unbroken tradition that the people of Ireland should be provided with uninterrupted commentaries on both Railway Cup finals on St Patrick's Day. This year Radio Éireann has broken that tradition ... The GAA refuses to be a party to the overseas broadcast of such a feature because, by doing so, they would be false to their tradition and principles. On the same grounds, they refused Radio Éireann to interrupt the home broadcast of the Railway Cup hurling final with an interim commentary on an alien game. The responsibility for the difficulties which have arisen rests with Radio Éireann alone.

The 1950s was the Railway Cup's era of prosperity, the attendance for the 1954 final nearly 8,000 more than the previous highest in 1952. From the 1960s, however, as television came into people's homes, the competition began to lose popular appeal. In more recent times, it has been on life-support, no longer enjoying St Patrick's Day billing, a castaway played in random venues across the country, and occasionally abroad, in front of pitifully small gatherings.

Munster had won 11 Railway Cup titles since 1942 with only

Connacht's victory in 1947 denying them a twelve-in-a-row. As it was, the six-in-a-row from 1948 to 1953 was the longest winning streak in the history of the competition. But the low-scoring 1954 final, in which defences ruled, ended the sequence. Leinster led from pillar to post to win their first title since 1941.

Christy Ring, Munster's captain, became synonymous with the Railway Cup and his haul of 18 medals has no rival. He lived to see the competition's decline and 10 days after his death in 1979, Munster failed to reach the hurling final for the first time. By then, attendances were averaging a couple of thousand. In the same year, there was a break from tradition when the hurling final, reflecting its declining status, provided the curtain-raiser to the All-Ireland club football final.

To have any chance of ending Munster's grip in 1954, Leinster realised they needed to restrain Ring and they managed it, the maestro impressively shadowed by Tullaroan's Jim Hogan. Ring scored three points, two from frees, although Kevin Matthews, the Dublin goalkeeper, denied him with an outstanding save from goal attempts in each half. John D. Hickey wrote of Ring's contribution in the *Irish Independent*:

> He scored three points, one of which was the best score of the game and he was denied a goal when Kevin Matthews made an almost incredible first-half save.

Kilkenny had the highest county representation, including the midfielder John Sutton who had an exceptional match. Another Noresider, Jim Langton, won his first inter-provincial medal in 13 years. Dublin's Norman Allen put in a solid shift in the middle of the field with Sutton, but his part was cut short when he was sent off in the second half, along with Tipperary's John Hough, after the pair had what was described as a 'heated exchange'.

The final that brought together the cream of Munster and Leinster hurling didn't produce a score until the quarter hour mark, Sutton finding Langton who pointed from 40 yards. John Kiely of

Waterford had Munster's first score in the 21st minute with a long-range point, but Leinster continued to hold sway at midfield, and Sutton and Langton added two more points to leave them 0–5 to 0–1 ahead. After Ring had his first goal attempt foiled, Leinster led at the interval 0–6 to 0–2.

They increased their advantage in the second half through Allen and while Matt Fouhy and Pat Stakelum hurled well for Munster, the Leinster backline stood firm. Ring scored another free, then got away from his marker to score an inspiring point from play. Three points down, they were denied an equaliser when Matthews again stopped a Ring piledriver. Sutton fired his province's ninth point in the second minute of injury-time to seal the win. Paddy Buggy was 'magnificent' in the final quarter, according to the *Irish Press* observer Padraig Puirseal, while Ned Wheeler 'mastered' Josie Hartnett.

Puirseal wrote of 'a game that while too rugged and ragged to leave much room for brilliant hurling, blazed into a tense and exciting final quarter'.

Little did Railway Cup enthusiasts realise what desolate days lay ahead. And the old ideologues could not have believed that one day the 'aliens' would be allowed play in Croke Park with the GAA's blessing.

LEINSTER: K. Matthews (Dublin); J. Hogan (Kilkenny), P. Hayden (Kilkenny), M. O'Hanlon (Wexford); P. Buggy (Kilkenny), N. Wheeler (Wexford), J. McGovern (Kilkenny); N. Allen (Dublin, 0–1), J. Sutton (Kilkenny, 0–2); M. Ryan (Dublin), D. Carroll (Kilkenny), T. Flood (Wexford, 0–1); J. Langton (Kilkenny, 0–3, 1f), P. Fitzgerald (Kilkenny, 0–1), M. Kelly (Kilkenny, 0–1); Subs: J. Morrissey (Wexford) for M. Ryan, B. Rackard (Wexford) for M.O'Hanlon.

MUNSTER: T. Reddin (Tipperary); G. O'Riordan (Cork), J. Lyons (Cork), J. Doyle (Tipperary); J. Finn (Tipperary), P. Stakelum (Tipperary), M. Fouhy (Cork); J. Hough (Tipperary), J. Kiely (Waterford, 0–1); W.J. Daly (Cork), J. Hartnett (Cork), S. Bannon (Tipperary, 0–1); J. Smyth (Clare), D. McCarthy(Limerick), C. Ring (Cork, 0–3, 2fs).

Referee: I. Flaherty (Galway)

Attendance: 49,021

43. The Hurling Immortal

1954 ALL-IRELAND FINAL (Croke Park, 5 September)
Cork 1–9 Wexford 1–6

Some of the Cork team had five or six All-Ireland medals. We hadn't one.
We were as green as the grass we walked on.
Ned Wheeler[1]

CROKE PARK WAS no place for the meek on 5 September 1954, the day Christy Ring won an eighth All-Ireland medal and a unique place in the game's history. In the *Irish Independent*, John D. Hickey recalled a tense and gripping encounter where 'every man was utterly unmindful of his personal safety'.[2] Not the best game of hurling, Hickey acknowledged, but in terms of suspense and physical attrition, he had seen few to surpass it.

For an unflinching warrior like Ring, those conditions would have held no fears. His latest triumph saw him overtake the Kilkenny quartet of Sim Walton, Dick 'Drug' Walsh, Dick Doyle and Jack Rochford, seven-time winners, and his feat remained unequalled for 11 years. John Doyle caught up with him in 1965, and both Doyle and Ring were surpassed by Henry Shefflin in 2012 (Noel Skehan's nine All-Ireland medals include three won as a substitute). But Ring has the distinction of being the trailblazer, going where no man had gone before. He secured his fortune when the championship was cut-throat – a straight knockout without reprieve.

A record attendance for an All-Ireland hurling final – 84,856 – watched history in the making. Like the Wexford hurlers, Ring had magnetic crowd appeal. He played in front of the largest attendance at a Cork county final and was also present when the biggest Munster final crowd – 62,175 officially, but estimated at close to 70,000 – was recorded in 1961. Earlier in the year, he'd hurled before the highest Railway Cup final attendance. Before television, the only way to see Ring was by attending matches. In his last outing playing for Glen Rovers, aged 46 in 1967, there were 9,504 present to see him score 1-2 against UCC.

The 1954 final was billed as a shootout between Ring and Nickey Rackard, Wexford's marksman. Both men were in their 30s – Ring almost 34, Rackard 32 – and still fêted and feared. Rackard's scoring had destroyed teams during Wexford's run to a second All-Ireland final in three years: his tallies included 5–4 against Dublin in the Leinster final and 7–7 in the All-Ireland semi-final against Antrim. In total, Wexford scored 25–33 in three games leading to September, but the final judgement day was marked by classic defensive play. Cork's 1–9 was the lowest winning score for 14 years.

While Ring took a great deal of the attention, Cork's backline laid the platform for victory. Their goalkeeper, Dave Creedon of Glen Rovers, had come out of retirement in 1952 when their first three choices were unavailable through injury and suspension. Creedon won three All-Ireland medals and only conceded one goal in three finals. In front of Creedon, Vin Twomey and Tony O'Shaughnessy were formidable figures in the Cork resistance. At full-back, John Lyons bottled up Rackard with nothing fancy, just adhesive marking, denying the big man clean possession at every possible turn. Wexford's defence also prospered. Jim English paid obsessive attention to Ring, who didn't have one of his most luminous hours.

Wexford led 1–3 to 0–5 at half-time with a goal from Tom Ryan, and suffered a hammer blow six minutes into the half when their inspirational full-back Nick O'Donnell had to leave the field with a broken collarbone. Ned Wheeler went to centre-back and Bobbie Rackard took up residence in O'Donnell's usual position. Critics of the move argued that while Rackard was still influential, his raking clearances were now landing too far from the Cork goal to have the same impact, and Wexford's attack suffered the consequences. 'They had plenty subs on the sideline and they have to break up nearly the whole team to make one change,' Wheeler lamented 60 years later. 'But Wexford hadn't an All-Ireland since 1910; that was an awful gap to bridge.'

In the third quarter, Wexford applied severe pressure without sufficient reward. The Leinster champions led 1–6 to 0–5 after 40 minutes, but it should have been more. Having soaked the pressure, Cork struck late. Johnny Clifford was their hero when he scored the vital goal in the 26th minute to put them a point up. Clifford had been an outstanding minor when Cork won the 1951 All-Ireland, and later went on to become a respected Cork manager.

Wexford tried to find a way back. Nickey Rackard had a free from an acute angle to level, but missed. Late points from Ring and Josie Hartnett steered Cork home. The defeat haunted Billy Rackard who blamed himself for not closing down Clifford quickly enough. 'I fatally hesitated,' he said, 'I shall never forget the misery and self-blame I felt at watching the green flag wave.'[3]

After the bitter fallout of the previous year, the 1954 final restored the game's communal values and was played in a spirit of sportsmanship typical of Wexford–Cork games of the period. Ring remarked that Wexford were the cleanest team he had faced. Cork had returned to win the All-Ireland in 1952 with seven newcomers, ending Tipperary's three-year rule of province and nation. The 1954 win completed a three-in-a-row that was the third in the county's history. When teams are riding that high, they can never imagine the fall, but 1954 was Ring's final medal and his second last All-Ireland final appearance. In 1955, Limerick caused a shock by winning Munster, after Clare sensationally floored Cork in the first round. Wexford would go on to better things, as Cork would discover to their cost.

CORK: D. Creedon; J. O'Riordan, J. Lyons, T. O'Shaughnessy; M. Fouhy, V. Twomey (0–1), D. Hayes; G. Murphy, W. Moore; W.J. Daly (0–1), J. Hartnett (0–1), C. Ring (0–5, 2fs); J. Clifford (1–0), E. Goulding (0–1), P. Barry. Sub: T. O'Sullivan for P. Barry.

WEXFORD: A. Foley; W. Rackard, N. O'Donnell, M. O'Hanlon; J. English, B. Rackard, N. Wheeler; J. Morrissey, S. Hearne; Paddy Kehoe (0–1), T. Flood (0–2), Padge Kehoe; T. Ryan (1–0), N. Rackard (0–3, 2fs), R. Donovan; Subs: T. Bolger for N. O'Donnell, D. Hearne for Paddy Kehoe.

Referee: J. Mulcahy (Kilkenny)

Attendance: 84,856

Wexford reach the summit

As Christy Ring had wished, Wexford won the 1955 All-Ireland, their first since 1910, overcoming Galway 3–13 to 2–8 in the final. Galway led 2–5 to 2–3 at half-time, but the Leinster champions dominated thereafter. Wexford's first two goals came from Nickey Rackard and Ned Wheeler, and a third from Tim Flood sealed the win, Centre-back Billy Rackard played an outstanding game; he had also been influential during the semi-final win over surprise Munster champions Limerick, when he subdued their dangerman Dermot Kelly. The 50,840 attendance at that game was a record for an All-Ireland semi-final.

After the final, Nick O'Donnell raised the MacCarthy Cup on Wexford's behalf. O'Donnell was a Kilkenny man and had been a member of the squad that had won the 1947 All-Ireland. After moving to work in Enniscorthy, O'Donnell transferred allegiance. He captained Wexford to victory again in 1960 and earned lasting recognition as one of the sport's best full-backs.

'We'd a few problem positions and one of them was full-back,' Billy Rackard explained years later. 'Nick O'Donnell sorted that out. It was like manna from heaven when we saw him coming.'

44. The Great Awakening

1956 ALL-IRELAND FINAL (Croke Park, 23 September)
Wexford 2–14 Cork 2–8

Hats, coats, everything you can think of have gone into the air and the whole of Croke Park has gone wild.
Michael O'Hehir[1]

The Wexford hurling team of the 1950s were at odds with the stereotype of that decade as being a grey and repressed time. They were stylish, larger than life and had a huge, captive audience. They were the genuine article, the first revolutionary force in hurling since Limerick in the 1930s.

The team of the decade, Wexford repeatedly charmed the nation and were central to some of hurling's most epic matches. 'There was no recession in Wexford,' Liam Griffin said of his county in the 1950s. Others followed suit – Waterford nailed an All-Ireland before the decade's end and Limerick won a Munster title against the odds – but Wexford were the pioneers. Having won the All-Ireland in 1955, the 1956 meeting with Cork would be their most famous hour, and one of the most memorable in hurling.

'In those days we had no money,' Ned Wheeler recalls. 'You were married to the hurling game. You went down to the field six nights a week. I used to walk about four miles down the road to the nearest pitch in Piercestown, hurl all evening and walk back. And that is all we did, unless maybe you'd go to the pictures on a Sunday night.' Such a simple life cried out for something extraordinary and uplifting.

The public was fascinated by Wexford. The attendance at the 1956 All-Ireland final was second only to the record set in September 1954. The 1956 league final, also involving Wexford, had established a new crowd record, as did that year's Leinster final when Wexford had beaten Kilkenny. And, unfailingly, they gave good value.

'Some went on pony and trap Saturday morning,' Wheeler remembers of the crowds leaving Wexford for Croke Park. 'It was a new thing that had happened in the county and, my God, they did take to it. You go back to the Oireachtas finals; up until then you had maybe 10,000 and when we'd play in them you had 45,000.'

An All-Ireland win confirms a team's superiority over the rest of the field. Wexford had achieved that goal in 1955. Greatness, though, requires at least a second title. So, having made the breakthrough in 1955, Wexford faced hurling's great empire, 19-time winners Cork, with Christy Ring attempting to win a ninth All-Ireland medal.

The atmosphere inside Croke Park on 23 September was electrifying. Before the start, an excited Michael O'Hehir captured the general air of anticipation when he wondered if this might turn out to be 'the game of the century'.

If the words of John D. Hickey are to be taken as gospel, it managed to meet expectations. 'I cannot recall a final that left me so utterly over-wrought at the end,' he reported. 'From the 12th minute of the second half to the end, it was a fusillade of hurling fury.'

Wexford had big men who were strong in the air, often electing to catch ball rather than bat or let fly with the hurl. In the 1956 final they were quick out of the traps. Tim Flood had a point inside a minute. Padge Kehoe goaled after three minutes. At one stage, they led 1–6 to 0–2, but Cork closed the half with three points to raise their spirits and headed into the half-time interval trailing 0–5 to 1–6. Wexford stretched their lead to six with early second-half points from Nickey Rackard and a 70 from his brother Billy. Martin Codd scored another point to put them seven up.

Cork were given a lifeline in a moment of controversy when Art Foley made a save and went to ground. The referee signalled a 21-yard free to Cork which Ring sent to the net. Then Ring pointed to trim the Wexford lead to a goal. Kehoe responded with a point. Paddy Barry replied with another for Cork and, in the 19th minute, the sides were level when Barry scored Cork's second goal. A minute later, Ring got free off Bobby Rackard and palmed a point. Cork were in front for the first and only time.

From there to the end, Wexford outscored them 1–4 to 0–0, Nickey Rackard contributing 1–3. He levelled within a minute of Cork going in front and two frees restored their goal-lead. There was a final twist that has become one of the legendary moments in the game's history. Ring got through and shot for goal, but Foley saved his effort. Wexford went back down the field and Tim Flood set up Rackard for the 28th-minute goal that made it safe, Tom Dixon scoring a point with time almost up to complete the job.

In an interview given to RTÉ radio 20 years later, Ring recalled Foley's crucial stop.

> Nick O'Donnell had a habit of batting the ball out and Bobby Rackard was breathing down my neck for the hour. I waited till the last minute and when Nicko batted the ball out, I went out and collected it. There were a lot of things happened between that and the goal, but I was kind of hampered a small bit, you know, Foley brought off a great save. I thought I had it, but he thought differently.

The story that he ran in to shake hands with the Wexford goalkeeper appears to be apocryphal and was disputed by Ring. 'No, I was coming out from behind him actually and I tapped him on the back and said, "Well done."'

In 1956, Wexford had eight of the team that had lost the 1951 All-

Ireland final to Tipperary. Along with holding the championship, league and Oireachtas titles, nine players were represented on Leinster's Railway Cup-winning side. Victory over Kilkenny earned Wexford their first Leinster three-in-a-row. In the All-Ireland semi-final, they had thrashed Galway 5–13 to 1–8 with Nickey Rackard scoring all five goals.

Cork had begun the summer with a team in transition, having lost to Clare the previous year. In the Munster championship, one of five newcomers, Mick Ryan of Ballyhea, scored 2–2 in a 5–9 to 2–12 defeat of Waterford at Fermoy. They came from behind to defeat Tipperary and, in the final, Ring, now 35, scored three late goals to help his team overcome the provincial champions Limerick who led with 15 minutes to go.

Wexford, though, proved one hurdle too many. After the final whistle, Nick O'Donnell kissed Ring's cheek, and he and Bobby Rackard lifted him shoulder high and carried him off the pitch. 'I think the sportsmanship was there before that happened and after it happened,' said Ned Wheeler. 'I never saw any of those lads pulling a dirty stroke. At times, Nick O'Donnell was assaulted in the square and never retaliated; the same with Nickey Rackard. The whole team had the same characteristics.'

WEXFORD: A. Foley; B. Rackard, N. O'Donnell, M. Morrissey; J. English, W. Rackard (0–1, 70), J. Morrissey; S. Hearne, N. Wheeler; P. Kehoe (1–1), M. Codd (0–2), T. Flood (0–3); T. Ryan, N. Rackard (1–5, 3fs), T. Dixon (0–2).

CORK: M. Cashman; J. Brohan, J. Lyons, T. O'Shaughnessy; M. Fouhy, W.J. Daly, P. Philpott; E. Goulding (0–1), P. Dowling; M. O'Regan (0–1), J. Hartnett, P. Barry (1–1); C. O'Shea, T. Kelly, C. Ring (1–5, 1–3fs); Subs: V. Twomey for O'Shaughnessy (inj.), G. Murphy for J. Hartnett.

Referee: T. O'Sullivan (Limerick)

Attendance: 83,096

The great escape

Wexford's win over Tipperary in the 1956 league final was one of the most extraordinary hurling comebacks. Facing a strong wind, they trailed 0–1 to 2–10 at half-time, with Paddy Kenny having scored 2–5. In the dressing room at the interval, Nickey Rackard admonished his men and accused them of 'playing like camogie players'. By the end of a stunning match, they had turned it around and won 5–9 to 2–14.

Rackard started the revival with a goal soon after half-time, and scored the last major before the final whistle as Wexford won their first league title. Tom Ryan also bagged two goals and Tom Dixon pitched in with one. Tipperary goalkeeping legend Tony Reddin, blamed for two of the goals, never played for the county again.

The crowd of 45,902 was a record for a league final. Present was one Gus Byrne, later to be Mayor of Wexford, who pedalled to Dublin with a gale wind to his back, having got out of bed in Arklow at 4.30 that morning.

> We must have done it in well under four hours, which was some going. We got to Croke Park to see Wexford being beaten at half-time. We were sick in more ways than one, at the thought of having to cycle home as well.[2]

That was all to change.

> [We] left Croke Park on a high. We went into one of the hotels to get something to eat and set out, with Wexford jerseys on us. Well I can tell you, that it was some journey through the city and down to Arklow. Every car that passed us was blaring and blowing. They were shouting out through the windows and there were flags and bonfires the whole way to Arklow, right into Wexford.[3]

45. Closing Time

1957 LEINSTER FINAL (Croke Park, 4 August)
Kilkenny 6–9 Wexford 1–5

As the popular Ned lay there, still unconscious and unaware of our humiliating defeat, I looked out of the ward window. The heavens had opened. That very moment for me was the nadir of the 1950s.
Billy Rackard[1]

HURLING HUMBLES THE mighty in the blink of an eye. This astonishing result ended Wexford's three-year reign as Leinster champions, marked the birth of modern coaching and served as the final salute for Nickey Rackard. Within a week, he had announced his retirement.

Rackard didn't go out all guns blazing – he was held scoreless from play by Jim 'Link' Walsh. The 35-year-old was denied a parting goal by a new star on the rise, Ollie Walsh. Kilkenny's goalkeeper had an outstanding day, beaten just once, when Tom Ryan scored before half-time. By then Wexford, who had won all in their wake in 1956, were finished. At one stage near the half-hour mark, they trailed 0–2 to 5–5. They recovered from the beating to win another All-Ireland in 1960.

In 1957, they were favourites to win a record fourth provincial title in a row. Kilkenny, studiously coached by a young priest called Tommy Maher, had defeated Wexford in the league at New Ross but faltered in the league final against Tipperary. They needed two matches to deal with Dublin in the Leinster semi-finals. Though outsiders, they had shown potential. In the 1956 Leinster final, they almost scored a winning goal near the end and, in 1955, they took Wexford to a replay.

Yet nobody predicted what was to unfold. Pat'O in his *Irish Times* column the day before the match wrote of his fervent hopes and expectations that this would be the hurling match of the year in what had otherwise been a dull season.[2] Later, he recalled the words of a follower he'd met leaving the ground who told him that Wexford had been 'hurled out of Croke Park'. It was a significant step in reviving Kilkenny's fortunes after 10 years without an All-Ireland. But not only that. It ushered in a new era of tactical coaching. Fr Maher's work would inspire others and create a direct link to the contemporary achievements of Brian Cody. Maher was a scholar of the game, with a keen analytical brain. His influence on Kilkenny and what they became was immense.

Wexford looked tired, having taken some time to dismiss Offaly in the Leinster semi-finals, and they were not long home from a trip to New York where they had spent much of June. Kilkenny spent most of the same month in Nowlan Park being drilled by Fr Maher. He coached his players to guide the ball low and not play, literally, into Wexford's hands with high trajectories. They would set the terms and conditions.

Bobby Rackard was missing, having suffered injury in a farm accident that ended his career. Wexford also lost Ned Wheeler in the early minutes when he was carried off unconscious after a blow to the head. Kilkenny had heroes from Walsh in goal up to Sean Clohosey in their full-forward line. They went one point up and then Wexford levelled before laying siege to the Kilkenny goal. Rackard had a go from 20 yards; Walsh was equal to it. Another goal attempt went narrowly wide. After 10 minutes, Wexford went in front for the only time in the match.

Then it all changed spectacularly. Dick Rockett began the carnage with a goal and, a minute later, another goal came off the stick of Billy Dwyer, who finished a rebound when a 21-yard free by

Mick Kenny was blocked. A point from Dwyer followed. At the other end, Walsh made another great save from Tim Flood.

The third goal came in the 20th minute when Clohosey got the final touch after a free from Kenny landed near the Wexford posts. Mick Brophy's point made it 3–4 to 0–2.

A Clohosey point was followed in the 25th minute by a goal from Denis Heaslip. Wexford were stunned. Within 60 seconds, Clohosey put his name to a fifth goal. In a strong challenge from Nick O'Donnell, Clohosey suffered injury and had to leave the game half an hour in – but his work was done. Even a late Wexford mini-revival before the interval did little to dent Kilkenny's authority, and they went in at the break 5–5 to 1–3 to the good. His replacement P.J. Garvan got the final goal near the end of the game.

After half-time, Wexford tried everything, but Kilkenny would not yield. Completing a perfect day, Kilkenny's minors won the curtain-raiser against Offaly, a 15-year-old Eddie Keher scoring 2–2. Kilkenny thundered on, winning their 14th All-Ireland and laying the foundation for greater prosperity.

The 52,272 attendance at the 1957 Leinster final wasn't bettered until the 1997 final when Wexford defended their Leinster title against Kilkenny, watched by 55,492. Kilkenny's win in 1957 avenged a 0–7 to 5–11 Leinster semi-final defeat to Wexford in 1954. They were back in charge.

KILKENNY: O. Walsh; T. Walsh, J. Walsh, J. Maher; P. Buggy, M. Walsh, J. McGovern; M. Brophy (0–1), J. Sutton (0–1); D. Heaslip (1–0), M. Kenny (0–3, 3fs), M. Kelly (0–1, f); D. Rockett (1–0), B. Dwyer (1–2), S. Clohosey (2–1); Sub: P.J. Garvan (1–0) for S. Clohosey.

WEXFORD: A. Foley; M. Morrissey, N. O'Donnell, T. Morrissey; J. English, W. Rackard, J. Morrissey; N. Wheeler, S. Hearne (0–2, 1 sideline); O. Gough, M. Codd (0–1), P. Kehoe; T. Ryan (1–0), N. Rackard (0–2, 1f), T. Flood.

Referee: B. Smyth (Meath)

Attendance: 52,272

A life less ordinary

Frequently mentioned in the same breath as Ring and Mackey, Nickey Rackard was the goal-scoring giant who catapulted Wexford into the big time. His life became a fascinating and at times tragic study, a personal battle with alcoholism leading to a later role of saving others from the same fate.

'Though retirement is inevitable in everyone's life,' wrote the engaging Wexford chronicler Nicky Furlong of the player's career end, 'it is doubtful if Nickey Rackard was mentally prepared for the silence that followed.'[3]

He had made his debut for Wexford in the 1942 championship, but it wasn't until 1951 that he won his first Leinster senior medal, adding three more and two All-Irelands, as well as a national league. He also won a Leinster senior medal in football in 1945. Rackard made 36 championship appearances for Wexford, scoring 59–96.

Notable performances include his tally of 5–4 in the 1954 Leinster final win over Dublin and his 7–7 against Antrim in the All-Ireland semi-final the same year, the latter a championship scoring record unlikely to be beaten.

The struggle with drink became part of his life story. In 1951, he quit and was on the dry when Wexford celebrated their All-Ireland wins in 1955 and 1956. But after the trip to New York in 1957, he resumed the habit until he finally managed to quit for good in 1970. He went on to work for Alcoholics Anonymous, helping people all over Ireland to tackle their addiction. Rackard died from cancer in 1976 at 53, reading the *Irish Field* in bed in St Vincent's Hospital in Dublin.

'I think as a family that that's the legacy we would be most proud of,' his son Bobby said in 2005, talking of his father's work with recovering alcoholics.

46. White Magic

1959 ALL-IRELAND FINAL REPLAY (Croke Park, 4 October)
Waterford 3–12 Kilkenny 1–10

As God is my judge, I believe there is an All-Ireland in this team.
Pat Fanning[1]

PAT FANNING, A master of all trades from manager to county board chief to GAA president, dared anyone to challenge his contention that Waterford had its own tradition, as important and valid as any of the great dynasties. It was, he said, a tradition 'of never giving up'. Beaten by Kilkenny in the 1957 All-Ireland final, their persistence was rewarded two years later.

1959 was not Waterford's first senior All-Ireland title – that had come in 1948 – but this was more fêted. Two years previously, they had lost to Kilkenny after leading by eight points with eight minutes left and they were fortunate not to lose to Kilkenny again in the 1959 drawn final, needing a stroke of good fortune to gain a replay.

The team of 1959 was one of their most talented ever. The season began with Tipperary as All-Ireland champions. In the league final, Waterford were defeated 0–15 to 0–7 by Tipperary, and when both counties safely negotiated first-round hurdles in the championship – Tipp seeing off Limerick and Waterford crushing Galway in their first year in Munster – the semi-final was staged in Cork with the blue and gold expected to advance. Instead, as Waterford's goalkeeper Ned Power memorably put it: 'We scandalised them.'[2]

Electing to play with a gale, Waterford ran amok, scoring eight goals to lead 8–2 to 0–0 at half-time. Tipperary made a recovery but nowhere near enough, losing 3–4 to 9–3. In the Munster final, Waterford had a goal to spare over Cork and went straight into the September decider against Kilkenny.

Only a late goal from Sean Clohosey carried Kilkenny past Dublin in the Leinster final. The drawn All-Ireland final was rated the best journalist John D. Hickey had seen, as he enthusiastically informed his readers in the *Irish Independent*. Kilkenny looked to have won until their full-back 'Link' Walsh deflected a shot from Seamus Power past Ollie Walsh with time almost up to level the match. Power had a chance to win the game but his point attempt went wide. Ollie Walsh had a starring role, pulling off three outstanding saves in the first half – even by his standards, this game is a serious contender for his finest hour.

A surprise influence in the drawn match was Tommy O'Connell, aged 19, who scored three goals for Kilkenny. On the second day, O'Connell failed to score. Until recent years, All-Ireland final replays were rare – this was the first since Limerick and Dublin had to play twice in 1934 – and it closed a memorable hurling decade with a popular winner. Waterford would play in three All-Ireland finals in this period, the last in 1963, and they should have won more than one title given the quality of players at their disposal.

The drawn match on 7 September had seen Waterford concede 5–5 and score 1–17. In the replay, Kilkenny started the better of the two and led 1–4 to 0–1 after 12 minutes, Denis Heaslip scoring the goal. But Waterford rallied and a goal from Mick Flannelly roused their spirits before a goal from Tom Cunningham levelled the game after 17 minutes. A third goal, from Tom Cheasty three minutes later, put them in front for the first time, a lead they never relinquished. By half-time, they enjoyed a 3–5 to 1–8 advantage. Kilkenny scored only two points in the second half, both from Eddie Keher, who had been added to the panel for the replay after appearing in the minor final and playing a couple of senior matches in the Oireachtas and Walsh cups. Frankie Walsh had a majestic day in the Waterford colours. Dick Carroll and John Barron were sent off with 15 minutes left – Carroll being the first Kilkenny player to be sent off in an All-Ireland senior hurling final since Dick Grace in 1916.

Waterford were much stiffer in their defensive resistance in the replay. 'I'd great backs,' stated Ned Power proudly years later. Of them all, Austin Flynn still held a special place in his affections well into old age.

Frankie Walsh went up the steps to accept the MacCarthy Cup, having played a captain's part. 'This, without doubt, was his match,' reported John D. Hickey. 'I cannot recall an occasion on which he was beaten, not even when the ball mischievously fell away from him as he essayed a point off a free. He hit it off the ground and sent it straight and true between the posts for a point.'

WATERFORD: N. Power; J. Harney, A. Flynn, J. Barron; M. Lacey, M. Óg Morrissey, J. Condon; S. Power, P. Grimes; M. Flannelly (1–1), T. Cheasty (1–2), F. Walsh (0–8, 6fs); L. Guinan (0–1), T. Cunningham (1–0), S. Kiely; Subs: M. O'Connor for M. Lacey, D. Whelan for T. Cunningham.

KILKENNY: O. Walsh; T. Walsh, J. Walsh, J. Maher; P. Buggy, M. Walsh (0–1, f), J. McGovern; P. Kelly, T. Kelly; D. Heaslip (1–1), M. Fleming, S. Clohosey (0–1); D. Carroll, B. Dwyer (0–5, 3fs), T. O'Connell; Sub: E. Keher (0–2) for J. McGovern.

Referee: G. Fitzgerald (Limerick)

Attendance: 77,285

Galway march on Munster

Defeated in three All-Ireland senior finals in the 1950s – two of which were contested without the benefit of a qualifying game – Galway hurlers competed in Munster from 1959 to 1969. It was not a happy holiday. They won one of their 12 championship games in Munster and took some heavy beatings.

The move differed from Galway's recent transfer into Leinster in that all inter-county teams participated, not just senior, as well as their club champions, but the venture did not succeed in bringing Galway closer to winning their first All-Ireland since 1923.

Their first match down south, against Waterford in 1959, ended in a 7–11 to 0–8 defeat at the Gaelic Grounds. In 1961, Tipperary ran seven goals past them after Galway had recorded their only victory in the province, defeating Clare 2–13 to 0–7 in Nenagh. Galway didn't win again in Munster and returned, chastened, to Connacht in 1969.

One curious legacy of the Munster invasion was the opportunity it offered other counties in Connacht to hoover up some silverware. In 1956, Galway had defeated Roscommon in the Connacht minor final by 49 points. In Galway's absence, the Rossies won five minor provincial titles. In 1965, Leitrim, fielding a team in the competition for the first time, defeated Mayo 8–5 to 0–0 in the Connacht final. They then faced Limerick in the All-Ireland semi-final played at Birr, losing by 37 points – 15–13 to 6–3. The story goes that the Limerick full-back was feeling charitable and allowed the Leitrim Number 14 to bag a hat-trick. It was also claimed that Leitrim fielded a 21-year-old on their first and last foray to the knockout stages of the minor championship.

47. Dublin's Light Declines

1961 ALL-IRELAND FINAL (Croke Park, 3 September)
Tipperary 0–16 Dublin 1–12

It was a tragedy ... that we lost that game.
Jimmy Gray[1]

THE 1961 ALL-IRELAND final was a missed opportunity for Dublin that left a nagging question: What might have happened had they won?

Instead of a victory to spark a hurling resurgence, defeat consigned them to a long spell in the wilderness. Jimmy Gray first stood in goal for Dublin in 1957 and finished in 1966, and says they were 'robbed' in a Leinster championship replay by Wexford in 1958. They beat Wexford in the 1959 championship and lost to a last-ditch Kilkenny goal in the Leinster final. That's how competitive Dublin were then.

A few years after he retired, Gray remembers Dublin having only 14 men in Nowlan Park for a championship game against Kilkenny and having to call on a selector, Christy Hayes, to play corner-forward. County board support and general organisation fell away and Gaelic football became the game of the masses.

In 1961, the team in light blue lined out with 14 native Dubs, having discarded their reliance on country men working in the capital. Paddy Croke of Killenaule was the sole exception, while Clonmel's Mick Kennedy was among the subs.

Even in defeat, the 1961 All-Ireland final performance should have been a new beginning for Dublin hurling; instead, the county didn't win another Leinster senior championship until 2013. Dublin failed to even reach a Leinster hurling final between 1964 and 1990. In the meantime, Kevin Heffernan's football teams captured the city's imagination. In terms of popular appeal, there was only one team in town.

The writer Breandán Ó Hehir maintained that Dublin were denied by 'loutish antics'.[2] But Dublin had destiny in their own hands and didn't seize it. 'We were lucky,' admitted Theo English, recalling the game years later, 'Dublin were all over us.'[3]

Dublin went in to the match clear outsiders, despite a Leinster final win over Wexford, who had claimed a shock All-Ireland win at Tipperary's expense in 1960. Tipperary returned in 1961 with renewed steel and focus and finished the year undefeated, having begun their campaign with an easy win over Galway. In the Munster final, they clattered Cork by eight points in a match clouded in controversy when Tom Moloughney went off after being struck on the head by a Cork player.

In the spring, Tipp had won the National League, but the All-Ireland final was as close as they came to losing a major game. Three key players went in with injury concerns – Kieran Carey, Tony Wall and Jimmy Doyle – and all required pain-killing injections. Wall struggled and the switch of Liam Devaney to centre-back helped Tipp steady their defence. They opened with three points in three minutes but Dublin settled, and Des Foley at midfield had the game of his life.

By half-time, Dublin trailed 0–6 to 0–10, then, six minutes after the restart, the game exploded when Willie Jackson goaled for Dublin and Achill Boothman, who tormented John Doyle throughout, had them level within 30 seconds. The remainder of the game was impossible to predict with any certainty.

At the back, Des Ferguson displayed a telling authority, the sole survivor of the team beaten by Cork in the 1952 final. Twelve minutes from the end, Dublin's dream was still very much alive when they led by two points, their pace and movement bamboozling Tipp's defence. Tipperary rallied and drew level with two frees from Doyle, Donie Nealon put them in front from play and then Doyle scored another free with six minutes left. Achill Boothman responded with a point within a minute. Dublin, a point down, pressed hard for an equaliser, a late free from Larry Shannon drifting wide. Tipp held on for an 18th title and went on to dominate the rest of the decade.

Dublin were a somewhat novel act. They had earned notice for impressive physical conditioning, being trailblazers in collective, gym-based winter training. Bernard Boothman sported an earring, a rare accessory for a GAA player at the time. Yet he and his brother Achill, from Crumlin, were quiet and reserved personalities. Achill's five points from play and his terrorising of John Doyle – who had his worst match in Croke Park[4] – is a lasting reminder of Dublin's unfulfilled promise. Promise that could well have been fulfilled if Lar Foley had not been sent off in the second half along with Tipp sub Tom Ryan.

Dublin had eight players on the Leinster team that beat Munster in the 1961 Railway Cup final, a measure of their standing in the game at the time. It did not last, but Tipperary were only starting; this was the first of four All-Ireland wins in five years.

TIPPERARY: D. O'Brien; M. Hassett, M. Maher, K. Carey; M. Burns, T. Wall, John Doyle; T. English, M. O'Gara (0–2); Jimmy Doyle (0–9, 7f), L. Devaney, D. Nealon (0–3); J. McKenna (0–1), B. Moloughney, T. Moloughney (0–1); Subs: T. Ryan for J. McKenna, J. Hough for M. O'Gara (inj.), S. McLoughlin for T. Wall.

DUBLIN: J. Gray; D. Ferguson, N. Drumgoole, L. Foley; L. Ferguson, C. Hayes, B. Lynch; D. Foley (0–1, f), F. Whelan; A. Boothman (0–5), M. Bohan, L. Shannon (0–3, 2f); B. Boothman (0–1), P. Croke, W. Jackson (1–2); Sub: E. Malone for M. Bohan.

Referee: G. Fitzgerald (Limerick)

Attendance: 67,866

Ring's end

The 1961 Munster final wasn't a classic – Tipp won by eight points and Cork managed only one score from play – but it was significant for two reasons. Christy Ring, who had stated that the GAA was only 'half-dressed' without Tipperary, played his last championship match against the blue and gold at the age of 40. His record against Tipp was eight wins, eight defeats and a draw. The other feature was controversial and left a cloud over Ring's exit. In the second half, a dispute between Ring and John Doyle escalated into a mêlée and Tom Moloughney, who was on the fringe of the group, was struck on the head by a Cork player's hurl, though neither Moloughney nor Doyle would disclose the identity of the culprit.

Ring's jaw had been broken when Cork had played Tipperary in the Oireachtas final the previous October. At the 1961 Munster final in Limerick, around 15,000 gathered outside the ground trying in vain to get in. Cork togged at the Railway Hotel and had to abandon their cars and walk because of the crowd swell. The disruption may have contributed to a poor first half; by half-time, they were 0–1 to 3–3 down.

The gates for the final were closed at noon for a 3.30 throw-in and the attendance was estimated at 70,000 even though the official figure was 62,175. 'I was 16, it was my first Munster final, and we were in the ground by 10.30 a.m.,' said Matt Aherne, a young Cork follower.

'There were fellas who went to that match that never went to another match after, they got such a fright; they thought they were going to die of a heart attack,' said Tipp hurler Theo English. 'They let in a terrible crowd that day. There were people coming out with their shirts off and they wringing with sweat. It was really frightening I heard. Lucky enough, they didn't rush the field.'[5]

48. Brawn *and* Class

1964 ALL-IRELAND FINAL (Croke Park, 6 September)
Tipperary 5–13 Kilkenny 2–8

I don't believe in fairies and I don't believe in hoodoos either.
Kilkenny county secretary, Paddy Grace[1]

KILKENNY WERE REIGNING All-Ireland champions when they squared up to Tipperary in the 1964 All-Ireland final, the first meeting of the counties in a championship final since 1950. Their poor record in these fixtures didn't spook the Kilkenny county secretary but Tipperary had demolished all in their path throughout the summer.

Clare leaked six goals in the Munster semi-final and lost by 20 points. Even Cork, Tipp's great rivals, weren't able to summon up a fight. They went down in the Munster final by 11 points, scoring just 1–5. And then Kilkenny suffered a similar battering, a 14-point loss. Tipperary were in a different class. This was their 20th All-Ireland and made them leaders on the roll of honour for the first time since 1937.

Tony Wall, a winner of five All-Irelands between 1958 and 1967, and loser in two more finals, recalled the Tipperary team of the time in the course of a newspaper interview in 2000. 'We expected to win every match, no doubt about it. We considered ourselves the best and we proved it. We should have won five in a row.'[2]

A report into the game produced by a Hurling Commission even worried that Tipperary were in danger of leaving all others behind.

John O'Grady, the Tipp goalkeeper in 1958, said:

The 1960s team had the most class and best balance between forwards and backs that Tipperary ever had. They were far more than brute force, but the reputation of being over-physical took seed. It was the day of the third-man tackle when goalkeepers and dandy forwards had good reason to be nervous.[3]

Even great, apparently invincible, teams have a shelf life and the 1964 final was probably the summit performance for this squad. Were it not for the surprise loss to Waterford in the 1963 Munster final, an All-Ireland five-in-a-row (never witnessed before or since) could have been theirs.

For Kilkenny, their hang-ups about Tipperary worsened. While they'd been pessimistic before defeating Waterford in the 1963 All-Ireland final, in 1964, they tended to see the glass half-full. The team contained 10 of the players from 1963 and a sprinkling of young talent, like Pat Henderson and Pa Dillon. Their coach Fr Tommy Maher told reporters in the lead-up to the game that they were 'fit and fearless'.

Kilkenny hadn't beaten Tipperary in the championship since the 1922 All-Ireland final but, as county secretary Paddy Grace pointed out, the counties hadn't met that often either. There was the 1937 defeat in Killarney, a comprehensive loss, and the other championship contests included Tipp's six-point win in the 1945 All-Ireland final, a one-point victory in the 1950 final and a five-point triumph in the 1958 All-Ireland semi-final.

Kilkenny's confidence was misplaced. They could not have bargained on the off-day endured by Ollie Walsh, who was at fault for at least two of the goals. An injury to Martin Coogan when they were two points down late in the first half was also a telling blow. But none of this offered total absolution.

A win over Tipperary in New York, in a game between the All-Ireland champions and the National League winners, had boosted Kilkenny's pre-match confidence. They placed a lot of hope in their youth and speed in a team with an average age of just over 23 –

Ollie Walsh was their oldest player at 27 and Tom Walsh their youngest at 20.

The skies fell in between the fourth and 16th minute of the second half, when Tipperary scored 2–4. At half-time, Tipperary were ahead 1–8 to 0–6 but when John Teehan got on the end of an Eddie Keher free to goal after the restart, Kilkenny had real hope. It was short-lived. Jimmy Doyle opened a three-point gap with a free and Nealon goaled in the 10th minute of the second half. They were eight points clear when Sean McLoughlin goaled and even though Tom Walsh's goal in the 49th minute and Paddy Moran's point reduced the deficit to seven points, Tipp would not let it rest. Nealon scored two more goals to round off his hat-trick. John McKenna had scored Tipp's first goal in the eighth minute of the first half. Nenagh's Mick Burns held Keher scoreless from play.

Tipperary had it every way. Their forwards were virtually unstoppable but their defence also gained acclaim and John Doyle ended up Hurler of the Year. 'Forwards could charge in those days and the backs' problem was to keep the forwards out,' said Wall. 'You needed big strong men to stand in the way. Doyle was big and strong. He would come running out looking like a big gorilla scattering small forwards in all directions. But you could not say that about any other teams since. Babs [Keating] preached hurling to his team. If anything they were too gentle.'[4]

Earlier in 1964, Tipp had destroyed Wexford 5–12 to 1–4 in the National League final, one of their five league titles in the 1960s – a decade in which they contested seven All-Ireland finals in nine years and were easily the hurling team of the decade.

The 1964 All-Ireland final came at a high cost for Phil 'Fan' Larkin whose man, Nealon, enjoyed a scoring feast. Fan accepted the blame for one of Nealon's three goals – the second was a long-range effort that should have been saved by Walsh – but he didn't play for Kilkenny again until 1970. 'The trouble with Kilkenny is that there's so many good hurlers, that when one lad goes out, there's always another to come in,' he explained.

KILKENNY: O. Walsh; T. Walsh, J. Walsh, J. Maher; P. Buggy, M. Walsh,
J. McGovern; M. Brophy (0–1), J. Sutton (0–1); D. Heaslip (1–0), M. Kenny
(0–3, 3fs), M. Kelly (0–1); D. Rockett (1–0), B. Dwyer (1–2), S. Clohosey (2–1);
Sub: P.J. Garvan (1–0) for S. Clohosey.

WEXFORD: A. Foley; M. Morrissey, N. O'Donnell, T. Morrissey; J. English,
W. Rackard (0–1), J. Morrissey; N. Wheeler, S. Hearne (0–2, 1 sideline);
O. Gough, M. Codd (0–1), P. Kehoe; T. Ryan (1–0), N. Rackard (0–1, f), T. Flood.

Referee: A. Higgins (Galway)

Attendance: 71,282

Minor massacre

Heavy defeats were the order of the day for Leinster's teams
in 1964 as Laois, a novelty act in the minor final, suffered a
horrendous tanking. Cork won 10–7 to 1–4, having led 3–3 to
0–4 at the interval. Laois' goal came in the second half; Cork
banged in seven.

A 30-point defeat in an All-Ireland minor final is astonishing,
given that Laois had been closely frisked through Leinster
which produced seven All-Ireland minor-winning teams in the
1960s. Laois had overcome Kilkenny in the Leinster final, 4–9
to 3–8. Their only previous All-Ireland minor final appearance
had been in 1934 when they had lost 3–5 to 4–3 to Tipperary.

The year also saw the publication of a Hurling Commission
report, driven by GAA president Alf Murray. One target was
that by 1969 all counties would have a minor team competing
in the hurling championship. That aspiration, along with a few
others, would prove far too ambitious.

49. Doyle's Eight

1965 All-IRELAND FINAL (Croke Park, 5 September)
Tipperary 2–16 Wexford 0–10

Nearly everyone now admits the game is not as good as it was.
Jim 'Tough' Barry[1]

TOUGH BARRY'S RATHER dismal diagnosis of the state of hurling was made in March 1965, during a time when Tipperary held the seat of power. Cork hadn't been able to raise more than token resistance, and Barry lamented that the last great All-Ireland hurling final had been the 1956 meeting of his own county and Wexford. If Tipperary were not quite at the peak of their powers, they didn't need to be – they were still too good for everyone else. Just like the previous year, they finished the season with a clean sweep of All-Ireland, National League and Oireachtas honours.

Barry started looking for clues and underlying ailments. He was old-school – direct play being his preferred option – and was critical of Cork's embrace of solo-running.

When Tony Wall, a modern thinker on the game, was asked about how hurling should be played, he had a more open-minded view and saw merit in a varied approach involving a mix of styles. Tipperary had the hard men of yore, they had the full-back line that had spawned the mythology of Hell's Kitchen, but they had hurling intelligence and imagination too. They were masters of all they surveyed. The 1965 All-Ireland final, though, was their final peak before a gradual decline.

The 1965 All-Ireland was embellished by John Doyle equalling Ring's record of eight All-Ireland medals won on the field of play. He would memorably and self-deprecatingly say that while Ring won them for Cork, Tipperary won them for him.

In Munster, Tipperary wiped out Clare 5–8 to 3–3 in the semi-finals and demolished Cork 4–11 to 0–5 at the Gaelic Grounds, qualifying them for the All-Ireland final automatically, like their Leinster counterparts. Wexford spiritedly regained the Leinster championship with a 2–11 to 3–7 defeat of Kilkenny. Tipperary had already beaten Kilkenny in the 1965 National League home final by nine points and Wexford in the 1964 version by 20 points.

Wexford were starting to make an impression in underage hurling and won the under-21 All-Ireland in 1965, with five of that team also playing in the senior final. Only six of the Wexford team who had lined out against Tipperary in the 1962 All-Ireland final started in 1965, with two more, Ned Wheeler and 'Hopper' McGrath, coming on as substitutes. Billy Rackard, the last of the brothers to retire, had gone, along with illustrious names like Tim Flood and Nick O'Donnell. 1965 also marked the end of the road for Wheeler and McGrath, and put Wexford into full-blown transition.

Two goals from Sean McLoughlin in the space of 30 seconds in the opening quarter sent Tipperary on their way to a comfortable victory. The winners led 2–5 to 0–6 at half-time after playing against the breeze.

Five points down at half-time, Wexford had the first score after the interval through Martin Codd but the rest of the match belonged to a dominant Tipperary with John 'Mackey' McKenna scoring five points. Tipp were never in danger and at the end, Jimmy Doyle, their prized attacker and captain, went up to collect the trophy. Doyle had also captained the side that had won the 1962 final but he had fractured his collarbone and was stretchered off, so Tony Wall accepted the cup on that occasion.

Tipperary's league home final win over Kilkenny in late May,

1965 had shown that they were in no mood to relinquish their grip on hurling. In a heated match, their defence was watertight and Len Gaynor nailed a position in the half-back line in the absence of the injured Mick Murphy. The final scoreline of 3–14 to 2–8 left Kilkenny exasperated as to what they needed to do to conquer their rivals. In a league match in Thurles six weeks earlier, Kilkenny had won by 7–10 to 5–5, a match in which Tom Walsh had scored three goals off John Doyle – come the league home final, he had to settle for one point.

The teams also met in October in the Oireachtas final with Kilkenny desperate to leave a meaningful impression. Tipperary trailed at half-time 0–2 to 1–6 but still turned it around to win 2–12 to 2–7 to round off the year with every title in their possession.

It wasn't until the 1966 league home final that Kilkenny achieved the long-awaited win over Tipperary in a national decider. By then, Tipp were showing signs of slippage – Limerick would also be waiting to ambush them in the Munster championship.

Wexford in 1965, though game, were not the Wexford of recent vintage, not the collection of characters who had stunned Tipperary in the 1960 All-Ireland final and given them plenty to think about in the 1962 final.

The 1965 All-Ireland victory was the eighth triumph for Tipperary under their celebrated trainer Paddy Leahy. In a team packed with quality players, it seemed appropriate that Jimmy Doyle, the prodigy who had played in four successive All-Ireland minor finals, the first at 14, should climb the steps to receive the cup. Doyle was their most prized forward, a left-handed player with a beautiful touch, a total hurler.

TIPPERARY: J. O'Donoghue; John Doyle, M. Maher, K. Carey; M. Burns, T. Wall, L. Gaynor; T. English (0–1, sideline), M. Roche; Jimmy Doyle (0–6, 6fs), L. Kiely (0–2), L. Devaney (0–1); D. Nealon, J. McKenna (0–5), S. McLoughlin (2–1).

WEXFORD: P. Nolan; W. O'Neill, D. Quigley, N. Colfer; V. Staples, T. Neville,
W. Murphy; P. Wilson, M. Byrne; J. O'Brien (0–4, 1f), J. Nolan, D. Shannon (0–3,
1f); P. Quigley, M. Codd (0–3, 3fs), J. Foley; Subs: N. Wheeler for J. Nolan,
O. McGrath for P. Quigley.

Referee: M. Hayes (Clare)

Attendance: 67,498

Wexford harvest

After winning four Leinster titles and two All-Irelands in the
1950s, it was no mean feat for Wexford to maintain the same
strike rate in the 1960s.

The 1960 win over Tipperary – 2–15 to 0–11 – served notice
of their intentions. Jim English, their captain in 1956, recalled
how much of a surprise the win in 1960 was.

> I was driving sheep on the Saturday afternoon before the game and
> a Carlow neighbour asked if we had a hope. I said it was 50/50. He
> went off and said to another neighbour that he thought I was stone
> mad.[2]

Wexford had remarkable staying power. In 1962, they still had
five of the team that had been beaten by Tipp in the 1951 final,
37-year-old Padge Kehoe being one of them.

50. Twelve Years a Slave

1966 ALL-IRELAND FINAL (Croke Park, 4 September)
Cork 3–9 Kilkenny 1–10

There was even talk about us taking pills; there were lots of post-mortems.
Martin Coogan[1]

SOME RESULTS MAKE no sense and fuel the wildest conspiracies. The day before a heavy league final defeat to Kilkenny in 1976, Clare's Pat O'Connor was taking his car for a service. To kill time while it was being worked on, he popped into a local pub to watch the match preview on television. Soon Pat's innocuous pub visit would become part of the fable that Clare had been drinking the day before the game – they were beaten so badly, there was no other way of explaining it.

Twelve years without an All-Ireland senior win is an eternity in Cork's world. Their longest stretch without an All-Ireland was 16 years from 1903 to 1919, but the drought in the middle of the same century was more traumatic. The scenes after they defeated Kilkenny in 1966 resembled those normally reserved for counties who are not blessed with much success.

In the previous year's Munster final, Cork had been demolished by Tipperary, 4–11 to 0–5, and the idea of them winning the All-Ireland of the following year seemed fanciful in the extreme – as did the idea that Tipperary would fall to Limerick in the first round.

Speculation over a possible return by Christy Ring who, at almost 46, remained highly influential with Glen Rovers, caused a flutter of excitement early in the year. The match programme for the Munster final against Waterford actually listed Ring's name among the subs. But he did not appear. The story goes that he met with the selectors and agreed to come back, but later became dissatisfied when he heard that the vote to reinstate him, while in his favour, had not been unanimous. Irrespective of the reasons, he decided he'd had enough.

Cork had an appropriately unsung hero in Colm Sheehan. There is a cloud over the claim to his third goal which even he, speaking 50 years later, was unable to clear up. He said he simply didn't know and he didn't care all that much either. Cork won, and that was all that concerned him.

If Sheehan 'scored' that goal now, there would be a choice of angles to view it from but, in 1966, hurling did not allow you to blink. The third green flag could just as easily have been John O'Halloran's, whose delivery towards the Railway goal, wind-assisted, came down off an upright and was directed past Ollie Walsh. Sheehan was in the vicinity but no one is sure who if anyone got the final decisive touch. However, there was no disputing his first two strikes. Sheehan had not been a cast-iron choice for the Cork team. In 1965, he'd been on the county intermediate team that had won the All-Ireland, but the headline-grabbing forward that summer had been Seanie Barry, their leading marksman.

In 1966, it was Barry's mishit 20-metre free in the first half that broke to Sheehan for the first goal, reeling in Kilkenny and trimming their lead to two points. Cork, young and hungry, made good use of the wind on the resumption and were well worth their victory and 20th All-Ireland triumph, leaving them five ahead of Kilkenny and one shy of Tipperary.

The match heralded the start of a new era for Cork, one without Ring as a central theme. Trained by Jim 'Tough' Barry, Cork won despite losing centre-back Denis O'Riordan to injury after he hurt his shoulder in a club football match two weeks earlier. Barry rated this, his 13th senior hurling triumph, as possibly his most satisfying and the celebrations went long into the night in the Spa Hotel in Lucan.

Cork's team in 1966 was one of bright, shining youth – they also won the All-Ireland under-21 title after three gripping matches against Wexford.

Kilkenny started the All-Ireland final with seven of the team that had won in 1963 and had four more who had played in the final they lost to Tipperary a year later.

Of the 77 All-Ireland senior finals that preceded 1966, Cork and Kilkenny had met in just 10 – but some of those matches were classics. Kilkenny were, however, the strongest of favourites. They had won the National League home final comfortably against Tipperary, laying a major bogey, having beaten Cork 4–11 to 1–8 in the semi. In Munster, Limerick had put out Tipperary in the first round. The cards appeared to be irresistibly stacked in Kilkenny's favour.

In terms of quality, the 1966 All-Ireland final was not one of the better contests between these rivals. The hurling was strewn with errors, devalued by poor striking and bunching. Cork were two points behind at the interval, trailing 1–2 to 0–7, but Sheehan's first goal had given them increased hope and came against the run of play. The favourites opened better: Kilkenny led 0–5 to 0–1 after 20 minutes, Keher with four points, three from frees.

Cork were level within five minutes of the restart and while Keher put Kilkenny back in front, Sheehan's second goal gave Cork their first lead. That came in the 41st minute from John Bennett's cross. Walsh scored a late goal for Kilkenny, by then a mere consolation.

Martin Coogan described it as his worst hurling day.

> We were red-hot favourites – we had a very good team with plenty of experience – but we made a lot of mistakes that day. Cork … played no-nonsense hurling. We were over-confident.[2]

CORK: P. Barry; P. Doolan, T. O'Donoghue, D. Murphy; T. Connolly, J. O'Sullivan, P. Fitzgerald; J. McCarthy (0–2, 1f), M. Waters; S. Barry (0–4, 2fs), J. O'Halloran, G. McCarthy (0–1); C. McCarthy (0–1), C. Sheehan (3–0), J. Bennett (0–1).

KILKENNY: O. Walsh; P. Henderson, J. Lynch, J. Treacy; S. Cleere, T. Carroll, M. Coogan; P. Moran, J. Teehan (0–1); E. Keher (0–7, 5fs), C. Dunne, S. Buckley (0–1); J. Dunphy (0–1), P. Dillon, T. Walsh (1–0); Subs: P. Carroll for P. Dillon, T. Murphy for T. Carroll.

Referee: J. Hatton (Wicklow)

Attendance: 68,249

Tough Barry

A little over two years after pioneering another Cork All-Ireland triumph, Jim 'Tough' Barry, one of the legendary figures in the game, died. His passing, following a stroke, brought to an end a celebrated coaching career that encompassed 13 All-Ireland senior hurling titles and one All-Ireland football success, and stretched from 1926 to 1966.

In his younger days, he had been an active member of the IRA's Cork City Brigade and was interned in 1921.

Barry had started out as a tailor and later worked for The *Irish Times* commercial wing based in Cork. He had his own sporting career, having competed as a swimmer, boxer, diver and also given service as a GAA referee. He was also a renowned tenor, with an interest in opera. Barry liked to dress colourfully and had a penchant for sartorial flourishes that made him stand out from the crowd. He was also partial to the occasional sherry.

Some of the wins he was associated with were milestones in the GAA's history. Cork's huring titles of 1926, 1928 and 1929 were followed by the famous victory of 1931 against Kilkenny. He was there for the Thunder and Lightning final in 1939. He later coached the four-in-a-row Cork team of the 1940s and three-in-a-row side of the 1950s.

He also trained Railway Cup teams in hurling and football from 1927, and Ireland teams that met American sides in the Tailteann Games in 1928 and 1932. While he is synonymous with Cork, Barry trained Limerick to win the 1934 All-Ireland senior hurling title.

It was Tough Barry who came up with the metaphor of mushrooms rising overnight to describe Cork's ability to emerge swiftly and unexpectedly. His last success in 1966 was the most striking example of that phenomenon.

51. Sweet 16

1967 ALL-IRELAND FINAL (Croke Park, 3 September)
Kilkenny 3–8 Tipperary 2–7

*Well, if you go into a Tipperary man's house, he'll do anything for you, there
is no one better. But it gets bitter enough at times, doesn't it, in pubs and
that. There could be rows.*
Dick Walshe[1]

KILKENNY'S 16TH ALL-IRELAND senior success is one of
their most cherished. Lory Meagher, not noted for public
displays of emotion, danced a victory jig outside the ground
afterwards. Tipperary had offered Lory little sympathy in 1937
on his last day in the black and amber in a runaway All-Ireland
final victory. And now that the 45-year losing championship run
against Tipperary was over, Meagher and Kilkenny were entitled
to celebrate.

It also meant that John Doyle's attempt to create a new record of
nine All-Ireland medal wins had fallen short. 'It is not by any means
a personal matter with me,' he said before the game of his prospects
of surpassing Ring. 'I have been a small cog in a big wheel for many
years. But having gone so far naturally I'd like to get it. I wouldn't be
human if I didn't. But I can tell you this – I won't die if I don't.'

It was only three short years since Kilkenny, the reigning
champions, had been demolished by Tipperary in an All-Ireland
final. The 1967 final, however, brought the wrecking ball to
Tipperary's acclaimed side. Among those exiting the inter-county
stage was Doyle, a hurling behemoth whose career ended at the

age of 37. A number of others, like Theo English, Kieran Carey and Tony Wall, also had their final curtain call. Tipperary were an ageing force, with eight of the side between 30 and 37; Kilkenny fielded an attack whose average age was in the mid-20s. And yet Tipp still caused Kilkenny irrational levels of anxiety. They had won five All-Ireland titles since 1958, and had been beaten in the 1960 final. In the same spell, they had won five leagues and, for a time, were regarded as almost infallible.

Kilkenny's 1966 National League home final win over Tipperary had been warmly welcomed in the county but the championship remained the ultimate prize.

The old saying about 'Kilkenny for the hurling and Tipp for the men', implying Kilkenny always struggled against the rugged power of their rivals, was now up for review. 'The prevailing view of the time was that Kilkenny bottled it when they met Tipp,' recalls Mick Lanigan, the new Kilkenny trainer. 'They hadn't won an All-Ireland for 10 years and to beat Tipp as well, it was a defining moment in the development of that particular team. And in actual fact, it started a downward trend for Tipp as well. The attitude of the players and the supporters was that Kilkenny were no longer going to be walked over.'

But the match that provided Kilkenny's long-awaited liberation was also notorious for an incident that overshadowed the celebrations. A serious injury to Tom Walsh, the dashing Kilkenny forward, resulted in him losing an eye and he never hurled again. He was just 23. The match took a large physical toll. Eddie Keher went off with a fractured wrist in the second half and Jim Lynch, who had scored four goals against Dublin in the Leinster semi-final, broke a finger – though he had to stay on the field because all the subs had been used. Kilkenny won, but they should have won by more than they did.

The problems had started before the game. Ollie Walsh had suffered a serious wrist injury and needed seven stitches after accidentally breaking a glass pane on the train to the match while playing cards. The goalkeeper's reputation was merely embellished by the incident, as he denied Tipperary with a string of high-class saves in the first half, at least six straight out of the top drawer, when Kilkenny faced a gale and repeated showers of rain. Walsh's performance, hailed as his best ever, would greatly influence his later selection as Texaco Hurler of the Year.

Tipperary were seeking a sixth All-Ireland title in 10 years and their 22nd in all. They had been shocked by Limerick in Munster the previous year and were aware that the clock was ticking. The team had an impressive haul of 50 All-Ireland medals but would they have the legs for another year? Under trainer Ossie Bennett, a Cork man living in Johnstown in Kilkenny, Tipp prepared assiduously for this final shot. There were ominous signs when they were well beaten by Kilkenny in March in the league – but Bennett was optimistic.

The trainer told Paddy Downey of *The Irish Times* in the days before the match, 'They have shown more enthusiasm than ever before. They want to go out on a winning note.'[2]

It wasn't a classic game of hurling but wind and rain throughout the game may be offered in mitigation. Despite conceding a goal to Paddy Moran after only five minutes, Tipperary led 2–6 to 1–3 at half-time with the assistance of the elements. On the resumption, Kilkenny took a grip on the match though their dominance took time to tell on the scoreboard. Facing a heavy-artillery Tipp attack, Kilkenny's defence laid the groundwork for their win. There were heroics throughout but Pat Henderson embodied the resistance in seeing off three opposing centre-forwards – John Flanagan, Michael 'Babs' Keating and Liam Devaney. Evidence of Kilkenny's defensive defiance was that Tipperary only scored one point from play and only managed one point in the second half, which came near the end of play.

After 10 minutes of the second half, Kilkenny were level, helped by Martin Brennan's goal. A goal from Tom Walsh in the 42nd minute gave them the confidence to drive on towards the line, even though

Keher went off shortly afterwards. Tipperary's midfield ailed badly, with English withdrawn, and the Kilkenny pair of Moran and John Teehan dominated, Teehan's job in curtailing Mick Roche still seen as another tactical triumph for Fr Tommy Maher.

Mick Lanigan, a hurdler, trained Kilkenny in nine All-Ireland finals. 'I remember bringing over the first showers, setting them up in Nowlan Park,' he says. 'Now, that shower was a garden hose, a tap and cold water. I brought a portable sauna over, there was no heat in the dressing rooms, no hot water, the dressing room itself didn't have a toilet. That was the norm. I am not suggesting that Nowlan Park was anything exceptional. Just the facilities for players were very poor. The saunas were being used by boxing clubs in those days.'

Lanigan recalls early innovations, like Fr Maher using a walkie-talkie that enabled him to watch the match from high in the stands and keep in touch with his fellow strategists on the sideline.

Teehan, a tough hurler more than a stylish one, kept Roche under tight guard. 'It was a move the hurlers on the ditch didn't approve of but Fr Tommy Maher was a very shrewd tactician – it was his move. That victory signalled the breakthrough,' Pat Henderson told Brendan Fullam.[3]

Both counties went directly into the final as provincial winners. In Munster, the All-Ireland champions Cork met an early demise when they lost in the first round to Waterford by eight points at Walsh Park. Tipperary defeated Waterford by 10 points in the Munster semi-final, then trounced Clare 4–12 to 2–6 in the final, with Babs Keating scoring 3–2.

The will to produce one last great performance in September was there, but the delivery didn't follow. Tipp had been tamed. Kilkenny won a famous All-Ireland but they, and the game, had also lost a beautiful hurler.

KILKENNY: O. Walsh; T. Carroll, P. Dillon, J. Treacy; S. Cleere, P. Henderson, M. Coogan; P. Moran (1–0), J. Teehan; E. Keher (0–3, 1f) , T. Walsh (1–2, 2fs), C. Dunne (0–2, 1f); J. Bennett, J. Lynch, M. Brennan (1–0); Subs: J. Kinsella for J. Bennett, R. Blanchfield (0–1) for E. Keher, P. Carroll for T. Walsh.

TIPPERARY: J. O'Donoghue; J. Doyle, K. Carey, N. O'Gorman; M. Burns, T. Wall, L. Gaynor; T. English, M. Roche (0–2, 1f); D. Nealon (2–0), J. Flanagan, L. Devaney; J. Doyle (0–5, 4fs), M. Keating, S. McLoughlin; Subs: L. Kiely for S. McLoughlin, M. Lonergan for M. Burns, P.J. Ryan for T. English.

Referee: M. Hayes (Clare)

Attendance: 62,241

Tom Walsh injury

Tom Walsh, who won his first All-Ireland in 1963 aged 19, suffered a career-ending injury in the 1967 final with only six minutes left to play when he and his marker Tony Wall were jostling while waiting for a lineball to be taken. His goal had helped turn the match in Kilkenny's favour. The day after the match Walsh had an eye removed at the Eye and Ear Hospital. That morning every Kilkenny player attended mass to pray for his recovery. Wall has always protested that the blow that struck Walsh was accidental and that he didn't realise he had inflicted serious injury.

Two years earlier, Wall had supported the introduction of helmets in a book he'd written on hurling. In January 1967, the UCC club put a motion forward to Cork convention supporting the use of light head gear, but it was rejected.

Micheal Murphy is acknowledged as the first man to wear a helmet, while playing for UCC in the Fitzgibbon Cup in 1969. Murphy's UCC colleague Donal Clifford was the first to wear one at county level, playing for Cork in 1969.

Wall explained why he had been an early advocate.

We were playing Limerick in the championship in Cork and I got a ferocious blow in the face under a dropping ball. I was in a bad way now, got concussed and got sick, but played the match after it. I said I would make a helmet, so I got a jockey helmet and riveted a faceguard piece to it and wore it a bit at training. I brought it out for the replay and there were 30,000 watching and I funked it, I didn't bring it out.

It wasn't until 2010 that the GAA finally made helmets compulsory.

52. Never Say Die

1968 ALL-IRELAND FINAL (Croke Park, 1 September)
Wexford 5–8 Tipperary 3–12

---

*I did not think we had a chance of winning at half-time, but by the time
Padge [Kehoe] was finished talking to us ...*
Vinnie Staples[1]

TWENTY MINUTES GONE and Babs Keating puts a rampant
Tipperary 0–8 to 0–1 clear with his third score. A fifth All-
Ireland of the decade looks imminent for the Premier County.
Mick Roche is having a majestic day at centre-back. Len Gaynor
beside him is a model of wiry resistance.

After 24 minutes, Donie Nealon stands over a lineball. His strike
is sweet and the ball sails towards the Wexford goal where, on its
descent, Jimmy Doyle gets a touch and the net billows. Tipp lead
1–9 to 0–3. Another point gives them a 10-point advantage. Even
the most optimistic Wexford followers have bowed their heads.

Jack Berry scores a goal out of nothing for Wexford, but the half
closes with Doyle pointing another Tipp score. They are 1–11 to
1–3 to the good – nobody could have anticipated what followed. 'We
were very fortunate to be only eight points behind at half-time,' the
Wexford goalkeeper Pat Nolan admitted years later. 'Tipp were all
over us – we were playing badly.'[2]

In the commentary box, Michael O'Hehir talked of the first half
being one you could easily have walked away from – it was hardly
a match at all. In the second half, O'Hehir found it hard to restrain
himself. An epic tussle unfolded and Wexford launched a comeback

to revive memories of their famous league win from 12 years earlier over the same county. This time, the deficit wasn't as severe, but having been down by 10 points in the first half, Wexford led by eight in the second before being brought back to a nervous two near the end. Those fortunate to have been present went home with their heads in a spin and a memory to last forever.

If Mick Roche was the outstanding player of the first half, then his Wexford counterpart Dan Quigley, the captain and farmer from Rathnure, was the most influential figure in the second. Quigley defended heroically after the interval and while Tipp were unfortunate to lose Jimmy Doyle who hobbled off early in the second-half, their forwards now found themselves more compressed. For most of the half, they only had one score, a point from Liam Devaney; their final two goals didn't come until the last few minutes.

Another huge driving force for Wexford was the young redhead Tony Doran. He had been eclipsed by Roche's elegant reading of the play in the first half, but switched to full-forward for the second. Doran scored two goals and caused terror whenever the ball came near him. Jack Berry scored 2–2, another player to have a dream day. Berry had the first score of the second-half, a point, and then the stadium erupted when the stylish Phil Wilson sent a ball into Doran, who feinted left, turned right and drove a great shot into the corner of the Tipp goal six minutes after the restart. After an absorbing passage of play, Berry added another point. The gap was down to a goal.

From there, anything seemed possible. Devaney finally nailed a score for Tipp but Jimmy O'Brien replied with a point and when Doran was fouled, Paul Lynch hammered the free to the net 16 minutes into the second half. They were level. Berry should have goaled when he was through, but his hand-pass was saved. Ten minutes left, the sides still tied, the excitement unrelenting.

Wexford had more. Doran struck another goal, O'Brien tapped on a point. Babs Keating went for a goal from a free but the shot was blocked, and when the ball went downfield Berry scored a fine goal. Doran added a point – Wexford 5–8, Tipperary 1–12. They were eight up with three minutes left when Tipp summoned a final effort. Two minutes from the end, McLoughlin scored a goal and a minute after that Keating netted from a free. But there wasn't enough time on John Dowling's watch for another late twist.

Oddly for a final involving Wexford the attendance – 63,461 – was the lowest for 10 years, down approximately 12,000 on the 1960 meeting between the same counties when Wexford also caused an upset.

In the days before the game, Wexford manager Padge Kehoe told Paddy Downey of *The Irish Times*:

> Wexford have the will to win – and they will win. This team has trained better than any I've seen since 1960, and a great deal of credit for that goes to our trainer, Ned Power, who has done a wonderful job with the minors as well as the seniors.[3]

Kehoe had been captain of Wexford when they'd been beaten by Cork in the 1954 All-Ireland, one of those mostly forgotten men who might have climbed the steps but didn't, and whose chance would never come again. He won three All-Ireland medals, and narrowly failed to land a fourth in 1962 aged 37. He'd seen his first All-Ireland hurling final during the epic three-game marathon between Kilkenny and Cork in 1931, when he was taken to Croke Park at six years of age by his father. There could be no more impressionable indoctrination.

The 1968 senior win completed a perfect day for Wexford whose minors were also triumphant. But it would be their last senior All-Ireland for 28 years. Kilkenny would soon gain an upper hand in Leinster and, by the 1980s, Offaly were a force, usurping Wexford as Kilkenny's chief provincial rival. The 1968 win was, in a real sense, the last successful link to the heyday of the Rackards and the incomparable men of the 1950s.

Doran and Berry were also the goal scorers, Doran with two, in their 3–13 to 4–9 Leinster final win over Kilkenny, who were the reigning All-Ireland champions but in a state of pique after a controversial six-month suspension had been served on Ollie Walsh following the home league final. Doran finished the senior championship season as top scorer with 6–3 from three matches.

Tipperary retained their Munster title with a 2–13 to 1–7 win over Cork, Clare stretching them a good deal more in the semi-final, scoring five goals but still losing 5–6 to 5–11. Their All-Ireland final meeting with Wexford was the fourth of the decade, the spoils evenly divided, though both counties were set for a spell of impoverishment.

WEXFORD: P. Nolan; T. Neville, E. Kelly, E. Colfer; V. Staples, D. Quigley, W. Murphy; P. Wilson, B. Bernie; P. Lynch (1–3, 1–2fs), T. Doran (2–1), C. Jacob; J. O'Brien (0–2), S. Whelan, J. Berry (2–2); Sub: J. Quigley for S. Whelan.

TIPPERARY: J. O'Donoghue; J. Costigan, N. O'Gorman, J. Gleeson; M. Burns (0–1, 70), M. Roche, L. Gaynor; P.J. Ryan, D. Nealon; M. Keating (1–3, 1-0 f), J. Ryan, J. Doyle (2–5, 4 fs); L. Devaney (0–2), M. McKenna, S. McLoughlin (0–1); Sub: F. Loughnane for J. Doyle.

Referee: J. Dowling (Offaly)

Attendance: 63,461

Press relations sour

Relations between the GAA and Gaelic games correspondents in the 1960s were normally cordial but in 1968 the Tipperary county board withdrew co-operation with six Dublin-based journalists. This was the result of their coverage of the National League home final, a two-point win by Tipperary over Kilkenny. The six blacklisted journalists were: Paddy Downey (*The Irish Times*), John D. Hickey (*Irish Independent*), Donal Carroll (*Evening Herald*), Mick Dunne (*Irish Press*), Gerry McCarthy (*Irish Press*) and Padraig Puirseal (*Sunday Press*).

In winning the 12 May final, Tipp reversed the result of the

All-Ireland final meeting of the previous September, but in the first-half, three rows broke out and a number of players were struck off the ball.

Near the half-time mark, a scuffle broke out near the Kilkenny goal during which Ollie Walsh was knocked to the ground by John Flanagan. The offender wasn't spotted and escaped punishment but later the GAA suspended him, and Walsh, for six months. It was generally accepted that Walsh was unfairly victimised.

Paddy Downey made the point to Keith Duggan in *The Lifelong Season* that the 1968 league final was 'responsible for Kilkenny changing their style subsequently and adapting a more physical game'.[4]

Kilkenny threatened to boycott the Leinster final against Wexford over Walsh's suspension.

53. Faithful Departed

1969 LEINSTER FINAL (Croke Park, 20 July)
Kilkenny 3–9 Offaly 0–16

---

*It was horrendous in the 1960s, how we got through ... I don't know. I
often look back and to see the bully boys who tried to bully a hurler, and
no appreciation for skill. If they couldn't beat you in hurling, they tried to
bamboozle you some other way.*
Johnny Flaherty[1]

GAA PRESIDENT ALF Murray, keen to broaden the hurling
church, must have been pleased to see Offaly raise some
dust towards the end of the 1960s. In 1969, they reached
their first Leinster senior hurling final since 1928, and they might
well have won the title for the first time with a bit more cunning
and *savoir-faire*. Ultimately, Kilkenny's knack of scoring goals at
crucial times bailed them out. When Pat Delaney got their third
goal seven minutes from the end, Offaly were two points up having
been ahead frequently during the match and level at half-time.

The big news of the season was Offaly's sensational 5–10 to
3–11 win over Wexford, the reigning All-Ireland champions, in
the Leinster semi-finals, with all five goals scored in the first-half.
Kilkenny had started out with a comfortable win over Dublin, 2–20
to 2–6 at Wexford, with Ollie Walsh making his comeback after
missing the previous year's championship because of a controversial
suspension. He received a hearty ovation from the Kilkenny
followers.

Offaly's win over Wexford at Croke Park confirmed a new arrival in Leinster hurling. They stormed into a 2–1 to 0–0 lead after six minutes and, by half-time, they were ahead 5–4 to 0–5. Paddy Molloy from Drumcullen, an experienced Offaly player who had been hurling for little reward since 1955, scored 3–4.

On 15 June, they began their campaign by demolishing Laois, 8–10 to 2–5, at Portlaoise, Molloy scoring 5–4. Laois had thrashed Westmeath 5–12 to 0–1 in the first round. Only two years earlier, Offaly had suffered defeat to Westmeath in a spiteful match in Birr that saw both teams reduced to 12 players and spectators invade the pitch. The referee, Jimmy Hatton of Wicklow, almost abandoned the game, and the defeat set Offaly back after they'd had encouraging wins in the league over Waterford and Tipperary earlier in the season.

'Looking back, it was a defining moment; from there on, we played hurling,' says Johnny Flaherty, who was one of those sent off that day. 'Offaly tried bullying instead of going out to win the game. Breaking up lads. We got rid of that mentality.'

Goalkeeper Damien Martin and Flaherty would still be hurling for Offaly when they eventually made a provincial breakthrough in 1980, but most of the players who contested the 1969 final were advanced in years. Martin revealed how he started his Offaly career with a first-round championship defeat to Westmeath.

> The players did not really know each other and a number did not even talk to each other. Neither was there even one training session or get-together. Then Brother Denis [Minahane], a Presentation Brother from Bantry, joined the Birr community. He got involved in the Offaly hurling team and we were on our way.[2]

Br Minahane was a unifying force and helped bring disparate elements together. For the first time, the players enjoyed regular training sessions and some refreshments afterwards. Better employment opportunities through Bord na Móna and the ESB also helped stabilise clubs who had traditionally lost players to emigration. Offaly had competed in four Leinster senior finals in the 1920s, losing them all.

Decades of defeats followed, but the signs of a new beginning were

there as the 1960s came to a close. Offaly lost the 1968 Leinster semi-
final to Kilkenny, the reigning All-Ireland champions, by only four
points, having played 50 minutes with 14 men after John Kirwan
was sent off for a foul on Noel Skehan. Br Minahane's efforts were
reaping some reward.

Paddy Molloy can remember Offaly not having any more than 13
players for a league game against Westmeath in Birr in the 1960s
and having to ask two of the crowd to help plug the gaps. A league
win over Tipperary in November 1966 was a key point in attaining
a belief in themselves and broadening their ambitions.

Molloy spoke of his unorthodox preparations for that match,
which Offaly won 3–13 to 2–7 at Birr, their first win over Tipperary
in a senior hurling competition and first league win in 10 attempts.

I had three acres of beet ready for drawing out. On the Friday night
before the match, my brother told me that if I wanted the tractor I
could have it for Saturday; after that he needed it. Without any help,
I loaded and unloaded seven trailers – no heeling the load; all thrown
in by hand and unloaded by hand. On Sunday morning, I couldn't lift
my hands. 'How can I face hurling Tipperary?' I said to myself. I went
to mass, came home, felt a bit better. I went out and picked up an axe
and swung it on a block several times; after that, the hurley felt light
in my hands. We hammered Tipperary. It was a great thrill.[3]

Molloy, despite his arduous day on the beet, still managed to finish
the match with 2–5 to his name. Offaly also defeated Waterford
in the same 1966–1967 league campaign. As a measure of their
progress, Offaly had been hammered by Tipperary in the league in
Roscrea in February 1962, by an eye-watering 11–11 to 1–2, having
failed to score in the first half. The day had been extremely cold and
some spectators in the crowd of around 750 lit a fire on the grass
bank to keep warm. They met again in November in the league at
Birr, when Tipp won 10–10 to 2–4.

In the 1969 Leinster final, they planted a seed for their future
breakthrough. 'Anything that can be said in commendation of
Offaly's performance yesterday is wholly deserved,' wrote Paddy

Downey in *The Irish Times*. 'They were simply magnificent. They hurled with supreme confidence when they might have been excused for faltering in awe of Kilkenny, or under the strain of a tense occasion; they hurled with speed and vigour, but above all with astonishing dexterity.'[4]

In the early stages of the match, Offaly set out their stall and took the game to Kilkenny. They led by three points late in the first half and a goal from Joe Millea before half-time brought Kilkenny level, 2–4 to 0–10. The first Kilkenny goal came after 14 minutes when Offaly had led 0–5 to 0–2, Delaney having his palmed effort saved by Martin but getting a second chance which he finished emphatically.

After the third goal seven minutes from the end, Kilkenny went in front and held their lead, scoring two more points to Offaly's one, but Ollie Walsh had to pull off an important save two minutes from the end from Declan Hanniffy.

Barney Moylan did a fine marking job on Kilkenny captain Eddie Keher, limiting him to one point from play. Paddy Moran had a big game in the middle of the field for Kilkenny, and Paddy Molloy again finished Offaly's top scorer with 0–8. But they could not get through for a goal, having scored 13 in their two games before the final. That was their undoing.

'The resurgence in Offaly is complete,' wrote Paddy Downey, 'a new team has joined the hurling elite.'

KILKENNY: O. Walsh; T. Carroll, P. Dillon, J. Treacy; W. Murphy, P. Henderson, M. Coogan; P. Moran, M. Lawlor; P. Lalor, P. Delaney (2–0), E. Keher (0–5, 4fs); J. Millea (1–1), J. Lynch (0–1), M. Brennan (0–2); Subs: J. Kinsella for P. Lalor, S. Buckley for J. Lynch.

OFFALY: D. Martin; P. Spellman, D. Flanagan, J. Murphy; B. Moylan, J. Kirwan (0–1, 70), E. Foxe; J.J. Healion (0–1), D. Hanniffy (0–2); G. Burke, P.J. Whelahan, J. Flaherty (0–3); P. Mulhaire (0–1), W. O'Gorman, P. Molloy (0–8, 1 sideline, 4fs); Subs: P. Moylan (44 mins) for E. Foxe, M. Kirwan for D. Flanagan (50), A. Dooley for G. Burke (56).

Referee: J. Gray (Dublin)

Attendance: 21,201

54. Drinks, Shoots, Leaves

1970 ALL-IRELAND FINAL (Croke Park, 6 September)
Cork 6–21 Wexford 5–10

Eddie would have been flamboyant and that would not have to be to their liking; they would have been conservative. He grew a beard at one stage, there wouldn't have been many inter-county players wearing beards. They would have frowned on things like that.
Matt Aherne[1]

THE FIRST 80-MINUTE All-Ireland final produced a scoring avalanche and a fleeting sensation called Eddie O'Brien, the Cork man who bagged three goals and never played for his county again. Old scoring records tumbled but a re-enactment of the great 1950s tussles between Cork and Wexford it was not. Cork won at their leisure, with the biggest winning scoreline for an All-Ireland senior final. The combined scores produced a new high too, but account must be taken of the extra 20 minutes.

As John D. Hickey put it in the *Irish Independent*, the match had a riot of scores but precious little entertainment. And an uncharacteristically downbeat John D. felt that Cork hadn't played terribly well either, describing their performance as more 'workmanlike' than magnificent.

The day's star player was undoubtedly O'Brien of Passage who had, to his chagrin, been taken off at half-time in the previous year's final against Kilkenny. He finished the day with 3–1 to comfortably redeem his reputation, the last hat-trick man in an All-Ireland senior hurling final until Lar Corbett's fireworks in

2010. It was O'Brien's valedictory performance in the red jersey. He was only 25.

Travel and romance played a part. Cork flew to New York for the away league final on 20 September and while there O'Brien met his future wife, leading to a number of return visits before he settled and married. The plan had been to bring his wife, of Italian descent, back to live in Ireland, but that didn't work out.

His lifelong friend Matt Aherne explains: 'All her family were at the airport and you know how emotional the Italians can be; they were all bawling crying and she said she could not go.' So O'Brien stayed and has been there since, enjoying a successful career in security and raising a family. He still comes home to Ireland on vacation.

O'Brien played minor for Cork in 1963 at corner-forward, with Charlie McCarthy in the other pocket. He was on the Cork team that had won the 1966 under-21 All-Ireland and he'd played senior for Cork in 1965, but he didn't make the senior squad the following year when they won the All-Ireland for the first time in 12 years. He returned in 1969, but Aherne felt O'Brien was worth his place earlier.

'Eddie was very unorthodox,' says Aherne. 'Not alone did his opponent not know what he was going to do, he didn't know himself. The first goal in the 1970 All-Ireland final, no other player would have done that.'

For the goal in the 11th minute, Willie Walsh crossed from the wing and with his back to goal O'Brien used his hand to flick the ball to the net when most players would have caught it or used the hurl. 'He was unmarked outside the square. I never saw a goal like it being scored. If he missed, they'd have been saying, "What was he doing?",' says Aherne.

The second goal in the 34th minute was deflected home with the hand and the third, seven minutes from the end, involved the most labour. He took a ball from a deep position and started a run, Eddie Colfer giving chase. 'Ned Colfer was flaking him with the hurley as he ran with the ball,' says Aherne. 'I heard someone describe it as like seeing a fella batin' a bullock up a boreen. Near the goal, he dropped the stick, which you could do then, and palmed it to the net.'

When O'Brien scored his second goal, Cork led 3–10 to 2–1. They increased this to 3–12 to 3–2 at half-time. Pat Quigley and Tony Doran each scored two goals for Wexford but they never looked capable of stopping Cork from winning a 21st title.

The feat is made all the more unusual by the admission by O'Brien that he treated himself to 'eight or nine' pints in Dublin the evening before. Some players have taken drink before big games to help them sleep or calm their nerves, but eight or nine pints was perhaps overdoing the pre-match hydration. 'I knew him all my life,' says Aherne, 'he was a fair drinking man, but I never saw him drunk. I never met anyone who didn't like him. He would be extremely popular with the Cork players.'

Aherne remembers a time when O'Brien gave a virtuoso performance for his club after a night on the tiles. 'He would be known as a better footballer than a hurler. I would say the best ever in our club. Long before Maurice Fitzgerald, he was kicking frees off the ground with left and right. Before the semi-final of a championship, we were told he had been out all night – I know a chap who drove him home – and he scored 13 points that morning, seven with the right and six with the left.'

Despite O'Brien's scoring feat and Man-of-the-Match accolade, he was not Cork's top scorer. That honour went to Charlie McCarthy, the team's free-taker, who finished with 1–9. Justin McCarthy sat out his second All-Ireland final as he'd suffered a horrendous leg injury shortly before the 1969 final.

A notable feature of the 1970 final was the appearance of four Quigley brothers on the Wexford team, unrivalled in the history of the game. Dan, the captain in 1968, was centre-back and the other three – Pat, John and Martin – were along the half-forward line. Wexford's cause wasn't helped by injuries to key players Willie Murphy, Phil Wilson and Ned Buggy, but it's arguable whether or not they would have made a huge difference had they played.

Paddy Downey in *The Irish Times* was not impressed, stating that the final was 'a bad advertisement for the image of hurling. There were several nasty incidents, comprising false strokes, vicious pulling, rough tackles, deliberate provocation – all most disedifying on hurling's biggest day of the year.'[2]

He added that it was fortunate that none of the incidents had escalated. At least one player on each side was lucky not to be dismissed, Downey wrote, adding that the referee Jimmy Hatton was 'not inclined to enforce the full rigour of the law'.[3]

Cork, who had been fortunate to defeat Tipperary in the Munster final by two points, finished the year league and championship winners, adding the minor and under-21 titles.

They also had the Hurler of the Year in Pat McDonnell. While Martin O'Doherty, his successor as Cork Number 3, was seen as the first modern full-back, McDonnell had similar attributes, being more than a traditional stopper.

Cork piled further misery on Wexford hurling in early November when they trounced them in a replayed All-Ireland under-21 final at Croke Park. The 0–8 to 5–17 reversal was a grim portent of Cork's supremacy over Wexford in the 1970s. Paddy Ring, a nephew of Christy, scored two goals from 21-yard frees.

Eddie O'Brien wasn't the only Passage clubman who played in the 1970 All-Ireland final. Quiz buffs take note: Wexford centre-forward Pat Quigley was also a Passage player, having moved to Cork and joined the club from Rathnure not long before the final.

CORK: P. Barry; A. Maher, P. McDonnell, J. Horgan; D. Clifford, P. Hegarty, C. Roche; G. McCarthy (0–2, 2fs), S. Looney; T. Ryan (0–6, 4fs), W. Walsh (1–2), C. Cullinane (1–0); C. McCarthy (1–9, 9fs), R. Cummins (0–1), E. O'Brien (3–1); Sub: S. Murphy for D. Clifford (HT).

WEXFORD: J. Nolan; E. Colfer, M. Collins, T. Neville; M. Browne (0–1), D. Quigley (1–0, f), T. O'Connor; D. Bernie (0–3), M. Jacob (0–1, 70); M. Quigley, P. Quigley (2–0), J. Quigley; M. Butler (0–3, 3fs), T. Doran (2–0), J. Berry; Subs: T. Byrne (0–2, 1f) for M. Butler (54 mins), J. Russell for T. Neville (62 mins).

Referee: J. Hatton (Wicklow)

Attendance: 65,062

Time stretch

The decision to extend games to 80 minutes, taken at Annual Congress at Easter 1970, applied to inter-county matches – but only provincial finals, and All-Ireland semi-finals and finals would be affected. All other games were run over an hour, as before.

The change lasted for five seasons and led to record-scoring feats but wasn't universally popular. In 1975, the GAA introduced a uniform 70-minute rule for all inter-county championship matches in hurling and Gaelic football. That year was the first 70-minute All-Ireland senior final.

Also at GAA Congress in 1970, Galway were allowed to opt out of the Munster senior hurling championship after 11 years.

A proposal to penalise players charging the goalkeeper in both codes was beaten at the same congress. However, the rule was changed for hurling at Congress in 1975, and goalkeepers breathed a huge sigh of relief.

the locals 6–10 to 2–8, with just nine of the team who had lost the county final. To complete a memorable day, Tadhg O'Connor returned home to hear that his wife Mary had given birth to their first child, a baby daughter. 'Tadhg's wife went into hospital as we were leaving,' recalls Minogue. 'Hurling that time here in Roscrea, it was a kind of life-and-death situation. Tadhg decided to travel, we could understand if he didn't.'

Loughgiel would have their day in the sun, becoming the first Ulster team to win an All-Ireland club title in 1983 and repeating the act in 2012. After Roscrea's first and only win, the competition was dominated by the Cork city clubs – Blackrock, Glen Rovers and St Finbarr's – who shared seven of the next eight titles. Ballyhale Shamrocks are the most successful club in the competition with five wins. The 1970 final was Roscrea's sole All-Ireland final appearance.

The build-up to the first All-Ireland club final was subdued with newspapers paying more attention to a round of National Football League fixtures on the same day, primarily the meeting of Dublin and Kerry at Croke Park.

'We hadn't great preparation going into it, having lost the county final,' recalls Damien Martin, the long-serving St Rynaghs and Offaly goalkeeper who played county from 1964 to 1986.[3] Losing, he says, wasn't traumatic. 'Not a bit in the wide earthly world, it was a glorified tournament, that's what it was at the time. I am sure Roscrea enjoyed it and we would have too, but there was none of this dreadful sick feeling of losing an All-Ireland.'

St Rynaghs won a junior championship title in 1963 and with no intermediate grade at the time, they were launched into senior hurling. In their first year, trained by Tony Reddin, they reached the county final. In 1965, they began an amazing sequence of senior wins that claimed 10 of the next 12. As Martin says, 'That was some rise from oblivion.'

The *Tipperary Star*, reporting on a famous Roscrea victory, noted how the half-back line of Patsy Rowland, O'Connor and Jimmy Crampton was the rock on which St Rynaghs perished. The trio were the 'stumbling block for many a St Rynagh's attack and the springboard for Roscrea offensives'.[4]

Other county players on the Roscrea team included Kieran Carey, Francis Loughnane, Tadhg Murphy, Mick Nolan, Joe Tynan and Jack Hannon. Damien Martin, Barney Moylan, Padraig Horan, Paudge Mulhare, Gerry Burke, and Frank and Pad Joe Whelahan of Offaly were hurling for their opponents. The future Cork secretary Frank Murphy was in charge, reputedly paying his first visit to Birr.

Roscrea led 2–4 to 0–1 at half-time in conditions described as deplorable, but both teams played excellent hurling. St Rynaghs were undone by a slow start when facing the wind, not scoring for 29 minutes until Brian Lyons pointed. Barney Moylan had an early second-half goal to fuel their hopes but a Tynan solo run midway through the same half led to a Roscrea goal that killed their challenge. Tynan finished up with two of their four goals.

Roscrea captain Donie Moloney received a shield in recognition of the feat. That was later replaced by the Tommy Moore Cup which is contested today, first presented to Blackrock after they defeated Rathnure in 1974. At the end of the year, Roscrea's hurlers celebrated their year with a dinner-dance at the Pathe Hotel, both All-Ireland trophies gracing the occasion. 'I can assure you we treasure that All-Ireland,' states Minogue. 'Only two Tipperary clubs have won it since, and look at all the clubs that haven't.'

ROSCREA: T. Murphy; M. Hogan, K. Carey, B. Maher; P. Rowland (0–2), T. O'Connor, J. Crampton; M. Minogue, D. Moloney; F. Loughnane (0–3), J. Hannon, J. Cunningham (1–0); J. Tynan (2–0), M. Nolan (1–0), B. Stapleton.

ST RYNAGHS: D. Martin; L. Horan, F. Whelahan, N. Gallagher; S. Moylan, P. Horan, P. Moylan; B. Johnstone (1–0), R. Horan; H. Dolan, P.J. Whelahan, B. Lyons (0–1); P. Mulhare (0–1), B. Moylan (1–3), G. Burke.

Referee: F. Murphy (Cork).

56. Barefoot Chic

1971 ALL-IRELAND FINAL (Croke Park, 5 September)
Tipperary 5–17 Kilkenny 5–14

'Twas a very lean period and a very frustrating period. The longer it went on, everyone became selectors, saying this team and that team should be picked, this sort of thing. It brought us down to earth really with a bang and when we started winning again, we really appreciated it.

Len Gaynor[1]

THE 1971 ALL-IRELAND final was a day of milestones and farewells. It was the first hurling final broadcast in colour by RTÉ and, more notably, Eddie Keher shot the lights out, scoring 2–11 – an All-Ireland record that stood until 1989. It was Kilkenny goalkeeper Ollie Walsh's last All-Ireland final appearance after a career straddling three decades. And it was a final curtain call too for Jimmy Doyle, the delightful left-hander who had come out of retirement to win his sixth medal.

Between minor and senior, Doyle played in 13 All-Ireland finals. 'He was the classiest hurler I ever saw,' declared Babs Keating, the Texaco Hurler of the Year for 1971, a year when he finished Tipperary's leading marksman. 'When it came to real skill, he was the Ballesteros of hurling, he had all the shots ... He had shots no one else had, he used his hands like no one else could. He saw things that the rest of us would never see.'[2]

Doyle, hampered by a back injury for much of the season, came off the bench but failed to score, Tipp's 5–17 total featuring just 0–4 from frees. Nine of his team-mates, though, were playing in their first All-Ireland senior final, a new era after the fêted generation of the 1960s. Four Tipp players were honoured at the year's end in the new All Stars scheme dreamed up by journalists and sponsored by the tobacco company Carrolls.

In the big picture, 1971 delivered Tipperary's 22nd title, leaving them the undisputed kings of hurling, one ahead of Cork and five ahead of Kilkenny in the roll of honour. How they slid from this lofty position on 5 September 1971 to the desolation that followed is difficult to fathom.

Tipperary didn't win another All-Ireland until 1989 and it was 16 years before they won Munster again. There was even a 10-year spell when they didn't win a single championship game. How on earth did it happen? Complacency, certainly, played a part. So consumed by the good times that they thought they'd never see a bad day again. Tipperary had won their 12th All-Ireland minor title in 1959. Kilkenny had only four by then; Cork were on six. After winning their 12th, Tipp didn't land another minor title until 1976. From 1962, they went 11 years without winning even a Munster minor championship.

Len Gaynor won a Munster minor medal as a player in 1962 and he was a selector when they won the next one in 1973, later playing in the Munster senior final against Limerick. 'The senior team was doing really well and people were saying we could put out two teams, and I would say there was a bit of carelessness about the minors. There wasn't enough heed paid to them,' Gaynor says. 'As well as that, Paddy Leahy – who was chairman of the selectors, or manager in today's world – was there for years and years and 'twas very steady and everyone knew where they stood with him. Even if Tipp didn't win or play well, there was no doubt he would be there the next year. That brought consistency.'[3]

In the 1970s, he remembers constant change and turbulence. After 1973, their only All Star winners over the remainder of the decade were Tadhg O'Connor, who won in 1975 and 1979, Tommy Butler (1978) and Pat Moloughney (1979). In the National League, Tipp made some headway, winning the title in 1979 with a huge

3–15 to 0–8 win over favourites Galway and having started out
the season in Division 2. Tipp lost the 1975 league final to Galway
by three points and suffered relegation from Division 1 in 1978.
The 1979 win was their first league success in 11 years and
first silverware of note since the 1971 All-Ireland win, the 1972
Oireachtas Cup aside.

Another factor was Cork's prominence which would see them win
three All-Irelands in succession. Clare also emerged as a serious
contender, unlucky not to make Munster breakthroughs while
winning leagues in 1977 and 1978, and then Limerick blossomed
and reached All-Ireland finals in 1980 and 1981.

There was little sense of imminent decline as Tipp celebrated
in September 1971. Beforehand, trainer Ossie Bennett sounded
confident. 'The boys are superbly fit and I honestly think that it will
take a super team to beat them. Kilkenny may be good – but not
that good,' he told *The Irish Times*.

Kilkenny might have felt victory was within their grasp, but
Tipperary finished powerfully, finding the response when needed
in the last seven minutes. The hurling didn't produce a classic
spectacle, compensating with a hard, spirited contest. A tame first
half was followed by a more intense second.

Roger Ryan scored two goals from full-forward and Tipperary,
2–10 to 2–4 ahead at the break, were only in arrears once. They
trailed momentarily 25 minutes into the second half when a goal
from Kieran Purcell after a solo-run was rapidly followed by a point
from Frank Cummins. With the wind at their backs, Kilkenny were
4–12 to 3–14 ahead and looked a good bet to win. The lead lasted
just three minutes.

Ryan goaled after a free from Mick Roche and, after Ollie Walsh
hesitated, Dinny Ryan scored another and Tipp were firmly in
charge. Walsh was also suspect for a goal early in the second half
when he misjudged a ball and Ryan finished. The concession was
a big blow to Kilkenny who had managed to whittle down Tipp's
half-time lead to just two points. Dinny Ryan's goal came with four

minutes to go and left them seven points up, Eddie Keher added 1–1 from frees to reduce the margin but Tipp could not be caught.

Peter O'Sullivan, who had been fingered for some blame when Tipperary conceded six goals to Galway in the semi-finals, gave a fine display. Francis Loughnane was also outstanding and scored four points. But it was Babs Keating, the man who would eventually lead Tipp out of the doldrums in 1987, who stamped his mark by discarding his boots and socks and playing barefoot.

Described by Michael O'Hehir as the 'barefooted wonder', he explained that his boots had been stolen before the final and he was relying on an old pair that started to rip. He kicked them off and then found the socks were loosening on his feet so he threw those off too. Keating was Tipperary's leading scorer all year, having accumulated 6–19 in three championship matches leading to the final. He would have to settle for a relatively modest 0–7 on the first Sunday in September but he was still their chief score-getter.

One final distinction belongs to the 1971 All-Ireland final. Kilkenny's 5–14 was – and still is – the highest losing score in an All-Ireland final.

Had Gaynor been told what was to come, what would he have thought? 'You would not have believed that at all. We saw ourselves as being in the running every year, even though we were not going to win every year.'[4]

TIPPERARY: P. O'Sullivan; L. King, J. Kelly, J. Gleeson; T. O'Connor, M. Roche, L. Gaynor; S. Hogan, P.J. Ryan (0–2); F. Loughnane (0–4), N. O'Dwyer (1–0), D. Ryan (1–1); J. Flanagan (1–2), R. Ryan (2–0), M. Keating (0–7, 4fs); Subs: J. Doyle for S. Hogan (57 mins), P. Byrne (0–1) for J. Flanagan (59).

KILKENNY: O. Walsh; F. Larkin, P. Dillon, J. Treacy; W. Murphy, P. Henderson, M. Coogan; P. Lalor, F. Cummins (0–2); M. Murphy (1–1), P. Delaney, E. Keher (2–11, 2–8fs); M. Brennan, K. Purcell (1–0), E. Byrne (1–0); Subs: P. Moran for W. Murphy (HT), P. Cullen for M. Brennan (62 mins), T. Carroll for F. Larkin (66).

Referee: F. Murphy (Cork)

Attendance: 61,393

57. The Great Escape

1972 All-IRELAND FINAL (Croke Park, 3 September)
Kilkenny 3–24 Cork 5–11

Best ever? It would have to be the 1972 final.
Mick Lanigan[1]

My biggest disappointment in hurling.
Justin McCarthy[2]

THIS WAS A surprise outcome and a blitz on the senses. And yet, even with the constant spinning of the scoreboard – and the twist that saw Cork lead by eight points, only to lose by seven – it was a man charged with keeping the score down who turned out to be one of the day's epic figures.

Understudy to Ollie Walsh for eight years, Noel Skehan spent much of his time on the bench, a spectator at five All-Ireland finals, including the previous year's loss to Tipperary. Now at 27, his patience was generously repaid. Four first-class saves in the opening half denied Cork goals and kept Kilkenny in the game.

In 1972, he was also captain, all his birthdays coming at once. His road had been long and character-building. In 1963, he was reserve keeper for the All-Ireland senior final victory over Waterford. A car accident ruled him out of hurling for almost a year, but he returned as deputy keeper for the All-Ireland finals of 1966, 1967, 1969 and 1971, winning medals in 1963, 1967 and 1969 as a substitute. Though a highly accomplished goalkeeper, it was his misfortune to have come up against a goalkeeper of Walsh's stature.

And what a match to start off with, one of the most spectacular All-Irelands of all time. 'About midway through the second half, Con Roche sent in a ball from about 90 yards,' Skehan told Brendan Fullam in *Hurling Giants*. 'I looked up and watched it as it sailed over my goal at the Canal End. I think it left us trailing by eight points. I felt that was it. I felt very downhearted. I just grabbed the ball and pucked it out with a feeling of complete indifference as to where it was going or how far it was going. Around that time, [Eddie] Keher was brought out from the corner to the wing and Martin Coogan came on at right full-back. In less than 15 minutes, we were in the lead and the next thing is I am going up on the Hogan Stand to collect the cup, having won by seven points.'

The *Irish Independent*'s John D. Hickey captured the moment when the 1972 final took off midway through the second half.

> I found myself with a match in my mouth and frantically attempting to light it with a cigarette! That is the kind of epic it became as Kilkenny unleashed a brand of power hurling that almost caused me to regret that I had not some affinity with the county – no matter how tenuous.

Newspaper accounts of visits to the training camps tell of Cork moving at an impressive pace and Kilkenny looking leaden by comparison. Blessed with exceptional forwards, Cork were already league champions. The conventional view was that their younger stickmen would outrun Kilkenny on a warm day – and it was warm – over 80 minutes. With 18 minutes to go, Cork looked victory-bound, leading 5–11 to 1–15. What followed is described by Mick Lanigan, Kilkenny's trainer, as 'a magnificent recovery'. Ultimately, Kilkenny were seen to have saved their energy for the day that mattered.

The result earned Kilkenny an eighth All-Ireland final success from 13 encounters against Cork. Having been 0–12 to 2–8 down at half-time and eight points in arrears 18 minutes into the second half, they rattled off 2–9 without reply. To manage that in any match is worthy of applause; to do it against a highly rated Cork side in oppressive heat in an All-Ireland final lent the accomplishment a special distinction.

Cork's Justin McCarthy cites overtraining after their Munster final win – 'We were killed from the training.'[3] – as the chief reason for his team's collapse. Cork hurled to expectations in the first half. Ray Cummins had a fourth-minute goal, set up by McCarthy, who was back playing in his first final since 1966. Mick Malone got Cork's second net-shaker later in the half. Kilkenny had managed to draw level early in the second half when Malone scored his second and Cork's third goal. Seanie O'Leary and Cummins scored points to open a five-point lead. Keher responded with 1–1, but Kilkenny had no time to settle on their gains. Cork hit back with two goals in the next couple of attacks, from Cummins and Seanie O'Leary, and, in the 27th minute, they moved eight points up when Roche scored a huge point from 80 yards that many felt had to be the clincher. They were rampant – but, remarkably, they would not score again.

If Skehan embodied Kilkenny's resilience at one end, Keher provided the cutting edge at the other, his move from corner to wing a telling influence. His first goal from out on the left touchline was a fortunate score that looped over Paddy Barry. He scored his second goal from a free and, with 15 minutes left, Frank Cummins went off on a solo-run, the ball hopping on his stick, and his shot ended up in the Cork net. The introduction of Coogan also roused Kilkenny. Pat Henderson had another colossal performance at centre-back, discovering his best form in the final.

Both Cork and Kilkenny had ridden their luck getting to September. Cork had been 10 points down with 17 minutes left against Tipperary in Munster, and managed to force a replay. Kilkenny were 11 points behind Wexford in the Leinster final soon after half-time and, even with Mick Brennan sent off, they managed to secure a draw. Pa Dillon came out of retirement and went on at full-back in the drawn game.

The 1972 All-Ireland final was the day Kilkenny hurler Pat Delaney demonstrated what became known as the 'Delaney Bounce' when he tapped the ball off the ground from his stick while on a solo. The innovation, which allowed him an extra catch, quickly spread. In the 1960s, Christy Ring's instructional film on skills advised players when raising a ball not to take it into the hand immediately but instead roll it on the stick, thereby allowing the player an extra catch.

This was the first of three Kilkenny All-Ireland wins in four years, watched by a record All-Ireland final attendance for the decade.

A young witness recalls seeing Keher and Brendan Bowyer standing on seating in the Kilkenny dressing room after the game, singing 'The Rose of Mooncoin'. In his biography of Fr Tommy Maher, Enda McEvoy ranks the 1972 All-Ireland final win as Kilkenny's greatest achievement to that point. It was, he said, a day of 'sheer, crazy exhilaration'.[4]

KILKENNY: N. Skehan; F. Larkin, P. Dillon, J. Treacy; P. Lawlor, P. Henderson (0–1 f), E. Morrissey; F. Cummins (1–0), L. O'Brien (0–5, 3fs); M. Crotty (0–2), P. Delaney (0–3), J. Kinsella (0–1); E. Byrne, K. Purcell (0–2), E. Keher (2–9, 1–7fs); Subs: M. Murphy (0–1) for E. Byrne (HT), M. Coogan for F. Larkin (49 mins), P. Moran for J. Kinsella (75).

CORK: P. Barry; T. Maher, P. McDonnell, B. Murphy; F. Norberg, S. Looney, C. Roche (0–2, 1f); J. McCarthy, D. Coughlan; G. McCarthy, M. Malone (2–1), P. Hegarty; C. McCarthy (0–4, 3fs), R. Cummins (2–3), S. O'Leary (1–1); Subs: E. O'Brien for F. Norberg (36 mins), D. Collins for P. Hegarty (69).

Referee: M. Spain (Offaly)

Attendance: 66,137

Minor massacre

Hurling's poverty gap was illustrated in the 1972 minor hurling championship which produced some frightful beatings for teams unfortunate enough to run into either of the eventual finalists, Cork and Kilkenny.

Kilkenny's summer started with a 13–6 to 1–3 win over Laois. They then beat Wexford 7–10 to 0–4 in the Leinster final and it was 7–9 to 2–8 against Galway to reach the September final.

Cork were not to be outdone. Waterford (7–8 to 1–3), Tipperary (10–5 to 2–3), Limerick (4–11 to 0–3) and Antrim (13–6 to 1–3) fell to the Young Rebels.

It was all set for a grand finale and a busy day for the scoreboard operators. Cork, featuring Jimmy Barry-Murphy at full-forward, were seeking a record fourth All-Ireland in a row. They had defeated Kilkenny a year earlier, but Kilkenny, captained by Brian Cody, foiled them to celebrate their first minor title win in 10 years.

Cork led 2–7 to 1–3 at half-time before being overhauled. Billy Fitzpatrick scored 3–4 and Kilkenny at one point led 6–6 to 2–7. The final score read: Kilkenny 8–7, Cork 3–9.

58. Rain Men

1973 All-IRELAND FINAL (Croke Park, 2 September)
Limerick 1–21 Kilkenny 1–14

I'm optimistic. We have a fair chance.
Jackie Power[1]

BY 1973, LIMERICK feared their opportunity might have passed and that the side beaten in the 1971 Munster final by Tipperary had carried their best chance of an All-Ireland. Spring tidings were not promising. Wexford had nine points to spare over Limerick in the National League final and they lost by 12 points to Kilkenny in the Leinster final.

In 1971, Limerick won the National League for the first time since 1947, a late Richie Bennis score giving them a one-point win over Tipperary. A first win over Cork in the championship since 1940 followed before they lost the Munster final to Tipperary in Killarney after holding commanding leads. 'I stayed in Killarney for a week,' Richie Bennis told author Henry Martin in *Unlimited Heartbreak.* 'I drank out of sorrow, there was no singing and roaring I can tell you.'

Until September 1973, Limerick hurling was a tale of unrequited ambition. After narrowly losing the 1972 league final to Cork, the summer ended in catastrophe with defeat by Clare in Ennis. It cost Joe McGrath his job as coach, in spite of the obvious improvements that had come about under his supervision and the fact that he had no control over team selection. Mick Cregan stepped in and dedicated himself to making them the fittest team in the land. But

McGrath's foundation work should not be ignored, nor was it by many of the players who were unhappy with his removal. Before he came along, Limerick had been making little impact and were notoriously inconsistent in their training methods. The major upset in 1966, when Eamonn Cregan inspired them to a shock defeat of Tipperary, was an isolated moment in a lost decade. As Cregan revealed, 'When I trained for the 1965 championship match against Waterford, we had only four players training.'[2]

In 1973, their luck began to change. As a result of conceding 2–2 to Tony Doran in the league final, Ned Rea was dropped and watched the opening win over Clare in the Munster championship as a spectator. An inspired decision to try him out as a full-forward before the Munster final paid dividends. Rea had the unusual experience of marking his brother Gerry in the All-Ireland semi-final against London, a 1–15 to 0–7 win for Limerick at Ennis. He overcame that odd arrangement to be one of the pivotal figures in the final, a physical nuisance for the Kilkenny defence, but he had really made his mark in the Munster final in Thurles.

Come September, Kilkenny had critical losses. A mix of emigration and injury meant that household names – Jim Treacy, Eddie Keher, Kieran Purcell and Eamon Morrissey – were all unable to play. Pat Delaney went into the match suffering the effects of flu and, in the second half, Frank Cummins had to leave injured while the match was still alive. No team could expect to survive such blows.

Beating Tipperary in the Munster final gave Limerick a huge surge of confidence and, with Kilkenny weakened, the prospect of a famous win grew significantly. Over 80 minutes in slippy, rainy conditions, they applied themselves with gusto to the task in a tightly contested match. Purcell came off the bench for Kilkenny but was clearly impaired and, given their losses, the performance of Kilkenny was notably brave and persistent.

The teams were level six times in the first half and twice in the second. Limerick were 0–12 to 1–7 in front at half-time, with Pat

Delaney scoring the Kilkenny goal after 20 minutes, giving them a 1–3 to 0–5 lead. Cregan, playing at centre-back, rewarded the selector's tactical gamble with a controlled display of skill and intelligence. Sean Foley shone beside him and Bennis' free-taking punished Kilkenny repeatedly. When he levelled the match – 1–10 to 0–13 – for the eighth time, seven of Limerick's points total were from Bennis frees.

Kilkenny restarted the match after the interval with three points to go in front. The third, from Mick Crotty, seemed destined to end up a goal but Seamus Horgan made an outstanding reflex save. Bennis put Limerick level, and then Noel Skehan's puckout was fielded and returned by Liam O'Donoghue and, in a scramble, Moss Dowling finished the ball to the Kilkenny net. Rarely has a less attractive goal been scored in an All-Ireland final but it did not make it any less important. Bertie Hartigan added a point immediately and a gap of four had opened up. Claus Dunne reduced it to two with a brace of frees but Limerick, backed vociferously, now had the bit between their teeth.

In the next 10 minutes, two great scores from play by Bennis and Eamonn Grimes pushed the lead out to five for the first time, but Kilkenny stayed in contention, and were only four adrift with eight minutes left. Then their resistance snapped. Grimes stretched it to five again. A mammoth score from Bennis made it six and a peach of a score from Frankie Nolan widened it to seven. When Liam O'Brien pointed in reply, the crowds had already gathered behind Horgan's goal waiting to invade. There wasn't time for the puckout and Mick Slattery called for the ball.

There is a story that before the final started, J.P. McManus, the gambler and financier from South Liberties and devoted Limerick follower, made a dramatic entrance through a window in the dressing room, helped in via a tight passage by some of the players. It is not known where he was when Slattery blew his last whistle of the day. By then it was every man for himself.

Limerick's first success since 1940 brought emotional scenes and the players returned home to a delirious reception on Monday night. A 40-foot CIÉ float brought them the last six miles from Castleconnell to Charlotte Quay, when the train stalled on the city's outskirts. Castleconnell is Ahane country, the club of the Mackeys, once the most powerful club in Limerick.

Among the local councillors there to welcome the victorious players was J.P. 'Rory' Liddy who once captained the Limerick minors. Liddy, a Claughaun man, was twice Lord Mayor and once received President Richard Nixon while wearing the mayoral chain, but it is doubtful that that would have held a candle to his pride on the evening he greeted the Limerick hurlers on their homecoming in 1973.

Eamonn Grimes had the honour of accepting the Liam MacCarthy on Limerick's behalf and was later voted Texaco Player of the Year, having made his senior championship debut against Tipperary in 1966. Limerick would reach the 1974 All-Ireland final, but there hasn't been another success since then. The gap, now 41 years, is longer than the one that preceded their success in 1973.

LIMERICK: S. Horgan; W. Moore, P. Hartigan, J. O'Brien; P. Bennis, E. Cregan, S. Foley; R. Bennis (0–10, 7fs), E. Grimes (0–4); L. O'Donoghue, M. Dowling (1–1), B. Hartigan (0–1); F. Nolan (0–2), N. Rea (0–2), J. McKenna (0–1); Sub: T. Ryan for B. Hartigan (69 mins).

KILKENNY: N. Skehan; P. Larkin, N. Orr, P. Cullen; P. Lawlor, P. Henderson, B. Cody; L. O'Brien (0–2), F. Cummins; C. Dunne (0–7, 7fs), P. Delaney (1–1), P. Broderick; M. Crotty (0–3), J. Lynch, M. Brennan (0–1); Subs: K. Purcell for P. Broderick (HT), W. Harte for F. Cummins (64 mins), J. Kinsella for J. Lynch (76).

Referee: M. Slattery (Clare)

Attendance: 58,009

Richie's cool hand

Limerick's win over Tipperary in the 1973 Munster final is a match that is often recalled, a 70 from Richie Bennis earning a narrow win in spite of Tipp claims that the shot was wide. Before Bennis struck the ball, Babs Keating appeared to say something to him, later admitting he was trying to psyche him out. Bennis claimed he was undaunted.

Mick Slattery, the match referee from Clare who also took charge of the All-Ireland final, informed Bennis that it was to be the last puck. John Flanagan had drawn Tipp level only 90 seconds before.

But Bennis – the prospect of winning his county's first Munster title in 18 years resting in his hands – held his nerve and his score sealed a dramatic 6–7 to 2–18 win.

Tipp had led 2–9 to 3–2 at half-time, with Limerick storming into a 2–1 to 0–0 lead inside 12 minutes, Frankie Nolan and Bennis, from a 21-yard free, the goal scorers. Moss Dowling had their third goal after 24 minutes. Two goals from Francis Loughnane had helped Tipp overturn the deficit.

Tipp went six points up and Limerick looked in bother before a goal by Nolan revived them. A Cregan goal and Bennis point drew them level. Ned Rea's new life as a full-forward was also bearing fruit and he set up both of Cregan's second-half goals. Cregan's second goal had Limerick 6–3 to 2–12 clear but Tipp rallied and it was unbearably tense in the final minutes as they traded scores.

59. Perfect Ambush

1976 LEINSTER FINAL (Croke Park, 18 July)
Wexford 2–20 Kilkenny 1–6

---

*We expected to beat them this time, but our supporters didn't have much
faith in us. And we couldn't blame them for that.*
Tony Doran[1]

IN APRIL 1976, the spirits of Wexford hurling people sank on
hearing of Nickey Rackard's death at the age of 53 after a long
illness. Rackard would have enjoyed this sensational win over
rivals Kilkenny, the defending All-Ireland champions and roaring
favourites, only three months later. It was headline news. Kilkenny
hadn't lost to Wexford in championship hurling since 1970. They'd
beaten Clare by five goals in the National League final on 20 June,
and they had won the previous two All-Irelands and contested the
last five finals – but none of this saved them from their heaviest
Leinster final defeat since 1896. It was their worst championship
loss since the 1937 All-Ireland final.

Wexford had made noticeably hard work of beating Kildare in
the Leinster semi-finals at Athy, eventually winning 2–19 to 2–15.
Kildare hurling exists in a sort of twilight zone for the most part
but, for a few years in the 1970s, they attracted notice and punched
above their weight. Their defeat of Dublin in the first round by two
clear goals was one such moment and they had taken Offaly to a
replay the year before. They pushed hard against Wexford too with
Henry Butler, Wexford's goalkeeping debutant, denying Kildare
full-forward Michael Moore a goal three times in the first half with
superb saves. That Kildare came so close was also largely down to

a Wexford man, John Murphy, living in exile in Kill, who finished with 0–12, evenly split between frees and open play.

Kildare led Wexford 0–9 to 0–2 after half an hour playing with the wind, and were 0–11 to 1–4 up at half-time. Pat Dunny was outstanding at centre-back for Kildare but they couldn't hold out and 10 minutes from the end, Wexford had gone six points clear. That stretched to nine before a late resurgence, with two Kildare goals, put a kinder look on the score.

Where did Kildare go from there? They defeated Westmeath the following year but lost to Wexford 0–9 to 2–25 and Offaly beat them by 12 points in 1978. By 1979, they had withdrawn from the Leinster championship, along with Laois and Westmeath, and have been a peripheral concern ever since, but during this brief period of modest prosperity, they reached two Leinster senior semi-finals and one of their players, Johnny Walsh, earned a replacement All Star. His club Ardclough beat Buffer's Alley in the 1976 Leinster club championship.

Struggling to get past Kildare made Wexford look ill-equipped to handle Kilkenny. Did the late Rackard inspire them? Speaking to the journalist Paddy Downey of *The Irish Times* ahead of the All-Ireland final against Cork later in the year, Colm Doran admitted that he had been in their thoughts:

> We want to win this All-Ireland in commemoration of him. He was the father-figure of modern Wexford hurling … he brought the team up from nothing at that time; he inspired everyone. There was nobody like him.

Wexford failed to win the All-Ireland but the Leinster final was a fitting tribute to Rackard's memory. Kilkenny only scored one point from play, courtesy of Matt Ruth, and only registered a solitary score in the second-half, from Liam O'Brien's free, failing to score for the last 23 minutes. Kilkenny's exceptional team that had dominated the decade had started to unravel. Only for Noel Skehan, Wexford would have won by a great deal more.

Wexford had heroes all over the field. Jim Prendergast did an excellent job marking Mick Brennan who had been one of Kilkenny's main attacking threats. The team was coached by Tom Neville, a corner-back when they had won the 1960 and 1968 All-Irelands, and was captained by Tony Doran, now 30 years old.

Kilkenny never led the match, but were level three times in the first-half. They scored a 14th-minute goal from an Eddie Keher penalty but Wexford hit 1–4 nearing half-time to lead 1–11 to 1–5 at the interval. John Quigley was their goal scorer, taking a Doran pass. Five minutes after the game's resumption, Doran burst through and palmed to the net. Wexford were coasting 2–13 to 1–5, and the match was as good as done.

Clues for Kilkenny's collapse might be found in their heavy schedule of games leading into the summer. When they drew with Clare in the league final, it meant the replay wasn't played until late June. In the meantime, they upped and left for the US. The league semi-final had also gone to a replay and the matches were taking their toll. To add to the load, the Kilkenny county board fixed a round of knockout championship matches for the weekend before the Leinster final.

Kilkenny had beaten Westmeath, conquerors of Offaly, 5–22 to 1–12 in the Leinster semi-final two weeks after demolishing Clare in the league final replay. There were no obvious signs of what was to come. The result confirmed that Wexford were on the rise again. As for Kilkenny, it was time for some rest and reflection.

WEXFORD: J. Nolan; T. O'Connor, W. Murphy, J. Prendergast; L. Bennett, C. Doran, N. Buggy (0–4, 0–1 70, 3fs); M. Jacob, W. Rowsome; J. Murphy (0–1), M. Quigley (0–2), J. Quigley (1–3); M. Butler (0–8, 3fs), T. Doran (1–2), C. Keogh.

KILKENNY: N. Skehan; F. Larkin, N. Orr, B. Cody; P. Lawlor, P. Henderson, G. Henderson; F. Cummins, L. O'Brien (0–4, 0–1 70, 3fs); M. Crotty, M. Ruth (0–1), B. Fitzpatrick; M. Brennan, P. Delaney, E. Keher (1–1, all fs); Subs: K. Purcell for M. Crotty (44 mins), J. Hennessy for B. Cody (49).

Referee: J. Rankins (Laois)

Attendance: 25,000 (estimate)

Wexford fall short

Hopes of another Wexford All-Ireland were dashed in September by Cork, who won by 4–11 to 2–21 in the first leg of a three-in-a-row. Wexford also lost the 1977 final to Cork by three points. They reached the final after defeating Galway in a replay, while Cork enjoyed a bye after winning the Munster championship.

Wexford surged into an eight-point lead after six minutes on the first Sunday in September but Cork reeled them back in to win their 22nd All-Ireland, joining Tipperary at the top of the winners' list. Ray Cummins became the first Blackrock man since Eudie Coughlan in 1931 to captain a victorious Cork All-Ireland team. He'd also scored Cork's first goal, kicking to the net on the half hour after losing his hurl.

60. Rebel Treble

1978 All-IRELAND FINAL (Croke Park, 3 September)
Cork 1–15 Kilkenny 2–8

We'll be back when the cuckoo comes.
Christy Ring

V AL DORGAN'S BOOK on hurling's greatest player opens
with a story from the 1978 All-Ireland final. The crowds have
deserted the stadium and Christy Ring returns to the pitch
to search for a watch he'd lost when rushing on to greet players at
the final whistle. He'd been given it as a gift for 25 years' service
with Irish Shell and had worn it for the first time that weekend.
The watch was never found on a field where Ring was rarely found
wanting. Nobody knew it at the time but the 1978 final would be his
final Croke Park salute; he died the following March aged 58.

He departed on a winning note, a prized team selector as Cork
won their fourth three-in-a-row, the first since Ring's own playing
days. Ring had been a part of hurling – many would argue he was
the hurler – since he'd started with the Cork senior team in 1939,
winning eight All-Irelands and an incredible sweep of 18 Railway
Cups. 'Ringey's presence in the dressing room was awesome,'
Johnny Crowley said. 'He spoke little but what he said was dead on.
He could read players, read referees, read the play like no one else.'[1]

Television footage shows the victorious dressing room with
Ring, face aglow, asked for his thoughts. 'We were ready for
Kilkenny this time,' he said, 'and when we are ready for them, we
can beat them.'

This was an All-Ireland Cork badly needed to win. The scorer of the crucial goal, Jimmy Barry-Murphy, explained their need by noting that Kilkenny were the only leading county they hadn't defeated since they had begun their three-in-a-row run in 1976. Needling defeats to Kilkenny in the All-Ireland finals of 1972 and 1969 had also driven them on.

The day also saw the sun set on the coaching career of Fr Tommy Maher, whose far-reaching role in Kilkenny's Renaissance had started with their win in the 1957 Leinster final. There was talk after Kilkenny's loss of whether Eddie Keher should have been coaxed out of retirement, or Pat Delaney, because the Kilkenny attack malfunctioned. Their first goal was a scrappy affair and only three of their eight points came from play. None of their forwards could be said to have played well. But Maher stressed that the changes they had made had helped get them to September. No one had been complaining up to then.

They had ended Wexford's reign as provincial champions and Wexford didn't win another Leinster title until 1996. The Leinster final was a thrilling match: a late Matt Ruth goal, along with points from Liam O'Brien and Ruth, earned Kilkenny a 2–16 to 1–16 win. In the Munster final, Cork scraped past a talented if ill-fated Clare team.

One of Maher's pupils, Brian Cody, hurled at full-forward in the 1978 All-Ireland final and his experience has often been recounted. At the homecoming on Monday night, some booing was allegedly heard when his name was called. Aside from the lamentable nature of such behaviour, there is a constituency who would say he was not quite as abysmal as the impression sometimes given. Martin O'Doherty was one of Cork's standout players, but while Cody didn't play well, he didn't play shockingly badly either. He was a goal scorer in the opening championship win over Offaly and had earned the selectors' trust. The whole attack failed to sparkle; his was just one of a number of subdued displays.

Cody had built his reputation as a defender and while the practice of converting backs into forwards was well established, ultimately, it didn't work for this team. He suffered inter-county exile as a result but came back to win two more All-Irelands, one as captain, before his spectacular success in management.

Pat Henderson also retired, a staunch figure in numerous Kilkenny rear-guard displays during the 1960s and 1970s. He came on during the match in a move that brought his brother Ger out of centre-back to midfield. It was one of a number of Kilkenny tactical gambles viewed unsympathetically in the post-mortem. Cork's sideline was seen as having been wiser or more fortunate on the day. The relocation of Tim Crowley from the half-forward line to midfield to compete with Frank Cummins was one of a few telling calls. A huge score from Crowley in the second half from near the sideline roused Cork at a key time in the match.

This wasn't a great game of hurling, but it was tight and tense, with the teams tied eight times, five times in the first half. Barry-Murphy's goal in the 57th minute when Cork were two points up was a piece of opportunism and neither he – nor anyone else – would have expected to beat most goalkeepers with it, let alone one as good as Skehan. It hopped along the ground, deflected off Dick O'Hara and deceived the Kilkenny keeper. Michael O'Hehir declared it the goal to win an All-Ireland, and it was – in spite of a quick response from Billy Fitzpatrick, who goaled at the other end on the hour. Kilkenny had time to win it, but they couldn't overhaul Cork, who sealed victory with Charlie McCarthy's point in injury-time.

In the spring of 1978, Cork had been relegated in the league. Ring's cuckoo remarks proved wise. Relegation was forgotten in September as they toasted their 24th All-Ireland win and Charlie McCarthy went up to lift the prize. McCarthy was one of two survivors from the team that had won in 1966 (Gerald McCarthy was the other).

One of the highlights of the day was the encounter between the towering Ray Cummins and diminutive Fan Larkin, who had first played in an All-Ireland final 15 years earlier. Larkin had also played on Cummins in the 1976 All-Ireland club hurling final. 'He was all the time stuck under me rather than shoulder to shoulder,' was how Cummins explained the predicament years later. Cummins didn't stay on Larkin for the full match though, switching with Seanie O'Leary in another beneficial tactical move.

Kilkenny had their first goal after six minutes when Kevin Fennelly had a tap-in after the ball broke in the square from Ruth's delivery. By half-time the game had yielded an unprepossessing 1–4 to Kilkenny, 0–7 to the champions. The second half went along the same lines, the teams level three times up to the 49th minute. When Tim Crowley gave Cork the lead in the 50th minute, they didn't relinquish it. Cork surged three clear, Liam O'Brien's free reduced it to two and then came Barry-Murphy's goal. Cork would not be caught.

CORK: M. Coleman; B. Murphy, M. O'Doherty, J. Horgan; D. MacCurtain, J. Crowley, D. Coughlan; T. Cashman (0–1), P. Moylan; J. Barry-Murphy (1–1), G. McCarthy (0–2), T. Crowley (0–2); C. McCarthy (0–7, 5fs), R. Cummins (0–1), S. O'Leary (0–1); Subs: J. Allen for T. Cashman (51 mins), K. O'Donoghue for S. O'Leary (67).

KILKENNY: N. Skehan; P. Prendergast, F. Larkin, D. O'Hara; J. Hennessy (0–1, 70), G. Henderson, R. Reid; L. O'Brien (0–4, 4fs), F. Cummins; K. Fennelly (1–0), M. Crotty, B. Fitzpatrick (1–1); M. Brennan (0–2), B. Cody, M. Ruth; Subs: T. Malone for K. Fennelly (55 mins), P. Henderson for L. O'Brien (57).

Referee: J. Rankins (Laois)

Attendance: 66,155

No encore for Eddie

Some people felt that Eddie Keher could, or should, have been brought out of retirement against Cork in 1978. But Keher had made his call after losing the 1977 Leinster final to Wexford, a second successive summer defeat to their rivals that had followed a hammering in the 1976 provincial final. He was on the Kilkenny senior team while a minor in 1959. At 37, he felt he had given his all.

Keher became a familiar sight in Kilkenny's campaigns during the 1960s and 1970s and later went into management, being part of the setup when Kilkenny won the All-Ireland in 1979. His father was from Roscommon and came to Kilkenny as a member of the gardaí. Eddie learned his hurling in Rower-Inistioge and St Kieran's College, and became one of the game's best forwards.

He hurled four years at minor for Kilkenny, narrowly failing to win an All-Ireland in 1959, but he went on to win six All-Ireland senior medals and was captain of the 1969-winning team.

His record of 50 championship appearances was eventually overtaken by D.J. Carey in 2004, but his scoring tally of 36–307 stood until 2010, when he was surpassed by Henry Shefflin. He won five All Stars and was Hurler of the Year in 1972.

The 1977 Leinster final defeat to Wexford, 3–17 to 3–14, was his last appearance for Kilkenny and came just shy of his 36th birthday.

61. No Surrender

1980 LEINSTER FINAL (Croke Park, 13 July)
Offaly 3–17 Kilkenny 5–10

They had to be tutored to believe that in the last 10 minutes they could win. Any team will stick with a team for three-quarters of an hour – it's the last quarter that matters. That's where skill and temperament comes in. Physical fitness won't do; it's the skill you rely on. It's pure skill in the last 10.
Former Offaly trainer, Dermot Healy[1]

THIS RESULT, WHICH delivered Offaly's first provincial senior hurling title, was hailed as one of the monumental shocks in hurling history – the question is why hadn't anyone seen it coming?

After all, Offaly had beaten Kilkenny in the league in Nowlan Park earlier in the year, just as they had beaten them in Birr the previous year. They had run Wexford to a point in the 1979 Leinster semi-final at Athy when a bad refereeing decision had cost them at least a draw. Their under-21s had won the 1978 Leinster title and eight of that side had graduated to the senior squad by 1980. Birr Community School was becoming a serious force in colleges hurling thanks to the efforts of Brother Denis Minihane from Cork, who had arrived in the town at the start of the 1960s, preaching lessons of hurling skill and strategy above brawn and timber.

St Rynaghs from Banagher had won two Leinster club titles in the 1970s, their achievements raising standards and helping clean up hurling in the county. This, in turn, had sparked a revival in traditional hurling heartlands, such as Coolderry and Kinnity. A swashbuckling forward from Kinnity called Johnny Flaherty had returned home after spending most of the 1970s in America and – along with goalkeeper Damien Martin, an All Star in 1971 – was a link with the team that had beaten All-Ireland champions Wexford in 1969 before losing the Leinster semi-final to Kilkenny by two points. In the autumn of 1979, the Offaly county board had even recruited a young Kilkenny coach, Dermot Healy, to work on skills and tactics. In the winter, Offaly manager Andy Gallagher had led a campaign that ended the cartel-style arrangement that had kept Kilkenny and Wexford on opposite sides of the Leinster championship draw for over 20 years.

By July 1980, surely it was obvious that something was stirring in the midlands? The answer is a definite no judging by the response to Offaly's victory. But within the county, some of the faithful were clearly beginning to believe. The *Midland Tribune*'s Leinster final preview included a team photo framed beside a poem submitted by a reader. Based on a Japanese warrior's prayer, it was entitled 'Testing Times Now!' with the warrior hoping:

> For sharpness in aiming/For coolness in danger/For three eyes for cunning/For two hearts for plunging/For hope to the last gasp in the gut.

Sharpness, cunning, coolness, heart and hope – it could be a mantra for every hurling team. Offaly needed those qualities and more during an almighty battle that captivated the 9,631 attendance in Croke Park. The crowd included a large group of Spanish students at the Railway End goal – the *Irish Independent* writer Mitchell Cogley noted in his column a few days after the match that they were vocal in their support for the black and amber. They experienced a game that Paddy Downey of *The Irish Times* described as being full of 'endeavour by both sides, plentifully endowed with skilful hurling, rich in a flood of scores and swaying fortunes and topped off by the unremitting excitement of a close and tense struggle'.

The Iberian brigade must have been pleased enough at half-time when Kilkenny led 3–6 to 1–10, very much against the run of play. A Johnny Flaherty goal in the third minute set Offaly on their way and they were 1–4 to 0–1 ahead after eight minutes – five different players having scored. Joachim Kelly and Brendan Keeshan held sway over Frank Cummins and Joe Hennessy at midfield, so much so that Cummins, the engine room of the great team of the 1970s, was taken off at half-time. The Kilkenny half-forward line made little ground against a classy Offaly trio of Ger Coughlan, Pat Delaney and Aidan Fogarty.

But while many of their team-mates floundered, Billy Fitzpatrick and Matt Ruth took the fight to Offaly. Ruth scored an oddly opportunistic goal in the 14th minute when, after being pushed in the back, he fell into the net with the ball trailing behind him. Six minutes later, he was fouled for a penalty converted by Fitzpatrick. At the other end, Padraig Horan had a penalty saved by Noel Skehan, the first of many stops, but Horan's frees and points from Bermingham and Paddy Kirwan kept the scoreboard ticking over for Offaly until Ruth popped up again for Kilkenny's third goal.

And when Skehan made two fine saves early in the second half and Fitzpatrick pointed a free to push Kilkenny a goal clear, the familiar plot was expected to unfold. 'Offaly had been expected to put up a good show for part of the game and then succumb quietly,' reported *The Irish Times* the day after the match. This time, though, the roles were reversed. Offaly were the team playing the more measured hurling, sniping away with points to regain a one-point lead by the 45th minute, and Kilkenny were forced into route-one manoeuvres. Billy Fitzpatrick set up substitute Mick Crotty for a goal in the 54th minute. Fitzpatrick then pointed a free to leave Kilkenny 4–10 to 1–16 in front. Offaly struck back with a 59th-minute goal from a penalty – Horan's strike was saved, but Bermingham who had won the penalty beat Skehan on the rebound to level the game.

The game-changer came two minutes later, in the shape of a goal that encapsulated the advances in Offaly's style. Damien Martin saved a Kilkenny 70 under the crossbar and rather than just lash it out the field, he considered his options. As the *Irish Independent* reported:

> He delicately flighted his clearance to unmarked midfielder Brendan Keeshan and he found skipper Horan with a crossfield pass. Horan, in turn, sent a perfect delivery into the raised hand of veteran Flaherty and in a twinkling the ball was nestling in the Kilkenny net.

Flaherty scored the goal with one of his trademark handpasses.

There was no score during the next seven minutes of furious hurling until Horan pointed a free to make it 3–17 to 4–10 and marginally becalm the frazzled Offaly supporters. However, the suspense became unbearable in the 69th minute when Ger Henderson struck a 70 that bounced off the crossbar and Matt Ruth lashed it past Martin. A one-point game. Kilkenny had one last chance that fell to Matt Ruth – the epitome of the crafty Kilkenny hurler, but his shot for the equalising point forked wide. The match ended with Johnny Flaherty heading upfield in possession. Hopefully the Spanish students stayed on for the joyous pitch invasion of buck-lepping men, women and children that followed, and the whooping, hollering and crying that greeted Padraig Horan when he became the first Offaly captain's to raise the Bob O'Keeffe Cup.

He was told later that his father Thomas had died while listening to the match at home in Banagher.

> He was listening to it on the radio in the kitchen, but when the excitement got too much he went out to listen to it on the car radio. Then my two sisters' children, Laura and Greg, went out to the car. They came back to tell my mother that my father appeared to be asleep in the car, but my mother knew what had happened.
>
> We're all very shocked but the fact is that he probably died a happy man. He died just as the final whistle was going. He knew we had won.[2]

OFFALY: D. Martin; P. Moloughney, M. Kennedy, P. Fleury; A. Fogarty, P. Delaney (0–1 f), G. Coughlan; J. Kelly, B. Keesham; M. Corrigan (0–4), B. Bermingham (1–2), P. Carroll; P. Kirwan (0–4), P. Horan (0–6), J. Flaherty (2–0); Subs. E. Coughlan for P. Moloughney (51 mins), M. Cashin for J. Kelly (62).

KILKENNY: N. Skehan; J. Henderson, B. Cody, D. O'Hara; R. Reid, G. Henderson, N. Brennan; J. Hennessy (0–1 70), F. Cummins; G. Fennelly (0–1), J. Wall (0–1), K. Fennelly (0–1); M. Brennan, B. Fitzpatrick (1–5), M. Ruth (3–1); Subs: L. O'Brien for F. Cummins (HT), M. Crotty (1–0) for K. Fennelly (45), M. Kennedy for M. Brennan (64).

Referee: N. O'Donoghue (Dublin)

Attendance: 9,631

62. Banished Misfortunes

1980 ALL-IRELAND FINAL (Croke Park, 7 September)
Galway 2–15 Limerick 3–9

---

*Is iontach an lá inniu a bheith mar Ghaillimheach. Tá daoine ar ais
i nGaillimh agus tá gliodar ina gcroíthe, ach freisin caithfidh muid
cuimhneach ar dhaoine i Sasana, i Meiriceá, ar fud an domhain agus tá siad
b'fhéidir ag caoineadh anois faoi láthair.*
Joe Connolly[1]

T HE PAST IS another country, they do All-Ireland celebrations
differently there. When the whistle blew on the 1980 hurling
final, Croke Park was engulfed by a pitch invasion and dam-
burst of emotion that it had never witnessed before and never will
again in this era of health-and-safety nannyism. The Galway crowd
went stone mad, and why wouldn't they? They'd waited since 14
September 1924 for a second senior hurling title. When Joe Connolly
and his team-mates reached the Hogan Stand, the captain delivered
an eloquent, off-the-cuff speech in Irish along with cúpla focail in
English, concluding with the rallying cry, 'People of Galway, we
love you.' The emotional barometer went off the scale when Joe
McDonagh took the microphone to sing a few verses from Thomas
Davis' 'The West's Awake'.

Joe Connolly's reference to emigrants in England, America and
all over the world would have meant a lot to Galway people who had
scattered in the 1940s and 1950s – decades when their hurlers had
gone so close to winning an All-Ireland. Between 1945 and 1953,
Galway lost two All-Ireland semi-finals by a point and another by

The Roscrea captain Donie Moloney (middle) receives the shield awarded to the first winners of the All-Ireland senior club championship in December, 1971. Also pictured are the GAA Director-General, Seán O Síocháin, on left, and John Joe Maher, the Roscrea hurling club Secretary. Maher served in that role from 1928 to 1975.

Cork captain Paddy Barry raises the Liam MacCarthy after the 1970 All-Ireland victory over Wexford. John Horgan, their fair-haired defender, is pictured (centre), while President Eamon de Valera is among the dignitaries looking on.

The Tipperary senior hurling team that won the 1971 All-Ireland final, the county's last for 18 years. Back: Michael Keating, Roger Ryan, John Flanagan, Liam King, John Kelly, Seamus Hogan, Mick Roche, Noel O'Dwyer. Front: John Gleeson, Francis Loughnane, Dinny Ryan, Tadhg O'Connor, Len Gaynor, P.J. Ryan, Peter O'Sullivan.

Kilkenny's Pa Dillon and Cork's Ray Cummins contest a high ball in the 1972 All-Ireland senior hurling final, a thriller won by Kilkenny by 3-24 to 5-11. Preparing to lend assistance are Cork's Seanie O'Leary and Kilkenny's Fan Larkin.

Limerick captain Éamonn Grimes lifts the Liam MacCarthy cup after his county's last win in 1973. Also in the picture is President Erskine Childers, far left, and Taoiseach Liam Cosgrave, far right. Limerick defeated the holders Kilkenny 1-21 to 1-14.

The Cork team that defeated Kilkenny in the 1978 final to complete an All-Ireland three-in-a-row. Front: Tom Cashman, Dermot MacCurtain, Sean O'Leary, Charlie McCarthy (capt.), Martin Coleman, Brian Murphy, Gerald McCarthy. Back: Fr. Bertie Troy (coach) Jimmy Barry-Murphy, John Crowley, Tim Crowley, Ray Cummins, Martin O'Doherty, Pat Moylan, John Horgan, Denis Coughlan.

Cork's John Horgan sends a typically relieving clearance downfield in the 1978 All-Ireland senior hurling final as Brian Cody, converted to attack, attempts a block.

The Galway team that defeated Limerick in 1980 to win the county's first All-Ireland title since 1923. Back: Conor Hayes, Steve Mahon, John Connolly, Michael Connolly, Michael Conneely, Frank Burke, Noel Lane, Sean Silke. Front: Niall McInerney, Seamus Coen, Jimmy Cooney, Joe Connolly (capt.), Sylvie Linnane, PJ Molloy, Bernie Forde.

Offaly's veteran scoring ace Johnny Flaherty broke Galway hearts with a late goal that inspired Offaly to an historic first All-Ireland win in 1981. He is seen being hotly pursued by Galway's Seamus Coen and Sylvie Linnane.

The Offaly team that won the county's first All-Ireland title by defeating Galway 2-12 to 0-15 in the 1981 final. Back: Paddy Kirwan, Pat Fleury, Joachim Kelly, Liam Currams, Pat Delaney, Eugene Coughlan, Aidan Fogarty. Front: Tom Donoghue, Johnny Flaherty, Damien Martin, Padraic Horan, Ger Coughlan, Pat Carroll, Mark Corrigan, Brendan Bermingham.

Cork goalkeeper Ger Cunningham shows Offaly's Joe Dooley (nearest) and Padraic Horan a clean pair of heels in the 1984 All-Ireland final, played in Thurles to mark the birthplace of the GAA in its centenary year. Cork, who had lost the previous two All-Ireland finals to Kilkenny, won by 3-16 to 1-12.

The rivalry between Galway and Tipperary was the fiercest in hurling during the late 1980s. Here Conor Hayes and Tipperary's Nicky English compete for possession during the 1988 All-Ireland final when Hayes captained Galway to back-to-back All-Ireland titles.

Tipperary captain Bobby Ryan raises the MacCarthy Cup following Tipperary's first All-Ireland victory in 18 years. They defeated surprise finalists Antrim by 4-24 to 3-9 after effectively sealing the title with victory over Galway in a controversial semi-final.

Offaly celebrate victory over Clare in the 1989 All-Ireland minor final, captained by a future star of the game Brian Whelahan. This was the county's third All-Ireland minor success in four years, and laid the foundations for two senior All-Ireland victories in 1994 and '98.

Jim Nelson's Antrim team pictured before they slayed favourites Offaly in the 1989 All-Ireland senior semi-final to reach the final for the first time since 1943. Back: Brian Donnelly, Dessie Donnelly, Dominic McKinley, Niall Patterson, Terence Donnelly, Paul McKillen, Dominic McMullan, James McNaughton. Front: Terence McNaughton, Olcan McFetridge, Ciaran Barr, Donal Armstrong, Gary O'Kane, Leonard McKeegan, Aidan McCarry.

Babs Keating, Tipperary manager, adopting an unusual pose during the 1991 All-Ireland final between Tipperary and Kilkenny, the first between the counties for 20 years. Tipperary won, as they had when Babs was a player in the '71 final.

two, in a losing streak that concluded with the turbulent 1953 All-Ireland final defeat to Cork. They had fine hurlers, but something seemed lacking in their mentality – Galway were perceived as game and gallant, but invariably likely to buckle in the closing minutes of tight matches.

The 1947 team was exceptional. Representing Connacht, they defeated Christy Ring's Munster Galacticos in the Railway Cup final, but that year's All-Ireland semi-final in Birr was a result that put the gall into Galway hurling. They led by two points at the end of normal time, but Kilkenny scored three points in 'lost time' to nick it. Mistaking a whistle for a free as the signal for full-time, Galway supporters had invaded the pitch in premature celebration before retreating back to the terraces to watch Kilkenny sharpshooter Jimmy Langton drive home the final nails.

Seanie Duggan was the goalkeeper on that team and in an interview before the 2012 All-Ireland final, he maintained that Galway's many misfortunes in those years were down to their competitive isolation in Connacht rather than dodgy refereeing decisions and the general mí-ádh which was supposed to include an infamous priest's curse laid after a Galway team had left mass early to get to a game.

'We were close, but we couldn't get through because we weren't crafty enough and in the end we'd be making mistakes, beaten by a short head because we didn't have that competitive experience,' recalled Duggan.

> But there were some great players on that team ... they were equal to anything that was in Cork or Tipperary or Wexford or Kilkenny, but it was like sending a carpenter to do a job with no hammer. We didn't have the experience.[2]

The GAA, forever tinkering with hurling championship structures, had given Galway a bye straight into that 1955 All-Ireland final, which they lost to Wexford, and they went in cold again for the 1958 final where they were hammered by Tipperary. After that, they were sent to Munster with lamentable results – winning one game in 11 seasons. Disenchantment and decline set in after the near misses of the 1940s and 1950s. Galway hurling turned in on itself as local club rivalries took precedence. The county team's fortunes bottomed out with a 5–28 to 3–7 beating from Kilkenny in the 1972 All-Ireland semi-final followed by a 4–7 to 3–5 All-Ireland quarter-final defeat to London in Ballinasloe in 1973.

It all looked fairly hopeless, but the senior team's form didn't reflect what had been going on in the background since 1965 when a juvenile hurling board had been formed to renew the game from the roots up. Underage competitions were revamped. Outsiders, such as Tipperary star Donie Nealon, were brought in to coach the best of the promising players at summer camps that were the forerunner of today's development squads.

Hurling revolutions, as Dublin are finding out, don't happen overnight, but Galway won an All-Ireland under-21 title in 1972 – beating Dublin – and lost the 1973 minor final to Kilkenny by a point. The senior team won the 1975 National League title, beating Cork, Kilkenny and Tipp in the knockout games. In the All-Ireland semi-final, they ambushed Cork – Galway's first championship victory over the Rebels – but they never had a chance in the final against a Kilkenny side packed with legends.

Four years later and managed by Babs Keating, Galway produced another semi-final tornado to halt Cork's bid for a four-in-a-row. That performance made them favourites for the final against a supposedly average Kilkenny team. A cracking Noel Lane goal gave them a 1–8 to 1–6 lead after 48 minutes, and then they stalled. The following, describing the closing stages of the game, could have been written about any number of Galway–Kilkenny clashes in the intervening years:

> Yet on the cusp of victory the westerners' challenge floundered. Despite the urging of their supporters, Galway failed to register another score and were left disconsolate as Kilkenny ground out a win.[3]

The final score was 2–12 to 1–8. Galway's hopes ended when John Connolly had a penalty blocked in the 61st minute. An unfortunate lapse by goalkeeper Seamus Shinnors, outstanding in the semi-final, gifted Kilkenny the clinching goal and that was it for Galway who had also lost the 1979 league final to Tipperary by 3–15 to 0–8.

The revival that had begun in 1965 appeared to be heading down a cul de sac. Babs departed and was replaced by Cyril Farrell. Expectations were low but Farrell had big ambitions. He had been a 23-year-old rookie when he'd managed the Galway side that had lost the 1973 All-Ireland minor final to Kilkenny by a point. Five years later, he had been in charge of the under-21 team that had defeated Tipperary in an All-Ireland final replay – Conor Hayes, Seamus Coen and Bernie Forde from that team had immediately made the senior grade and others would follow. As a player, Farrell had helped his club, Tommie Larkins, to win a county senior title in 1971 and he had also captained UCG to a Fitzgibbon Cup title. He got a run out with the Galway seniors, scoring two goals off Cork's John Horgan in a challenge match in 1977, but he didn't make the cut. He focused his energies on management and UCG was his finishing school.

> I came across people from several other counties and quickly realised that they were no different to us in Galway. They all had their doubts, their insecurities, their secret fears and that applied in hurling matters too. It was just that they managed to disguise them better.[4]

Farrell inherited a squad with plenty of big-name players, such as John Connolly, Joe McDonagh, Iggy Clarke, Sean Silke, Frank Burke and P.J. Molloy. John Connolly had started playing for Galway in 1967 and even in the lean years was acclaimed nationally for his talents, winning an All Star in 1971. When Farrell looked around the dressing room, he saw plenty of hurling talent but he had doubts about their mindset.

> It irked me to think that some of the more senior players might be more interested in looking for excuses than in actually getting down to it and proving that they were the best in the country.[5]

Training began on 6 January 1980, but Galway still looked as flaky as ever in the All-Ireland semi-final against Offaly. A Bernie Forde goal put them 4–8 to 1–9 ahead by the 58th minute but that was their last score. Sylvie Linnane had been sent off in the 52nd minute and using their extra man around midfield, Offaly scored 2–1 in the last eight minutes as the rain poured down on Croke Park. Galway were mightily relieved when referee J.J. Landers of Waterford blew the whistle 52 seconds early, but they had lost their most influential defender Iggy Clarke to a shoulder injury. There were also big question marks about goalkeeper Michael Conneely after his poor performance.

Farrell showed his mettle in how he dealt with both issues. He helped restore Conneely's confidence by using some basic sports psychology and pairing him with P.J. Molloy for extra shot practice. Conor Hayes, who had been on a student working holiday in Europe after breaking his thumb in a club game, was summoned back to Ireland and named at corner-back in the team for the final.

Both Conneely and Hayes made vital contributions in a final performance that veered between convincing and nerve-wracking. Galway led by 2–1 to 0–0 after nine minutes, Bernie Forde and P.J. Molloy both slicing the defence apart as Galway threatened to overrun the Munster champions, who badly missed the steadying influence of Pat Hartigan at full-back.

Eamonn Cregan took the fight to Galway, scoring a goal with an overhead flick in the 10th minute. He added two quick points, but with Frank Burke blotting out the influence of Limerick's centre-back Sean Foley, and with Bernie Forde and Noel Lane going to town in the corners, Galway led 2–7 to 1–5 at half-time. One of the highlights was a vintage John Connolly point from the sideline, adding to the sense that Galway's day had come.

Two points from Forde put them seven ahead by the 52nd minute when Limerick's full-forward Joe McKenna, who had been scoring goals for fun all year, broke the cover of Niall McInerney. Game on. A few minutes earlier, Conneely had produced a stunning save from

McKenna. Cregan added a point after McKenna's goal before Forde pushed the lead back to five. Cregan ended the game with 2–7 – his second goal from a penalty strike in the 61st minute putting a chill into Galway veins.

Joe Connolly calmed the situation with a pointed free. Possibly the most decisive intervention came in the 68th minute when Conor Hayes repaid his airfare by intercepting a pass from Cregan meant for McKenna who was unmarked within easy scoring distance of goal: Galway clung on with substitute John Ryan scoring the insurance point. Cregan had a late shot from a 21 deflected over the bar and that was that, as Noel O'Donoghue blew the whistle that ended Galway's decades of misery.

The atmosphere of the day was reflected in the opening line of Paddy Downey's match report in *The Irish Times*:

> At last, at long last, the hurlers of Galway are teeming through the garden of the golden apples and at the gate, all the dragons, and the ghosts of dragons, are dead.

Alas, the hurling dragons hadn't finished with Galway. They would soon be back, with reinforcements.

GALWAY: M. Conneely; C. Hayes, N. McInerney, J. Cooney; S. Linnane, S. Silke, S. Coen; M. Connolly, S. Mahon; F. Burke, Joe Connolly (0–4, 3fs) P.J. Molloy (1–0); B. Forde (1–5), John Connolly (0–2), N. Lane (0–3); Subs: F. Gantley for M. Connolly, J. Ryan (0–1) for P.J. Molloy.

LIMERICK: T. Quaid; D. Murray, L. Enright, Dominic Punch; L. O'Donoghue, M. Carroll, S. Foley; J. Carroll, David Punch; P. Fitzsimmons, J. Flanagan, W. Fitzmaurice; O. O'Connor, J. McKenna (1–1), E. Cregan (2–7, 1–5fs); Subs: P. Herbert for M. Carroll, B. Carroll (0–1) for J. Flanagan, E. Grimes for W. Fitzmaurice.

Referee: Noel O'Donoghue (Dublin)

Attendance: 64,895

63. Here Comes Johnny

1981 ALL-IRELAND FINAL (Croke Park, 6 September)
Offaly 2–12 Galway 0–15

That game came a bit late for me … A few years before, I could dominate a
match from out the field … I was well past my best … Still, I felt if they could
only work it up to me, if they'd puck it up to me, I'd be able to do something
with it. They did, and sure I managed to get the ould goal.
Johnny Flaherty[1]

IN THE 1500s, the mentally fragile burghers of Galway had an inscription carved above the western gate into the city that read: 'From the ferocious O'Flahertys, Lord preserve us.' These were the same merchant class of people who had outlawed hurling in 1527 and also forbade anyone with an 'O' or a 'Mc' in their name to 'strut and swagger' through the city's streets. In 1981, a Flaherty – without an 'O' but with plenty of swagger – ransacked Galway by plundering a goal that was the winning of Offaly's first hurling All-Ireland.

Even before Johnny Flaherty's goal, Galway were arguably a beaten team. They had squandered many chances, but still led by four points, 0–15 to 1–9, on 61 minutes when Offaly centre-back Pat Delaney soloed from inside his own half and, without a Galway player laying a hand on him, landed a majestic point on the run. Two minutes later, Offaly goalkeeper Damien Martin made a tremendous instinctive save to deflect Noel Lane's high, angled shot out for a 65, which was driven wide. At the other end, Flaherty, warming up for the main act, flashed over a point with five minutes left.

It was down to two points with five minutes left and Offaly swept forward for the winning scores, but Iggy Clarke briefly repelled them with a fine clearance that was won in the air by Delaney. With Galway men flailing in his trail, Delaney set off on another solo – this time sending a perfect stick pass to Brendan Bermingham who was about 30 yards from goal. He transferred to Flaherty who was momentarily unmarked on the edge of the square. And even though he was swallowed up by goalkeeper Michael Conneely and corner-back Seamus Coen, the Kinnity man – back to goal – still found the target with one of his trademark palmed flicks of the ball. It was the palm of God as far as Offaly supporters were concerned. Slow motion replays definitely prove a subtle striking action even though the crestfallen Galwegians protested it was a throw.

Martin saving at one end and Flaherty goaling at the other was a suitably blockbuster-style combination of split-second heroics to win an All-Ireland title. They were the two links with the 1969 team that had almost made the breakthrough. An All Star in 1971, Martin enjoyed a high-profile career despite Offaly's difficulties, but Flaherty had emigrated to America before returning in 1978 and helping Kinnity win a county championship. He was a stylish player who adapted his game as the years passed. Instead of calling the shots out the field, he had reinvented himself as a poacher.

Flaherty won an All Star in 1981 as did the late Pat Carroll whose goal had given Offaly a badly needed foothold during a first half that Galway controlled completely as they landed a stream of spectacular points from distance with the breeze at their backs. They led 0–13 to 1–4 at half-time. Three of the Offaly points were long-distance frees by Pat Delaney, a truly inspiring figure at centre-back as the game progressed.

Offaly manager Dermot Healy has always maintained that he was convinced at half-time that Offaly would win. In the 1980 semi-final against Galway, they had cut a nine-point gap to two in the final 10 minutes and were spoiling for an equaliser when the game ended a minute or so too early. Healy's logic was that even though they were champions, Galway would revert to the bumbling brittleness of old if there was less than six points in it with 10 minutes left.

And he was right, even if the reality of what happened is a little more complex. It's not taking anything away from Offaly's endless fighting spirit, admirable method and the special contribution of players like Damien Martin, Pat Delaney, Liam Currams, Pat Carroll, Mark Corrigan and Johnny Flaherty, but any consideration of this game also has to reflect on Galway's second-half collapse.

John Connolly had a goal disallowed in the first half for an accidental clash with Damien Martin after the ball had landed in the net, but they were going so well that it hardly seemed to matter that much. Six ahead at half-time, they went seven clear when Joe Connolly pointed a free just after the resumption. After that, they only managed one point in 31 minutes – Noel Lane scoring in the 48th minute. They hit 14 wides in the second half.

Too many of their key men were visibly out on their feet during the last 10 minutes. Offaly had done the hard physical work over the winter and reached a league final, whereas Galway – and who would blame them – had enjoyed the high life and had only got down to business after scraping past Wexford in May to secure their Division 1 league status. Offaly went straight from the league into a testing Leinster campaign. They almost lost their Leinster crown in the semi-final against Laois where they led by five points with a few minutes left before conceding two late goals. Paddy Kirwan from Ballyskenach scored a point from a 90-yard free in injury-time to save the day – Offaly 3–20, Laois 6–10. Offaly also lived dangerously at times against Wexford in the Leinster final before winning by 3–12 to 2–13 in a game where Wexford full-forward Tony Doran had to go off after 16 minutes with a head wound.

Meanwhile, Galway needed a late free from substitute Finbarr Gantley to draw 0–11 to 1–8 in a torrid All-Ireland semi-final against Limerick who were down to 14 men after Sean Foley was sent off in the eighth minute. Galway rediscovered some form to win the replay by 4–16 to 2–17 against opponents with an ever lengthening injury list after the drawn game and punishing provincial campaign. 'Limerick felt they simply ran out of men and that with a full squad they would have beaten us. They might well be right,' wrote Galway manager Cyril Farrell in his autobiography.[2]

After the All-Ireland defeat, Galway were accused of being too cocky and complacent, but Cyril Farrell was more inclined to rue the absence of the injured Conor Hayes and Damien Martin's save from Lane. He was mystified by the forwards' loss of form, writing that they would be expected to score more than a single point from 50 yards in 30 minutes on a dark night, never mind a pleasant afternoon in Croke Park.

There was a grisly sequel when the teams met in a National League tie at Birr the following month. An infamous club game in Offaly back in the 1960s had been immortalised as the 'Battle of Birr', a description that was also attached to this hour of timber and score-settling. The *Midland Tribune* ran an inventory of the wounded on its front page:

> Offaly ... Liam Currams – stitches in ear; Eugene Coughlan – fractured bone in hand; Johnny Flaherty – four stitches in wound at back of head; Sean O'Meara – blurred vision from a head injury. The Galway toll: Brendan Lynskey – broken ankle; Joe McDonagh – cracked ribs; Frank Burke – injured thigh; Frank Canning – 8 stitches; Seamus Coen – 6 stitches; Noel Lane and P.J. Molloy – stitches.[3]

Galway won the game by 1–20 to 1–7, Sylvie Linnane scoring 13 points from placed balls. It was ferocious stuff.

OFFALY: D. Martin; T. Donoghue, E. Coughlan, P. Fleury; A. Fogarty, P. Delaney (0–5, 4fs), G. Coughlan; J. Kelly, L. Currams (0–1); P. Kirwan, B. Bermingham, M. Corrigan; P. Carroll (1–1), P. Horan (0–2, 2fs), J. Flaherty (1–2); Subs: B. Keeshan for Donoghue (inj.), D. Owens (0–1) for P. Kirwan.

GALWAY: M. Conneely; S. Coen, N. McInerney, J. Cooney; S. Linnane, S. Silke, I. Clarke; M. Connolly (0–1), S. Mahon (0–2); F. Gantley, J. Connolly (0–8, 6fs), P.J. Molloy (0–1); B. Forde, J. Connoly, N Lane (0–3); Subs: Fr Burke for F. Gantley, P. Ryan for B. Forde.

Referee: Frank Murphy (Cork)

Attendance: 71,348

64. Centenary Classic

1984 MUNSTER FINAL (Semple Stadium, 15 July)

Cork 4–15 Tipperary 3–14

The greatest match I ever took part in.

Ger Cunningham[1]

THERE IS A story John Fenton tells about a man from his own hometown of Midleton who, on the day of the 1984 Munster final, left a feverish Semple Stadium downhearted and resigned to defeat. Five minutes remained when Noel O'Dwyer scored during a phase of rampant Tipperary pressure, extending their lead to four points. Destiny was theirs, or so it appeared.

On his journey home, the Cork man avoided the radio, suffering in silence, imagining raucous celebrations around Liberty Square, toasting Tipperary's first Munster senior hurling title since 1971. When he got to his destination, his wife told him that Cork had won. Finding this incredible, he had to check the news to be sure she wasn't having him on.

Fenton remembers the noise and the tumult when Tipperary were in control during those frantic moments, something he describes as unique in his career. Tipperary desperately wanted to win this match and very nearly did, but hurling doesn't always favour the brave. Two late opportunist goals from Tony O'Sullivan and Seanie O'Leary earned Cork an unlikely escape to victory.

This final was dear to Tipperary because it was the centenary year of the GAA, and Thurles was where it had all started. Since their last All-Ireland in 1971, the county had gone through a harrowing and puzzling period of impoverishment, scarcely believable in the context of their tradition and the lavish success of the 1960s. When they scraped past Clare in the 1984 Munster semi-final – relying on a late, late goal – they had achieved the distinction of reaching their first Munster senior final since 1973. That's how lean their times had become. But reaching the provincial final would not be enough; they wanted this title more than any other.

For the Munster final itself, the match was significant for restoring the old familiar pairing that had helped to create its reputation as a fixture apart. The old snobbery that held there was no Munster final to rival one between Cork and Tipp still had currency, in spite of Tipp's failings. The previous two Munster finals had seen Cork annihilate Waterford – the fixture needed a great match and, certainly in the second half, the 1984 final was a gripping encounter with a strong claim for epic status.

Donie Nealon, Len Gaynor and Pat Stakelum, great names from the past, were part of the management team trying to fashion the triumph the county craved. Nicholas English was an All Star forward in his second year, but the team did not heave with star players. Tipp needed to be more than the sum of their parts and they were; their defeat was heartbreaking but heroic. In losing, they managed to resurrect the ferociously competitive spirit synonymous with Tipperary. In some way, they probably sowed the seeds of the revolution that would overthrow Cork three years later and restore Tipperary as a force in the game.

Munster is now consistently competitive but in centenary year, with all the will in the world, the reality was that Cork ruled. The first-round match between Clare and Waterford, who had been in the previous three Munster finals, drew a crowd of 5,000 to Thurles. Even Cork had their issues. In the previous two years, they had lost All-Ireland finals, something that haunted and inspired them in equal measure. Fenton talks of playing their first match in the league the previous October and coming off the field convinced they'd win the All-Ireland. And they would, overpowering Offaly in Thurles the following September, but the Munster final was a match they could, and probably should, have lost.

Cork and Tipp had not played in the Munster final since 1970. In 1984, Cork led 2–10 to 3–5 at half-time, Jimmy Barry-Murphy getting their goals, with English, Seamus Power and Donie O'Connell raising green flags for the Premier County. By the 48th minute, Tipperary were level. Liam Maher put them in front and the crowd and the team seemed to be working in perfect symmetry, finding a unity of purpose, and though Cork soon drew level, the next push from the blue and gold yielded four scores in a furious drive for home.

Ultimately, in the time that the Midleton man was probably getting to his car, the match had wheeled away from Tipp in the most crushing manner. Cork reeled off 2–2 in the final six minutes, including injury-time. Fenton scored a free in the 65th minute, then a shot parried by John Sheedy fell kindly to O'Sullivan and he steered it into the goal. Level again, and the whole dynamic of the game changed with three minutes of normal time left.

Tipperary, sensing alarm, attacked and began the move that is seen as the defining moment in the game. Michael Doyle, son of the legendary John, got bottled up and hand-passed across the face of Cork's goal – a decision that would exact a terrible retribution. Denis Mulcahy intercepted and drove a long clearance, O'Sullivan gained possession and shot for a point. Sheedy brought it down, just not tidily enough, so it broke and O'Leary stole in and applied the stake through the heart. With Tipp reeling, Fenton added a free.

'When Noel O'Dwyer put them four up, it was the first and only time in my life when I really was aware of the noise coming from a crowd,' recalls Fenton, the Cork captain. 'I thought the roof was going to come off the stand that day. That more than anything woke us up.'[2]

Defeat invariably brings a post-mortem, and Tipperary followers would later question whether the selectors were wise in moving Power, their most effective attacker, out of full-forward and placing him left corner-back in the later stages. Power's aggressive play had unsettled Cork's defence and forced the substitution of Donal O'Grady. There were injury concerns over Dinny Cahill and Pat Fitzelle, but both were selected. Ultimately, even allowing for their predatory forwards, the ball bounced for Cork on the day. Tipperary were beaten but there was hope that the darkness was finally giving way to some light.

Doyle, too, would have that hand-pass forensically analysed over the long winter that followed. In 1987, he would have his day in the sun, scoring two goals as Tipperary won the Munster title for the first time in 16 years.

Being the son of eight-time All-Ireland winner John Doyle couldn't have been easy. 'He could have played a much bigger part if he had accepted the regime and our attitude to fitness,' Babs Keating maintained in his autobiography. 'Michael was a heavy smoker and he was not the best attender at training. He had a lot of skill and could have filled in at centre-forward or full-forward, but he never gave us the message that he was prepared to do the work necessary. It was unfortunate that he did not have the right approach to training because he had everything else.'[3]

CORK: G. Cunningham; D. Mulcahy, D. O'Grady, J. Hodgins; T. Cashman, J. Crowley, D. MacCurtain; J. Fenton (0–7, 6fs), P. Hartnett (0–1); P. Horgan (0–3), T. Crowley, K. Hennessy (0–3); T. Mulcahy, J. Barry-Murphy (2–0), S. O'Leary (1–1); Subs: J. Blake for D. O'Grady (51 mins), T. O'Sullivan (1–0) for T. Crowley (55), D. Walsh for P. Horgan (62).

TIPPERARY: J. Sheedy; J. Bergin, J. Keogh, D. Cahill; P. Fitzelle, J. McIntyre, B. Ryan; R. O'Callaghan, P. Kennedy (0–2, 0–1 70); N. English (1–0), D. O'Connell (1–2), L. Maher (0–1); M. Doyle, S. Power (1–6, 0–1 pen, 3fs), N. O'Dwyer (0–2, 1f); Subs: J. Doyle for D. Cahill (12 mins), B. Heffernan for P. Fitzelle (29), P. Dooley (0–1) for B. Ryan (45).

Referee: J. Moore (Waterford)

Attendance: 50,093

Legends on parade

The centenary All-Ireland hurling final in Thurles, which had been carefully planned to mark the foundation of the GAA in the town in 1884, didn't live up to to the occasion. Cork defeated Offaly with some ease (3–16 to 1–12), thereby avoiding the fate of losing three All-Ireland finals in a row.

One of the day's highlights was a parade of surviving All-Ireland hurling captains, including Eudie Coughlan of Cork who had been victorious in 1931, the earliest winning captain alive at the time, right up to the most recent winner, Liam Fennelly from 1983. Cheer of the afternoon was reserved for Jack Lynch, the former Taoiseach, when he was introduced to the crowd of 59,814 packed into Semple Stadium.

65. Thurles Tornado

1986 ALL-IRELAND SEMI-FINAL (Semple Stadium, 10 August)
Galway 4–12 Kilkenny 0–13

A lot of Noresiders felt sad as if something had been taken from them. After all, this was Galway's first win over Kilkenny in the championship since 1953. The majority hadn't suffered the experience before. It wasn't easy to accept. This wasn't part of the All-Ireland script.
Kilkenny People (15 August, 1986)

I T'S SAID THAT if you can't hurl in Thurles, you can't hurl anywhere. It might be true for teams that have been playing championship games there for decades, but the holy ground in the heart of Tipperary was, until recent times, unfamiliar and intimidating terrain for Galway. In 1984, they had been beaten there 4–15 to 1–10 by Offaly in the All-Ireland semi-final. It was a shocking performance, a throwback to the worst of the old days.

When the inquests had finished, Cyril Farrell returned as manager after a two-year break. He built a new team around a core of veterans from 1980 and the pick of the Galway minor and under-21 sides that had won All-Ireland titles in 1983. Against all expectations, they defeated Cork by 4–12 to 5–5 in the 1985 All-Ireland semi-final played in a deluge at Croke Park before an attendance of 8,205 spectators. Inexperience and erratic shooting undermined Galway's challenge in the final against Offaly who were on a recovery mission themselves after a chastening defeat against Cork in the centenary All-Ireland final. Two goals from Pat Cleary helped Offaly to a 2–11 to 1–12 victory.

Even allowing for their progress in 1985 and the obvious talent of the new generation of players such as Tony Keady, Peter Finnerty, Gerry McInerney and Joe Cooney, Galway, in the words of a *Sunday Tribune* headline the day of the game, weren't given a prayer against Kilkenny in the 1986 semi-final. The Cats had reasserted themselves by clipping Offaly 4–10 to 1–11 in the Leinster final and faced Galway with nine of the team who had completed back-to-back All-Irelands in 1983. Another September lap of honour beckoned for players like John and Ger Henderson, Paddy Prendergast, Christy Heffernan, Kieran Brennan, and Liam and Ger Fennelly. What happened next wasn't part of anyone's script except Farrell's.

It wasn't just their experience that made Kilkenny such strong favourites to sweep Galway aside. Three months earlier, the teams had fought out an extremely physical National League final in Thurles. In the end, Kilkenny had won easily, a late Conor Hayes goal from a penalty putting a gloss on the 2–10 to 2–6 scoreline for Galway. 'There was a near arrogance about the manner in which Kilkenny had blown us apart in the league final,' recalled Farrell in his autobiography. 'Kilkenny believed we would never beat them. They reckoned that when the real heat came, Galway would melt into a subservient mess in the corner. God, that infuriated me.'[1]

Trying to match such a hardened Kilkenny side in the 'physicality' stakes was clearly not going to work, so Farrell opted for a game-plan that would maximise his forwards' edge in speed and skill. Hurling in the 1980s was a fairly straightforward sport tactically. Players tended to stick closely to their starting positions and there was still a considerable amount of ground hurling which made a lot of possession a lottery. Farrell, however, was an advocate of the hand-pass and solo-running as a means of maximising possession and scoring opportunities. The purists didn't approve, but they had to revise their opinions after this game where Galway bamboozled Kilkenny from start to finish.

Taking a player out from corner-forward to the half-forward line or midfield is routine today but in 1986 the 3–3–2 midfield and forward formation that Farrell unleashed on Kilkenny was almost revolutionary. Galway played a two-man full-forward line of Joe Cooney and Noel Lane. The nominal centre-forward, Anthony Cunningham, drifted in and out between the lines and the corner-forward, the pacey Martin Naughton, also ran at the Kilkenny defence from deep. The iron man of the team was Brendan Lynskey who did much of the graft, as did Tony Kilkenny at midfield with Steve Mahon. Behind them, Gerry McInerney played a stormer on his championship debut alongside Keady and Finnerty. Sylvie Linnane holding Kilkenny's ace Liam Fennelly scoreless was another bonus.

The fluidity and pace of Galway's attack wrong-footed the Kilkenny backs as the system Farrell had drilled into his players at training in Athenry clicked in the home of hurling. Farrell cited the second goal as the 'perfect execution of what we had planned. Cooney, whose sense of vision suggested he had eyes on all sides of his head, won possession. Cunningham was already making his run so that he was running at full pace by the time Cooney fed him. The gallop through and the hand-passed goal. Sweet and virtually unstoppable. We could do no wrong. Kilkenny were completely mesmerised.'[2]

Cunningham scored that goal in the 27th minute and Galway led 2–7 to 0–5 at half-time. Cooney scored the third goal 25 seconds after the restart and added the fourth in the 50th minute to wrap up the result. Kilkenny only scored seven points from play on a day when the Hendersons' defiant rear-guard action in the second half was their one consolation.

Inevitably, what had worked so sweetly for Galway in the semi-final turned sour in the All-Ireland final against a Cork side managed by Johnny Clifford. Galway's game-plan demanded utmost precision, but it malfunctioned badly. Cork corner-back Johnny Crowley stayed in position and was lord of all he surveyed, mopping up an amount of aimless ball from Galway's outfield players. Galway reverted to the orthodox 2–3–3 in the second half but by then Cork had their tails up. The fleet-footed Thomas Mulcahy scored a 48th-minute goal that turned the game for the Munster champions. Galway argued that he had taken an inordinate number of steps. Cork saw it differently:

> Thomas Mulcahy careered through on a splendid solo-run and with courage, conviction and great ball control finished the sliotar to the net. That was the signal for Cork to take command and a second goal from Kevin Hennessy crowned a wonderful performance.[3]

Dowtcha boys!

It ended 4–13 to 2–15 and the winners were quick to scorn those who had written them off. The Lord Mayor of Galway John Mulholland had put his mayoral chain in it during the build-up to the final by making some ill-advised comments about homecomings in Eyre Square. He got it back with interest.

> 'And finally,' said Tom Cashman gleefully as he raised the MacCarthy Cup, 'Lord Mayor of Galway take a look at this.' It was the ultimate riposte to the apparent arrogance of the Galway folk whose supreme confidence in victory had been voiced by their first citizen on television the previous day. It had been a light-hearted remark, but it served to instil a furious desire to win in the hearts of the Cork players.[4]

It was another sickening defeat for Galway. They had been outmanoeuvred again and while Farrell accepted they had been beaten by the slicker team, he was angered by Dublin referee John Bailey's performance. He was especially aggrieved by what he claimed was the 'special attention' dished out to Brendan Lynskey, the fulcrum of the 3–3–2 strategy against Kilkenny.

> [He] got more belts in the first half than a player might reasonably expect to get in a life-time ... One first-half tackle in front of the Hogan Stand was appalling.[5]

Galway could protest all they wanted, but the day belonged to Cork. It was their 26th title, moving them three ahead of Tipperary and Kilkenny in the grand hurling scheme of things. It was Jimmy Barry-Murphy's final game for Cork, and he departed with all the élan that distinguished his 15 years in the red jersey.

GALWAY: J. Commins; C. Hayes, S. Linnane, O. Kilkenny; P. Finnerty, T. Keady, G. McInerney; S. Mahon (0–1), T. Kilkenny (0–1); P. Piggott, A. Cunningham (1–3), B. Lynskey (0–1); M. Naughton (0–2), J. Cooney (2–2, 2fs), N. Lane (1–1); Subs: P.J. Molloy (0–1) for P. Piggott.

KILKENNY: K. Fennelly; P. Prendergast, J. Henderson, F. Holohan; J. Hennessy, G. Henderson, S. Fennelly; R. Power (0–1), G Fennelly (0–3 3fs); P. Walsh, C. Heffernan, K. Brennan (0–2); L. Ryan, L. Fennelly, H. Ryan (0–2); Subs: J. Mulcahy (0–4, 3fs) for Prendergast, J. O'Hara for Walsh, B. Fitzpatrick (0–1) for H. Ryan.

Referee: Terence Murray (Limerick)

Attendance: 28,000

66. Tipp, Tipp Hooray!

1987 MUNSTER FINAL REPLAY (Fitzgerald Stadium, 19 July)
Tipperary 4–22 Cork 1–22 (after extra-time)

'We grew up with an inferiority complex as regards Cork.'
Richie Stakelum[1]

NEAR THE END of the 1987 Munster final replay, Donie O'Connell ended up in a heap in the Cork goal but the ball was there too and the score stood. Tipperary's fourth green flag was a mere embellishment – they had already ensured victory through a two-goal blast from Michael Doyle – but it was the goal that really sparked the celebrations. It pushed Tipperary nine points clear and even those of more fatalistic disposition, wounded by repeated failure and haunted by the trauma of Thurles in 1984, knew there was no way back for their fierce rivals.

Supporters came onto the field, wild with delight. Some clambered on top of O'Connell, others danced in giddy triumph on the ground where, 16 years earlier, Tipperary had won their last Munster senior title. Their famine – which Richie Stakelum would memorably declare over in his acceptance speech afterwards – is one of hurling's most intriguing. Tipp didn't just stop winning All-Irelands over that barren period after 1971, they stopped winning Munster titles. They didn't just stop winning Munster titles, they stopped reaching Munster finals. A hurling county that had struck fear in the hearts of opponents in the 1960s somehow became ordinary and everyday.

The hands of the giants of old were all over subsequent

attempts to climb back up the ladder. Tony Wall had a go at management. Len Gaynor was involved too. And then along came the ebullient Babs Keating whose view of Tipperary seemed brazenly unreconstructed. His belief in Tipperary was unshakable and while the talent at his disposal was obvious, his conviction appeared to make the difference.

Tipperary's win over Cork in 1987 is a pivotal moment in their long and storied rivalry. Cork, chasing a record sixth Munster title in a row, were favourites, but in extra-time their power and authority finally wilted under the great will and desire of the Premier County. After coming on as a sub in extra-time Doyle's two goals were lethal blows to the champions, driving a clear gap between two sides that had been inseparable for 160 minutes.

What relief for a county that had lived in the shadow of the great sides of the 1960s and early 1970s. By 1987, Theo English of the all-conquering side of the 1960s was 20 years retired and now joined Keating and Donie Nealon, another 1960s legend, as a selector. Tipp began the year in Division 2 and ended it Munster champions. Heads were in a spin. It marked the end of their longest period in the wilderness.

Speaking about the final, Richie Stakelum, Tipp's captain on the day, said:

> What I found very interesting is that while a lot of those players went on to win more Munster titles and All-Irelands, many cite that as the greatest buzz they ever got. Maybe it was because it was in Killarney, maybe because it was Cork, or the extra-time, I don't know.[2]

Stakelum had noble breeding. His uncle Pat had captained the team that had won the 1949 All-Ireland, the prequel to the most intense spell of conflict between Cork and Tipp. His first cousins, Bobby and Aidan Ryan, also hurled on the team of 1987. He'd been reared on stories of better times.

We grew up with an inferiority complex as regards Cork. That's why it took so long to win in 1987; we were looking over our shoulders all the time, you needed to be a lot better than Cork to beat them.[3]

Tipperary had lost the centenary Munster final to a late Cork rally, taken a sound beating the following year and blew a commanding lead in the drawn final in Thurles in 1987. 'Cork flew into an early lead in the replay and the first half was as people had predicted,' recalled Stakelum. 'The masters would now take control.'[4]

And that is how it looked. Cork, fortunate to escape on the first Sunday, began the replay imperiously. Tipperary were nervous and error-ridden in comparison. In the drawn match, Tipperary had led for 67 minutes and were the better team but had still needed a late score to earn a replay. Cork had struck late with a goal from Kieran Kingston and a point from John Fenton. Kingston's goal had given them the lead for the first time, three minutes from the end, and Fenton's point put them two up. Pat Fox rescued Tipp with two frees. The picture had looked much different when a goal from Nicky English put Tipp seven up 15 minutes into the second half, English kicking to the net after losing his hurl.

If the first day looked hard to surpass, the replay managed to raise the bar even higher, though you wouldn't have thought so in the opening 25 minutes. Cork took off at a blistering pace and went into a five-point lead after 10 minutes. Aidan Ryan scored Tipp's first point from play after 22 minutes. Undeterred, Tomás Mulcahy sent over a huge score in response: 0–8 to 0–2.

Kingston had a goal attempt saved by Ken Hogan and then, out of nothing, came a goal from English, hitting the ball off his stick on the turn, a great strike against the run of play in the 26th minute, reducing the difference to two points, 0–8 to 1–3. Again, Cork responded, with Mulcahy scoring a goal from an acute angle. By half-time, they were 1–10 to 1–5 clear.

Gradually Tipp improved and the match, though a slow-burner, found an intensity to match expectations. With Fenton striking immaculately, Cork opened a six-point lead again early in the second half, but Tipp were making a deeper impact and began to eat into the lead. With 12 minutes left, Fox scored from play to level at 1–14 apiece and a great roar rose around the ground.

From here to the end of normal time, the play was energy-sapping. Teddy McCarthy made a huge leap and fetch, and his drive was finished to the net by Tony O'Sullivan but the umpires harshly ruled a square ball. Back came Cork, McCarthy winning another ball and delivering it forward and O'Sullivan snapping it up and pointing. Ten minutes to go and Cork were up by one again. Martin McGrath, a Tipp sub, got a second score from distance to level at 1–15 apiece. Fenton's third 65 restored Cork's lead. Another score from McGrath, a lovely score on the spin, left them deadlocked once more. Fox put one wide. Fenton pointed a free won by the lion-hearted McCarthy, Fenton's ninth. Just over four minutes to go and Cork were ahead by one. With a minute left on the clock, Paul Delaney missed a 65 and Cork might have escaped.

Twice before – in 1905 and 1979 – the Munster six-in-a-row had eluded Cork. Seconds left and Ger Canning, the match commentator, asked if Cork were on the threshold of history. Then, a stunning end. English ran on to a huge Ken Hogan puckout, lifted the ball with incredible speed and, pursued feverishly by Corkmen, elected to hand pass over the bar. An unforgettable score. From Cunningham's puckout, the whistle sounded, the teams were deadlocked, 1–17 apiece. The crowd applauded in warm appreciation and prepared for extra-time.

'The whole team would be wound up when they'd be meeting Cork,' recalled Theo English in 2005 of this famous rivalry. 'The minute the ball was thrown in, sure, there'd be hurleys flying. They'd be sorting out the men from the boys. It's whoever comes out then, or dies in the battle as the fella says.'[5]

The teams re-emerged for extra-time and whatever Fate would ordain. By the end of the first period, Cork led 1–21 to 1–20. Then, early in the final period, Fox levelled from a free, followed by a startling sight – Fenton put a free wide, his first miss of the day. By now, he was up front, tired and not fully fit, a leg heavily strapped. It seemed a portent of things to come. Soon O'Connell was tearing on to a loose ball and scoring, putting Tipp ahead for the first time. Doyle's first goal widened the gap. A free from Fenton reduced Tipp's lead to a goal with eight minutes to go, but Cork looked beaten.

Confirmation of their demise came quickly. Nicky English nicked the ball off Richard Browne who was coming clear and Pat Fitzelle cleverly sent it immediately back inside to Doyle, all alone, who scored a second goal. That was it, even with six minutes left.

Fenton went for goal from a 20-metre free, which was saved, and then O'Connell scored the fourth goal and Tipp's celebrations began in earnest. Tipp, with an average age of 23, looked to the future with renewed optimism.

The game marked the end of Fenton's county career, which had seen him win five successive All Stars at midfield up to 1987. In his final summer, he scored one of the most breath-taking goals ever seen in hurling, whipping a ball off the ground first-time to the net from 45 yards against Limerick in the Munster championship. He'd had the honour of being captain of Cork when they won the centenary All-Ireland in 1984 and was later named Hurler of the Year. He bowed out in Killarney in defeat, but still at the top of his game.

TIPPERARY: K. Hogan; J. Heffernan, C. O'Donovan, S. Gibson; R. Stakelum, J. Kennedy, P. Delaney (0–2, 65s); C. Bonner, P. Fitzelle (0–1); G. Williams, D. O'Connell (1–1), A. Ryan (0–3); P. Fox (0–11, 7fs), N. English (1–1), B. Ryan; Subs: (normal time) M. McGrath (0–3) for G. Williams (27 mins); (extra-time) M. Doyle (2–0) for P. Delaney (11), G. Stapleton for C. O'Donovan (25).

CORK: G. Cunningham; D. Mulcahy, R. Browne, J. Crowley; J. Cashman, P. Hartnett, D. Walsh; J. Fenton (0–13, 0–3 65s, 10fs), T. Cashman; M. Mullins, T. McCarthy (0–3), T. O'Sullivan (0–3); K. Kingston, K. Hennessy, T. Mulcahy (1–2); Subs: (normal time) G. Fitzgerald (0–1) for M. Mullins (48 mins), P. O'Connor for T. Cashman (65), J. Fitzgibbon for K. Kingston (66); (extra-time) S. O'Gorman for J. Cashman (at start), M. Mullins for J. Fitzgibbon (7), D. McCurtain for J. Crowley (26).

Referee: T. Murray (Limerick)

Attendance: 45,000

67. The Hunger Games

1987 ALL-IRELAND FINAL (Croke Park, 6 September)
Galway 1–12 Kilkenny 0–9

All this Galway team requires is the single-mindedness and self-possession to match the skill they have inherited from the generations who kept the game alive during the hungry years.
Breandán Ó hEithir[1]

BREANDÁN Ó hEITHIR, a native of the Aran Islands, knew all about the hungry years of Galway hurling. As a young man in the 1940s, he had cycled to Ennis and Birr and returned home despondent after Galway teams had repeatedly buckled within sight of the finishing line in tight games against Kilkenny and Cork. The 1987 victory must, then, have been immensely satisfying for Ó hEithir and his contemporaries – 1980 had been the glorious release from the 56-year sentence in the hurling house of pain, but this was the day Galway came of age by beating one of the traditional powers in a final that was more a battle of wills than a test of sporting prowess.

The 1987 final marked the centenary of the first All-Ireland hurling championship and while 13 counties had won titles since 1887, Cork (26), Kilkenny (23) and Tipperary (22) had amassed 71 wins between them. Leaving aside the titles won in the 1920s by countrymen moonlighting as Dubs, only Limerick in the 1930s and Wexford in the 1950s had offered sustained resistance to the big three, who remain the measure of the chasing pack's ambitions. In the elitist hierarchy of hurling, a county isn't considered to have truly arrived until it has beaten one of them in an All-Ireland final. That's why there had been some low-level sniping from some quarters about Galway's win in 1980. It was lovely to see the poor oul' divils finally win one, but beating Offaly and Limerick hardly constituted a 'real' All-Ireland.

Most of the Galway players in 1987 were still so young that they probably weren't even aware of this consideration. In any case, they had a far more pressing motivation. After losing the previous two All-Ireland finals to Offaly and Cork, they were at risk of being branded hurling Fancy Dans if they failed again and became the first team to lose three successive finals. Nine of the Kilkenny team they faced had won All-Ireland medals in 1983 and some of them were multiple medallists, but the Leinster champions also had an unusually intense motivation. Losing the 1986 semi-final to Galway by 13 points was considered a stain on the county's honour that could be swiftly erased by victory in this decider.

'They came back with virtually the same 15, as if to say: "Last year was a freak, let's settle it this time,"' wrote Cyril Farrell in his autobiography. 'We had played them in a challenge game earlier that summer and I knew for a fact that they were not impressed by us. Word filtered back to me that they were convinced they had been the victims of a freak in 1986 and that they felt there was no chance that we would beat them again. Frankly, I think they saw us as chokers.'[2]

Galway had almost 'choked' against Clare in the 1987 league final in Thurles where Gerry McInerney miscued a late opportunity that could have produced a winning goal for the Banner. Galway won by 3–12 to 3–10 to break a losing sequence in finals that had also included the 1986 league decider against Kilkenny. After that, they cut loose against Tipperary in one of the most celebrated of All-Ireland semi-finals. There had been an almost carnival atmosphere for that game which was played on a fast sod in the sun. Galway had been hoping for another fine day to unleash their high-tempo game-plan, but it rained heavily in Dublin the night before the final and the day itself was wet and grey. A sustained blast of thunder and lightning would have been appropriate for the battle that ensued.

For once, the statistics really do tell most of the tale. Galway led by 0–5 to 0–4 at half-time after both defences had dug in for what old-timers would have described as a teak-tough, hard-hitting encounter. Kilkenny centre-back Ger Henderson played on, despite having his hand split by an accidental pull from Joe Cooney when the duo were contesting a high ball. Gerry McInenery and Steve Mahon were influential figures for Galway in the middle third, where Tony Keady policed the red-headed giant Christy Heffernan who had scored 2–3 in the 1982 final against Cork.

Kilkenny only scored three points from play in the 70 minutes and their six starting forwards managed just one point from play – Ger Fennelly kept them in the game with six points from frees. The Leinster champions badly missed the dead-eye accuracy of Billy Fitzpatrick who had retired after the 1986 semi. Harry Ryan was now their main scoring threat and if it hadn't been for the 2–5 he posted in the All-Ireland semi-final against Antrim played in Dundalk, Kilkenny could well have suffered their most sensational defeat since the 1943 All-Ireland defeat in Belfast. Kilkenny got out of Dundalk with a 2–18 to 2–11 win, but had only taken the lead in the 64th minute before tacking on six points without reply.

Not even Ryan, though, could make headway against the Galway full-back line of Ollie Kilkenny and the well-seasoned Conor Hayes and Sylvie Linnane who got the better of a fiery personal battle with the equally combative Ryan. Hayes managed to keep the other Kilkenny dangerman Liam Fennelly scoreless. Some Kilkenny people maintain the game turned midway through the second half when Fennelly slipped Hayes only to see John Commins block his hand-passed effort for goal – one of several fine saves from Commins. The deciding goal came at the other end in the 62nd minute when Noel Lane finished off a move begun by a powerful Joe Cooney solo-run. In keeping with the tension of the day, Lane's shot just about trickled over the line after Kevin

Fennelly – one of the four Ballyhale brothers who started the final – got a half-block on it.

The bulk of Kilkenny's players were in their late 20s to early 30s and they wilted in the closing minutes against a much younger Galway side. Twenty-three-year-old centre-back Tony Keady had the last score, a mood-lifting 80-yard point from play. He was flanked by 22-year-old Gerry McInenery, not long back from America, who was later that night named RTÉ Man of the Match.

The good times were set to roll for Galway, while the earlier victory of a golden generation of Offaly minors over Tipperary raised hopes that the second century of the championship would fork off, for a few years at least, on a different direction to the first. Success for the Offaly minors, Breandán Ó hEithir had written in his *Irish Independent* essay, 'would be a hopeful sign that hurling is about to break out of the corral in which that great enemy of progress, sentimental tradition, has kept it for far too long'.[3]

GALWAY: J. Commins; S. Linnane, C. Hayes (capt), O. Kilkenny; P. Finnerty, T. Keady (0–2, 0–1 65), G. McInerney; S. Mahon (0–2), P. Malone; M. McGrath (0–1), J. Cooney (0–5, frees), M. Naughton (0–1); E. Ryan, B. Lynskey, A. Cunningham (0–1); Subs: N. Lane (40) (1–0) for M. Naughton, P.J. Molloy for A. Cunningham, T. Kilkenny for M. McGrath.

KILKENNY: K. Fennelly; J. Hennessy, P. Prendergast (capt), J. Henderson; L. Walsh, G. Henderson, S. Fennelly; G. Fennelly (0–7, 6fs), L. Ryan; K. Brennan, C. Heffernan, R Power; P. Walsh, L. Fennelly, H. Ryan (0–1); Subs: T. Lennon (0–1) for P. Walsh, L. McCarthy for R. Power.

Referee: T. Murray (Limerick)

Attendance: 65,586

68. Tale of the Unexpected

1989 ALL-IRELAND SEMI-FINAL (Croke Park, 6 August)
Antrim 4–15 Offaly 1–15

Some lads had booked holidays and had to cancel.
Terence 'Sambo' McNaughton[1]

NOBODY – INCLUDING THE Antrim hurlers – anticipated this outcome to the 1989 All-Ireland semi-final. Their team captain, Ciaran Barr, had planned his wedding the day before they played Tipperary in the All-Ireland final, never considering, seriously at any rate, the possibility of walking up the aisle on Saturday and out the tunnel in Croke Park on Sunday.

'Looking back at it, our captain away getting married was probably not the best preparation, we were naive, lambs to the slaughter to be honest,' said Terence McNaughton.[2] Neither McNaughton nor any of the rest of the team attended Barr's big day. As for the win over Offaly, McNaughton felt it was no fluke.

> It always annoys me that people see it as a one-hit wonder. We had been knocking at the door for five, six or seven years. I felt if we had beaten Kilkenny in the semi-final in 1987 we would have been more ready to play the final in 1989.

The final ended in an 18-point defeat but to qualify was a major landmark for hurling in Antrim. In areas around the Glens, the game is cherished as fervently as it is in any of the blueblood strongholds down south.

An Antrim team had last reached a senior final in 1943, when

Kilkenny had been stunned in the semi-final at Corrigan Park in Belfast, Galway falling the round before that.

In the final 10 minutes, Antrim seized the moment. They abandoned the old default position of failure and cut loose with relish and soaring confidence, tearing the Offaly backline to pieces. A young Brian Whelahan, who would go on to captain the Offaly minors in their All-Ireland triumph the following month, came on late in the match, heralding the dawn of a new generation for the Faithful County after their run of success in the 1980s. At the end, shocked as they may have been, they memorably formed a guard of honour and clapped Antrim's hurlers off the field.

As a sporting gesture, it completed a perfect day that had been rich in novelty and drama, and yet the form Antrim had been showing should not have been readily dismissed. There had been few signposts of intent along the way. In 1986, the eventual All-Ireland champions Cork had been given plenty of it by the Saffrons in their semi-final, before advancing on a scoreline of 7–11 to 1–24. The following year, Kilkenny had met some of the same tough resistance in the semi-final at Dundalk before prevailing 2–18 to 2–11. In 1988, it had been Tipperary's turn; they'd won 3–15 to 2–10 after another trying contest. In the National League, Antrim had been promoted to Division 1 and were holding their own.

On the ground, the game in Antrim was in decent health. In 1989, O'Donovan Rossa in Belfast reached the All-Ireland club final, denied a famous victory by Buffer's Alley. Six years earlier, Loughgiel Shamrocks had made history by becoming the first Antrim club, indeed the first Ulster club, to win an All-Ireland senior title when they defeated Offaly's St Rynaghs in the final after a replay. The Antrim goalkeeper in 1989, Niall Patterson, was part of that success.

In 1989, the Ulster championship was revived after a long lapse that went back to 1946. But the competition has gone into decline again and has become increasingly peripheral. Antrim's dominance is now total, and they have won every title since 2002, but the value of the championship to Antrim has waned considerably. That has largely been down to their move into Leinster in recent years, with the high point being a 2010 win over Dublin that saw them contest, impressively, an All-Ireland quarter-final against Cork. Playing in an All-Ireland final now looks as remote a possibility as ever.

In 1989, they didn't look set to reach the final either as Offaly made a confident start. Fourteen minutes into the match, they were 0–5 to 0–1 clear and led 0–7 to 0–4 after 20 minutes. An Aidan McCarry penalty goal fuelled Antrim hopes, but it was short-lived; inside a minute, Vincent Teehan had goaled after Patterson had batted down a Joachim Kelly centre. Offaly were 1–10 to 1–6 up at the break. But for 13 wides, they would have been further ahead.

Thirteen minutes into the second half came a crucial twist. With Offaly two points ahead. Olcan McFetridge, a junior club hurler and deadly predator popularly known as 'Klute', hit the net. Antrim were in front and, this time, they consolidated it with points from McCarry and McFetridge. Another goal from McFetridge put more daylight between the teams with half an hour played in the half. Five points divided them. Pat Delaney reduced it to four from a free, but then Antrim goaled again, McCarry this time, before Dom McKinley rounded off the scoring with a point. On the day of the final, Sambo McNaughton noticed they were taking part in a parade in Croke Park for the first time. They had another slow start only this time they did not recover.

We were so naive it was unbelievable some of the things that were going on. For the first time in our lives, [television] cameras were at our training sessions; we all got carried away. Before, we couldn't get a cup of tea, next thing we were getting jackets. It was all crazy stuff. We forgot about the match. [Ciaran] Barr's wedding was only one aspect of a lot of naivety. See, the last Antrim team to play in an All-Ireland final was during the war. We had nothing to compare it to.[3]

No Antrim county team has reached an All-Ireland senior final since 1989. No Antrim team has played in a senior semi-final since 1996. 'You have to have hope,' says McNaughton. 'You have to aspire. That is what it is all about.'[4]

ANTRIM: N. Patterson; G. O'Kane, T. Donnelly, D. Donnelly; J. McNaughton, D. McKinley (0–1), L. McKeegan; P. McKillen (0–1, f), D. McMullen; B. Donnelly (0–1), A. McCarry (2–4, 1–0 pen, 1f), O. McFetridge (2–3, 1f); D. Armstrong (0–2), C. Barr (0–1), T. McNaughton (0–2); Sub: D. McNaughton for D. McMullen (58 mins).

OFFALY: J. Troy; A. Fogarty, E. Coughlan, M. Hanamy; R. Mannion (0–1), P. Delaney (0–3, 0–2 65s, 1f), G. Coughlan; J. Kelly (0–1), J. Pilkington (0–1); J. Dooley (0–3), D. Regan (0–2), M. Corrigan (0–3, 2fs); V. Teehan (1–0), M. Duignan, D. Pilkington (0–1); Subs: P. Corrigan for V. Teehan (43), D. Owens for M. Corrigan (53), B. Whelahan for D. Pilkington.

Referee: T. Murray (Limerick)

Attendance: 64,127

The match was part of a double-header along with the other semi-final between Galway and Tipperary.

69. Winner Takes All

1989 ALL-IRELAND SEMI-FINAL (Croke Park, 6 August)
Tipperary 1–17 Galway 2–11

The importance of this game is almost frightening. A victory would take much of the sting away from the previous losses and put us well in line of the national title; a defeat would positively stamp us irretrievably inferior [to Galway] and prove that closeness is our utmost in this particular confrontation.
Culbaire, *Tipperary Star* (July 1989)

IT SHOULD HAVE been the hurling showdown of the decade; instead, the 1989 All-Ireland semi-final descended into a snarling grudge match between counties pursuing agendas that reflected how much the hurling landscape shifted during the 1980s. Having won three titles from six All-Ireland final appearances in nine years, Galway were the team of the decade and were chasing greatness in the form of a three-in-a-row. In a complete reversal of the traditional roles, Tipperary were the desperadoes and under incredible pressure from their supporters, craving a first All-Ireland title in 18 years.

The last thing Tipp had anticipated when they ended their Munster title 'famine' in 1987 was that a maroon-and-white roadblock would impede the path to the Liam MacCarthy, but, over the next two years, they failed to get past Galway in three attempts at Croke Park. The first clash, the free-wheeling 1987 semi-final, was, in pure hurling terms, one of the games of the decade. It was the age of innocence in the teams' rivalry as Galway came with a late flourish and a Noel Lane goal to win by 3–20 to 2–17. The second, the 1988 All-Ireland final, was a grittier affair – Galway edging it by 1–15 to 0–14 after setting the pace and again finishing the stronger side with another late goal from Lane. The 1989 league final saw Galway maintain the whip-hand, winning a thriller, albeit one with a slight air of shadow-boxing, by 2–16 to 4–8.

Against that backdrop, Culbaire, the *Tipperary Star*'s columnist, wasn't exaggerating the significance of the 1989 All-Ireland semi-final. Another demoralising defeat to Galway could have halted the entire blue-and-gold revival project for a few years. Winning Munster for three years in a row without adding at least one All-Ireland would have constituted failure. Heads – both management and players – would have rolled.

There was another element to Galway's hoodoo over Tipp. They had beaten them in the 1978 and 1983 All-Ireland under-21 finals and a dozen players, six for each team, from the 1983 final figured in the 1989 showdown. Ken Hogan, Colm Bonnar, Nicky English, Joe Hayes, Conor O'Donovan and John Kennedy had come through for Tipp. In the maroon corner, there was Peter Finnerty, Ollie Kilkenny, Michael Coleman, Michael McGrath, Gerry Burke and Eanna Ryan. It should have been seven, only for Tony Keady's misadventures in New York.

No matter which angle you approach the 1989 semi-final from, there's no escaping the 'Keady Affair'. To this day, Galway supporters insist the three-in-a-row would have been won if Keady, the 1988 Texaco Hurler of the Year and Man of the Match in the 1988 final, had played in 1989. Instead, he sat the game out in the dugout.

After Galway had toured America with the All Stars in May, Keady had stayed behind in New York where he kept his eye in by training with the Laois club managed by a Galway man. He made a fatal mistake by playing for Laois as 'Bernard Keady' in a New York championship game against the Tipperary club. The false name indicates that the paperwork wasn't in order and Keady had his reservations about playing, only making up his mind when he got to the ground:

> Anyway, I went down to the pitch with my gear. I'll never forget it. I
> was standing in a corner, only 30 or 40 yards from the dressing rooms.
> The next thing, one of the doors opened and out came a blue-and-gold
> jersey. Sure 'twas like a red rag to a bull. I think I had my boots, togs
> and helmet on before I even got to the dressing-room door. That's what
> the sight of the Tipp jersey did to me.[1]

Laois won well, but Tipperary club officials objected. The New York board upheld the objection and suspended Keady and two other Galway illegals for two games. That should have been the end of it until the Games Administration Committee in Croke Park got involved. Keady was suspended for a year over breaches of rules governing transfers and playing in New York. The decision caused outrage in Galway and beyond as the GAA was accused of making an example of Keady for their clampdown on the trans-Atlantic movement of players. The controversy rumbled on, only ending the week before the semi-final when an appeal to Central Council was defeated by 20 votes to 18. Some of the Connacht delegates voted against Galway who were convinced Keady's suspension was part of a plot by the GAA and the traditional hurling powers to 'put manners' on Galway.

Tipperary did the honourable thing by pleading on Keady's behalf. If they were going to beat Galway, they didn't want their victory tainted.

> The county's representative was instructed to vote in favour of
> reinstatement and county secretary Tommy Barrett not alone voted
> for reinstatement, but argued it with such force that he was publicly
> thanked by the Galway hurling board secretary and team selector
> Phelim Murphy. Tipp had done all it could.[2]

Galway then threatened to withdraw from the championship altogether. Little wonder that the players looked jittery and distracted in the pre-match parade in front of a full house in Croke Park, still buzzing after Antrim's shock win over Offaly in the first semi-final. Tipperary, by contrast, marched with a purposeful, martial bearing. They appeared far more attuned for battle in what was the de facto 1989 All-Ireland final.

Eanna Ryan scrambled an opportunistic goal for Galway after 40 seconds, but Tipp looked the sharper and possibly fitter team in the first half. Sean Treacy, Keady's replacement, played a fine game at Number 6, but Pat Fox and Nicky English, Tipp's most influential forwards, were winning their battles against Conor Hayes and Sylvie Linnane, who had repeatedly frustrated them in the 1988 final. John Leahy, a spiky 19-year-old newcomer, seemed on a mission to stop Galway's dynamic wing-back Peter Finnerty from hurling and the Mullinahone man escaped without even a caution for a wild pull across Finnerty in the early exchanges.

Eanna Ryan, who was shaping up as Galway's liveliest forward, was also felled in an off-the-ball incident that went unpunished. These were two of the bad calls made by referee John Denton who was slated by neutral analysts for his performance. 'He blew up for fouls which no one but himself saw, ignored blatant fouls and made other decisions which were totally baffling,' wrote Donal Keenan in his match report in the *Irish Independent*.

Galway didn't help their cause by overreacting and losing their discipline. They were down to 13 men by the final whistle and had five more players booked. Tipperary escaped with five bookings.

Joe Cooney missed the target in the 18th minute from a free that he would normally have converted without a second glance at the posts. That miss reflected how rattled Galway were. By then, Tipp led 0–8 to 1–1, the Galway point coming from a Sean Treacy free. It was 0–11 to 1–3 approaching half-time before Eanna Ryan poached another goal against the run of the play. He was the only Galway forward to score in the first half with the champions badly missing the influence of the injured Noel Lane, Martin Naughton and Anthony Cunningham.

Cooney had made little impact at full-forward against Conor O'Donovan, but he drew a great save from Ken Hogan just after half-time. Two minutes later, Fox cut through the Galway defence to score a rousing goal for Tipp who were awarded a penalty in the 42nd minute for an apparent foul by Linnane on English. Leahy missed from two attempts.

Four minutes later, Linnane was sent off after English went to ground. Galway played their best hurling in the period between Linnane's sending off and Michael McGrath's dismissal 10 minutes from time for a wild charge on O'Donovan. Cooney opened up when switched to midfield alongside Coleman who, along with Ryan and Treacy, had done much to keep Galway in the game. Tipperary were the jittery looking team by then and it was 1–15 to 2–9 before McGrath got the line. It was 1–16 to 2–11 with three minutes left after Cooney had gone very close to threading a pass through to Ryan for a possible shot on goal.

Tipperary held on to the three-point lead and 'narrowly avoided the catastrophe of losing to 13 men which would have made the county a laughing stock. And there was, too, a feeling that perhaps a couple of the Tipp players while not meriting marching orders might on the day have contributed towards the bad feeling which destroyed the game,' wrote the Tipperary hurling historian Seamus Leahy.[3]

How would it have ended if Keady had played? It can be argued that Tipperary had been catching up on Galway anyway, the margin of defeat reducing from six in 1987 to four in 1988 and two in the 1989 league final. They were close to their prime, whereas time and injuries were taking a toll on some of Galway's key men. Would Keady's sojourn in New York have blunted his edge against opponents who had trained as never before? Or would the sight of the blue-and-gold jersey have inspired another one of his bravura displays that sent confidence surging through the Galway team? Who knows.

One telling postscript to the game came when a man, who

identified himself as the chairman of the New York Tipperary club, appeared outside the Tipp dressing room in Croke Park. 'He was approached by the county chairman Noel Morris and told he was not welcome.'[4]

TIPPERARY: K. Hogan; J. Heffernan, C. O'Donovan, N. Sheehy; C. Bonnar, B. Ryan, P. Delaney (0–3 fs); D. Carr, D. Ryan (0–1); M. Cleary (0–1) J. Hayes, J. Leahy; P. Fox (1–2), C. Bonnar (0–2), N. English (0–8, 3fs); Subs: J. Cormac for J. Hayes, J. Kennedy for P. Delaney, C. Bonnar for C. O'Donovan.

GALWAY: J. Commins; S. Linnane, C. Hayes, O. Kilkeny; P. Finnerty, S. Treacy (0–1 f), G. McInerney; P. Malone, M. Coleman (0–1); M. McGrath (0–3), B. Lynskey, R. Duane; G. Burke (0–2), J. Cooney (0–3, 1f), E. Ryan (2–1); Subs: A. Cunningham for R. Duane, P. Nolan for G. Burke.

Referee: John Denton (Wexford)

Attendance: 64,127

The match was part of a double-header along with the other semi-final between Antrim and Offaly.

70. A Rare Vintage

1989 ALL-IRELAND UNDER-21 FINAL (O'Moore Park, 10 September)

Tipperary 4–10 Offaly 3–11

We played in great games over the years. In Cork and Thurles against Cork. Great games against Galway in Ennis and Limerick. Of all the games this is the one that stands out.

Danny Morrissey[1]

HOW MANY PEOPLE attended this classic in Portlaoise? Nobody knows for sure, but it seems safe to say that the crowd descending on the midlands town well exceeded 30,000. The hordes filing into O'Moore Park caused chronic traffic congestion and a throw-in delay of 10 minutes but they witnessed an exceptional contest. In the annals of under-21 hurling, this may stand supreme.

Jack Nolan, the Laois PRO of the time, was involved in producing the match programme.

> We usually sold one to every three people, that was the ratio, and we had 10,000 ready. They were sold 10 or 15 minutes before the game started. We could have sold a lot more.[2]

By that measure, there were at least 30,000 present but the true number was probably closer to the capacity at the time of 35,000. The official attendance given was a laughable 18,000 – apparently because all the turnstiles didn't have counters installed. At the very least, the crowd set a new record for an under-21 hurling final, and it is likely that it is the highest of all time: greater than the 31,415 who attended the second of Limerick's three All-Ireland wins in a row, against Wexford in Thurles in 2001.[3]

The game had major crowd-pulling appeal. 'Offaly had a huge following,' says Michael Duignan, their under-21 captain in 1989. 'We played Kilkenny twice in Portlaoise in the Leinster minor championship in 1986, and played Dublin and Wexford and there were massive crowds following the team. Suddenly, you had all these young players and it was a swashbuckling kind of a team with great skill. They captured the imagination. There was no dirt, it was just pure hurling.'[4]

A week earlier, Tipperary had won the All-Ireland senior title, their first since 1971, and three players from that senior team – Declan Ryan, John Leahy and Conal Bonnar – were now seeking an under-21 title, their first since completing the under-21 three-in-a-row (1979–1981). Future senior players and management figures, like Liam Sheedy, Michael Ryan and George Frend, were also on the team, but Offaly were just as star-studded, having won the All-Ireland minor title three years earlier.

The Offaly team captained by Duignan featured an impressive spread of talent, including four of the minor team – Brian Whelahan, Johnny Dooley, John Troy and Adrian Cahill – who had won the All-Ireland a week earlier. The mainstay of the team were the graduates of Offaly's first All-Ireland minor-winning team of 1986, and there were also hurlers from the team that had retained the minor title in 1987. Other illustrious names included Johnny Pilkington, Declan Pilkington, Daithi Regan and Billy Dooley. Ten of those who played for Offaly in the 1989 All-Ireland under-21 final would go on to win senior All-Ireland medals in the next decade. Joe Errity would have played but for injury and Shane McGuckin could not get on the team. Even Tipperary would concede they were up against it; even Tipperary would admit they were lucky to win an absorbing match.

In 2011, Duignan described losing the 1989 under-21 final as the biggest disappointment of his career, and argued that it delayed

Offaly's re-emergence as a force in senior hurling. In his book, *Life, Death & Hurling*, he also took issue with the victory speech made by Declan Ryan. He said it smacked of 'that brand of arrogance that Tipp have been famed and disdained for ... In a sneer at the fact that we had lost to Antrim in the senior semi-final he said, "I'd like to thank Antrim for the game ... oh, sorry, I mean Offaly."'[5]

The Tipperary selector Danny Morrissey said he was shocked to hear Duignan's views.

> There isn't an ounce of arrogance in Declan Ryan. It was a major achievement for us to have beaten Offaly. I was surprised, it sounded more like sour grapes.[6]

More recently, Duignan appears to have softened his line and believes it was not in Ryan's nature to be malicious and that the delivery was probably nothing more than a clumsy attempt at a joke. 'I don't think it would be his form. We were only young lads.'[7]

Morrissey had served with manager Mick Minogue when Tipp won three All-Ireland under-21 titles in succession from 1979 to 1981. They were installed as the senior management team for one year, 1982, looking after senior and under-21 simultaneously, but drew Cork in Cork and with a young side they were out in the first round. They weren't given a second chance.

In 1989, they were brought back as the county's under-21 management team. Tipperary had been the first All-Ireland under-21 champions in 1964, in a team that featured Mick Roche, but success at the grade had dried up. 'When we came in for 1978 we had only one All-Ireland in those intervening years,' says Morrissey. That management group remained more or less intact until 1985, before being recalled in 1989.

They needed a long-range score from Declan Ryan to gain a draw early in the campaign against Cork, and won the replay in Thurles. Kerry fell in the semi-finals and Limerick were easily dismissed in the Munster final, before they got past Galway in a match made edgy by the intense rivalry that existed at senior level at the time.

Dan Quirke, a full-forward from Clonoulty-Rossmore, scored 3–2 to become an unlikely hero. He never played championship for the Tipp senior team, but his contribution to the under-21 side was immense and he destroyed Offaly's hopes, all three of his goals coming in the first half.

Offaly led by seven points after 17 minutes, Billy Dooley scoring their second goal to leave them 2–3 to 0–2 up. Declan Pilkington had banged in their first. But with Quirke finding the net, Tipperary stormed back to level at 2–4 to 1–7 by the 24th minute. They upped the tempo even more before the break and went in at half-time 3–7 to 2–4 ahead. They strengthened their hand when a penalty from Michael Nolan left them 4–8 to 2–8 clear 12 minutes into the second half.

That lit a huge resistance fire in Offaly. Johnny Dooley landed a free, a sideline from Johnny Pilkington roused huge cheers and the ground shook when Daithi Regan scored a goal. They drew level at 4–8 to 3–11. The sending off of the full-back Damien Geoghegan was also a blow to Offaly, but they were still pressing hard at the last whistle. Tipp responded with two points to lead with time almost up. Then Offaly launched a final frantic bid to save the day. Declan Pilkington created a goal chance for Regan but he put it wide. Another chance from a 21-yard free from Roy Mannion was deflected out for a 65 which was dropped in and cleared and the whistle sounded.

'By and large we found that fellas who were on the senior panel they really enjoyed the under-21 scenario, there was less pressure and more pleasure, they loved it I must say,' says Morrissey. 'When I meet these guys they often recall the fun and the carefree time we had at under-21 level. We always thought under-21 did not have the same physical intensity and for that reason it was probably more free-flowing.'[8]

In 2010, they had a reunion and remembered their team-mate Seamus Maher, the wing-back from Thurles Sarsfields, who died in an accident in Doolin, County Clare, in 2001. 'He was a real gentleman,' says Morrissey. 'He might have been captain as Sarsfields were club under-21 champions, but we wanted Declan Ryan to captain the team and Seamus was very gracious about it.'[9]

His last thoughts on the match?

We were playing a team that on paper was a better side, we were struggling a bit throughout the game but our determination kept us in it. Dan Quirke's goals kept us in front long enough but it was a hectic finish. When they got that 21-yard free, I turned my back; I couldn't look.[10]

Duignan had his eyes firmly fixed on what took place. 'Mannion hit Michael Ryan on the shoulder, Mick never saw it I'd say. He mightn't admit that!'[11]

TIPPERARY: B. Bane; L. Sheedy (0–1 f), M. Ryan, G. Frend; J. Madden, C. Bonnar, S. Maher; J. Leahy (0–1 f), Declan Ryan; P. Hogan (0–1), C. Stakelum (0–3), Dinny Ryan (0–1); M. Nolan (1–1, 1–0 pen), D. Quirke (3–2), T. Lanigan; Subs: J. Cahill for S. Maher (19 mins), D. Lyons for T. Lanigan (44), K. Ryan for J. Cahill (55).

OFFALY: J. Troy; B. Whelahan (0–1, 70), D. Geoghegan, B. Hennessy; R. Mannion, B. Kelly, G. Cahill (0–1); J. Pilkington (0–2), A. Cahill; B. Dooley (1–0), D. Regan (1–2), J. Dooley (0–5, 3fs); R. Byrne, D. Pilkington (1–0), M. Duignan; Sub: J. Kilmartin for R. Byrne (44 mins).

Referee: P. Long (Kilkenny)

Attendance: 18,000 (official figure)

71. Donkeys and Derbies

1990 MUNSTER FINAL (Semple Stadium, 15 July)

Cork 4–16 Tipperary 2–14

People around Cork have already resigned themselves to Tipp winning a fourth Munster title and don't expect much. I don't think we should be written off that easily.

Mark Foley[1]

THE STORY OF this game centres around a player who made his living telling people to 'open wide' and a manager who might have been better advised to ignore that instruction. At the end of play, Cork hurling had a new and unlikely hero in a relatively unknown dentist, Mark Foley. Tipperary had a shock defeat and a chastened manager in Babs Keating, who was arraigned over comments he'd made in an RTÉ interview broadcast the day before the game.

After this unexpected win, the Cork manager Fr Michael O'Brien revealed how his team had been wound up by Keating's assertion in that interview that 'donkeys don't win derbies'. Keating used those words but later argued that they were taken out of context by the wily priest to motivate his team. Keating insisted in his autobiography, written six years later, that the comment was not directed at Cork and had been taken completely out of context.

According to the recollections of Tipperary forward Michael Cleary, Keating was answering a question on the general influence of managers. 'He made no specific reference to Cork.'[2]

GAA managers tended to be guarded in their media dealings. Not Babs. The team reflected his own vivacious style and he was highly opinionated. The night before they had played Kerry in the first round of the 1987 Munster championship, he had ensured the whole panel stayed at a five-star hotel. He'd insisted that the players were made to feel special and were well looked after. But it wasn't all style and no substance. That had raised their profile and the new glamour was matched by some dazzling hurling on the field.

Ger Fitzgerald, the Cork and Midleton forward, says the RTÉ interview was 'mentioned' but he doesn't remember it being a huge factor.

> I think it undermines the work the Canon [as Michael O'Brien was later to become] had done beforehand, I thought we were in a very good place, we had trained very well; we had a good victory over Waterford.[3]

He described their manager as being interested in 'nothing but winning' and was 'driven to be successful'. Cork had last won the All-Ireland in 1986, then they'd relinquished their grip on Munster to Tipperary. They went into the match in 1990 without the injured pair, Teddy McCarthy and Tomás Mulcahy.

As well as clever use of psychology, Cork were helped by indifferent Tipp form. They had already beaten Tipp in the league and Tipp made heavy weather of putting away Limerick in the Munster semi-final. But not even Cork could have banked on Foley, the dentist from Timoleague, filling his boots with 2–7 from play. It remains a record haul from play for a Munster final.

Foley, who had been commuting from England earlier in the year, never reached the same heights again, and reminded people in Cork of a Glen Rovers hurler named Jackie Daly. In 1956, Daly gave an exhibition of hurling in a county championship game against St Finbarr's that was so impressive he was drafted into the Cork senior panel for the All-Ireland final against Wexford. He wasn't used in that historic final and never played senior championship hurling for the county. Daly was known to local hurling followers as 'one fine day'.

Ger Fitzgerald argues that while it was almost impossible for a player to reach those levels again, Foley had a big say in the All-Ireland final that year, scoring 1–1. Irrespective of what came after, Foley is immortalised for his performance on 15 July 1990.

'The side were so committed to proving all sections of the media wrong,' Canon O'Brien hummed to the waiting media after the game as he savoured the win against the odds. 'One thing we objected to mostly was the inference that I was trying to make racehorses out of donkeys.'

He described Foley as 'so laid back he gives the impression he is not trying. I often have to shout at him, "You won't go to sleep on me now, Mark?"'

The Cork trainer Gerald McCarthy described beating Tipp as the 'sweetest victory I was ever associated with'.

Tipperary had been Munster title holders for the previous three years. They had never won four back-to-back and did not give up their title without a fight, subjecting Cork to two periods of intense pressure, before half-time and again in the final quarter. With seven minutes left, there was only one point between the teams, yet Cork finished eight ahead, with a sweeping finale that reaped 2–2. Of their total score, only one point came from a free.

Apart from Foley, Cork also had an outstanding contribution from Jim Cashman, their stylish centre-back. Cashman kept Declan Ryan in check and the half-backs excelled, Kieran McGuckin and Sean McCarthy alongside Cashman forming a formidable line of red resistance.

Cork were 0–6 to 0–3 ahead after 28 minutes but had enough play to be more in front. Cleary gave Tipp hope with a goal seven minutes before the interval that tied the match. John Leahy and Nicky English added points and then an English goal handed Tipp a lead of 2–5 to 0–6. Up stepped Foley, his flicked goal leaving Cork in touch at the interval; Tipp led 2–5 to 1–6.

Cork restarted in a fury. Two points by midfielder Brendan O'Sullivan had them level within three minutes. English edged

Tipp back in front before Fitzgibbon punished them with the first of his goals, giving Cork a 2–8 to 2–6 lead. From there, Cork hit five points to one in return from Tipp, to strengthen their lead. With 14 minutes played in the second half, Cork led 2–13 to 2–7.

The move of Colm Bonnar to midfield in place of Declan Carr helped rouse the Tipp midfield engine room and lifted the overall team performance.

But the last decisive push came from Cork. Foley pointed and then struck for his second goal in the 65th minute. Leahy replied with a point, then Fitzgibbon goaled again and Foley completed a wonderful day with another point.

CORK: G. Cunningham; J. Considine, D. Walsh, S. O'Gorman; S. McCarthy, J. Cashman, K. McGuckin; P. Buckley, B. O'Sullivan; D. Quirke (0–1), M. Foley (2–7), T. O'Sullivan (0–5); G. Fitzgerald (0–1), K. Hennessy (0–1, 1f), J. Fitzgibbon (2–0); Subs: A. O'Sullivan for D. Quirke (48 mins), C. Casey (0–1) for P. Buckley (60).

TIPPERARY: K. Hogan; J. Madden, N. Sheehy, B. Ryan; Conal Bonnar, J. Kennedy, P. Delaney; D. Carr, J. Hayes; M. Cleary (1–5, 3fs), Declan Ryan (0–1), C. Stakelum (0–2); P. Fox, J. Leahy (0–2), N. English (1–4); Subs: Denis Ryan for P. Fox (HT), Colm Bonnar for D. Carr (43 mins).

Referee: J. Moore (Waterford)

Attendance: 49,782

72. Rebel Heaven

1990 ALL-IRELAND FINAL (Croke Park, 2 September)
Cork 5–15 Galway 2–21

Before the speeches came, a united chorus of 'De Banks' that could be heard all the way to the top of Patrick's Hill. Proud Cork men and women sang from the soul.
Cork Examiner (4 September 1990)

IF THERE IS a next world, there is probably a corner reserved for Cork hurling supporters, with the recording of this game showing permanently on a big screen as merry Rebels clink their otherworldly glasses of Murphy's and Beamish in eternal delight.

Winning the 1990 championship was a coup that ranked alongside 1931, 1952 and 1966 on the shortlist of the most gratifying of the 27 All-Ireland hurling titles Cork had amassed in the century since Aghabullogue won the first in 1890. Cork celebrate every All-Ireland victory as proof that all is well in the world, but this one was special – an affirmation of the qualities that move some Rebels to proclaim themselves Irish by birth, Cork by the grace of God. Backs to the wall, they summoned up an old-school display of defiance, sideline cuteness and opportune goals to escape to victory from a high-octane shootout.

Discounted by the pundits at the start of the 1990 championship, Cork had 'mushroomed' in Munster to topple Tipperary, but the mushroom appeared to have come and gone 10 minutes into the second half of the All-Ireland final when Galway led by seven points.

Cyril Farrell's team had spent the winter brooding over the

injustices of the 1989 semi-final. They were relegated in the league, but had regrouped in the early summer and overran Offaly by 1–16 to 2–7 in the semi-final. Keady was back at Number 6, flanked by Peter Finnerty and Gerry McInerney. Michael Coleman was maturing into a midfield powerhouse and the flair forwards – Joe Cooney, Michael McGrath and Eanna Ryan – were hitting their prime. There were concerns about the full-back line where Conor Hayes and Sylvie Linnane had been replaced by Dermot Fahy and Sean Treacy, and it looked ominous when Kevin Hennessy whipped home a goal after 45 seconds. Teddy McCarthy and John Fitzgibbon added points within four minutes and that opening flurry against the wind would prove priceless.

After the shaky start, Galway took control in the second quarter and led by 1–13 to 1–8 at half-time. Joe Cooney was in virtuoso mood at centre-forward, scoring 1–6 from play off Cork's accomplished centre-back Jim Cashman. Cork manager Canon Michael O'Brien and his selectors bided their time and weren't panicked into taking the Blackrock player off and Cashman repaid their faith in the second half, holding Cooney scoreless. They did make one critical call when they switched Sean O'Gorman onto Noel Lane late in the first half after the veteran Galway forward had given Denis Walsh the runaround. With Keady and Coleman driving Galway on, Cooney's goal in the 19th minute had signalled a wave of attacks. Cork were outscored by 1–7 to 0–2 before the break. Eanna Ryan also had a 27th minute goal disallowed by referee John Moore who instead called back play for a free. A goal then would have pushed Galway eight clear, but Cork hung on – the dual star Teddy McCarthy scoring a point and Kieran McGuckin adding another from a sideline cut.

Galway were seven points ahead before Cork captain Thomas Mulcahy took route one for a 45th-minute goal that ignited a scoring spree. The Glen Rovers man had switched out from the corner onto Keady with Mark Foley going to the wing – one of the Cork mentors' match-winning moves. Foley cut loose for goal in the 56th minute as

Galway came under severe pressure from Ger Cunningham's wind-assisted puckouts. Noel Lane levelled the game in the 58th minute with a shot that could have whizzed under rather than over the bar.

There was almost a score a minute but, after a brief lull, John Fitzgibbon scored two goals in the 62nd and 63rd minutes to push Cork 5–13 to 1–19 in front. There was no stopping them. Brendan Lynskey had been sent on in the 62nd minute to give Galway's resistance an abrasive edge. He blasted a terrific goal in the 64th minute for a short-lived lifeline, but Mulcahy and Tony O'Sullivan scored two quick points and that was that. 'In that last quarter, the whole Cork team played like supermen, proving once again that 15 players in those famous red jerseys should never be underrated,' reported Paddy Downey the following day in *The Irish Times*.

Praise for their contribution to a classical exhibition of hurling that was rarely interrupted by the referee's whistle was hollow consolation for Galway who have yet to break their Cork hex. Farrell later wrote that one of the regrets of his management career was that 'we never beat Cork in an All-Ireland final. That would have buried the myth of the "golden circle" once and for all.'[1] As in 1986 and 1989, Galway also had complaints about the referee. It was beginning to sound like a broken record, but the gripes appeared legitimate.

Apart from Eanna Ryan's disallowed goal, there were questions asked about a bizarre decision in the 48th minute when Martin Naughton's shot on goal struck Ger Cunningham on the head and deflected over the endline. It should have been a 65, but the umpire signalled a wide at a time when the score was 1–17 to 2–10.

'Why immediately afterwards did he [the referee] not award a free out to Galway after their centre-back Tony Keady was fouled and Tony O'Sullivan picked up a breaking ball to score a vital point for Cork. And why did he not note the number of steps [eight] taken by John Fitzgibbon before he scored the second of his two goals for Cork in the 63rd minute?' asked Paddy Downey in the *Times*. He hastened to add that 'these questions, pertinent though they are, must not imply that Cork were lucky to win. Masterly switches directed from the dugout played a major part in their victory.'

Three weeks later, Teddy McCarthy played at midfield for Cork footballers when they defeated Meath in the All-Ireland final to complete the famous double. The Liam MacCarthy and Sam Maguire cups were paraded together through the streets of Cork and Thomas Mulcahy remembered it as the evening Bishop Buckley told the crowd: 'Tonight there are two kinds of people in Ireland – Cork people and those who wish they were Cork people.'[2]

CORK: G. Cunningham; J. Considine, D. Walsh, S. O'Gorman; S. McCarthy, J. Cashman, K. McGuckin (0–1, cut); B. O'Sullivan, T. McCarthy (0–3); G. Fitzgerald (0–1), M. Foley (1–1), T. O'Sullivan (0–2); T. Mulcahy (capt) (1–2), K. Hennessy (1–4, 3fs), J. Fitzgibbon (2–1); Subs: D. Quirke for K. McGuckin (45), C. Casey for T. O'Sullivan (49).

GALWAY: J. Commins; D. Fahy, S. Treacy, O. Kilkenny; P. Finnerty, T. Keady (0–1), G. McInenery; M. Coleman (0–1), P. Malone; A. Cunningham (0–1), J. Cooney (1–7, 1f), M. Naughton (0–4); M. McGrath (0–1), N. Lane (0–4), E. Ryan (0–2); Subs: T. Monaghan for P. Malone (55), B. Lynskey (1–0) for A. Cunningham (62).

Referee: John Moore (Waterford)

Attendance: 63,954

73. Through the Barricades

1991 MUNSTER FINAL REPLAY (Semple Stadium, 21 July)
Tipperary 4–19 Cork 4–15

The most exciting would have to be the 1991 Munster final replay in Thurles. It had everything; speed and skill, a high-scoring match. The crowd even got involved at one stage.
Declan Ryan[1]

I N A SPECTACULAR and somewhat chaotic send-off to the last 'traditional' Munster final for nine years, the fever was too much for Tipperary supporters who repeatedly invaded the pitch in the second half as their team closed in on victory. The drawn game in Cork two weeks earlier had invoked Tipp's grittier virtues as they clambered out of a hole eight points deep; in the replay, they resurfaced from nine points down to win by four without their injured star forward Nicky English.

Cork secretary Frank Murphy protested at what he claimed was poor Thurles stewardship, and there were complaints that Ger Cunningham had been impeded on his puckouts by marauding Tipp fans. More seriously, it was alleged that Cunningham had been pelted by coins and even a crutch. On radio commentary, Micheál Ó Muircheartaigh spoke of one pitch incursion being led by a man in a wheelchair. Cunningham, another claim went, sought help from an umpire only to be told to 'get on with it'. The Rebels headed south with their Munster and All-Ireland titles pillaged, and a sour taste in their mouths.

Speaking about the incidents in July 2014, Cunningham

mentioned the intense rivalry and the excitable nature of Tipp's comeback in mitigation.

> I think it was pure emotion and there had been something similar when we beat them in 1990, in fairness. I couldn't take the steps back for the puckouts because of the crowds gathered around the goal so it did get a bit complicated, but we still felt the match could be saved.[2]

But the incursions were a concern to Tipp too. 'As a player, they were a nuisance,' explains Michael Cleary. 'You were focused on the job in hand, we had some momentum at the time and I remember thinking, *This is doing us harm*. We had Cork on the rack.'[3]

Cork were also aggrieved over a broken finger suffered by their centre-back Jim Cashman. Declan Ryan was the man accused of a bad stroke, but he maintains there was no malicious intent. But Cashman, who had been outstanding up to then, waned as an influence after the incident and it impacted on the play.

'A lot of people put a lot of importance on the incident because Tipperary went on to win the All-Ireland and we weren't going well at the time. People saw it as changing the course of the game,' Ryan recalled years later. 'I suppose it was a small factor in a larger pool of facts. Tipperary happened to play very well that day. People put a lot more significance on the incident than they should have done.'[4]

Much Cork anger was directed at the referee, Terence Murray, for not stopping the play to bring about crowd control. Gerald McCarthy, the Cork trainer, said that it was one of his regrets that he did not take the Cork team off the field in protest until order was restored. After the high of 1990, this was a bitter experience for Cork – though they recovered to win the Munster title again in 1992, before losing the All-Ireland to Kilkenny. The All-Ireland they surrendered in 1991 took eight more years to regain.

Tipperary showed a marked improvement on the previous year's Munster final performance. Pat Fox, taken off in 1990 after failing to score, helped himself to 1–5 and was later voted Hurler of the Year. Declan Carr, also substituted in 1990, made amends with a more imposing display, scoring 1–1. Tipperary rejigged their defence and it was noticeable that Mark Foley, Cork's scoring hero of 1990, did not raise a flag.

Tipperary had easily defeated Limerick 2–18 to 0–10 in their semi-final, the losers were without Ciaran Carey and had Anthony Carmody sent off; Cork had only a goal to spare over Waterford – losing leads of eight and nine points would haunt Cork over the closed season and beyond. Tipperary powered on from there and laid to rest a few ghosts of their own. Galway, their arch-rivals of the previous decade, were no match, losing 1–9 to 3–13, and they overcame a hardy challenge from Kilkenny, two-point winners over Antrim in the semi-finals, to win their second All-Ireland in three years. It was the first final between Kilkenny and Tipperary since 1971, and was the last fling of the Babs Keating era. After this game, the team began to go into gradual decline, a shock defeat to Clare in 1994 ending Keating's reign.

'We had a disaster in 1990,' says Cleary, who scored 1–7 in the 1991 replay in his only championship appearance at left corner-forward. '1991 started terribly, Offaly beat us 1–7 to 0–7 in the league semi-final and championship was make or break, it looked like we were just going to fade into oblivion. We got over Limerick and met Cork in the Páirc where they hadn't lost in 70-odd years or whatever. There were doubts over the team. People felt we had still to prove ourselves, having won a "handy" All-Ireland in 1989 and been beaten by Cork the year after.'[5]

Cork led 2–7 to 1–7 at half-time. John Fitzgibbon hit a goal in the 18th minute, Ger Fitzgerald a second after 27, Cleary firing one home for Tipp in reply. Twelve minutes into the second half Kevin Hennessy netted, leaving Cork 3–13 to 1–10 to the good. Tipp found themselves nine points down two minutes later. From that unpromising position, they went into overdrive, scoring 2–5 in a blistering 13-minute spell, the goals from Fox and Aidan Ryan. A sideline point from Cathal Casey was the only response Cork could muster and with eight minutes left, Tipperary were in front. Pat

Buckley levelled the match with a minute remaining to raise the prospect of extra-time. But in the six minutes of added time played, partly because of the pitch incursions, Tipperary produced a surge to the tape.

John Leahy's move to midfield helped strengthen Tipp's hand as the comeback set sail and after Buckley had appeared to set up extra-time, the substitute Aidan Ryan blocked Richard Browne and ran through to goal. They were five points up when Fitzgibbon goaled again, from a 30-metre free, before Cleary added two points to make Tipp safe. Their spirit was embodied by a crunching Michael Ryan tackle on Tomás Mulcahy in the second half. Ryan had played full-forward in the league semi-final loss to Offaly, but saw out the season as a left corner-back.

Babs Keating admitted he had feared the worst.

> It was a game I thought was gone on us when we were nine points down. I didn't think they'd recover, but the breaks came and the breaks haven't always come our way. I've been watching Cork–Tipp games since 1952 and this game and the one a fortnight ago lived up to all the ones I've seen. This was a great day for Tipperary hurling.[6]

TIPPERARY: K. Hogan; P. Delaney, N. Sheehy, M. Ryan; J. Madden, B. Ryan, Conal Bonnar; D. Carr (1–1), Colm Bonnar; D. Ryan (0–2), D. O'Connell, J. Leahy (0–2); P. Fox (1–5), Cormac Bonnar (0–1), M. Cleary (1–7, 2fs); Subs: A. Ryan (1–1) for D. O'Connell (HT), J. Hayes for J. Madden (40 mins).

CORK: G. Cunningham; S. O'Gorman, R. Browne, D. Walsh; C. Casey (0–1, sideline), J. Cashman (0–3, 1 70, 1f), P. Hartnett; B. O'Sullivan, T. McCarthy; T. Mulcahy (0–1), M. Foley, T. O'Sullivan (0–6, 4fs); G. Fitzgerald (1–2), K. Hennessy (1–0), J. Fitzgibbon (2–1, 1–0f); Sub: P. Buckley (0–1) for B. O'Sullivan (25 mins).

Referee: T. Murray (Limerick)

Attendance: 55,000

74. Fenian Flame

1993 ALL-IRELAND FINAL (Croke Park, 5 September)
Kilkenny 2–17 Galway 1–15

People were saying I couldn't play on a dry day. I had to show them.
Pat O'Neill[1]

GALWAY'S DEFENCE HAD undergone significant change since 1990, the county's last final appearance. Only Gerry McInerney remained of the half-back line, with Tony Keady retired and Pete Finnerty a peripheral influence. McInerney manned the centre, flanked by Tom Helebert and Padraig Kelly, a nimble and stylish hurler from Sarsfields.

In the All-Ireland semi-final, it was this new defence that had helped to frustrate a highly rated Tipperary attack, which had earlier destroyed Clare in the Munster final. But Kilkenny in a final would be the supreme test. D.J. Carey was destined to win Hurler of the Year and would need close surveillance. Galway performed admirably, limiting Carey to one point from play, but they hadn't banked on P.J. Delaney scoring 1–4.

A 20-year-old from the Fenians club in Johnstown, Delaney buried Galway's hopes of an upset with a classic show of Kilkenny stealth and timely opportunism. After a brave Galway comeback in the second half, it was Delaney's goal three minutes from time that sealed their fate and meant he ended the day as top scorer. Padraig Kelly won the Man of the Match accolade despite being on the losing team.

Delaney looked set to have a long career but his last appearance came as a 63rd-minute sub in the 1999 All-Ireland final defeat by Cork when he was 26. A week after that final, he was the victim of a vicious assault in Thurles that left him with head injuries and in a coma fighting for his life. Four years later, having made a good recovery, he spoke to the *Sunday Independent*:

I'm just glad to be alive. I think after you go through something like that, you have a different outlook on life as well. You say, 'I'll give up the hurling, I'll be all right.' You take things easier, you don't get worried about things, you see how good you have it.

Carey's 6–23 over the course of the 1993 season contributed massively to Kilkenny's success, but Galway reduced his influence in the final, drawing praise from their manager Jarlath Cloonan afterwards.

Our backs played like tigers, and while the forwards battled very hard, they missed too many chances, which proved very costly in the end. Naturally, we are bitterly disappointed with the result, but I think that we showed enough out there today to convince people that this team will win an All-Ireland before very long.[2]

In *The Irish Times*, the veteran match reporter Paddy Downey described the 1993 climax as 'one of the most sporting finals ever played'. He cited a free count of 21 as being illustrative of the good-natured exchanges. Donal Keenan in the *Irish Independent* lauded Pat O'Neill's role at centre-back for Kilkenny: 'He dismissed a succession of direct opponents with a display of great power.'

Kilkenny goaled in the 10th minute through Adrian Ronan after Richie Burke saved from Delaney. They led by five points after 16 minutes, Paddy Downey writing about how Galway at that stage looked set for a 'hiding'. But in the 23rd minute, a long-range effort from Liam Burke deceived Michael Walsh and gifted Galway a goal against the run of play. Watched by his father Ollie – the manager and revered goalkeeper from Kilkenny's past – Walsh made amends with a first-half penalty save from Michael Coleman and some important stops after the interval. Though dominant, Kilkenny led just 1–8 to 1–6 at half-time.

Three Joe Rabbitte points in succession over 10 minutes meant that the teams were level after 51 minutes and Joe Cooney landed a 65 to put them in front for the first time three minutes later, 1–12 to 1–11. A surprise looked on. Liam McCarthy and Power responded for Kilkenny before Rabbitte struck again to level on the hour mark. A minute after that came a crucial call by the referee Terence Murray who harshly reprimanded Rabbitte for over-carrying. Carey nailed the free. Kelly hit back with an inspirational score for Galway but Carey replied again – then came Delaney's goal. Two more points from Delaney and Carey, his first from play, provided added decoration in stoppage time.

This was the fifth All-Ireland in a row won by a traditional county but there were rumblings of insurrection among the less well-heeled. Cork, the National League winners after a three-day affair with Wexford, were shocked by Clare in a low-scoring Munster championship semi-final in Limerick in which Anthony Daly starred at full-back. Wexford's league final appearance created hope of greater democracy in Leinster but in the provincial final, Kilkenny again proved their masters in a replay, concocting a brilliant score to earn a draw the first day, a move that was quintessential Kilkenny: composed, erudite and technically brilliant. The replay win, by seven points, was controversial as Wexford accused Carey of taking too many steps for a crucial goal.

The greatest upset happened in Walsh Park where Kerry put out Waterford in the Munster championship. A year before Nickey Brennan spoke of a crisis in hurling at GAA congress, some green shoots were beginning to appear above the ground. Wexford would have to lose another Leinster final in 1994, their third in succession, and Clare would have to lose another in Munster, but their shackles were about to come off. But, first, Offaly would show them how.

Kilkenny were about to suffer their worst championship run since the 1920s. Galway, in spite of Jarlath Cloonan's optimism, couldn't imagine the frustration that lay ahead.

KILKENNY: M. Walsh; E. O'Connor, P. Dwyer, L. Simpson; W. O'Connor, P. O'Neill, L. Keoghan; B. Hennessy (0–1), M. Phelan; L. McCarthy (0–3), J. Power (0–1), D.J. Carey (0–4, 3fs); E. Morrissey (0–2), P.J. Delaney (1–4), A. Ronan (1–2); Subs: J. Brennan for E. Morrissey (64 mins), T. Murphy for M. Phelan (68), C. Heffernan for P.J. Delaney (70).

GALWAY: R. Burke; P. Cooney, S. Treacy, M. Killilea; T. Helebert, G. McInerney, P. Kelly (0–2, 1f); M. Coleman, P. Malone (0–3); B. Keogh, J. McGrath, J. Cooney (0–4, 0–1 65, 3fs); M. McGrath (0–2), J. Rabbitte (0–4), L. Burke (1–0); Subs: J. Campbell for J. McGrath (49 mins), P. Finnerty for B. Keogh (68).

Referee: T. Murray (Limerick)

Attendance: 63,460

75. The Great Hurling Heist

1994 ALL-IRELAND FINAL (Croke Park, 4 September)
Offaly 3–16 Limerick 2–13

Johnny went for his goal himself. He took responsibility, he went for goal, he got it. That sparked off the rest of us. After that we could do nothing wrong. For 65 minutes, we didn't deserve to win. For five minutes, we did.
Eamonn Cregan[1]

'HURLING IS DYING on its feet,' declared Kilkenny county board chairman Nickey Brennan at the 1994 GAA Congress. Alarm about the game's perilous health was a hardy congress annual, and Brennan's diagnosis that hurling was rapidly losing ground to other codes saw the GAA prescribe its favourite cure-all. GAA President Jack Boothman announced the setting up of a 'special committee' to examine the 'crisis' affecting the game. 'Hurling is unique and particularly Irish,' said President Boothman.[2] 'At its best we have a living art form, equalling if not surpassing our drama, our music and our dancing. Every effort must go into the new hurling drive. We cannot afford to fail in restoring this most ancient of Irish games.'

If the 'special committee' members were looking for some ideas, there were probably a dozen or more hurling revival masterplans lying in some corner of Croke Park. The GAA's inability to expand hurling's territory in any meaningful way beyond its 1884 borders is one of the great mysteries of Irish life. Twenty years after Nickey Brennan's warning, what has changed? The outgoing GAA President Liam O'Neill told the 2014 congress that 2013 had been 'hurling's greatest year'. Arguably it was in terms of drama and quality, but the divide between the hurling haves and have-nots is widening rather than closing. Playing numbers have increased, the Dublin 'revolution' does look permanent and competitions such as the Ring, Rackard and Meagher cups – why not a Mackey? – have raised standards in 'the weaker counties' but, for all this progress, the pool of contenders for top honours is as shallow as ever.

In 1981, Offaly became the 13th county to enter the All-Ireland roll of honour – they were also the last 'new' county to win an All-Ireland. Which county will be the 14th and when? Meanwhile, the Faithful's freefall from hurling grace illustrates how difficult it can be for a county with a limited playing base to compete long-term against the superpowers. The talk now in Offaly is not of winning an All-Ireland, or even a Leinster title, but of 10-year plans to restore pride and credibility. Let's hope they succeed because the game is a poorer place without their cussed spirit and eccentric panache.

Offaly's sad surrenders to Kilkenny and Tipperary in the 2014 championship are a world away from September 1994 when they celebrated a third All-Ireland title after the greatest heist ever seen in Croke Park. 'In all my years reporting hurling for this newspaper, or before it, I have never seen such a dramatic finish to an All-Ireland final … it was as if a fairy godmother or some magician waved a magic wand for Offaly and then they were winners,' wrote Paddy Downey whose career as a GAA writer for *The Irish Times* spanned four decades. And you have to go back to well before even his time to find a parallel to what Offaly achieved in the final five minutes when they scored 2–5 to convert a five-point deficit into a six-point victory.

Mesmerised probably best describes how Limerick looked as the goals and points flowed in a torrent from Offaly. Those fateful final five minutes have become such a part of the game's folklore that hurling followers far beyond the Midlands can almost recite the sequence blow by blow. For the record, here's how it happened.

In the 65th minute, Billy Dooley was fouled and his brother Johnny addressed the free. 'I thought, if I got a point it wouldn't be enough to lift us,' he said. 'We needed a goal at that stage so I made up my mind up. I had nothing to lose because I hadn't been playing well up to that. If I had missed I probably would have been shot.' He didn't miss, firing a low shot to the net at the Hill 16 end past the Limerick cover blinking against the sun.

Limerick's Man of the Match Ger Hegarty actually won possession from Joe Quaid's puckout, but Offaly sub Michael Duignan rattled into him and the ball broke to Johnny Pilkington who lobbed it back into the square where it took two perfect bounces for Pat O'Connor, another Offaly substitute, who whacked home goal number two. Every ball now seemed predestined for an Offaly hand or stick. The two goals were followed by two points in a minute from Johnny Dooley and John Troy. When Billy Dooley delivered a trio of points in less than 90 seconds from almost the same patch of ground on the Cusack side of the pitch, it really did feel as though an unseen hand had intervened.

It was an unprecedented reversal of fortunes in an All-Ireland final, and you have to go back to 1922 for the nearest comparison. On that occasion Kilkenny scored two goals in the last three minutes to defeat Tipperary, 4–2 to 3–6.

There was immense and genuine sympathy for Limerick, while there was an almost tragic cast about the predicament of Eamonn Cregan. Over the winter, along with fitness trainer Derry Donovan, he had whipped a group of underachievers into shape and cajoled them into fulfilling their talent. An All-Ireland medallist with Limerick in 1973 and part of the losing 1974 and 1980 sides, Cregan had taken the Offaly job in 1993, never imagining he would be facing his own county in an All-Ireland final.

No one else had either because neither county was considered a realistic contender early in the season when back-to-back champions Kilkenny were clear favourites to win their first 'proper' three-in-a-row. Offaly ended that ambition by dismissing the champions 2–16 to 3–9 in the Leinster semi-final, when Kilkenny scored two of their goals in the closing minutes. Offaly were equally convincing when they defeated Wexford by seven points in the Leinster final and Galway by six in the All-Ireland semi. Their brilliant underage players from the late 1980s had finally started to give an appropriate reply to the sniping that had suggested that, for all their talent, they had a soft centre and were more fond of the bar stool than the hard slog. Ten of the players and subs used in the 1994 final had featured on the 1986, 1987 and 1989 All-Ireland-winning minor teams.

Limerick didn't have this kind of prodigious firepower to call on, but they had been building for a couple of seasons. They rallied from 2–4 to 0–2 down against Cork to win 4–13 to 4–10 before overrunning Clare by 0–25 to 2–10 in the 1994 Munster final. Only two late goals saved any face for Clare, but nine of the same team would do duty in 1995. Limerick then overwhelmed Antrim by 18 points in their All-Ireland semi-final, and there were times in the first half of the final when they seemed just a score or two away from routing the Leinster champions.

Ger Hegarty, Ciaran Carey, Mike Houlihan and Dave Clarke controlled the game and full-forward Damien Quigley scored 2–3 to leave his side 2–8 to 1–5 ahead at half-time. Offaly's goal had come in the second minute when Joe Dooley had a penalty saved and his brother Johnny scrambled home the rebound. Limerick shot 12 wides when playing with the breeze, but despite some Offaly switches and improved performances from Kevin Kinahan, Whelahan and Johnny Pilkington, Limerick still led 2–13 to 1–11 before being struck by the whirlwind.

It blew again during the following year's Leinster final in what was perhaps the best performance ever produced by this group of Offaly players who obliterated Kilkenny in a match delayed by a spectacular thunderstorm. The teams clattered into each other in the first half, playing bone-crunching ground hurling that was a throwback to another era. Offaly revealed an inner hardness

failure. Thurles loomed large in that tale of misfortune. Munster finals devoured one Clare team after another. They lost them everywhere, but the road home from Thurles became especially synonymous with heartbreak.

Ger Loughnane was part of Clare's wretched losing tradition but he had no truck with hard-luck stories. His was an approach based on science and pragmatism rather than voodoo or superstition. Not for him the wrath of Biddy Earley who was said to have cursed the county's hurlers. Loughnane recognised Thurles had a forbidding aura and he set out to cure all related phobias. This was the crucible in which most Clare title dreams had perished and it is where, driven by duty more than optimism, Banner followers headed on 9 July 1995 for another Munster final attempt.

Clare had lost 11 Munster senior finals since 1932. The team of 1955 had defeated the All-Ireland champions Cork, then taken out Tipperary, only to collapse in the final against Mick Mackey's Limerick. A very good Clare team had lost successive Munster finals in the late 1970s. Two years before 1995, they had lost the Munster final to Tipperary by 18 points and the writer Raymond Smith argued that it was time they considered hurling in the B championship.

In 1994, they were back in the Munster final but lost again, this time by nine points to Limerick. In the dressing room afterwards, Len Gaynor fielded media questions. Gaynor had restored Clare to being a contender but he saw first-hand how Munster finals spooked them. While he answered questions, Loughnane, a team selector, stood in silence by a dressing-room wall. In a few months, he would be the new manager.

Yet Clare did not look destined for a long summer when they lost the National League final to Kilkenny by nine points in Thurles in early May. When Loughnane talked of winning the Munster championship after the game, it sounded like bluster. They had good fortune on their side against Cork in the Munster semi-final. Three goals came in the final five minutes, the most decisive being Ollie Baker's winner when he met a Fergie Tuohy lineball in the air.

They made hard work of it, shooting 20 wides, and at the death a vital block by Frank Lohan saved Clare from a winning Cork goal. The victory meant Clare qualified for their third Munster senior final in a row, which was unprecedented. They faced Limerick, the previous year's All-Ireland finalists and raging favourites.

Playing with the wind, Limerick were 0–5 to 0–2 up after 23 minutes. The difference this time was that Clare didn't let the opposition out of their sight. On the half hour, they got a break when Mike Nash was deemed to have fouled Conor Clancy and from the penalty Davy Fitzgerald finished before accelerating back to his goal. Clare had some luck on the day – Damien Quigley lashed a strike off the bar soon after the penalty – but by half-time, they led 1–5 to 0–7. They were not rolling over.

In the 51st minute, a long-range free from McMahon put them three points up. Then a pivotal moment: Quigley wheeled past Michael O'Halloran, ran in on goal but kicked wide. This was a huge let-off, which Clare seized on by scoring four points to Limerick's one over the next five minutes. P.J. O'Connell, the tanned, long-haired centre-forward whose job it was to run Ciaran Carey, had four points from play. Jamesie O'Connor scored 0–6, including four points from play, and had a characteristically central role in Clare's win.

In the final stages, they started to pull clear but no Clare follower could believe, or allow themselves believe, it was over until they heard Johnny McDonnell's final whistle. Soon, the pitch was a festival of celebration. 'It's an unbelievable feeling,' said O'Connor. 'After losing the last two finals we could not have faced another defeat. We knew that, we had talked about it and we were determined it would not happen again.'[3]

Loughnane went back to the league final defeat by Kilkenny.

I knew we needed to make three or four changes; we had to bring in fast ball players, fellas who can run because in Thurles you have to run. That's what we did and it worked.

Another important factor for us was Sean McMahon. There was a doubt about his fitness but normal rules don't apply to McMahon. He epitomises this team, he's a fantastic fella on and off the field. He kept the head down and battled away. I have never seen a team so relaxed before a Munster final ... it was just another game ... for once things worked out for us in Thurles.[4]

McMahon had broken his collarbone against Cork, but played for the final quarter of an hour as Clare had used up their subs. He won the lineball that led to Clare's winning goal and made it back to play in the final. 'There was a desperate focus on the match,' said Anthony Daly, their inspirational captain. 'We were going out that door that day and we were going to hurl for 70 minutes. If we were beaten we were beaten, but at least we weren't going to come off the field saying we choked.'[5]

CLARE: D. Fitzgerald (1–0, pen); M. O'Halloran, B. Lohan, F. Lohan; L. Doyle, S. McMahon (0–1, f), A. Daly; O. Baker, J. O'Connor (0–6, 2fs); F. Tuohy (0–1), P.J. O'Connell (0–4), F. Hegarty (0–1); S. McNamara (0–1), C. Clancy (0–2), G. O'Loughlin (0–1); Subs: J. McInerney for F. Tuohy (69 mins), C. Lyons for C. Clancy (71).

LIMERICK: J. Quaid; S. McDonagh, M. Nash, D. Nash; D. Clarke, C. Carey, T. Herbert; M. Houlihan, S. O'Neill; F. Carroll (0–1), G. Kirby (0–6, 0–1 65, 5fs), M. Galligan (0–3); T.J. Ryan, P. Heffernan (0–1), D. Quigley; Subs: T. Hayes for T. Herbert (HT), B. Tobin for F. Carroll (59 mins), D. Barry for T. Hayes (62).

Referee: J. McDonnell (Tipperary)

Attendance: 46,361

Sponsor's dream

The summer of 1995 saw the arrival of Guinness as chief sponsor of the senior hurling championship. In spite of some reservations regarding the link between a sports organisation and an alcoholic drinks company, the move proved novel and popular. It was also exceedingly well timed. Clare's breakthrough captured the public imagination, and Guinness carried an impressive promotion and marketing campaign. Catchy advertising slogans appeared on billboards depicting hurlers as mythological figures. The following year, Guinness was raising a glass to Wexford, winners of the All-Ireland for the first time since 1968.

77. Passion Play

1995 ALL-IRELAND FINAL (Croke Park, 3 September)
Clare 1–13 Offaly 2–8

So my girlfriend at the time and I were driving into Doolin and we passed all these people screaming and roaring on the side of the road. It turned out it was the day of the hurling championship and Doolin hadn't won it in 80 years. So we got into the town and the place was apoplectic. They were going nuts. We pub-crawled for the night. It was great.
Quentin Tarantino[1]

DOOLIN IS MANY things to many people, but it did not win the 1995 All-Ireland hurling final as Quentin Tarantino mistakenly assumed when passing through the village while Clare celebrations were in full swing in September of that year. Clare might have settled for a Munster title. But Ger Loughnane was soon devoting every ounce of his being towards landing the ultimate prize.

Two weeks before they played Offaly in the All-Ireland final, the Clare manager ordered the players into the dressing room at Cusack Park, furious over a lack of intensity during training. Stephen McNamara, the fast-heeled corner-forward from Ennis, recalls what happened next:

> Davy Fitz was always first in and he let fly at him and worked his way around and then he absolutely hit me a box right in the stomach. His next statement was along the lines that if I was feeling sick now, it was

nothing; sick is when you come out of Croke Park after being beaten by Offaly.

He probably thought there was a softness coming into the dressing room. Whenever he had us in a circle and he'd be walking around talking to us, you felt his eyes were on you all the time. Players were genuinely afraid of him.[2]

McNamara, who was 22, felt he got off lightly compared to some of the more established players. 'Jamesie [O'Connor] got an amount of verbal abuse. Brian [Lohan] got a lot of it. Seanie [McMahon]. They were his lieutenants and he wanted those right.'

Loughnane was single-minded and devoid of sentiment. He used his influence to stop five senior players hurling with the county's under-21 team, which had reached the Munster final against Tipperary in late July. Senior trainer Mike McNamara was the county under-21 manager and backed the decision. Loughnane felt nothing should be allowed compromise the senior team's quest to win the MacCarthy Cup for the first time since 1914. And so when the under-21s played Tipperary in Thurles, losing by six points, five of their best hurlers were in Croke Park getting used to the ground ahead of an All-Ireland semi-final date with neighbours Galway a week and a half later.

This was a controversial decision – Clare didn't win a Munster under-21 title until 2009 – but such was the sweep of hysteria surrounding Loughnane's team that most were willing to go along with his plan. Sceptics were more assured when a blistering start against Galway laid the platform for a thrilling victory and a place in the All-Ireland final, leaving them 70 minutes from their first title win in 81 years.

They were outsiders in spite of the team's extraordinary momentum and feverish support. Offaly had won the All-Ireland the year before, profiting from a rich seam of talent coming off three All-Ireland-winning minor sides. They boasted some of the most stylish hurlers in the game and, on paper, they were more accomplished. In the Leinster final, they had loudly advertised their talents by demolishing Kilkenny.

Clare did not make it easy on themselves. They hit 16 wides. Jamesie O'Connor, their key score-getter, had a deeply frustrating day and failed to score from play. Both Offaly goals were charitable concessions – the first a half-hit shot from Michael Duignan that Davy Fitzgerald fumbled, the second a scrappy finish from Johnny Pilkington when Clare should have cleared their lines. Brian Lohan felt his hamstring tear with 20 minutes to go but there was no question in the management's mind of him coming off.

'Passion. Passion is what Clare hurling is all about,' said Loughnane after the match. 'Passion with a clear head. Our game is based on heart. People admire heart. Everybody has time for a person with heart. We weren't going to lie down for anyone.'[3]

The final unveiled an unlikely Clare match-winner in Fergie Tuohy, the Clarecastle forward who scored four points from play. The Clare defence, the two goals aside, limited Offaly's exalted assembly to eight points – Brian Lohan was immense. The hurling was intense, though far from classic. In compensation, there was endless suspense and uncertainty and a carnival atmosphere, a riot of colour and ground-shaking noise.

The scoreline was the lowest since 1987 and only one other final had been as miserly in the preceding 30 years. Offaly started full of confidence and were two points up when Ollie Baker landed a sideline and a long-range strike from Seanie McMahon had Clare level and more settled. In spite of Duignan's goal in the 34th minute, Clare went in at half-time only two points adrift, 1–6 to 0–7, closing the half with a beautifully flighted point by Ger O'Loughlin. This led to the memorable exchange between Marty Morrissey of RTÉ and Loughnane as the teams were about to resume for the second half.

'Are you going to do it?' asked Morrissey bluntly.

'We're going to do it,' was Loughnane's instant reply.

Clare dug in and Offaly struck just one score from play in the second half, that being Pilkington's goal in the 54th minute. The captain's goal put Offaly three points up, 2–7 to 0–10, but they managed only one more point and Clare responded with 1–3. The Offaly lead held for nine minutes, then Tuohy pointed, and after 66 minutes Anthony Daly's free came off a post and Eamon Taaffe, who had slipped quietly on as a sub, whipped the rebound to the net.

Taaffe had been due to start at full-forward in the opening match against Cork, but had failed a fitness test. He'd recovered fitness before the All-Ireland semi-final and had Brian Lohan for company in training matches. But in Croke Park the night the county under-21s were playing Tipperary, he broke down again, his hamstring problem recurring. He wasn't on the subs list for the final, but with 17 minutes left, he came on, though he made little visible impact. In fact, he hit only one ball – but it was a priceless connection.

They were preparing to take him off again when he made his mark. 'I wasn't right,' he recalls. 'I was a stone and a half overweight. I remember trying to follow Kevin Martin out the field, sure he left me for dead. It was just after that the ball came in and hit the post. Kevin Kinahan just missed it. I can still see it, he put hand up to catch it on the bounce. [When the goal went in] the roar that went up was unbelievable.'[4]

The remaining moments were tension-filled, with Johnny Dooley levelling from a free within a minute and Daly scoring a 65 in the 68th minute, assuming the duty from McMahon, the usual dead-ball striker from distance. In injury-time, O'Connor put a little more daylight between the sides with a free. As he wheeled away, the whistle sounded.

'For us, there was going to be no turning point today,' said Loughnane in the afterglow of victory. 'I never thought we were going to lose, it never entered my head.'[5]

CLARE: D. Fitzgerald; M. O'Halloran, B. Lohan, F. Lohan; L. Doyle,
S. McMahon (0–3, 0–2 65s), A. Daly (0–1, 65); J. O'Connor (0–2, 2fs), O. Baker
(0–1, sideline); F. Tuohy (0–4), P.J. O'Connell, F. Hegarty (0–1); S. McNamara,
C. Clancy, G. O'Loughlin (0–1); Subs: E. Taaffe (1–0) for S. McNamara (50 mins),
C. Lyons for C. Clancy (60), A. Neville for E. Taaffe (66).

OFFALY: D. Hughes; S. McGuckin, K. Kinahan, M. Hanamy; B. Whelahan,
H. Rigney, K. Martin; J. Pilkington (1–0), D. Regan (0–1); Johnny Dooley (0–5,
0–1 65, 3fs), J. Troy (0–1), Joe Dooley; B. Dooley (0–1), P. O'Connor, M. Duignan
(1–0); Subs: D. Pilkington for P. O'Connor (49 mins), B. Kelly for Joe Dooley (60).

Referee: D. Murphy (Wexford)

Attendance: 65,092

78. Border Crossing

1996 LEINSTER FINAL (Croke Park, 14 July)
Wexford 2–23 Offaly 2–15

And the colours that you hold over your head are purple and gold. That flag over your head is a symbol of everything that we stand for.
Liam Griffin[1]

ON THE WAY to Dublin on 14 July 1996, the bus carrying the Wexford hurlers stalled at the border with Wicklow and Liam Griffin, their manager, had them walk across the county boundary. He gave a hair-raising speech about their ancestry and the hurling idols of the 1950s. He referenced the fighting tradition of Vinegar Hill and the revolutionary lore of their forefathers. In mind and body, they were now ready for battle.

That evening on the journey back – having won their first Leinster senior title in 19 years – it was clear that the ancestral spirit had been reawakened. Their performance against Offaly had been all Griffin could have asked for, and they were now being welcomed home by their people as heroes. Griffin, the fast-talking hotelier from Rosslare, was being hailed as a Messiah.

Local opinion of Griffin had not always been as favourable. When Clare had won their first All-Ireland in 81 years the previous September, efforts were underway to have him sacked. It was Wexford's good fortune that the move failed. Griffin – who had hurled for Wexford and Clare, the home of his father – had taken the job in the autumn of 1994 and begun the process of instilling belief into the team. There were many mishaps along the way.

His first year ended with defeat to Offaly in the Leinster championship when Liam Dunne was stripped of the captaincy for playing a club game in breach of house rules. 'It destroyed our chances but we had to do it,' Griffin explains. 'We were trying to get a work ethic, it wasn't us trying to be heavy disciplinarians.'[2] He brought a professional approach to preparations that included new diet plans and training objectives, but players took time to adjust. There were stories of his instructional leaflets being tossed out of players' car windows after training.

Offaly had won back-to-back Leinster titles, but Wexford toppled them by producing their most complete performance in Griffin's time in charge. What made the experience richer was that Offaly played exceptionally well. In the final minutes, mistakes crept into their game and a three-point Wexford lead morphed into eight. The high skill levels and gung-ho intensity made it easily the game of the year and probably the decade.

You couldn't say it was coming. A league defeat to Meath, who would come within six points of Offaly in the 1996 Leinster quarter-final but were rarely seen in high society, was one of those moments along the way that tested Griffin's and the players' faith. Griffin was told by followers that he knew nothing about hurling. He was spat at. He received hate mail. But there was a trace of light when they lowered Offaly in the 1996 National League quarter-finals. If the defeat in the league semi-final to Galway was dispiriting, it at least meant they came into the summer under the radar. And the team underwent key positional changes: Liam Dunne from wing to centre-back, Ger Cushe from centre to full, Damien Fitzhenry from wing-back to goal. In the Leinster championship quarter-finals, they defeated Kilkenny for the first time since 1988, winning 1–14 to 0–14, the veteran Billy Byrne getting the vital goal.

Wexford defeated Dublin by six points in the semi-final to set up the day of reckoning with Offaly, who were going for their third provincial title in a row. Together, they produced an epic of first-time hurling. This was hurling played very differently to today's game. Players moved the ball instantly, whipping on the ground and in the air. They ploughed fearlessly into challenges. At a time when team formations were more orthodox, players holding conventional lines, space was more confined and scoring more difficult. The 20-point-plus sprees we have now were not as commonplace. Wexford's 2–23 against a team of Offaly's class was remarkable. It was the highest winning tally in a Leinster final since 1973, leaving aside Offaly's one-sided win over Laois in 1985, which was only a point higher. Their half-forward line of Rory McCarthy, Martin Storey and Larry Murphy scored 0–12 from play. Tom Dempsey hit 1–5. Fitzhenry goaled from a penalty and made a series of outstanding saves.

And yet Offaly were still in the game with five minutes to go. They had made the better start. A 13th-minute goal from Billy Dooley had put them 1–2 to 0–1 in front, but Fitzhenry's penalty came five minutes later and Storey's first point had levelled the teams 1–5 apiece after 21 minutes. Offaly went two ahead, Wexford drew level again. Eamon Scallan put them ahead for the first time, Offaly levelled a third time, before Wexford came again to lead 1–10 to 1–9 by the interval.

Wexford came out and raised it another gear. A point from Storey and three from Murphy, the last a huge distance-defying score from the sideline, opened a five-point gap in eight minutes. Johnny Pilkington, who had a magnificent match, pulled one back and Gary Laffan had a great goal chance saved by Liam Coughlan. Offaly were within three of Wexford when Fitzhenry made a brilliant reflex save to deny Joe Errity a goal. Johnny Dooley reduced it to two. Dempsey made it three again.

Offaly suffered a major blow when Joe Dooley, a constant threat, went off with a head wound. Then worse followed when Adrian Fenlon's long sideline broke and Dempsey dived to poke it home in the 55th minute. Six up, Wexford looked destined for victory. From the next play, Michael Duignan smashed home a goal to leave nerves on edge. Pilkington pointed again. Back to two. Wexford responded, the outstanding Larry O'Gorman finding Murphy and his point had them 2–17 to 2–14 clear with five minutes to go.

Then Wexford broke free. An incredible point by Dempsey was added to by another from Storey. Dempsey popped up to score again. Six in it. On came Billy Byrne and his fellow veteran George O'Connor to share in the drama. In spite of heroic defending from Martin Hanamy, Wexford kept streaming forward and scoring. Storey landed another point. Pilkington replied. Storey again. And then Dempsey to finish.

Sean Kilfeather wrote in *The Irish Times* that he could only hope that the crowds attending the upcoming Tina Turner and Neil Diamond concerts in Croke Park would be 'a fraction as fulfilled' as those privileged to be in attendance.

Storey, who had often pulled wistfully on his cigarette while speaking to reporters outside a losing Wexford dressing room, gave his reaction. 'I told everyone during the week that we would win and they just laughed at me. Well, the other defeats don't matter now, because I have my Leinster medal.'[3]

WEXFORD: D. Fitzhenry (1–0, pen); C. Kehoe, G. Cushe, J. O'Connor; R. Guiney, L. Dunne, S. Flood; A. Fenlon, L. O'Gorman (0–2); R. McCarthy (0–3), M. Storey (0–5), L. Murphy (0–4); T. Dempsey (1–5), G. Laffan, E. Scallan (0–4, 3fs); Subs: B. Byrne for G. Laffan (68 mins), G. O'Connor for R. McCarthy (71).

OFFALY: L. Coughlan; S. McGuckin, K. Kinahan, M. Hanamy; B. Whelahan, H. Rigney, K. Martin; J. Pilkington (0–4), M. Duigann (1–1); Johnny Dooley (0–4, 2fs), J. Troy, Joe Dooley (0–3); B. Dooley (1–2), J. Errity, D. Pilkington (0–1); Subs: D. Regan for D. Pilkington (HT), P. O'Connor for Joe Dooley (inj. 55 mins), P. Mulhare for D. Regan (63).

Referee: A. MacSuibhne (Dublin)

Attendance: 34,365

Wexford see it out

Liam Griffin's team may not have hurled at quite the same level but they still managed to carry on and win the county's first All-Ireland since 1968. Following Clare's win the previous year, hurling was now experiencing a full-blown revolution, Offaly having replaced Kilkenny as champions in 1994. 'The Galway game was more rugged and in the final we had a man sent off [Eamon Scallan] and we had to play a different game in the second half,' Griffin recalls. Wexford defeated Galway 2–13 to 3–7 in the All-Ireland semi-final, while the final was won with their lowest championship score, 1–13 to Limerick's 0–14, on 1 September. The season, in which Griffin described hurling as the '*Riverdance* of sport', saw two great performers retire, Cork's Jim Cashman and Tipperary's Nicky English.

79. Banner Nirvana

1997 ALL-IRELAND FINAL (Croke Park, 14 September)
Clare 0–20 Tipperary 2–13

I have a savage hunger – a more fanatical hunger to win than I had the first time. We have to get another All-Ireland. If we do, this side will be regarded as a great team ... and our job will be done.
Ger Loughnane[1]

WHEN THE MEDAL presentations to Clare's All-Ireland-winning teams at senior and minor were held in Ennis in 1997, Ger Loughnane chose the words of Robert Frost when addressing the large audience. Not Robert Frost the Clare county board chairman, he quickly clarified, but the famous poet. The lines he laid emphasis on were: 'Two roads diverged in a wood, and I took the one less travelled by.'

This was, Loughnane explained, the path Clare had chosen. They had traded the old road of failure for the more difficult and ambitious route and here – he pointed to the two winning cups – were the prizes that rewarded it. They were champions at minor, for the first time ever, and senior, for the second time in three years.

Clare were on top of the hurling order, having set out to prove that 1995 had not been a once-off but evidence of a new beginning, a new force, one there to stay. In triumphing, they enjoyed the perfect winning streak. Having easily disposed of Kerry in the Munster quarter-finals, Clare beat their way past hurling's aristocracy: Cork, Tipperary, Kilkenny – and Tipperary again.

Their season contained a selection of treats: a third championship win over Cork in five years, a first Munster final win over Tipperary, a first championship win over Kilkenny – and in a historic first, an All-Ireland final featuring teams from the same province, when they survived a fierce challenge from Tipp to deservedly finish champions.

The winning score, in a nod to aesthetics, came from the refined stick of Jamesie O'Connor. The player who had had a forgettable day in the final two years earlier ensured he did not miss the opportunity to leave his mark a second time – form that earned him recognition as Hurler of the Year. O'Connor took a pass from another of Clare's outstanding players, Colin Lynch, and struck off his left, whipping the ball over the bar.

While the final of 1995 didn't score highly for technical virtuosity, the 1997 final stood in comparison with, and probably surpassed, any of the previous 20 years. This may in some way explain Loughnane's outburst later that evening at the victory banquet when he lit on RTÉ analyst Eamonn Cregan. The earth hadn't moved for the Limerick man, who had once managed Clare, as he felt the game, while absorbing, wasn't an epic. This prompted an angry response from Loughnane when he went on air live soon afterwards. He described what he had heard as a '10-minute rant'. The Clare manager had started to become increasingly confrontational.

Earlier in the year after the Munster final, which Clare had led by eight points but had ended relieved to see John Leahy miss a late goal chance, Anthony Daly had made a typically rousing victory speech. In it, he stated that Clare were 'no longer the whipping boys of Munster' – later picked up on by Tipperary PRO Liz Howard who referred to it as 'conduct unbecoming' of the GAA.

Out of this, things went a little crazy. Loughnane wrote a lengthy open letter to Howard in the *Clare Champion* where he took her to task, citing examples of Tipperary arrogance he had encountered, and warned her to expect a backlash if she ever were to repeat the charges.

Letters zipped back and forth between the editor of the *Champion* and various Tipperary newspaper titles for a while and when the two teams ended up meeting again in the All-Ireland final, the scene was set for a dramatic and tense season finale. There had been much anticipation of a dream final between Clare and Wexford until Tipperary upset those plans when they defeated Wexford in a surprise result coming through the new back-door route (a journey that had begun with a slightly surreal quarter-final encounter against Down in Clones).

The new championship structure allowed the defeated Munster and Leinster finalists back into the competition with the creation of two new quarter-finals. These comprised the Leinster and Munster runners-up, Galway and the winners of Ulster. Previously, Ulster winners had the privilege of a ticket straight into the semi-finals.

Clare also broke new ground with the practice of dummy selections. Niall Gilligan, who went on to have a big match in the final, wasn't named on the official team. Fergal Hegarty had been down to play but was used as a decoy and Gilligan started instead. There were misgivings about this policy but Loughnane was unapologetic, arguing that it offered protection to new players from excessive exposure.

'The idea of the dummy teams came about from the temperament of certain players who, if they knew they were expected to play, would get nervous or overexcited and not do themselves justice on the big day,' he explained.[2]

Gilligan, who had started and was taken off against Cork, scored three points, making him the joint-top points scorer from play along with O'Connor.

There was some worry about the impact on the new back-door format if Tipperary won the final. They were clearly wound up for revenge for the provincial final defeat in Cork and in the first half they attacked Clare. Declan Ryan and John Leahy were in rampant form and their markers, Sean McMahon and Liam Doyle, were in trouble. By half-time, Clare trailed by four points, 0–6 to 0–10, having faced the wind. But Doyle set the example at the start of the second half with a huge point and gradually, they eliminated Tipperary's advantage and built one of their own.

They drew level at 0–11 apiece and when David Forde came on, he picked off two scores during a spell of Clare dominance. With 10 minutes left, they led 0–17 to 0–12. Clare, who hit 17 wides, had been notorious all year for letting leads slip. This would be no different. Liam Cahill came off the bench and kicked a goal and when Tommy Dunne's free broke in the square with four minutes to go, Eugene O'Neill batted to the net. That he was Brian Lohan's responsibility seemed a cruel twist of fate given Lohan's stellar performance up to then. Tipp led by a point.

The television cameras missed the next score, Ollie Baker catching the quick puckout and pointing to level. And that's how it sat until O'Connor's score decided it. The final heart-stopping scene involved Leahy stealing some yards on the right side of the field and striking to the far corner for goal. The ball hopped and Fitzgerald got down smartly to shove it clear to his right and out of danger. Conor Gleeson, the Tipp captain, had one snap chance from long range to level but it drifted wide. The match finished soon afterwards in the Tipp half of the field.

CLARE: D. Fitzgerald; M. O'Halloran, B. Lohan, F. Lohan; L. Doyle (0–1), S. McMahon (0–1, f), A. Daly; O. Baker (0–2), C. Lynch (0–2); J. O'Connor (0–7, 4fs), C. Clancy (0–1), P.J. O'Connell; N. Gilligan (0–3), G. O'Loughlin (0–1), F. Tuohy; Subs: F. Hegarty for F. Tuohy (28 mins), D. Forde (0–2) for P.J. O'Connell (47), B. Murphy for F. Hegarty (60).

TIPPERARY: B. Cummins; P. Shelly, N. Sheehy, M. Ryan; L. Sheedy, Colm Bonnar, Conal Bonnar; T. Dunne (0–5, 3fs), C. Gleeson (0–1); L. McGrath, D. Ryan, J. Leahy (0–4, 1f); M. Cleary (0–1), E. O'Neill (1–1), B. O'Meara (0–1); Subs: A. Ryan for L. McGrath (HT), L. Cahill (1–0) for M. Cleary (57 mins).

Referee: D. Murphy (Wexford)

Attendance: 65,575

Burning rivalry

For a spell in the 1990s, the rivalry between Clare and Tipperary was the most intense in hurling and, at times, it threatened to spill over.

One of the flashpoints came in Ennis in 1999 when the counties met in the Munster under-21 final. The Tipp senior team hadn't defeated Clare since the 1993 Munster final and lost four senior championship meetings up to 1999.

'That was the worst night of all,' Len Gaynor recalled. 'You could cut the tension with a knife and that shouldn't happen. We had young players there to play a game and all of a sudden there seemed to be a war on. It was time to call a halt.'[3]

Nicky English would strongly deny charges that he was 'laughing at Clare' when he smiled broadly having scored a point in the runaway Munster final win of 1993. Clare admitted they milked the moment in later years for motivation.

Clare put Tipp out of the championship the following year in a major shock and then defeated them twice in the championship in 1997. Tipp should have won in 1999 but were held to a draw before Clare ran riot in the replay.

Tipp finally broke their duck in the 2000 championship meeting, winning by eight points, with English as manager. Loughnane stepped down afterwards, marking the end of an era.

80. The Empire Strikes Back

1999 ALL-IRELAND FINAL (Croke Park, 12 September)
Cork 0–13 Kilkenny 0–12

A lot of us laid to rest an awful lot of ghosts out there.
Jimmy Barry-Murphy[1]

THE TUNNEL SURROUNDING Páirc Uí Chaoimh doubled as a running track for Cork hurlers' winter training in the 1990s. They'd begin with eight circuits to warm up and then break into a series of sprints on the grey concrete. Cork were top of the class in hurling knowledge but they were posting alarmingly low grades for physical preparation at a time when other counties were radical and innovative.

Clare had set the bar with torturous training regimes and 6 a.m. starts. 'Clare were supposed to be training 28 out of 29 nights, or something like that,' says Teddy Owens, who Jimmy Barry-Murphy brought in as team trainer and coach in 1998. Clare had beaten them in their four previous championship meetings and Barry-Murphy realised Cork had to catch up.

Owens consulted experts in the field. Sean McGrath and Donal O'Gorman held qualifications in exercise physiology and, drawing from their knowledge, Owens drew up a training and coaching plan.

> Jimmy [Barry-Murphy] gave me fierce leeway in terms of the hurling training and the drills. We wanted continuous assessment. We looked at nutrition. I remember the first session when we had pasta and chicken, some of the lads had never seen pasta before, they were saying, 'What kind of shit was this?' It was all chips before that.

We never went in for high-frequency training. We saw the importance of rest. There was a whole different emphasis to drink. The old attitude after a match was that lads deserved a few pints but that began to change and players took that on board.[2]

For the first round against Waterford, they even changed their pre-match routine by going to Dundrum House, a country retreat away from Thurles, rather than the Anner Hotel which had been their normal port of call. Owens argued that they would benefit from greater solitude and more open space to stretch their limbs and puck around.

There was also a new focus on tactics, an area Cork tended to treat indifferently or ignore altogether. Cork trusted their hurlers 15-on-15, but new challengers introduced pioneering ideas that forced Cork to change their habits. When Clare defeated Cork in the 1998 Munster championship, they picked a dummy team, making changes before the throw-in. Cork were not on the same frequency.

'I remember going to Jimmy and saying, "Look at these stats, this guy is great in this, great attitude,"' says Owens. 'I had all the physical stats and Jimmy turned round and said, "But, Ted, can he hurl?" Jimmy had a great eye for a hurler. He would not be a great man for tactics. We played Clare one Friday night in Páirc Uí Chaoimh and Clare were training the following morning. I went down to see them train, they wouldn't have known who I was. One thing that struck me was that their drills were all timed and controlled, and that created a greater intensity. It was only a simple thing.'

Cork's improved and more scientific preparations did bear fruit in 1999, but there were few positive signs leading up to the first match against Waterford. They were trounced in two challenge games against Tipperary and, in the second game, Owens remembers Nicky English indicating to the referee that he should blow it up as an act of goodwill.

Shortly before the Waterford game, Owens got a phone call from a Cork selector urging that Barry-Murphy should step down when – not if – they lost the match. Barry-Murphy is revered in Cork, but his time as manager had been a trying one. In 1996, they had lost to Limerick by 16 points, their first home championship defeat in 73 years. Alarm sirens sounded and RTÉ ran that evening with a report of a group being formed to save Cork hurling from ruin.

In 1997, they had run Clare to the wire in the championship but, in 1998 having won the National League, they had been torched in the summer by Clare who won by eight points. When they faced Waterford in 1999, it was win-or-bust time for Barry-Murphy's management. He started six debutantes on a team that had an average age of 23. They won and the manager's celebration dance at the end summed up the enormity of his relief and joy. The Munster final win over Clare that followed was the one they craved and, after an epic semi-final match against Offaly, they were back in the All-Ireland final for the first time since 1992.

Kilkenny were in a cycle of transition. Losing the 1998 All-Ireland final to Offaly had led to a management change that saw Brian Cody arrive with little enough in the way of management experience. Nobody could have envisaged how much he would redefine hurling over the next 15 years. Nobody could have envisaged either how ruthlessly the fledgling rebellion of the lower orders would be quashed by the 'big three'. Cork's win in 1999 was the first of 15 straight All-Ireland triumphs for the top three, with Kilkenny winning nine times. The sequence was finally ended in 2013 by Clare.

At half-time on 12 September 1999, there was pressure on Barry-Murphy to take off Seanie McGrath, a delightfully skilful hurler with a jockey's physique who had announced himself on the championship stage with a brilliant five-point return against Clare in 1997. McGrath hadn't scored and had missed some chances but Barry-Murphy persevered. It proved a richly rewarding decision.

McGrath scored three invaluable points at a key stage late in the game despite the rainy conditions as Cork timed their winning run to perfection.

Kilkenny felt they blew it. Four points is not much of a lead in hurling but in 1999, in a game played in relentless rainfall where scores were at a premium, it counted as a sizeable investment. They had that advantage with 17 minutes left. D.J. Carey could have stretched it to five but he missed, and the complexion of the game began to alter. Having scored 13 goals in their three previous championship games, Kilkenny failed to put one past a watertight Cork defence. It was the first time an All-Ireland senior hurling final failed to produce a goal. In 2004, the same counties repeated the feat. In the past 60 years, only two All-Ireland finals have had a lower aggregate score than 1999.

The first half had Kilkenny marginally ahead, 0–5 to 0–4, with both sides accumulating a high wides count. Kilkenny hit a good spell after the interval which brought four points without reply. Kevin Murray broke their momentum with a point after coming on as a sub and McGrath then delivered on his promise. Between the 55th and 62nd minutes, he scored three times, the third a beautiful finish. Cork had five in a row and Kilkenny couldn't rescue the match in time.

Cork had lost five of their previous six finals to Kilkenny, two of those defeats when Barry-Murphy was captain. This explains their manager's allusion to ghosts being exorcised. The win struck a blow for hurling tradition. Until the 1990s, hurling's top three had never gone more than two years without winning an All-Ireland. By the time the last championship of the millennium arrived, tradition was at the end of a five-year losing streak. The decade had witnessed a rebellion from counties challenging the old order. But the century closed with a familiar presence, an old-money duel between Cork and Kilkenny under sullen skies.

CORK: D. Cusack; F. Ryan, D. O'Sullivan, J. Browne; W. Sherlock, B. Corcoran, S. Óg Ó hAilpín; M. Landers (0–1), M. O'Connell; T. McCarthy (0–3), F. McCormack, N. Ronan; S. McGrath (0–3), J. Deane (0–3, 2fs), B. O'Connor (0–1); Subs: A. Browne (0–1) for N. Ronan (HT), K. Murray (0–1) for M. Landers (51 mins).

KILKENNY: J. McGarry; P. Larkin, C. Brennan, W. O'Connor; M. Kavanagh, P. O'Neill, P. Barry; A. Comerford (0–2), D. Byrne (0–1); D.J. Carey, J. Power (0–1), B. McEvoy (0–1, sideline); K. O'Shea, H. Shefflin (0–5, 4fs), C. Carter (0–2); Subs: P.J. Delaney for J. Power, N. Moloney for C. Carter (both 65 mins).

Referee: P. O'Connor (Limerick)

Attendance: 62,989

81. Derry Heirs

2000 ULSTER FINAL (Casement Park, 9 July)

Derry 4–8 Antrim 0–19

We are looking to improve Derry hurling, and winning the Ulster title would be a massive lift to the sport in the county ... it's a big incentive for the players to go out and create history.

Kevin McNaughton[1]

FIVE MINUTES FROM the end of the 2000 Ulster final, John O'Dwyer scored Derry's fourth goal and the reality of the county's first Ulster title since 1908 moved a step closer. 'The ball broke in and I would be a bit of a poacher and I got on the end of it,' O'Dwyer recalls. 'That put us a point up and I thought, *We could actually win this.*' The six to one outsiders held their nerve in the final stages to end a 92-year wait.

O'Dwyer was a long way from Killenaule, his home place in County Tipperary. Derry's liberator had hurled at under-21 for Tipperary in 1993 alongside Tommy Dunne and Brendan Cummins and had also won an All-Ireland B title with the county's senior football team. Romance led him north after he met a Derry girl in 1992 during the Trip to Tipp music festival. They began a long-distance relationship where, because he didn't have a car, he'd take the bus to Dublin and then hop on another bus to Derry – a full day's travelling. In 1995, he moved there and they married in 1998.

Hugo McCusker was the Derry hurling manager and invited him to a trial match at Celtic Park where he scored a goal with his first touch. He then had to find a club. He signed up with Banagher in his wife's parish and he is still there, managing the senior team.

Jonathan, the eldest of their two sons, is on the Derry hurling squad.

His arrival coincided with Derry's emergence as a serious challenger in the province. He was on the field when they ran Antrim to three points in the 1998 Ulster final and when they were beaten again by Antrim in the 1999 final. Reaching a third final in succession, they realised it was time to make their mark. They felt better equipped, having played the likes of Kilkenny, Tipp and Cork in Division 1 of the National League during the spring.

Kevin McNaughton from Cushendall came in as manager and one of Derry's most dedicated hurling souls, Lavey's Tom McGill, took over the coaching. 'I played 12 years I think with them,' says O'Dwyer. 'I just came at the right time. At the start, there would have been a fairly big drinking culture because they were playing Division 3, they were not too worried, then McNaughton came in and said no more sessions after games. He said we had a team that could win an Ulster title.'

Derry's hopes took a severe dent in the lead-up to the 2000 Ulster final when Geoffrey McGonigle, their main attacking spearhead from Dungiven, was ruled out through suspension. Also unavailable was their captain, Emmet McKeever, sent off in the Ulster semi-final win over Down. To make matters even worse, the experienced midfielder Oliver Collins became an injury doubt after breaking his jaw. Collins played, but he struck eight wides in the first half, later admitting that he was ring-rusty.

This was the last time Ulster had a truly competitive hurling championship before Antrim took over and monopolised the competition (they've won every title since 2002). Antrim aside, Derry were the last county to win the province, and when they played Down in the 2001 final, it created a new landmark – it was the first time a final hadn't involved Antrim since the championship's revival in 1989. In 1997, Ulster's ticket to the All-Ireland semi-finals was rescinded, downgraded to a quarter-final spot. In 2006, Antrim, Ulster champions again, played in the Christy Ring competition and the county went into Leinster in 2009. In a further morale blow, the 2013 Ulster final wasn't played until February 2014.

Compared to now, Ulster was a thriving competition when Derry made their breakthrough in 2000, with Down also serious bidders. Yet Antrim looked on course to win again when they led by four points with 10 minutes to go, taking over completely after the interval and hitting 10 points in a row. O'Dwyer's goal changed the course of the game and gave Derry renewed hope, edging them one-point ahead. Antrim substitute Chris Hamill tied the sides again. A draw and replay looked likely until Collins sent over a free on the stroke of full-time. Antrim won a 65 in injury-time, but the referee ruled that time was up.

Among Derry's heroes was their goalkeeper, Kieran Stevenson, who made four critical saves. Gregory Biggs came off the bench and scored a vital late point and set up the goal. Seeing them brave the Antrim storm, Kevin McNaughton hailed the team's 'incredible determination' in the closing stages.

In the first half, Antrim struggled badly and were 0–5 to 3–4 down at half-time playing into a wind. Their manager Sean McNaughton did not mince his words: 'It is the worst performance that I have ever seen.'

O'Dwyer enjoyed the experience, even if he was an outsider.

It was great to win it, for me, but the lads, they really appreciated it more being Derry men and they had experienced nothing like it before. They went bananas. Even [his son] Jonathan can't get over the crowds that were at our games back then. The Ulster final was seen as a proper competition.

Ollie Collins was the man, he was something else. Every game, he drove us on. Huge man and a brilliant hurler. Everything went through him. They went to all the clubs with the cup for nearly two weeks afterwards, great nights, fantastic nights in Derry. They stopped at Toomebridge on the border on the way back after the Ulster final and walked the cup over the bridge into Derry which was new to me. I was saying, 'Why are we stopping here?'[2]

O'Dwyer scored the winning point as Derry retained their title in 2001, defeating Down in the final, but the following year, their reign ended, when Down beat them in an Ulster semi-final replay.

DERRY: K. Stevenson; C. McGurk, C. Murray, N. Mullan; B. Ward, C. McEldowney, D. Cassidy; O. Collins (1–2, 2fs), M. Conway; K. McCloy (0–1), K. McKeever (1–0), R. McCloskey; Gary Biggs (1–3, 2fs), M. Collins, J. O'Dwyer (1–1); Sub: Gregory Biggs (0–1) for M. Conway (60 mins).

ANTRIM: S. Elliot; E. O'Hara, Ciaran McCambridge, D. McKillip; M. McCambridge, M. Molloy, K. Kelly; J. Connolly (0–1), C. Cunning (0–1); Conor McCambridge (0–6, 0–3 65s, 1f), Gary O'Kane, R. Donnelly; A. Delargy (0–1), Gregory O'Kane (0–4, 3fs), A. Elliot (0–3); Subs: C. Hamill (0–3, 1 sideline) for E. O'Hara (24 mins), A. Mort for R. Donnelly (69).

Referee: J. McDonnell (Tipperary)

Attendance: 3,000

Derry go down fighting

Derry did Ulster hurling proud when frightening favourites Offaly in the 2000 All-Ireland quarter-finals. Offaly led by eight points in the first half and by five at half-time, but 22 minutes into the second-half, Derry sensationally drew level. That sparked an Offaly resurgence and they won 2–23 to 2–17 – but Derry left the match with enormous credit.

Having retained Ulster in 2001, Derry discovered Croke Park wasn't quite as agreeable on their return as Galway won their quarter-final meeting by 21 points. Since then, they have played in just two Ulster finals, in 2003 and 2012, and were heavily beaten each time.

Derry currently compete in the Christy Ring Cup and in the third tier of the National League.

82. Stars in Stripes

2000 ALL-IRELAND FINAL (Croke Park, 10 September)
Kilkenny 5–15 Offaly 1–14

*There are a lot of good young lads now in this squad and Kilkenny hurling is
in a good old state. I reckon we'll be a force for a while now.*
John Power[1]

A SPELL OF PENURY ended and one of unimaginable
prosperity began with Kilkenny's All-Ireland win in
2000. They were led there by 33-year-old captain Willie
O'Connor, one of only three survivors from the last team to win
an All-Ireland seven years earlier, who was nearing his career's
end. O'Connor came from a family of nine in Glenmore. His brother
Eddie had captained Kilkenny in 1993. On succeeding him as victorious
captain in 2000, Willie remembered their mother, who had died on
1 March. 'Mammy loved hurling. She'd have the gear ready for you and
things like that. At the end of the day, she was an inspiration to me.'

For a while, he contemplated retirement but the decision to
play on was rewarding. Following Cork's win the previous year,
this was further evidence that the revolution driven by Clare and
Wexford in the previous decade had been quashed. Kilkenny were
not short of motivation. The loss to Cork in the 1999 final hurt
deeply, the defeat to Offaly in 1998 was still raw. In 2000, they
defeated Offaly in the Leinster final for the third year in succession,
but Offaly recovered to floor the All-Ireland champions Cork with
a sensational performance. To lose three All-Ireland finals in a row
would be unprecedented. Were Kilkenny spooked by what Offaly

could offer? No. As John Power would say afterwards, nothing was going to stop them achieving their goal.

'I remember even shortly before the All-Ireland even up to the last week, we were training under Mick O'Flynn and some of the players asked to do more running,' says Willie O'Connor. 'There was no way we were going to be beaten. Kilkenny were in such a mood that year, I don't think it mattered who was going to be [opposing them] in the All-Ireland.'

O'Connor came on to the team in 1988 but by 2000, he, D.J. Carey and Power were the only Kilkenny players still hurling with All-Ireland medals. A week after Kilkenny had lost the 1999 All-Ireland senior final, the county had won the All-Ireland under-21 championship. The following season, Brian Cody promoted players from that panel and gave them game-time in the league. He wanted self-motivated characters but there was such a prevailing will to win in Kilkenny that he was working with an extremely driven bunch. Kilkenny also upped their training intensity to match modern trends.

O'Connor said the win brought enormous relief. It also launched an unrivalled era of dominance. Of the 10 All-Irelands contested in the 2000s, they won seven. 'I would be training greyhounds,' says O'Connor, 'and good dogs will make a good trainer if you nourish them and look after them. And that is what he [Cody] did, he nourished them and looked after them.'

Since 2000, the county has been involved in every final, bar three, up to and including 2014. In the three years they didn't feature on the last day, they reached the semi-final twice, losing to Galway in 2001 and 2005 – 2013 was a rare exception, when they failed to make the semi-finals for the first time since 1996 and didn't play in Croke Park for the first time since 1951. In these years, they hurled in seven All-Ireland finals in succession.

But in 2000, they were delighted to win just once. Henry Shefflin, 21 years old, gave a fine performance in a full-forward line that demolished Offaly and picked up his first All-Ireland medal. No player embodied Kilkenny's work ethic and core principles more than the Ballyhale player, who had not been a prodigious underage talent. He practised religiously and became an outstanding hurler.

2000 also marked the end for Offaly as a force, though the signs had been on the wall. The county won Leinster minor and under-21 titles the same year but the follow-through didn't materialise. In 2004, they lost a Leinster senior final to Wexford and they haven't been in one since, nor have they added to their underage stockpile. Kilkenny beat Offaly by 11 points in the 2000 Leinster senior final, having won the previous year's provincial final by 10 points and the one before that by five. In 2005, they managed a 31-point win over Offaly. In the 2014 Leinster championship, Offaly's decline continued, placed in stark relief by a 26-point hammering from Kilkenny in the quarter-finals.

'Their full-forward line of Charlie Carter, D.J. Carey and Henry Shefflin was devastating as they teased and tormented the Offaly defence into submission,' Martin Breheny reported in the *Irish Independent* after the 2000 final. Between them, Kilkenny's three inside-forwards scored 4–10.

For Carey, there was personal redemption after two quiet finals. He was declared the Man of the Match, although there was uncertainty about whether or not he scored the second goal, as Shefflin's effort looked to have already crossed the line when Carey came charging in.

Carey's emphatic goal after just six minutes had set Kilkenny on their way. The next goal on nine minutes is the one that has variously been attributed to Carey and Shefflin, but the newcomer looked like he had done enough to make it his. It put Kilkenny eight points clear. Offaly managed to reduce the lead to five points in the 29th minute but Kilkenny responded with 1–2, Charlie Carter getting the goal shortly before half-time. Leading 3–8 to 0–7, Kilkenny never looked like they would relinquish control.

In the second half, Offaly reprised the tactic that had worked so well in the 1998 final and moved Brian Whelahan to the attack. It made no difference. After Offaly got to within eight points of Kilkenny, Shefflin demoralised them with another goal. Johnny

Kilkenny's hunter-gatherer John Power stoops to collect the sliotar under pressure from Galway's Gerry McInerney in the 1993 All-Ireland senior final. Kilkenny retained their title but did not win again for seven years.

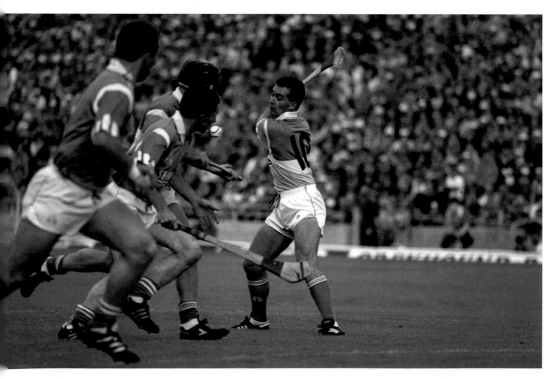

Johnny Dooley about to strike the goal that sparked Offaly's dramatic late fusillade against Limerick in the 1994 All-Ireland senior final. Limerick's five-point lead was turned into a six-point defeat in the final five minutes.

Clare manager Ger Loughnane clutches the MacCarthy Cup after guiding his county to their first All-Ireland since 1914.

Premature celebration as Offaly score their second goal in the 1995 All-Ireland final against Clare. Offaly players, from left, Declan Pilkington, John Troy, Johnny Pilkington (the goalscorer) and Joe Dooley show their delight, while Anthony Daly (partly hidden) and Brian Lohan look on in dismay. Clare recovered from the blow to win their first All-Ireland in 81 years.

The Wexford team that won the 1996 All-Ireland final, defeating Limerick, ending a wait of 28 years. Back: Rod Guiney, George O'Connor, Garry Laffan, Adrian Fenlon, Larry Murphy, John O'Connor, Ger Cushe. Front: Liam Dunne, Tom Dempsey, Martin Storey (captain), Damien Fitzhenry, Sean Flood, Eamonn Scallan, Colm Kehoe, Rory McCarthy. Sean Flood did not play due to injury. Larry O'Gorman, who did and ended up Hurler of the Year, is missing from this shot.

Brian Whelahan helped inspire Offaly to a famous win over Clare in the 1998 All-Ireland semi-final, his county eventually prevailing on the third day in Thurles. Offaly overcame a management upheaval, that saw Babs Keating replaced by Michael Bond, and went on to win the final against Kilkenny in which Whelahan starred in an uncustomary attacking role.

Seanie McGrath shows the delicate stickplay that was a memorable feature of the 1999 All-Ireland final, closely policed by Willie O'Connor, while Mickey O'Connell looks on. Cork won the championship for the first time in nine years, coming from behind to defeat Kilkenny 0-13 to 0-12.

Derry's Oliver Collins (blue helmet) was one of his county's great servants and got his reward when he won an Ulster Championship in 2000, after defeating favourites Antrim. Derry had last won the title in 1908.

DJ Carey about to strike in the 2000 All-Ireland final when Kilkenny ended a seven-year wait, winning comfortably against Offaly. Carey scored their first of five goals and atoned for the previous year's disappointment of losing to Cork. It was the first of Brian Cody's All-Ireland wins as manager.

The 2002 Munster final brought Waterford's first title win since 1963 when they overcame favourites and All-Ireland champions, Tipperary. Here, Peter Queally and James Murray contest with Conor Gleeson and Tommy Dunne of Tipp.

Eoin Kelly celebrates a crucial first half goal, with Dónal Óg Cusack still on the deck during the 2004 Munster final, a famous victory for Waterford, who finished with 14 men.

Kilkenny finally mastered Cork in 2006 with a policy of suffocating marking and effective counter-tactics. The new approach is captured here as Timmy McCarthy is caught in a sandwich between Derek Lyng and James 'Cha' Fitzpatrick in the All-Ireland final.

In 2008 Kilkenny became only the second team in hurling history to complete a four-in-a-row of All-Ireland senior titles. Waterford were the victims of a Cats' masterclass in the final, losing by 3-30 to 1-13. Back: Richie O'Neill, Sean Cummins, Willie O'Dwyer, James Ryall, Noel Hickey, Canice Hickey, Brian Hogan, Michael Grace, Jackie Tyrell, Derek Lyng, Michael Fennelly, Henry Shefflin, P.J. Delaney, T.J. Reid, Michael Rice, Eddie Brennan, John Dalton, Damien Fogarty, Martin Comerford, John Tennyson. Front: David Herity, Aidan Fogarty, Michael Kavanagh, Richie Hogan, P.J. Ryan, Richie Power, J.J. Delaney, Eoin Larkin, Tommy Walsh, Eoin McGrath, Eoin Reid, James Fitzpatrick.

The third of Lar Corbett's goals in the 2010 All-Ireland final, which ended Kilkenny's dreams of five-in-row, goalkeeper PJ Ryan and full-back Noel Hickey unable to intervene. Corbett's hat-trick was the first in an All-Ireland final since 1970.

Clare's hat-trick hero, Shane O'Donnell, raises the MacCarthy Cup after the 2013 All-Ireland final replay against Cork. The 2013 championship was possibly the most open and exciting ever.

Brian Cody experiences that familiar winning feeling at the final whistle in the 2014 All-Ireland final replay. Kilkenny's 2-17 to 2-14 win over Tipperary marked Cody's 10th All-Ireland success in 16 seasons. The drawn game ended dramatically when Hawk-Eye score-detection technology showed a 97-metre free to win the game from Tipp's John O'Dwyer was marginally wide.

Pilkington scored a goal on the hour which did no more than lessen the indignity. Near the end, Eddie Brennan came on and scored a fifth goal.

Kilkenny were clearly the best team of the 2000 championship, scoring 12–71 in four games, winning by margins of 15, 11, eight and 13 points. And they were only getting started.

KILKENNY: J. McGarry; M. Kavanagh, N. Hickey, W. O'Connor; P. Larkin, E. Kennedy, P. Barry; A. Comerford (0–1), B. McEvoy; D. Byrne (0–4), J. Power, J. Hoyne; C. Carter (1–3), D.J. Carey (1–4), H. Shefflin (2–3, 2fs); Subs: C. Brennan for B. McEvoy (28 mins), E. Brennan (1–0) for C. Brennan (67).

OFFALY: S. Byrne; S. Whelahan, K. Kinahan, N. Claffey; B. Whelahan (0–1), J. Errity, K. Martin; Johnny Dooley (0–8, 0–1 65, 6fs), G. Oakley; J. Pilkington (1–1), G. Hanniffy (0–1), B. Murphy (0–1); M. Duignan, J. Ryan, Joe Dooley (0–1); Subs: D. Franks for N. Claffey (45 mins), J. Troy for J. Ryan (48), P. Mulhare (0–1) for B. Murphy (52).

Referee: W. Barrett (Tipperary)

Attendance: 61,493

Offaly shock Rebels

The 2000 All-Ireland semi-final defeat of champions Cork by Offaly was the shock of the year, the Faithful posting a 0–19 to 0–15 win with a consummate show of skill and cunning. Gary Hanniffy subdued Brian Corcoran, and Johnny Pilkington hit four points from play. The old refrain of Offaly being 'never bet' was given a few renditions in the bars that evening as they relived a famous win, coming back from being three points down early in the second half.

The defeat marked the end of the road for Jimmy Barry-Murphy as Cork manager and began a period of chronic instability for the county that included much management upheaval and a fractious relationship between players and the county board.

83. Déise Delirium

2002 MUNSTER FINAL (Páirc Uí Chaoimh, 30 June)
Waterford 2–23 Tipperary 3–12

I am 50 years old this year and this was the first time I saw Waterford win a Munster senior title.
Paddy Joe Ryan[1]

WATERFORD'S HURLERS WERE championship contenders from the late 1990s but they appeared damned by a fickle streak. In 2001, they went out of the championship after leading Limerick at one stage by 11 points. The defeat brought an end to Gerald McCarthy's five years as manager. He made Waterford serious contenders but could not make them champions.

While Waterford had failed to emulate the liberating Munster wins enjoyed by Limerick and Clare, they had still come a long way. In 1993, they were eliminated by Kerry in the Munster championship and, in 1995, they were tenderised by Tipperary by 21 points. McCarthy, an admirer of the Waterford teams he remembered as a child, laid the groundwork but their inconsistency was exasperating.

'It's been one of our big problems, this great inconsistency that's in the team,' he stated in the losing dressing room in 2001. 'We can hurl and out-hurl the best of teams for periods of a game and then sink so low that you wouldn't believe it's the same team. It's a big, big bugbear.'[2]

When he left, another Cork man, Justin McCarthy, stepped in.

Paddy Joe Ryan, the Waterford county board chairman, welcomed all outside help.

> I always maintained that a county like Waterford needed an outside coach with experience. Both Gerald and Justin brought great expectations with them. Both were winners in their own time.[3]

The Munster final win of 2002 was Waterford's first since 1963. Tipperary, reigning All-Ireland champions and strong favourites, qualified for the final with wins over Clare and Limerick. Waterford put out Cork on a rainy day with a winning point from Ken McGrath. They didn't look like world-beaters but the victory was invaluable, earning them entry to a Munster final for only the second time in 20 years. It paved the way for a new era in Waterford and Munster hurling. Of the 12 Munster finals played since then, Waterford have contested seven and won three.

Most forecasters were made eat their words. The day before the match, the outspoken Babs Keating had gone on radio and said that Waterford people would be leaving with 10 minutes to go. He expected a comfortable Tipperary win. Keating later claimed his comments were flippant and not meant to cause offence. He offered his mea culpa: 'I got it wrong; simple as that.'

The surprise result completed the most open period and democratic period in Munster championship history, a competition mostly dominated by Cork and Tipperary. Every county except Kerry had captured a Munster title at least once in the previous 10 years, and Kerry had left their imprint with the sensational win over Waterford in 1993.

Justin McCarthy was a coach to his fingertips, and a perfectionist who fussed over the smallest details. He took players' hurls home for a polish in his workshop. He requested that their shorts be changed from white to blue, a wish that Paddy Joe Ryan made sure won approval at the next county board meeting. McCarthy also changed their pre-match habits. On the day of the Munster final, they went direct to the ground from a training pitch in Midleton. Sean Kelly, the cyclist, was a surprise guest at training one night where he gave a talk on different aspects of physical and mental preparation. Members of the Waterford team of 1963 were brought in to talk to the players too.

They didn't just win the 2002 Munster final, they did it in style with a stirring demonstration of free-spirited hurling. McCarthy had coached Clare during the 1970s, and Antrim in 1970. He'd won with Cork too, without ever feeling that his work had been appreciated. In Waterford, it was and, in 2002, his coaching refinement appeared to release the genie from the bottle.

Waterford trailed 1–9 to 1–10 at half-time after playing into the breeze. In spite of Benny Dunne getting two goals in seven minutes in the second half for Tipp, the challengers were able to respond each time. Ken McGrath, after a frustrating start, led the scoring with seven points from play. John Mullane had four. Paul Flynn scored their other goal from a 20-metre free. Eoin Kelly matched Flynn's feat with a goaled free for Tipp and teed up both majors for Dunne in the second half.

Waterford went at Tipp throughout and it paid dividends. The champions caved in over the final 20 minutes, conceding 1–6 without reply. 'We wanted to play fast hurling,' said Ken McGrath afterwards. 'We've a fast team.'

Yet for any team striving to break through after a long time in the doldrums, belief is key. Dunne's second goal put Tipp level at 3–10 to 1–16. A point from Conor Gleeson nudged them in front. Ken McGrath levelled and Tommy Dunne restored the Tipp lead, 3–12 to 1–17. They didn't score again.

Eoin McGrath tied the teams with a point and, in the 18th minute of the second half, Tony Browne stole in behind the Tipp defence and pulled to the net. Waterford led by a goal and, from there, they cut loose, scoring five points in a rip-roaring finale.

At the end, Fergal Hartley threw his arms aloft and walked towards the euphoric Waterford supporters. Hartley had been there when they lost to Kerry in 1993 and when they were destroyed by

Tipp in Páirc Uí Chaoimh in 1995. Waterford had been miles off. He had good reason to savour the moment.

On the field at the final whistle, Brian Greene fell on his knees in thanksgiving that their day had come. Another experienced hurler, this was a day to treasure. His father Jim had hurled in vain for the county for years and had taken two horrendous beatings in Munster finals from Cork in the early 1980s.

Peter Queally, their wing-back, summed up the day. 'I went straight to my parents. I knew where they were in the stand and my wife and her family. A very emotional moment, something I'll remember for the rest of my life.'[4]

Their manager had added another string to his bow:

Obviously, there was some sort of celebration after 39 years; that is bound to happen. We had to wind down and build it back up again. That was my 13th Munster final to be involved in. I had work the following morning – that was it.[5]

WATERFORD: S. Brenner; B. Flannery, T. Feeney, B. Greene; E. Murphy, F. Hartley, P. Queally; T. Browne (1–0), J. Murray; E. Kelly (0–3), S. Prendergast (0–1), P. Flynn (1–6, 1–5fs); J. Mullane (0–4), K. McGrath (0–7), E. McGrath (0–1); Subs: D. Bennett (0–1) for B. Flannery (52 mins), M. White for P. Flynn (61), D. Shanahan for E. McGrath (69), A. Moloney for S. Prendergast (69).

TIPPERARY: B. Cummins; T. Costello, P. Maher, D. Fahey; E. Corcoran, D. Kennedy, P. Kelly; T. Dunne (0–2, 1f), N. Morris; B. Dunne (2–2), C. Gleeson (0–2), B. O'Meara; E. Kelly (1–4, 1–3fs), J. Carroll (0–1), L. Corbett (0–1); Subs: E. Enright for N. Morris (44 mins), P. Ormonde for D. Kennedy (55), M. O'Leary for T. Costelloe (59), P O'Brien for C. Gleeson (63).

Referee: A. MacSuibhne (Dublin)

Attendance: 40,276

Second chance saloon

A new hurling qualifier system was unveiled in 2002 that, for the first time, gave beaten teams up to and including the provincial finalists another chance in the All-Ireland championship.

Though defeated by Tipperary in the first round in May, Clare were able to dust themselves off and use the qualifiers to their advantage. They beat Dublin and Wexford to reach the quarter-finals where they overcame Galway and then, in the All-Ireland semi-finals, surprised Waterford. Kilkenny took the conventional route, winning a fifth Leinster title in succession and dethroning the reigning champions Tipperary in the other semi-final, Jimmy Coogan's goal the key moment when he was set up by D.J. Carey. They went on to win the final, a repeat, with the same outcome, of the 1932 All-Ireland final between the two counties.

84. Setanta's Tears

2003 ALL-IRELAND FINAL (Croke Park, 14 September)
Kilkenny 1–14 Cork 1–11

The All-Ireland you win today is the greatest ever final.
Brian Cody[1]

HAVING WON THE All-Ireland in 1999, a young Cork team were expected to win more. To their dismay, the next three years brought stagnation and internecine strife rather than medals and further glory. Jimmy Barry-Murphy stepped down as manager after the 2000 All-Ireland semi-final defeat to Offaly and was replaced by Tom Cashman, who lasted a year. Cork lasted one day in the 2001 championship, losing to Limerick by a point. The bus due to take them to Páirc Uí Chaoimh never showed and they were left with no choice but to take cars through the crowded streets where they became a curious distraction for followers of both persuasions. Brian Corcoran retired, temporarily as it turned out, after the Limerick defeat.

The next year, under Bertie Óg Murphy, they reached the National League final but by then revolution was fermenting. The Gaelic Players' Association (GPA) had been established in 1999 and Cork became a focal point of player unrest. Players like Joe Deane, Mark Landers and Donal Óg Cusack were to the forefront of demands for better playing conditions. In the 2002 league final, Cork players lined up for the parade with their shirts out and socks pulled down, a protest designed to draw attention to their cause. But in the championship, they bombed. After losing to Waterford in Munster, they crashed out to Galway in the qualifiers.

Seeking better treatment from a county board that was in no
mood to shower gifts, the net result was a players' strike that forced
the board's hand and meant an agreement had to be brokered using
a third party. Later in the decade, the Cork hurlers would go on
strike again to resolve other issues. They were militant by the
acquiescent standards of previous generations, but what they were
looking for wasn't outlandish. The battle, however, was more about
principle than specific demands.

Out of this turmoil, they found a degree of stability and focus
that would propel them to renewed success and even coax Corcoran
out of retirement. Donal O'Grady was at the helm in 2003 and he
brought a modern coaching approach, with detailed preparation
and a strong line on discipline. The players responded positively.
Clare had caused a big surprise beating Tipperary in the Munster
championship, but Cork dealt with them comfortably in the semi-
finals and, in the final, they put in a strong second half to overcome
reigning champions Waterford.

The O'Grady era ushered in new levels of tactical planning and a
radical style change. The short-passing game with the emphasis on
possession divided opinion in Cork but, as long as they had success,
most could live with it. The success of Newtownshandrum in the
club championship provided the catalyst for change. Newtown's
short passing had worked on the national stage and the county
team followed suit. With Jerry and Ben O'Connor on the team, they
had the players capable of hurling with that kind of precision, with
enough skill and speed to make it work.

Cork came up marginally short in 2003, as Kilkenny retained
the All-Ireland title, a third in five attempts for Brian Cody. The
champions had their own issues. During the year, Charlie Carter
had left the panel in frustration at not getting more game-time.
He was team captain. The captaincy then moved to his club-mate
D.J. Carey, who led the team to back-to-back titles.

Cork were inspired by their new forward weapon Setanta
Ó hAilpín, a tall and athletic hurler with a goal-scoring swagger

who quickly became a summer sensation. He goaled against Waterford in the Munster final and netted again in the All-Ireland final when his goal in the second half levelled the scores. Cork had trailed by six points at half-time but turned the match around and looked more likely winners entering the final 10 minutes. After their goal, a point from Niall McCarthy had Cork in front for the first and only time. But two missed point chances let Kilkenny off the hook and then Martin Comerford, outstanding throughout, tied up the match.

Kilkenny found a second breath. Henry Shefflin, subdued by his standards for much of the game, made a telling late input. He scored two points and helped set up the crucial goal for Comerford in the 65th minute. Shefflin went into the season as Hurler of the Year and, at 24, collected his third All-Ireland medal. It wasn't Kilkenny's best performance in a final, but they timed their run to perfection. Their biggest contributions came from men at opposite ends of the field: Comerford, the full-forward, and Noel Hickey who held Deane to a point from play.

'To have lost would have been a major, major blow,' admitted Cody. 'It would have made bits of the things we had achieved, and that's being honest because 1999 is a short time ago and it lived in our memories. There's no point saying it didn't – it lived in mine. To start off by losing to Cork in the final and to finish up four years later with the same thing happening again – if we had lost, the skill of the team would never have been questioned. What would have been questioned was their toughness, their heart and their ability to grind and battle.'[2]

O'Grady pinned Cork's failure on a poor first half when they hit 11 wides while playing with the breeze.

Every game is different, you know, some days things go over the bar. The Munster final against Waterford, we came out after half-time and everything we hit went over.[3]

Cork's win over Waterford in Munster was the first of many epic tussles between the two neighbours through the decade. John Mullane scored three goals and still ended up on the losing team. In a thrilling All-Ireland semi-final, Wexford had drawn with Cork but were no match in the replay.

In the other semi-final Kilkenny defeated Tipperary by 3–18 to 0–15, storming clear after a tightly contested opening half, with the day's star player the Tipperary goalkeeper Brendan Cummins. A new lighter sliotar introduced over the previous 18 months and used in the 2002 All-Ireland final began to attract greater notice and provoke debate, being deemed by many as too zippy and difficult to control. It had a new polyurethane core and appeared to have a bigger bounce. But Kilkenny, as ever, adapted better than most.

Earlier in the year they had defeated Tipperary in a high-scoring National League final. In September, they rounded off the league and championship double to leave the young Setanta Ó hAilpín in tears at the final whistle. Later that year, Ó hAilpín went to Australia to try his hand at Aussie Rules, and he never wore the Cork shirt again. But Cork had a trump card that they would play when the new season came around. Brian Corcoran didn't know he was it at the time; he watched this one from the stands.

KILKENNY: J. McGarry; M. Kavanagh, N. Hickey, J. Ryall; S. Dowling, P. Barry, J.J. Delaney; D. Lyng (0–1), P. Mullally; H. Shefflin (0–6, 4fs), J. Hoyne, T. Walsh (0–3); D.J. Carey, M. Comerford (1–4), E. Brennan; Subs: C. Phelan for T. Walsh (45 mins), A. Comerford for P. Mullally (60), R. Mullally for J. Ryall (60), J. Coogan for E. Brennan (69).

CORK: D. Óg Cusack; W. Sherlock, D. O'Sullivan, P. Mulcahy; T. Kenny, R. Curran, S. Óg Ó hAilpín; J. Gardiner, M. O'Connell; B. O'Connor (0–1), N. McCarthy (0–2), T. McCarthy (0–1); S. Ó hAilpín (1–0), J. Deane (0–5, 4fs), A. Browne; Subs: J. O'Connor (0–1) for M. O'Connell (38 mins), S. McGrath (0–1) for B. O'Connor (66).

Referee: P. O'Connor (Limerick)

Attendance: 79,383

85. Camán, Lights, Action

2004 NATIONAL LEAGUE DIVISION 1B (Páirc Uí Rinn, 28 February)

Cork 2–13 Wexford 0–9

We want every county to have the chance to train under lights so they can get used to it and be familiar with playing under these conditions. It's a question of getting more grounds with lights and quality playing surfaces.
Sean O'Laoire[1]

THE FIRST DECADE of the 21st century saw the GAA actively encourage counties to invest in floodlit facilities. They recognised the practical benefits, but were also curious about how the public would embrace Saturday-night games.

Tipperary claim to be the first hurling side to play under floodlights when, in 1931, they played a team in San Francisco during a tour of the US. But the meeting of Cork and Wexford in February 2004 was the first competitive hurling match played after dark in Ireland.

The switching on of the lights at Páirc Uí Rinn, the ground named after hurling's great maestro from Cloyne, proved the most exciting part of the evening. The hurling was less than illuminating. Cork easily dispatched a Wexford side with whom they had shared a thrilling draw in the previous year's All-Ireland semi-final. Cork had won the replay comfortably and this game didn't overstretch them either, even with an experimental side. Brendan Lombard, a forward from Ballinhassig, hit two goals either side of the interval in a match played within a week of the 25th anniversary of Ring's death.

While Gaelic football had already embraced floodlit matches, hurling appeared to be more sceptical. With a small ball rising higher distances, there was concern about players being blinded, mistakes being made, even injuries. 'Any worries that floodlights might prove difficult for hurling were universally dismissed and the only thing lost in their powerful glow was Wexford,' Sean Moran wrote in *The Irish Times*.

Wayne Sherlock, who hurled in the Cork defence, says his players were used to training under lights. He was part of a Blackrock team that had played a Cork selection at the same venue earlier and he was supportive of the idea. 'It was an occasion. The one thing that stood out was the atmosphere, it added a bit to it and that can he hard to get in the league.'

Around the same time, a number of Cork clubs installed floodlit facilities on sand-based pitches which meant that Cork were now hurling earlier while undergoing the usual physical hardship during the winter months. Sherlock said that hurling under lights was no different to hurling in natural daylight.

In 1989, the Cork county board had bought Páirc Uí Rinn, formerly the Flower Lodge soccer pitch, and took four years to develop it, at a cost of almost £1 million. On 23 May 1993, the venue was officially opened by GAA President, Peter Quinn. Floodlights were added in 2003 and the first game played under lights was in the National Football League meeting of Cork and Kerry on 1 February 2004.

In the weeks leading up to the match against Cork, Wexford had been preparing for hurling under lights, having had challenge matches against Dublin and WIT at Craanford, a floodlit facility between Gorey and Enniscorthy. The Cork manager Donal O'Grady didn't think the lights created a playing hazard.

It was the same as a daylight match but there seemed to be a good atmosphere – possibly better than you might get on a cold Sunday afternoon. Wexford have played a couple of matches under lights and so have we and the feedback from the players is that it makes no difference.[2]

Wexford manager John Conran had no issues with the lighting, though he was disgruntled by the refereeing. 'None at all. I think it's a great facility to be able to have lights and be able to play out there. It had absolutely nothing to do with how we played.'

Damien Fitzhenry played in goal for Wexford that evening, the only competitive game he played under lights, even though he continued to play for Wexford for another six years.

> The only thing I was a small bit worried about was how I was going to adapt to the lights if there was a high ball coming in. Trying to keep my eye on it without the glare of the lights; that was the only concern.[3]

In recent years, Dublin launched a spring series of National League football and hurling double-headers on Saturday afternoons in Croke Park using the floodlight facilities. 'There is a very strong status-quo thinking in hurling and a reluctance to move away from the status quo, and floodlight hurling might be seen to move away from that,' said Pat Daly, Head of Games in Croke Park. 'But people are realising how they can benefit and that there are no real complaints when they take place.'

In 2010, the first Munster hurling final was held under floodlights when Waterford defeated Cork in a replay on a Saturday evening, but it attracted an attendance of just over 22,000. The following year Davy Fitzgerald, the Waterford manager, claimed the lights had partly contributed to Shane O'Sullivan receiving a red card in the league against Tipperary. Fitzgerald maintained that the player lost sight of the sliotar in the glare at Semple Stadium.

The ultimate endorsement of hurling under lights though arrived in the 2013 All-Ireland senior final replay, which started at 5 p.m. on Saturday, 28 September. There were some reservations expressed in advance, as neither team had played at the venue under those conditions, but it did nothing to hamper a classic shootout between Clare and Cork. The lights had been switched on for a brief period during the 2011 final between Kilkenny and Tipperary because of grey and gloomy conditions, but they were later switched off. They were also turned on momentarily during a rain-lashed, ultra-grey August day in 2014 as Limerick and Kilkenny hurled up a storm in their All-Ireland semi-final. They had another run when the 2014 All-Ireland went to a replay on a Saturday evening.

Speaking in 2013, Croke Park stadium director Peter McKenna explained some of the technicalities.

> There are different settings for hurling, football, soccer and rugby and the brightest of them is for hurling, based on the lighting specifications for cricket at the MCG in Melbourne. It means that more of the lights are operational and it cuts out dazzle and glare.[4]

Whatever stigma may have been there in the first place has been removed. In visual terms, the alignment of modern lighting and hurling at full throttle makes for a fascinating spectacle.

CORK: D. Óg Cusack; A. Fitzpatrick, D. O'Sullivan, W. Sherlock; G. Callinan, R. Curran, S. Óg Ó hAilpín; T. Kenny (0–2), A. Coughlan (0–1, f); J. O'Callaghan (0–4, 2fs), M. Byrne (0–1), T. McCarthy (0–2); S. McGrath (0–1), B. Lombard (2–1), E. Fitzgerald; Subs: N. McCarthy (0–1) for S. McGrath (50 mins), P. Tierney for T. Kenny (63), K. Hartnett for S. Óg Ó hAilpín (69), C. O'Connor for W. Sherlock (70).

WEXFORD: D. Fitzhenry; K. Rossiter, D. Ryan, M. Travers; D. Stamp, D. Ruth (0–1), M. O'Leary; T. Mahon, P. Codd (0–4, 3fs); M. Jordan, J. O'Connor, M. Jacob (0–4); B. Lambert, R. Codd, R. Jacob; Subs: P. Carley for T. Mahon (29 mins), D. Berry for M. Jordan (HT), B. Goff for R. Codd (50), D. O'Connor for J. O'Connor (52), M.J. Furlong for B. Lambert (72).

Referee: P. Aherne (Carlow)

Attendance: 6,000 estimated

86. Lucky Dipper

2004 MUNSTER FINAL (Semple Stadium, 27 June)
Waterford 3–16 Cork 1–21

That's better after all the criticisms about bottle and everything.
That's easily our most satisfying day.
Ken McGrath[1]

THEY CALLED IT 'the Dipper', the trick shot perfected by Paul Flynn, and this was the day it became part of Munster final legend. There were times when he'd tried the same shot and it hadn't come off, and nobody was any the wiser. But in the 52nd minute of this extraordinary match, he decided to have a pop.

Cork were aware of his flair for mischief but didn't appear to read the danger. Thirty metres out, at an angle from their goal, he looked out of range. Cork were a point up, a man up and playing with the wind. Waterford were in no place to be fooling around with gilt-edged scoring chances. They expected Flynn to take his point and reduce the Cork lead to the minimum.

'The farther out you are, the more distance and movement you can get on the ball,' Flynn explained. 'That gave you more latitude for the dip. I kept saying if it didn't actually dip, it would go over the bar and that was the safety net I was relying on.'[2]

Dan Shanahan was standing in front of the Cork goal, impeding the light and hampering the defence's view. He told Sean Óg Ó hAilpín to be ready, informing him that Flynn was going for goal. But he was only winding him up; Shanahan didn't expect it either. Flynn stood over the ball, took a look and let it go with lots of top-spin. The ball sailed in at a low trajectory, dipping at the last moment. Goal.

It was a crossroads moment in a terrific contest – it shook Cork and inflated Waterford. Waterford had looked doomed when John Mullane was red-carded for an off-the-ball incident early in the second half after he got involved with his marker, Brian Murphy. But from there, trailing by two points and facing the wind, Waterford were inspired.

Cork went on to win the All-Ireland and Waterford were left cursing their luck when they lost, without the suspended Mullane, the All-Ireland semi-final to Kilkenny. But regaining the Munster title was a significant marker. This was their third provincial final appearance in a row and second win in three years. It was their second championship win over Cork in that time and only their seventh Munster senior title.

Waterford's last All-Ireland win – in 1959 – had also been their most recent Munster final win over Cork.

They started poorly. Inside five minutes, a mistake by Stephen Brenner allowed a weak strike from Garvan McCarthy to trickle over the line. Eight minutes in, Cork led 1–3 to 0–1. The Waterford defence struggled and Brian Corcoran, who had come out of retirement earlier in the year, scored two points.

After losing the National League final against Galway, Waterford went out a week later and destroyed Clare by 19 points in the Munster championship. Their next victims were Tipperary in the semi-finals when substitute Paul O'Brien scored a late goal to carry them through. But Cork, the holders, started the final as favourites.

The Déise's stomach for battle had frequently been questioned but, in the 2004 Munster final, they thrived on adversity. Fifteen minutes into the first half, Eoin Kelly goaled after a long run that started on the right-hand touchline. He got hooked by Jerry O'Connor, recovered, and worked his way in along the endline before applying a deft finish from a tight angle. The score put Waterford back in the match, trailing just 1–5 to 1–4, and offered a foretaste of what was to come.

Waterford were five points down 10 minutes later when they snatched another lifeline, Shanahan scoring a goal after Kelly's shot dropped short. The Lismore man outfielded O'Sullivan and blasted home from close range. Cork led 1–10 to 2–5, which was not a true reflection of their dominance. Waterford were spiky and defiant. When Cork edged back in front, Ken McGrath responded with a massive point from his own half.

The second half started with an inspiring score from Mullane, clipping Cork's lead to a point, 1–14 to 2–8. Then, as Ken McGrath waited to take a free, the referee's attention was drawn to an incident near the Cork goal. Murphy lay on the floor. RTÉ's analyst Michael Duignan announced that he had seen Mullane strike Murphy in the face with the butt of his hurl. Waterford claimed Mullane had been provoked, but it was no use. He was sent off.

'If Cork had got a point or two then, you might have had the heads dropping. But I think we got the next score and we matched them score for score. They didn't use the ball the best,' says Flynn.[3]

The dismissal seemed to throw Cork. McGrath began to rule from centre-back and the defence tightened up, with Eoin Murphy tying down Joe Deane. A point from Ronan Curran had the lead at a goal, 1–16 to 2–10, after 45 minutes. Waterford closed to the minimum, but Ben O'Connor pushed Cork back out to two points in front with a glorious score from the sideline. When Shanahan won a free 30 metres from goal in the 50th minute, Flynn's famous goal that resulted put them in front for the first time, 3–12 to 1–17.

On the hour, Flynn landed a beautiful point to move them two up, 3–15 to 1–19. Cork closed to one. Then, with three minutes to go, a key sequence of play decided the match. Diarmuid O'Sullivan made a catch and booming clearance. The ball broke Cork's way, but a key interception prevented what might have been a winning goal. The ball was swept downfield. Seamus Prendergast gathered and nailed a massive score. With Mullane watching on nervously from the bench, Cork pressed again. They reduced the lead to a point but, repelling one final raid, Ken McGrath raised his hand, fielding heroically. He won a free and Waterford were safe.

They headed to Croke Park in confidence, but their win was clouded by Mullane's dismissal.

WATERFORD: S. Brenner; J. Murray, D. Prendergast, E. Murphy; T. Browne, K. McGrath (0–1), B. Phelan; D. Bennett (0–1 f), E. Kelly (1–1); D. Shanahan (1–3), M. Walsh, P. Flynn (1–7, 1–4fs); J. Mullane (0–2), S. Prendergast (0–1), E. McGrath; Subs: P. O'Brien for D. Bennett (50 mins), S. O'Sullivan for E. McGrath (66), J. Kennedy for P. O'Brien (71).

CORK: D. Óg Cusack; W. Sherlock, D. O'Sullivan, B. Murphy; S. Óg Ó hAilpín, R. Curran (0–1), J. Gardiner; T. Kenny (0–3), J. O'Connor (0–2); G. McCarthy (1–0), N. McCarthy, T. McCarthy; B. O'Connor (0–4, 0–1 65, 1f), B. Corcoran (0–2), J. Deane (0–9, 6fs); Subs: J. O'Callaghan for N. McCarthy (58 mins), K. Murphy for G. McCarthy (65 mins), P. Tierney for T. Kenny (46), M. O'Connell for J. Gardiner (70).

Referee: S. McMahon (Clare)

Attendance: 52,100

An epic rivalry

Between 2000 and 2010, a thrilling rivalry developed between Cork and Waterford, characterised by fascinating matches and high levels of skill and drama. Cork had better luck outside Munster, winning All-Irelands in 2004 and 2005.

It began with Waterford's one-point win over Cork in the 2002 Munster semi-final, the Déise striding on to win a first Munster title since 1963. A year later, they met in the Munster final where John Mullane's 3–1 wasn't enough to save Waterford from losing the title to Cork, going down 3–12 to 3–16.

After Waterford's win in 2004, they met twice in 2005. Cork won by two points in the Munster semi-final and they repeated the act when they defeated Waterford in the All-Ireland quarter-final, 1–18 to 1–13, the goal coming from Brian Corcoran.

More heartbreak followed for Waterford in the 2006 All-Ireland semi-finals. Waterford had a four-point lead and looked destined to make the final until late sub Cathal Naughton scored a decisive 1–1 for Cork.

They met three times in 2007. Waterford won a high-scoring Munster semi-final, 5–15 to 3–18. They later drew 3–16 apiece in the All-Ireland quarter-finals, with Waterford finally overcoming Cork in the replay, winning 2–17 to 0–20, when Dan Shanahan scored two goals.

The next meeting wasn't until the 2010 Munster final, when Waterford won after a replay.

87. Style Makeover

2004 ALL-IRELAND FINAL (Croke Park, 12 September)
Cork 0–17 Kilkenny 0–9

There was a saying in Cork one time that once you went outside Blackpool, there wasn't a hurler in the county. They're coming out for them now.
Bernie O'Connor[1]

THE NEW STYLE of hurling deployed by Cork traced its roots to Newtownshandrum in the north of the county, an area with little tradition until the local club won a first senior hurling title in 2000. Drawing from a parish of around 850 people, they added an All-Ireland club title in 2004 and reached another final, losing to Portumna. However, there wasn't universal approval for their playing method.

One man was seen as chief architect of their possession game. Bernie O'Connor came from Meelin, 20 miles from Shandrum. He married into the parish and two of his sons – twins, Ben and Jerry – became part of a successful juvenile team that he took over when they were 12. Using a running and link-up style he'd first experimented with in Meelin, O'Connor had huge success with the Newtown team up through the juvenile grades.

O'Connor was something of a maverick, but his system worked. In his own playing days, he became the first Meelin man to make the Cork minors, in 1967, and he went on to play county at under-21 and senior. For most of the 20th century, the city clubs of St Finbarr's, Glen Rovers and Blackrock ruled Cork hurling, but Newtown helped shift the power base away from the city. To play minor for

Cork, Bernie had to work much harder than his city equivalent. He would thumb a ride into Cork City, 45 miles from his home, and hitch back late at night.

> I think it's the way to hurl. You see lads belting balls 60 feet in the air into small forwards. Then you hear fellas saying, 'Ah, the forwards were hopeless.' Of course they were, when the ball is coming down from the clouds. I think it's total hurling, not hit-and-hope. You're hitting the ball with a purpose, you think when you get the ball. Most hurling is played off-the-cuff; get it and flake it. I don't think that is the right type of hurling.[2]

His running game demanded a high level of fitness.

> If you can name any team game in the world that the main emphasis is not on passing the ball, then I'll change my style. Why should hurling be so much different than any other game? You have good midfielders not playing well simply because the ball is being flaked up over their heads the whole time. They're inside in the middle like zombies running here and there, the ball flying over them. Now my argument is: put them on the ball.[3]

Cork, with the O'Connors, Pat Mulcahy and Cathal Naughton involved, were soon following the Newtown example.

But Cork took a step back in time, too. In April, Brian Corcoran returned to the hurling panel at 31, having retired in 2001. His career had started spectacularly in 1992 when he won Hurler of the Year at just 19 on a team that lost the All-Ireland final to Kilkenny. After seven barren years, he had avenged that defeat to win his first All-Ireland medal at Kilkenny's expense. But one All-Ireland from 10 attempts is a modest return for a Cork hurler. He'd watched their defeat to Kilkenny in 2003 from the upper deck of the Hogan Stand.

The 2004 final wasn't a classic, more a tough, error-ridden affair with little fluent hurling. With time almost up, Corcoran won a ball near the sideline and made an angle and shot off his left side – the sliotar landed just over the crossbar. He dropped to his knees and raised his arms in triumph. Corcoran scored two points and caused Noel Hickey, the star of the 2003 final, serious difficulty. So much so that Kilkenny moved their full-back to the corner and put James Ryall on Corcoran.

It is hard to believe, given the performances that would come later in the decade, that Kilkenny were held to nine points in an All-Ireland final. Their attack totally malfunctioned. D.J. Carey was held scoreless. So was Eddie Brennan. The team failed to score from play in the second half and only registered two points in that period, from placed balls. Cork outscored them 0–11 to 0–2 after the interval and Kilkenny went the final 23 minutes without raising a flag.

The 2004 final broke new ground in that, for the first time, both finalists had failed to win their provincial championships. Kilkenny had a fitful year and looked tired and possibly over-trained. Michael Jacob's late winning goal for Wexford had stunned them in the Leinster semi-finals, a crestfallen Brian Cody collapsing theatrically behind the Kilkenny posts when Jacob's shot hit the net.

From there, they embarked for the first time on the qualifier route. An abject Dublin were filleted in Dr Cullen Park by 26 points and league champions Galway felt Kilkenny's wrath in the next round, losing by 19 points in Thurles. Cody was volcanic on the line, haring after the referee Diarmuid Kirwan at half-time to protest over some grievance. Clare took them to a replay in the quarter-finals and then they overcame Waterford, 3–12 to 0–18, in their semi, Henry Shefflin scoring two goals. But the additional games and high emotion may have drained them and they looked out on their feet after half-time in September.

Cork ended up in the qualifiers after losing to Waterford in the Munster final. They went to Killarney and re-energised themselves by beating Tipperary. In the All-Ireland quarter-finals, they easily overcame Antrim, by 22 points, and Wexford were shown no mercy in the penultimate stage, the Rebels coasting 1–27 to 0–12 in a replay.

The final was the third in six years to feature Cork and Kilkenny.

They both started the day with 28 All-Ireland titles, vying for outright leadership on the roll of honour. The All-Ireland champions played most of the hurling in the first half but went in at half-time only 0–7 to 0–6 ahead, knowing their labours deserved better. Cork didn't score from play until the 31st minute, though Joe Deane had a goal chance, hitting the crossbar after 13 minutes. But in the second half, Cork ran the show. In the final a year earlier, Niall McCarthy had missed chances to consolidate Cork's lead over Kilkenny at a critical stage in the second half; this time his three points were critical in establishing Cork's foothold and guiding them towards victory.

They had one major scare when Shefflin had a snap shot but Donal Óg Cusack saved, with Cork leading 0–12 to 0–9 after 57 minutes – 10 minutes after Shefflin had got Kilkenny's final score. Shefflin's goal miss saw Kilkenny's influence wane. Cork won the last 23 minutes 0–9 to 0–0 to inflict on Kilkenny their heaviest All-Ireland final loss in 40 years.

A year later, Corcoran won another All-Ireland medal, but 2004 was special, and his last point was the one he later chose as his 'moment in time'. It was, he said, 'the ultimate way to finish the game, the year, the comeback'.[4]

As for Cork's style makeover, winning made it easier on the eye. 'People may say it's not traditional Cork hurling,' said Bernie O'Connor, 'but I don't care what hurling it is as long as it wins.'

CORK: D. Óg Cusack; W. Sherlock, D. O'Sullivan, B. Murphy; J. Gardiner, R. Curran, S. Óg Ó hAilpín; T. Kenny (0–1), J. O'Connor (0–1); B. O'Connor (0–3), N. McCarthy (0–3), T. McCarthy; K. Murphy (0–2), B. Corcoran (0–2), J. Deane (0–5, 5fs); Sub: J. Browne for B. Murphy (inj., 25 mins).

KILKENNY: J. McGarry; M. Kavanagh, N. Hickey, J. Ryall; T. Walsh, P. Barry, J.J. Delaney; D. Lyng (0–1), K. Coogan; H. Shefflin (0–5, , 0–1 65, 3fs), J. Hoyne, D.J. Carey; J. Fitzpatrick (0–1), M. Comerford (0–2), E. Brennan; Subs: C. Phelan for J. Fitzpatrick (62 mins), S. Dowling for K. Coogan (69).

Referee: A. MacSuibhne (Dublin)

Attendance: 78,212

88. All Guns Blazing

2005 ALL-IRELAND SEMI-FINAL (Croke Park, 21 August)
Galway 5–18 Kilkenny 4–18

If you'd told me before we were going to score 5–18, I would have said that wasn't going to happen.
Conor Hayes[1]

THE ODD THING about this contender for game of the decade is that, in the long run, the vanquished came back stronger. This was Kilkenny's last championship defeat until September 2010 – while Galway, in a familiar pattern, failed to build on their success. Brian Cody learned the lessons and tightened up his defence. Galway went on to lose the All-Ireland final and, the following year, were unable to handle a Kilkenny barrage when the teams met in the All-Ireland quarter-finals, falling 17 points behind with 25 minutes to go. They remained as scattergun as ever.

This was Cody's moment of realisation that serious change was required. Kilkenny dusted themselves down and came back with renewed aggression and a demonic will in 2006. There was also a changing of the guard. D.J. Carey, who finished his last day scoreless, put away his gun. Peter Barry from James Stephens was taken off and never saw duty again.

Galway's all-out attack brought about a remarkable transition in their fortunes. In late 2004, their manager Conor Hayes looked like a dead man walking. His two-year term expired in a 19-point defeat to Kilkenny in July, having won the National League earlier in the year. Another race to succeed him had begun. Mattie Murphy seemed set to win, but fell at the last hurdle. Hayes was given another two years.

For some time, the GAA had been agonising about how best to tackle Galway's western isolation. Hayes openly favoured a move to Leinster. Before being destroyed by Kilkenny in 2004, they had only played Down in a qualifier and hadn't been tested. Further structural changes in 2005 ensured that when they met Kilkenny again, they had three qualifier games behind them and a win over Tipperary in the All-Ireland quarter-finals. Serious momentum.

Ten of the players who had started against Kilkenny in the Thurles massacre were there in 2005 when the teams met again in Croke Park. Kilkenny were league champions, Leinster champions and strong favourites to reach a sixth All-Ireland final in seven years. What followed was pure Galway eccentricity. All out attack against Kilkenny was judged to be madness. No other county but Galway would have tried it and no other county would have been able to pull it off.

The 2004 defeat to Kilkenny had demanded a response. Ollie Canning recalled it later.

> Well, it was one of the worst defeats I ever had. You try to rationalise, you kind of hear people say that they were unbeatable on the day; I don't really believe in that. I think they got a run on us and really punished us, got a couple of goals near the end. Maybe we just weren't ready for the pace of the championship.[2]

Winning this match in the manner they did deepened Galway's mystique as a problem team for Kilkenny. Their surprise win in 2001 had forced Kilkenny to alter their approach and become more robust. The win in 2005 would also lead to a different strategy and some serious soul-searching. In the 2012 Leinster final, Galway did it again, sweeping Kilkenny off the field in the first half. They also drew with them in 2014 after being 10 points down, scoring three late goals.

In 2005, some things worked in Galway's favour. Kilkenny were without their regular full-back Noel Hickey who was injured, and his replacement, John Tennyson, struggled with the pace of the game. Niall Healy scored three goals and while Tennyson was not to blame for all three, Hickey's presence and experience were badly missed.

However, Galway had a start that must have sent shivers through their backline. After three minutes, Damien Joyce misjudged a low ball and it ran through to Eddie Brennan who goaled. Brennan soon had 1–2 and won a free that gave Kilkenny another score. Shane Kavanagh was moved on him and went on to have an outstanding match. Brennan still ended up with 2–4, exceeding Healy's haul.

Galway also had an exceptional marksman in Ger Farragher, a minor star for three years up to 2001 who hadn't always fulfilled his promise, in classic Galway fashion. This was his finest hour. Farragher finished with 2–9, eight points from frees. He put them 0–9 to 1–5 up nearing the half hour when Kilkenny conceded two goals in a minute. Both were his. The second was a follow-up after Damien Hayes was denied by James McGarry and illustrated how much Galway were tuned in. An inspirational score from David Tierney followed. Galway, 2–10 to 1–5 clear, were on fire.

The fun was only starting. In the 34th minute, porous defending allowed the ball to run through to Henry Shefflin and he pulled it into the net. David Forde hit a point in reply but, before the interval, Galway were exposed again. A misplaced pass by Kavanagh let in John Hoyne and his goal left Galway shaken but ahead, 2–11 to 3–5, at half-time.

The second half began in a whirlwind that never stopped. Kilkenny applied most of the early pressure and by the 42nd minute, the teams were level. With expert timing, Healy popped up with the first of his goals; Alan Kerins had a shot deflected by McGarry and Healy pounced.

Kilkenny were angered, not unjustifiably, by a couple of critical calls from the referee Seamus Roche. Peter Barry was fouled by

David Forde, but the free went the other way and Farragher nailed it. And when Kilkenny won a free, an agitated Barry was penalised for verbals and a throw-in was given instead. From there, the ball flew into Healy's paw, he turned his man and goaled again. Galway were seven points up with 20 minutes to go.

Kilkenny took off Barry, replaced him with Brian Hogan, but Galway continued to press. In the 56th minute, a long ball broke and Healy kicked to the net: 5–17 to 3–12. Surely that was it?

But Kilkenny weren't done. Over the remainder, they outscored Galway 1–6 to 0–1. A 65 from Shefflin reduced the margin to 10 points, Brennan slipped through for a goal and another Shefflin point had it down to six. Kilkenny went at Galway with all they had. They shaved the lead to three until Kevin Broderick relieved some of the pressure with a fine score near the end of normal time. Shefflin responded with a free, but Galway held on.

This was Kilkenny's darkest hour but a glorious dawn was near. They were about to wreak great vengeance.

GALWAY: L. Donoghue; S. Kavanagh, O. Canning, D. Joyce; D. Hardiman, T. Regan, D. Collins; F. Healy (0–1), D. Tierney (0–2); R. Murray (0–2), D. Forde (0–2), A. Kerins; G. Farragher (2–9, 8fs), N. Healy (3–0), D. Hayes (0–1); Sub: K. Broderick (0–1) for N. Healy (67 mins).

KILKENNY: J. McGarry; M. Kavanagh, J. Tennyson, J. Ryall; R. Mullally, P. Barry, J.J. Delaney; T. Walsh (0–1), D. Lyng; M. Comerford (0–1), H. Shefflin (1–9, 0–1 65, 7fs,), J. Hoyne (1–0); E. Brennan (2–4), D.J. Carey, E. Larkin (0–1); Subs: R. Power (0–2) for J. Hoyne (44 mins), B. Hogan for P. Barry (52), E. McCormack for D. Lyng (53), J. Tyrrell for E. Larkin (63).

Referee: S. Roche (Tipperary)

Attendance: 39,975

D.J. calls it quits

The Galway defeat was D.J. Carey's last appearance for the county, although his retirement wasn't announced until the following year. Carey had been a Kilkenny player since 1990 and is the county's third highest championship scorer with 34–195 from 57 appearances. He caused a sensation when he announced his retirement in 1998 at the age of 27, but reversed that call six weeks later after a huge appeal from the public. His personal highlight came when he captained Kilkenny to All-Ireland success in 2003 and, in a career of many great scores, one of his most memorable was an audacious point in the previous year's All-Ireland final win over Clare. He finished with five All-Ireland medals and nine All Stars. Talking about his retirement in 2006, he said, 'I just haven't the urge.'

89. No Limits

2006 ALL-IRELAND FINAL (Croke Park, 3 September)
Kilkenny 1–16 Cork 1–13

I believe that the greatest skill in hurling is tackling, the ability to block and put pressure on players. Anybody can hit the ball and do lovely things with the ball, but the game is so seriously intense now, and fitness levels massive, and without that you won't win anything.
Brian Cody[1]

FIFTEEN MINUTES INTO the 2006 All-Ireland final, Donal Óg Cusack prepared to puck the ball out after Kilkenny had levelled the game at 0–4 apiece. He looked up the field, surveying his options. Puckouts were Cusack's trademark speciality. He made a hand signal and then whipped the ball to his left, almost to the sideline. Jerry O'Connor made his run and fielded, perfectly on cue. He turned infield and, as he was about to send the ball into the Kilkenny half, James 'Cha' Fitzpatrick made a block. The ball spilled into open play and was swept along the ground back towards the Cork goal. Shefflin gathered with his back to goal and pointed. The score was a sign that Kilkenny had Cork's number.

There were several sequences of play like this, highlighting how Kilkenny cracked Cork's tactical code. They set up roadblocks in the channels where Cork expected a free run with the ball. They made short passing a high-risk venture. Brian Cody maintained all along that Kilkenny don't do tactics. But if that were true once, it wasn't any longer. They had studied the Cork running game in detail and were intent on disrupting it at every turn.

Kilkenny pulled their half-forwards back up the field on the Cork puckout to fill up space, and their midfielders retreated towards their own half-back line. Their players pledged to work like no Kilkenny team had worked before. And that is what they did. There were comparisons to the swarm tactics being employed by Ulster football teams like Tyrone, as on one occasion in the first half Seán Óg Ó hAilpín was hopelessly smothered by four or five Kilkenny players, and had to release the ball or be whistled for over-carrying.

Later in the match, Cusack had the ball in hand again, plotting another restart. Cusack wound back the hurl and let go. The ball zipped out to the left again, veering towards the sideline and into view came Niall McCarthy, the Cork centre-forward who had raced from his berth to gain possession. But the symmetry wasn't pinpoint and every half-second and inch counted; the ball beat McCarthy and went over the sideline to a huge roar from the Kilkenny crowd.

Brian Cody may have difficulty judging which victory has been the most satisfying, but the 2006 All-Ireland win is surely a serious contender. Three championship defeats – to Wexford, Cork and Galway – had left a deep wound and asked questions about whether Cody could come again, and if he was able to find a new way. The remarkable run of success that was about to follow started with this match. Kilkenny would go on to win four All-Irelands back-to-back. Old records that had looked as immovable as the ancient pyramids began to fall.

The 2006 All-Ireland win ended Cork and their three-in-a-row bid. Brian Corcoran retired and the county's established players gradually dropped away over the next few years without adding to their All-Ireland collection. John Allen's term as manager also came to a close. More internal unrest was also around the corner and, in Munster, Tipperary were about to usurp them.

Kilkenny's game became the new template. Fitness levels had been fundamental to the running game Cork employed; and they were just as essential to the game Kilkenny devised to spoil it. But power was critical too. Mick Dempsey, the former Laois footballer and manager who was a publican in Kilkenny, had come in as a physical trainer. He trained the under-21 team that had crushed

Tipperary in the 2004 All-Ireland final, and several of those players now hurled for the senior side. Kilkenny had big men. Their forwards were strong in the air and comfortable under a high ball.

All-Ireland finals produce unexpected heroes and 2006 belonged to 24-year-old Aidan Fogarty, nephew of the late Pa Dillon. Six and a half minutes into the match, he beat Pat Mulcahy to the ball, lost it, regained it, broke away, turned back and found the target. It put Kilkenny 0–3 to 0–1 up, his first point in the championship. Mulcahy, Cork's captain, would have a tough day dealing with Fogarty's pace and elusive left-handed game before being substituted in the second half.

In the 26th minute, Cork drew level, a dozen points evenly shared, with a perfect example of their playing method. Cusack went long, again to the left sideline. Deane raced out the field and gathered and spotted Jerry O'Connor steaming through the middle. A neat stick pass had the ball in O'Connor's hand and he finished confidently. They exchanged scores again and then, in the 29th minute, came the score that put daylight between the sides. Cork were never able to get back on equal footing.

A dropping ball from Martin Comerford popped out of the outstretched hand of Diarmuid O'Sullivan. Fogarty still had plenty to do, but his reactions were exceptional. He snatched the ball over Mulcahy and sent a belter past Cusack into the net. Ben O'Connor hit a quality score in reply but the half ended with one more from Kilkenny. When O'Sullivan was hooked under pressure and Brian Murphy under hit the clearance, Derek Lyng picked it up and pointed to leave Kilkenny 1–8 to 0–8 ahead after an absorbing opening 35 minutes.

Nothing seemed capable of stopping Kilkenny. In the weeks leading up to the final, they had suffered a major setback when J.J. Delaney was ruled out with a serious knee injury. They had only scored one goal in their three previous All-Ireland finals against Cork, but the one they scored in 2006 would be enough and was all they needed to keep Cork at bay.

Three points still separated them in the 53rd minute when Jerry O'Connor ran into traffic, lost the ball and Kilkenny worked it to

This league win wasn't the high point of their season – they went on to win the Munster championship – but as league wins go, it had real currency. Clare had a similar spell with a richly talented team in the 1970s, winning two league finals against Kilkenny, but falling short in the championship. Those league wins were warmly welcomed at the time and greatly celebrated in a county starved of success.

For Waterford, there was also the Kilkenny aspect. Waterford has a history with Kilkenny, living on their border and in their shadow, and had endured narrow All-Ireland semi-final defeats to Kilkenny in 1998 and 2004. This match was one to savour. Kilkenny had also a proud league track record – in 2007 they were aiming for a third title in succession – and took every game seriously. To beat them in a national final, you had to be on top of your game and Waterford were.

They held their composure in a thrilling finale, with two points in injury-time after the teams had been locked on 0–18 apiece. Embellishing the feat was the manner in which they managed to drag themselves out of a difficult spot to regain control of the match. Waterford led 0–11 to 0–9 at half-time but then hit a valley period when Kilkenny put five points over without a response to build a 0–14 to 0–11 lead. On came Paul Flynn in a bid to salvage the match and Shanahan was moved to the edge of the square. With John Mullane having little impact, Kilkenny appeared to have done enough.

Kilkenny still had a three-point lead, 0–15 to 0–12, with a quarter left when Waterford made their heave. Seamus Prendergast, Flynn and Shanahan all registered to level the match. Some loose Kilkenny finishing helped keep Waterford within striking distance, while their 2006 All-Ireland final Man of the Match Aidan Fogarty was being tightly guarded by Aidan Kearney in the Waterford full-back line. Eoin Murphy played at full-back on Cha Fitzpatrick and held him scoreless.

The game featured a first start for Henry Shefflin since the previous September's All-Ireland final, the Ballyhale player now in the autumn of his career. But his class showed and he got a tally of 12 points. Five of the Kilkenny wides were his, too, showing that even then he was short of match sharpness. Kilkenny had to field without regular centre-back John Tennyson, P.J. Delaney filling in as emergency cover.

The final 10 minutes had the crowd totally absorbed. Martin Comerford and Richie Power twice restored Kilkenny's lead, but suddenly Mullane found his range, equalising on both counts. Waterford warmed to the challenge. Michael 'Brick' Walsh began to wield greater influence from centre-back and Prendergast nudged Waterford ahead, 0–18 to 0–17.

Shefflin levelled again with a last-minute free, before the final push from Waterford. Eoin Kelly scored a huge point from long distance and Prendergast capped the win with their 20th score. Brick Walsh had the honour of receiving the cup, and Waterford were entitled to dream of even headier days in the summer ahead.

WATERFORD: C. Hennessey; A. Kearney, E. Murphy, D. Prendergast; T. Browne, K. McGrath (0–3, 3fs), J. Murray; M. Walsh, J. Kennedy (0–1); D. Shanahan (0–1), E. Kelly (0–8, 6fs), S. Molumphy; S. Walsh, S. Prendergast (0–3), J. Mullane (0–2); Subs: P. Flynn (0–1) for S. Walsh (49 mins), E. McGrath (0–1) for J. Murray (53), S. O'Sullivan for J. Kennedy (74).

KILKENNY: P.J. Ryan; N. Hickey, B. Hogan, J.J. Delaney; J. Tyrrell, P.J. Delaney, T. Walsh; D. Lyng (0–1), W. O'Dwyer; E. Brennan (0–1), M. Comerford (0–2), R. Power (0–2); H. Shefflin (0–12, 0–1 65, 9fs), J. Fitzpatrick, A. Fogarty; Subs: E. Larkin for J. Fitzpatrick (49 mins), E. McCormack for A. Fogarty (66).

Referee: S. Roche (Tipperary)

Attendance: 22,235

91. The Masterpiece

2008 ALL-IRELAND FINAL (Croke Park, 7 September)
Kilkenny 3–30 Waterford 1–13

From where I was, it was everything you could ask for in a team, I think that was the essential thing about it. They were a team and not about individuals, prima donnas or anything like that. They were the essence of everything a team could and should be.
Brian Cody[1]

IF THE FIRST Kilkenny three-in-a-row, achieved by the pioneering men of 1911–1913, contained the nagging rider of one title having been won in the boardroom, the county's second was above reproach. They honoured the moment with a performance of incontestable magnificence.

This was Kilkenny at their radiant best. Of the winning total, 3–24 came from play. They hit just two wides in the whole match. Eight players shared the scoring, with Eddie Brennan compiling 2–4, including two goals in the 20th and 22nd minutes to open up a 12–point lead. It was 2–16 to 0–5 at half-time, Kilkenny's first wide coming in injury-time from Martin Comerford. All of Waterford's first-half points were scored by Eoin Kelly from frees.

The most one-sided All-Ireland final since 1943 was so extraordinary that, in a break from tradition, Brian Cody received the RTÉ Man of the Match award in recognition of an exceptional team performance. The team was very much Cody's creation, the fruits of his principles and resolute work ethic. The award sealed his place as the greatest manager the game has known. His All-Ireland win count rose to six in nine years.

The build-up consumed Waterford, who had last won an All-Ireland in 1959, and their players found it hard to escape the manifold distractions. A farmer in Portlaw laid out 300 manure bags to carry the message 'Cats Beware'. In the four weeks between the semi-final and final, the local radio station WLR belted out the track 'Don't Stop Believing' 142 times. Houses and cars were painted blue and white in honour of the team's achievement in reaching the final judgement day. Kilkenny jerseys were placed on tackle bags in training.[2]

Waterford were hopeful that they could emulate their 1959 All-Ireland win over Kilkenny. 'The county just went cracked before the 2008 All-Ireland final. It is as simple as that,' Dan Shanahan stated in his autobiography. The two tribes were neighbours but poles apart historically. They had met in only two other finals – Kilkenny winning in 1957 and again in 1963 despite conceding six goals. Waterford hadn't been in a final since then, 45 years. In that same stretch, Kilkenny had contested 25 finals and won 15 – 2008 was their eighth final in 10 years. But Waterford were upbeat about their chances.

It had been a season of twists and upheaval. Earlier in the summer, a nine-point Munster first-round defeat to Clare ended Justin McCarthy's reign and Davy Fitzgerald took over as Waterford manager. McCarthy had lost the dressing room and been left in an untenable position. 'Some of the players just got bored listening to him,' said Shanahan.[3]

Fitzgerald seemed a curious choice but he was ambitious and keen to learn the ropes. One of his contentious early decisions was to plant Ken McGrath at full-back. Waterford were an attacking team by instinct and tradition, and Fitzgerald's natural caution ran somewhat against the grain.

Through the qualifiers, Waterford restored some stability and found momentum. They defeated Antrim 6–18 to 0–15 in the first round, then Offaly 2–18 to 0–18 in Thurles before seeing off Wexford 2–19 to 3–15 in the All-Ireland quarter-finals. They reserved their

best performance of the year for the semi-final when they out-
stayed the league and Munster champions, Tipperary. The team
was greatly miffed by a claim that Tipperary had already booked
their hotel for the final and made much use of this apparent display
of arrogance. Tipperary denied this and said they were merely
planning for the possibility that they might qualify.

After 2008, the chasm between Kilkenny and everyone else
seemed wider than ever, and the usual fretting followed regarding
the game's general health. Cork, in the semi-finals, came closest to
ruffling Cody's side – and they lost by nine points. Offaly lost the
Leinster semi-final by 18 points, Wexford the final by 19. The margin
in the All-Ireland final was 23 points, the sixth highest in history.
It is possible that one team's mastery over another will never be
demonstrated so emphatically in an All-Ireland final again.

Kilkenny were blitzing teams and finding new frontiers.

As for Waterford, Fitzgerald had used the boxer Bernard Dunne
as an occasional team motivator but he couldn't salvage the team's
morale in the dressing room at half-time. Seventeen points down,
they faced an impossible mission. Waterford's attempts to upset
some Kilkenny players before the start also backfired. 'Davy had
it in his head to target five lads on the Kilkenny team, to get into
their heads,' Shanahan revealed. 'That made no sense to me ... it
was alien to our players.'[4]

Kilkenny were not content to rest up after the interval, the
eventual Hurler of the Year Eoin Larkin striding through for a
third goal after a litany of early points by T.J. Reid. In the final
five minutes, Waterford scored 1–3, the goal a lucky one when late
replacement James McGarry failed to deal with a shot from Kelly.
McGarry's introduction was a nod to his time spent minding goal for
the county before he made way for P.J. Ryan and an appreciation
of the terrible time he had endured since the tragic loss of his wife
Vanessa the previous year. The late Waterford consolation was the
only goal Kilkenny conceded in the championship.

Kilkenny now looked at their most invincible, 14 championship games unbeaten since they were shocked by Galway in 2005. For the first time, 30 points were scored in an All-Ireland final. Cody felt the performance came 'from within the heart' of his players. The question was could any team stop them?

KILKENNY: P.J. Ryan; M. Kavanagh, N. Hickey, J. Tyrrell; T. Walsh, B. Hogan, J.J. Delaney; J. Fitzpatrick (0–2), D. Lyng (0–3); H. Shefflin (0–8, 0–1 65, 5fs), M. Comerford, E. Larkin (1–4); E. Brennan (2–4), R. Power (0–2), A. Fogarty (0–3); Subs: T.J. Reid (0–4) for M. Comerford (inj., 44 mins), J. McGarry for P.J. Ryan (61).

WATERFORD: C. Hennessy; E. Murphy, D. Prendergast; A. Kearney, T. Browne, K. McGrath, K. Moran; M. Walsh, J. Nagle; D. Shanahan, S. Molumphy, S. Prendergast; E. McGrath, E. Kelly (1–9, 9fs), J. Mullane (0–3); Subs: J. Kennedy for S. Prendergast, S. O'Sullivan for J. Nagle (both HT), P. Flynn for E. McGrath (52 mins), D. Bennett (0–1) for D. Shanahan (63), T. Feeney for D. Prendergast (63).

Referee: Barry Kelly (Westmeath)

Attendance: 82,186

Cats catch up

When Kilkenny won their first All-Ireland in 1904, their main rivals already had a head start, Cork and Tipp each having won six times. But Kilkenny didn't take long to make up some of the lost ground. They were level with Cork by 1912 and ahead of them by 1913. They finally caught up with Tipp in 1935 but didn't surpass them until 1983, when they won their 23rd championship. Their win in 2008 had them six clear of Tipperary and one ahead of Cork.

The 2008 season also saw a notable change in the championship structure, with the Munster and Leinster champions gaining automatic entry to the All-Ireland semi-finals, the provincial losers playing in the quarter-finals against those who made it through the qualifiers.

92. Primal Passions

2009 NATIONAL LEAGUE FINAL (Semple Stadium, 3 May)
Kilkenny 2–26 Tipperary 4–17 (after extra-time)

People ask, 'Does the league matter?' The league matters.
Everything matters. The game matters.
Brian Cody[1]

HURLING WASN'T READY for this. Invoking the county's ancestral fighting spirit and summoning up every ounce of will, Tipperary removed some of the aura surrounding a Kilkenny team that had looked to be in a league of its own. Tipperary's transformation was all the more astonishing because only six weeks earlier, Kilkenny had walloped them by 17 points at Nowlan Park in Round 4 of the National League. This time, Tipperary regained much of their self-respect and proved the championship wouldn't be a foregone conclusion.

It was unremittingly physical and at times bordered on feral. With Nowlan Park fresh in their minds, Tipperary wired into their vaunted opponents. They were bristling with indignation from the start, building a strong early lead and taking the match to extra-time after seeing their lead disintegrate during the second half. Kilkenny were shaken, but they took all the punches and remained standing and victorious at the end.

Teams don't delight in moral victories, but Liam Sheedy's players had taken a major leap forward. Kilkenny were not infallible. Tipp were not to be disregarded. The first chapter of a riveting new phase in an age-old rivalry had begun.

Tipperary went back to basics after the Nowlan Park debacle and emerged with a new confrontational rage. Brian Hogan ended up with a broken collarbone early in the game after a shattering shoulder charge from Seamus Callanan. Kilkenny men were met with full-blooded challenges, not all of which were within the rules. After only eight minutes, the favourites had conceded two goals.

How could Tipperary have imagined such a metamorphosis? The public, as evidenced by the modest attendance, was also caught by surprise. Temporary rules requiring players on yellow cards to be replaced – part of a campaign to root out cynical play – were held up to the light. Martin Comerford came on for the injured Hogan after 11 minutes and was off after 12 without touching the ball or even reaching his appointed station, instead becoming entangled with Tipperary's Declan Fanning, who was also dismissed. Henry Shefflin and Michael Kavanagh were also sent off on yellow cards.

Cork referee John Sexton could have red-carded three more players for a range of offences that included a wild pull, a head-high charge and a hurley thrown at an opponent. But the match remained captivating for the mercilessness of the exchanges, and had absorbing passages of play, driven by a heroic attempt by Tipperary to win and a typically obdurate resistance by a Kilkenny side determined not to lose.

The previous September, Kilkenny had destroyed Waterford in the All-Ireland final and they looked unstoppable as they carried that form into the following spring. Cork took a 27-point lashing. Clare went down by 13. Galway by 11.

Tipperary were leading Division 1 when they faced Kilkenny in the fourth round. By half-time, they were staring at the abyss, 0–4 to 5–9 behind. As the *Tipperary Star* said:

> Mothers' Day it was [and] Tipperary got the mother of all lessons in the first half of this one – an education on how the game should be played. Precision passing, pace, aggression in the tackle, unrelenting attacking, defensive acumen, midfield authority – Kilkenny were

simply awesome and tossed the Tipp lads about like rag dolls. It was boys hurling against men.

History didn't favour them either. Tipperary hadn't beaten Kilkenny in a league decider since the home final of 1968, another occasion when they had sought to assert themselves and gain some measure of retribution for a loss to their rivals the previous September in the All-Ireland final. That had been a bruising encounter and had spilled over into rows and suspensions. Tipperary's Nowlan Park defeat in March 2009 had highlighted a timidity in the team that needed to be addressed – their forwards lost possession almost 20 times on their way to the demoralising defeat.

But far from being another mismatch, the league final ushered in a renewed spell of competitive duels, with the Premier finally toppling Kilkenny the following year in the All-Ireland final and ending their long unbeaten run in championship hurling.

A good start was essential against a team that had earned a reputation for blowing teams off the field early. Goals from James Woodlock and John O'Brien gave Tipperary the morale boost they needed, and a lead they protected until well into the second half. By the interval, they were 2–7 to 0–8 ahead, and Callanan's goal early in the second half pushed the lead out to eight when Kilkenny had the breeze.

Immediately, Kilkenny retaliated; Richie Hogan, their top scorer on 1–10, struck with a well-timed goal in the 38th minute and, after 50 minutes, Aidan Fogarty, who finished with 1–5, had their second. From there, they gradually wore down the Tipp lead, until Hogan fired them in front for the first time with the match almost over. In injury-time, Noel McGrath, playing his first senior match aged 18, fired over the equaliser from a free to force extra-time. McGrath also scored 1–4 from play and set up O'Brien's goal.

In extra-time, Noel McGrath scored a fourth Tipp goal shortly before the break, but Kilkenny finished powerfully, outscoring Tipp 0–6 to 0–1, and Eddie Brennan completed the win with a monstrous strike between the posts from 100 metres.

'In many ways, it was the perfect way to win the league,' Cody stated in his autobiography. 'Had we beaten Tipp easily, it would have fuelled all this nonsense about Kilkenny being unbeatable. There's no such thing as an unbeatable team in any sport.'[2]

Physicality alone would not win All-Irelands or beat Kilkenny, but Tipperary left Thurles on 3 May 2009 infinitely more assured than when they'd arrived. If Kilkenny were going to win four-in-a-row, it would have to be done the hard way.

KILKENNY: P.J. Ryan; M. Kavanagh, J.J. Delaney, J. Tyrrell; T. Walsh, B. Hogan, J. Ryall; J. Tennyson, M. Rice; R. Hogan (1–10, 7fs), H. Shefflin (0–4, 0–1 65, 1f), E. Larkin (0–1); E. Brennan (0–2), T.J. Reid (0–4), A. Fogarty (1–5); Subs: M. Comerford for B. Hogan (11 mins), M. Grace for M. Comerford (yellow card, 12), J. Fitzpatrick for H. Shefflin (yellow card, 42), S. Cummins for M. Kavanagh (yellow card, 79).

TIPPERARY: B. Cummins (0–1, f); P. Stapleton, P. Curran, C. O'Brien; D. Fanning, P. Maher, S. Maher; T. Stapleton, S. McGrath (0–2); J. Woodlock (1–1), S. Callanan (1–7, 0–1 65, 6fs), L. Corbett; N. McGrath (1–5, f), M. Webster, J. O'Brien (1–1); Subs: B. Maher for D. Fanning (yellow card, 12 mins), H. Maloney for S. Maher (15), B. Dunne for H. Maloney (58), S. Hennessy for J. Woodlock (62), D. Fitzgerald for T. Stapleton (70), E. Buckley for P. Maher (89.)

Referee: J. Sexton (Cork)

Attendance: 17,098

93. The Late, Late Show

2009 ALL-IRELAND FINAL (Croke Park, 6 September)
Kilkenny 2–22 Tipperary 0–23

As me poor grandmother used to say, a Tipp man will die before he lets you bate him.
Dick Walshe[1]

SEASONED KILKENNY FOLLOWERS regarded Tipperary with appreciable caution as their team set out to match Cork's All-Ireland four-in-a-row from 1941–1944. Take the then 91-year-old Dick Walshe. A winner of a Leinster medal in 1945 and veteran supporter from Tullaroan, at 19 he cycled to the 1937 All-Ireland final in Killarney, Lory Meagher's last outing, and rolled home disheartened after Kilkenny's capitulation. By 2009, his eyesight starting to fail, he was compelled to watch Kilkenny's All-Ireland bid at home on television.

Before the teams went into combat, he shared his thoughts.

> Well, if you go into a Tipperary man's house, he'll do anything for you, there is no one better. But it gets bitter enough at times, doesn't it, in pubs and that. There could be rows.[2]

His memory is extraordinary. He recalls as a young child people discussing the 1922 All-Ireland final meeting of the counties, played in 1923. He also tells a story of a group of Tullaroan hurlers from the early years of the hurling championship who stopped off at old Mrs Walshe's house in Rathealy looking for nourishment on the way to Urlingford to play Tipperary. '"You will give us a sup of tea?"

they asked. "Tea, is it?" she said. "Tea, is it? And ye going to hurl Tipperary!"'

Any match between Kilkenny and Tipperary bows to that grand tradition, but their rivalry had low circulation after the All-Ireland final of 1971. The 2009 meeting was the first All-Ireland final between these acclaimed rivals for 18 years, and only the third in 38 seasons.

Former Kilkenny hurler John Power lives in Callan close to the Tipp border. He hurled through a period when Tipp were less prominent in Kilkenny hurling lives.

I hadn't an awful hatred built up, but the older generation, all my uncles, when we went to play that 1991 All-Ireland, the advice I was getting, 'twas unquotable. They suffered from Tipp during their day. We played them in 1991 and should have beaten them, they played very poorly.[3]

The 1991 meeting, when Tipperary won the All-Ireland, was the first encounter between the two since 1971, after that they didn't meet in a championship match again until 2002 in an exciting All-Ireland semi-final won by Kilkenny. One more rendezvous in 2003 was followed by a short Tipp recession and an incredible boom for Kilkenny. By 2009, Tipperary had resurrected themselves and were looked on as the only credible challenger to the greatest hurling force of all time.

Having won their third All-Ireland in a row by demolishing Waterford, Kilkenny were strongly fancied to quell all coup attempts. Tipperary were Munster champions but in the National League at Nowlan Park in March 2009, Kilkenny had slaughtered them 5–17 to 1–12. When the two counties met in the league final six weeks later, the match had an entirely different intensity, with Tipperary taking Kilkenny to extra-time.

Dick Walshe's concerns about Tipp fortitude were not misplaced when they reunited in September's All-Ireland final. Only three survivors from the successful 2001 expedition headed by Nicky

English played eight years later: Eoin Kelly, in the form of his life, Lar Corbett and Brendan Cummins. With a wave of new talented players like Paudie Maher and Noel McGrath embedded, they now declared themselves ready to emulate those earlier blue-and-gold trailblazers.

The match is exceptional not only for Kilkenny's record-equalling four-in-a-row, but also for its staggering physical intensity.

Hurling refereeing would come under the spotlight after the match. Diarmuid Kirwan opted for light-touch regulation, ignoring certain fouls, notably holding, to allow the game to attain momentum and flow. That suited a physically powerful team like Kilkenny, but Tipperary hurled to an exceptional standard and for the best part of the game, they had the look of champions. The teams were level seven times in the first half and five in the second. The first significant turning point, one of Tipperary's own making, came in the 54th minute. A Cummins puckout dropped between Tommy Walsh and Benny Dunne. Walsh raised his hand to fetch and Dunne wheeled round and swung, striking Walsh dangerously in the face. Kirwan had no choice but to issue a red card.

Tipperary held the lead until the 63rd minute, and Henry Shefflin's controversial penalty goal. Tipperary protested that Richie Power, bearing down on goal, had been fouled outside the penalty area. The call was crucial. Up stepped Shefflin to fire Kilkenny a point in front. Within a minute, Martin Comerford, who had been dropped from the starting line-up for the final, ran through for a second goal. Tipperary were unable to recover. Kilkenny goalkeeper P.J. Ryan was declared Man of the Match for a series of critical saves, further evidence of the pressure Kilkenny had to withstand.

The penalty award was the subject of a question put to Brian Cody in an interview after the match by RTÉ's Marty Morrissey. His prickly reaction became part of the day's folklore. Asked about it the next day, he explained his feelings.

If we were to dissect every mistake by every player and every official at every game, we'd go on forever. I never comment on referees after the game.

Six All-Ireland titles out of eight also established a new record. As for Tipperary, they were far from done. Their manager Liam Sheedy couldn't find fault with their effort.

These lads have done everything I've asked of them in the last eight months, everything I could possibly want them to. So to just come up short is very, very disappointing. We knew we were facing the best team in probably the history of the game.

After two poor finals, this was an overdue boost to the game's morale. A truly invigorating contest.

KILKENNY: P.J. Ryan; M. Kavanagh, J.J. Delaney, J. Tyrrell (0–1); T. Walsh (0–1), B. Hogan, J. Tennyson; D. Lyng (0–1), M. Rice; E. Brennan (0–3), E. Larkin (0–3), R. Power (0–1); R. Hogan (0–2), H. Shefflin (1–8, 1–0 pen, 7fs), A. Fogarty; Subs: T.J. Reid (0–1) for A. Fogarty (50 mins), M. Fennelly (0–1) for D. Lyng (52), M. Comerford (1–0) for R. Hogan (55).

TIPPERARY: B. Cummins; P. Stapleton, P. Maher, P. Curran; D. Fanning, C. O'Mahony, B. Maher; J. Woodlock, S. McGrath (0–1); P. Kerwick, L. Corbett (0–4), J. O'Brien; E. Kelly (0–13, 0–3 65s, 7fs), S. Callanan (0–3), N. McGrath (0–2); Subs: B. Dunne for J. O'Brien (47 mins), W. Ryan for P. Kerwick (66), M. Webster for J. Woodlock (69).

Referee: D. Kirwan (Cork)

Attendance: 82,106

Hurling men cry foul

There was widespread dismay, among hurling managers in particular, over experimental disciplinary rules introduced in 2009 in subsidiary competitions and the National League. The GAA was acting on concerns about dangerous tackling and cynical fouling in both Gaelic football and hurling.

Under the experimental rules, players could be sent off but replaced for what were termed 'highly disruptive' fouls. This included pulling down an opponent, tripping, body checking and bringing an arm or hurley around the neck of an opponent.

However, the experimental rules narrowly failed to win the two-thirds support required when they came before congress in April.

After the All-Ireland final, Tipperary considered putting a motion to congress seeking the introduction of technology to aid referees in making important decisions. This followed the penalty decision that proved pivotal and turned the final Kilkenny's way. They later decided against pursuing the matter.

2009 marked the start of a new phase of Tipp–Kilkenny rivalry that, over the next six seasons, saw them meet in four All-Ireland finals, a semi-final, a historic qualifier and three league finals.

94. Perfect Storm

2010 ALL-IRELAND FINAL (Croke Park, 5 September)
Tipperary 4–17 Kilkenny 1–18

---

*The five-in-a-row brings its own pressure and we just really focused
on our game and got our just rewards.*
Liam Sheedy[1]

NOWLAN PARK HAS seen some spectacular events, even
playing host to Bob Dylan in 2001, but in the final week of
August 2010 almost 8,000 turned up to watch a Kilkenny
training session ahead of an All-Ireland final date with Tipperary.
The traditional stoicism and composure associated with Kilkenny
All-Ireland final build-ups was gone. In its place, a fever swept the
county at the prospect of winning the game's first five-in-a-row.

There was an equally compelling subplot: would Henry Shefflin,
their most influential field general, be fit to hurl and win a record-
equalling eighth All-Ireland medal on the field of play? Shefflin
looked a no-hoper when he went off in the semi-final win over Cork
having torn the anterior cruciate ligament of his left knee. But an
extraordinary effort got underway to have him fit to play, a race
against the clock and a battle against the medical odds. At Nowlan
Park 10 days before the final, he took full part in a training match.
It seemed he had performed a miracle, and the Kilkenny faithful
must have felt the omens were on their side.

After three weeks of intensive physio under the direction of
Gerard Hartmann, and cryotherapy sessions that had started with
a dash to Wexford on the day they beat Cork, reports of Shefflin's
progress seemed miraculous. John Tennyson also had a serious knee

ligament injury and was also making headway but the spotlight was all on Shefflin, now 31 years old and still the team's on-field natural leader. Normally, such injuries take six to eight months of rehab after surgery. Shefflin returned in 17 days. One doctor interviewed at the time talked of 'absurd expectations' of recovery.

But the fans were willing to believe in the impossible and when they saw Shefflin score in the training match on 25 August, the cheer raised the roof. Like the 'drive for five', Shefflin's battle for fitness attracted obsessive levels of attention.

Meanwhile, Tipperary calmly prepared for another tilt at the champions after the previous year's heartbreaking defeat. They looked doomed when crashing to the biggest defeat from Cork in 68 years, 0–14 to 3–15, in the Munster championship quarter-finals, but rebuilt from the rubble through the qualifiers. They began with a win over Wexford in Thurles, then brushed off Offaly in Portlaoise to reach the All-Ireland quarter-finals. Galway provided the opposition and in a thrilling finish, Tipp scored the final two points to win 3–17 to 3–16. In the semi-final, they avenged the previous year's defeat by Waterford, winning 3–19 to 1–18.

Kilkenny's route was more conventional. They opened with a Leinster semi-final thumping of Dublin, 4–19 to 0–12, and held off Galway by seven points in the provincial final, the first Leinster showpiece to feature the westerners. They had 12 points to spare over Cork in the All-Ireland semi-finals, but the loss of Shefflin created understandable concern.

'The media circus in Kilkenny was getting out of hand and that suited us fine,' said Lar Corbett. 'By comparison, Thurles was a haven of peace and quiet.'[2]

Tipperary hit Kilkenny with a perfect storm. Eamon O'Shea's coaching had a marked influence in liberating their forwards who thrived by creating open space in their opponents' half of the field. Corbett's career had a new lease of life, his hat-trick was the first in an All-Ireland hurling final since 1970.

The win also left Kilkenny defeated in the championship for the first time since the loss to Galway in the 2005 All-Ireland semi-final. But the champions went down fighting. Even though the sides were only level for six minutes, the match remained unsettled for over an hour. Tipperary couldn't shake off Kilkenny's attentions until the final minutes when they had a string of scores, four from substitutes, and Corbett's third goal.

Tipp led 1–6 to 0–3 after the opening quarter. Shefflin broke down after only 13 minutes, but Brian Cody defended his selection. 'Henry had been back training, full training, for two weeks before the game.'

Kilkenny, even at below their best, were a hard and resilient opposition. Six points down and with Shefflin stricken, they mounted a spirited comeback, reeling off four points. Tipp stretched out to six again, then, three minutes from the interval, another Kilkenny rally produced a goal. Eoin Larkin's penetrating run and neatly placed pass to Richie Power was followed by a clinical finish past Brendan Cummins. Power clipped on two points. At half-time, Tipp led 1–10 to 1–9, then a beautifully executed sideline from T.J. Reid had the teams level early in the second half.

Tipp were not in the mood for a repeat of 2009. In the 42nd minute, Corbett scored his second goal, the opening made by a reverse hand-pass of untrainable instinct from Noel McGrath. Two minutes later, McGrath had a third, putting them 3–11 to 1–10 in front. Kilkenny hit the next four points to reduce the gap to a goal with 15 minutes left. Tipp went back to six entering the final 10 minutes and then they began to empty their bench. Seamus Callanan's point in the 62nd minute widened their lead to five and the previous year's fall guy, Benny Dunne, entered and pointed near injury-time to restore the five-point cushion. Finally, Kilkenny snapped. Seamus Hennessy, another sub, dashed through to point off the stick and Tipp moved nine points clear when Corbett completed his hat-trick. In the last play, Michael Rice scored a consolation point for Kilkenny, typically still hurling to the end.

Cody took the defeat graciously.

You take it, you take it on the chin, and you respect the fact you were beaten by a better team. And we were beaten by a better team on

Sunday. Tipperary were excellent. We're massively disappointed. I'm not trying to pretend we were geniuses as losers or anything like that. We're not. We hate losing. But we can't change it.[3]

Six days later, Tipperary routed Galway in the All-Ireland under-21 final in Thurles and the talk during the winter was that Kilkenny's era may have passed and that Tipperary's had arrived. Endless renditions of 'Slievenamon' carried them blissfully through into the New Year, but they had to defend their title without Liam Sheedy who had stepped down in October, citing pressures of work.

Sheedy had taken over towards the end of 2007, along with Michael Ryan and Eamon O'Shea, the county's fifth management team in six years. The worry now was that his absence might destabilise the team.

As for Kilkenny, they could point to the loss of Shefflin, the concerns over Tennyson's fitness and the loss of Brian Hogan with a broken finger picked up the night Shefflin wowed the crowd in Nowlan Park.

Tipp made hay through the middle of the Kilkenny rear-guard and their tactics left the Kilkenny backs isolated and exposed, but there was no guarantee Kilkenny would be so compliant when the teams renewed their rivalry in 2011.

TIPPERARY: B. Cummins (0–1, f); P. Stapleton, P. Curran, M. Cahill; D. Fanning, C. O'Mahony, Padraic Maher; B. Maher (0–2), S. McGrath; G. Ryan (0–1), L. Corbett (3–0), Patrick Maher; N. McGrath (1–0), E Kelly (0–7, 7fs), J O'Brien (0–2); Subs: C. O'Brien for C. O'Mahony (57 mins), S. Callanan (0–2) for J. O'Brien (58), B. Dunne (0–1) for S. McGrath (63), D. Young for D. Fanning (68), S. Hennessy (0–1) for B. Maher (70).

KILKENNY: P.J. Ryan; J. Dalton, N. Hickey, J. Tyrrell; T. Walsh, J. Tennyson, J.J. Delaney; J. Fitzpatrick, M. Fennelly; T.J. Reid (0–4, 1 sideline), H. Shefflin (0–1, f), E. Larkin; E. Brennan, R. Power (1–9, 8fs), A. Fogarty (0–1); Subs: M. Rice (0–1) for H. Shefflin (inj., 14 mins), D. Lyng (0–1) for J. Fitzpatrick (51), M. Comerford for E. Brennan (51), R. Hogan for A. Fogarty (55), J. Mulhall (0–1) for T.J. Reid (63).

Referee: M. Wadding (Waterford)

Attendance: 81,765

95. Darlin' Dubs of May

2011 NATIONAL LEAGUE FINAL (Croke Park, 1 May)
Dublin 0–22 Kilkenny 1–7

---

*I think the whole thing has changed, and Dublin are in the frame to win
an All-Ireland in the next five years. And that would be wonderful.*
Michael O'Grady[1]

THE SEEDS OF a spring regeneration that swept Dublin to a
first National League title since 1939 can, paradoxically, be
found in the 2010 championship collapse against Antrim in
Croke Park. It was a calamitous defeat that shook Anthony Daly's
belief in the Dublin hurling project and left him questioning his
own future as manager.

A championship win over Daly's native Clare set up the final-
round qualifier tie against Antrim, with the prize of an All-Ireland
quarter-final against Cork at stake. Six points up, Dublin had the
match in their grasp, and let it slip. The decision to take off a couple
of key players left them bereft of leadership when Antrim came at
them. The defeat was a psychological hammer blow.

Daly recalled leaving a traumatised dressing room.

I got into the car and just drove west and I didn't take the turn-off for
Galway [towards home]. I wound up in a hotel in north county Galway
somewhere looking up at the roof, spent the night there. Just booked a
room, couldn't face anyone. I got into the car the next day and drove to
the Burren and walked the beach in Fanore, drove around Black Head
for a long time.[2]

The setback stoked a renewed determination. There were also some significant team additions, including Conal Keaney who returned to county hurling, having left early in 2005. Though out of the game at county level for some years, he was still an integral part of a very accomplished Ballyboden club team and there had been repeated efforts to lure him back since Daly had taken over. His impact was immediate. Showing no sign of rust, he became Dublin's outstanding player of the spring.

Dublin also picked up a Tipperary hurler, Ryan O'Dwyer, who had been part of his home county's squad before spending some time abroad. When he took a teaching post in Dublin, he received an offer to join a Dublin club and then tried his luck with the county team. He proved another valuable addition. Dublin set out their stall early by defeating Kilkenny to win the Walsh Cup. In the National League that followed, they topped Division 1, suffering only one defeat, to Galway who won with a goal in stoppage time. They defeated Tipperary, the All-Ireland champions, at Croke Park and drew with Kilkenny. In the final round, they went to Cork and got a win to secure a place in the final, along with Kilkenny who finished runners-up.

Already, history was being written. This was Dublin's first league final since 1946 when Daly's uncles had played on the Clare team that defeated them in a replay. In 2011, Dublin started out the year as 66/1 outsiders to win the league, but in the evening of 1 May, Sean Óg Ó Ceallacháin read out the result that confirmed they had defeated Kilkenny to win their third league title, the first for 72 years. Ó Ceallacháin, himself, played on the Dublin team of 1946.

Kilkenny were missing some star names, including Henry Shefflin, Richie Power, Tommy Walsh and Michael Fennelly, and J.J. Delaney went off injured in the second half. They also had to hurl with 14 players when Eoin Larkin was sent off for striking after 24 minutes after winning a free off Conor McCormack. But the performance was unfeasibly flat for a Brian Cody side, easily their worst in his time in charge. The defeat was also the heaviest Kilkenny had endured in a national final since the 1964 All-Ireland loss to Tipperary, as well as their biggest loss in a major final since the Leinster final defeat to Wexford in 1976.

In contrast, the performance from Dublin was one of their finest in Daly's time there. Their touch was impeccable. They overran the Kilkenny defence with intelligent movement and smart use of the ball. They were powerful in the tackle and their finishing was of the highest order. Paul Ryan, finally establishing himself on the team, led the way with some spectacular scores. Limerick All-Ireland under-21 medal winner Maurice O'Brien scored a point with one hand, while Keaney had a monster from his own half near the sideline. He set up another for Johnny McCaffrey when showing exceptional vision with a cross-field ball.

Eddie Brennan had a goal after 12 minutes that might have rocked Dublin, but they didn't flinch. Kilkenny's final tally of 1–7 had little resemblance to their usual high totals, and only 1–1 came from play. After Brennan's goal, Dublin hit eight points in the next 15 minutes without reply to open a lead of 0–10 to 1–1. They had a goal ruled out because the half-time whistle had sounded, and went in at the interval 0–11 to 1–2 in front.

Kilkenny could not get back into the game, getting no closer than six points. Liam Rushe moved to centre-back when Joey Boland was forced to leave with a shoulder injury in the 44th minute. Because of that injury, the game had six minutes of stoppage time, during which Dublin went into overdrive and fired over six points.

Jackie Tyrrell did not conceal their dismay.

> It was the worst performance I was ever involved in with Kilkenny. It's not just one or two things – a lot of things in our game weren't up to scratch. Fair play to Dublin – they're really moving in the right direction but we seem to be going backwards.[3]

He felt that they needed to raise their game.

> Our training has dropped, our intensity levels have dropped. You'd be hoping over the next week that we'll have bruising sessions. That's the only way to get it back.[4]

Coming on the back of the loss to Tipperary the previous September, there was concern over Kilkenny's well-being and immediate future. Dublin looked ahead to the summer with rising confidence. Revolution, it seemed, was in the air.

DUBLIN: G. Maguire; N. Corcoran, T. Brady, P. Kelly; J. McCaffrey (0–1), J. Boland, S. Durkin; A. McCrabbe, L. Rushe; C. McCormack (0–1), R. O'Dwyer (0–2), C. Keaney (0–3); D. Plunkett (0–1), D. O'Callaghan (0–1), P. Ryan (0–9, 5fs); Subs: M. O'Brien (0–2) for J. Boland (45 mins), D. O'Dwyer for D. Plunkett (55), D. Treacy (0–1) for A. McCrabbe (63), S. Lambert (0–1) for L. Rushe (67), S. Ryan for D. O'Callaghan (72).

KILKENNY: D. Herity; J. Dalton, B. Hogan, N. Hickey; P. Hogan (0–1, f), J. Tyrrell, J.J. Delaney; T.J. Reid (0–5, 5fs), M. Rice (0–1); J. Fitzpatrick, M. Ruth, E. Larkin; C. Fennelly, E. Brennan (1–0), R. Hogan; Subs: M. Kavanagh for J.J. Delaney (56 mins), J. Mulhall for C. Fennelly (58), P. Murphy for M. Ruth (65).

Referee: M. Wadding (Waterford)

Attendance: 42,030

Cats' revenge

With their big names back in the fold, Kilkenny exacted revenge for their National League final defeat by handing Dublin a hefty beating in the Leinster final in early July. The win earned them a seventh straight success in Leinster, which was a new record, surpassing the six they had achieved from 1998 to 2003. Dublin recovered to defeat Limerick in the All-Ireland quarter-finals in Thurles. They pushed Tipperary, who had scored seven goals in a Munster final rout of Waterford, all the way in the semi-finals, losing 0–18 to 1–19. Paul Ryan finished the season leading scorer with 2–47 from five championship matches. It was the first year that Dublin qualified for the provincial finals at senior, under-21 and minor. But for Conal Keaney, the year was bitter-sweet. In July, he suffered serious injury in a motorbike accident, and missed the Limerick match and the All-Ireland semi-final.

96. Premier Downgrade

2011 ALL-IRELAND FINAL (Croke Park, 4 September)
Kilkenny 2–17 Tipperary 1–16

But if I am being honest this is by far our best achievement,
without a shadow of a doubt.
Brian Cody[1]

THE CELEBRATIONS HAD barely died down after Tipperary's 2010 All-Ireland success when Liam Sheedy announced he was stepping aside as manager. It caught the players totally by surprise. Lar Corbett, whose career was rejuvenated under Sheedy and his mentors Eamon O'Shea and Michael Ryan, had hoped to finish his career with the same crew in charge. 'The thoughts of starting all over again with a new crowd absolutely sickened me,' he stated in his autobiography. He said he felt 'betrayed'.[2]

It was hardly an auspicious beginning to their title defence when the player who had done so much to make it happen – the hat-trick hero and Hurler of the Year – reacted with an almost theatrical level of fatalism. Nor did it augur well for the new men at the helm, led by Declan Ryan, a deeply admired figure who was about to take on a role that measured success by nothing less than retaining the title. Before Ryan was confirmed as Sheedy's successor, Corbett was one of three players who door-stepped Nicky English, seeking in vain for him to return to the job.

Corbett admits he spent much of the season pining for what they once had, and perhaps that was symptomatic of Tipperary in general. Rather than kick on and consolidate, their period at the summit was temporary; they had already become fixated with loss. A new season was about to begin and they appeared, to some extent, to still have one foot in the past.

Benny Dunne – who came on in the 2011 All-Ireland final, his final match for the county – is less inclined to peddle that as an excuse. They had retained their Munster title in impressive style and reached the final in September for a third year in a row. Ultimately, he feels Kilkenny had the visceral yearning that had driven Tipp the year before.

> We didn't have the same hunger as we had in 2010. We might have thought we had, and Kilkenny, who have no love for Tipperary anyway, were meeting a team that stopped them winning the five-in-a-row. I would say it boiled down to that. I came on and they were more aggressive, physically they were all over us.[3]

Ceaseless motivation was a hallmark of the Cody years. 'That is why I would have huge admiration for the Kilkenny fellas,' says Dunne. 'How they keep coming back year after year. They will do anything to win nearly, and that is a great thing to have.'[4]

Tipperary were seeking to win their first back-to-back title since 1965. Instead, Kilkenny reclaimed top position and Henry Shefflin won a record-equalling eighth medal on the field of play, having recovered from his second serious knee injury. When they were plundered the previous September, Kilkenny had lost some of the mystique that had had teams half-beaten before a ball was struck. Cody's challenge was to revitalise his team, to show they could win another All-Ireland. A year earlier, Corbett had rifled three goals and Tipperary looked to have perfected an attacking game that had Kilkenny figured out. But, just as they had overcome the Cork running game five years earlier, Kilkenny found a way to neutralise Tipperary's strengths and impose their own personality. Corbett, watched feverishly by Jackie Tyrrell, was starved of good supply and failed to raise a flag.

Cody's instincts were right; his team was aching for a crack at the title holders. Tipperary went 0–5 to 0–0 down early in the match, and were left chasing the game throughout. Their opening score had to wait until the 16th minute from Noel McGrath, and by then the barometer had been set. No other Tipp forward scored from play for the rest of the half. Like the previous year's final, the exchanges were unshirking and referee Brian Gavin let play run, facilitating another crunching encounter. Later, concerns were voiced about the wisdom of this selective application of the rule book. At one point in the match during a short-lived scuffle, Gavin took an accidental dart from Tommy Walsh's hurl while trying to restore order, and had to leave the field to receive medical attention, blood weeping from a head wound.

The defeat, while not comprehensive, created the first doubts about Tipperary's constitution for the long road. The meeting of the counties for a third successive All-Ireland – which was unprecedented – spread further unease over a narrowing field of genuine contenders. The league final win by Dublin over Kilkenny earlier in the year had raised the prospect of change, but Kilkenny reversed that result tellingly in the Leinster final with an 11-point win. In the Munster final, Tipperary destroyed Waterford, who had won the province the previous year, by seven clear goals. It was left to Tipp and Kilkenny to fight it out again.

Tipperary were on the back foot from the moment Gavin threw in the ball. Their defence was under siege for the opening quarter, the five-point deficit a more manageable position than what might have been had their full-back Paul Curran not cleared a goal attempt from Eoin Larkin off the line after 12 minutes. Not for the first time, Kilkenny, having been repeatedly unhinged the year before, showed a granite resistance – J.J. Delaney and Walsh, whose battle with Patrick Maher was a match highlight, among the pillars of defiance. Brian Hogan, who missed the 2010 final, made the centre his territory. Paul Murphy thrived in his first season and the veteran Noel Hickey put the 2010 experience behind him, eager to show he was not finished.

With Tipperary striving to remain in touch, their situation worsened. On 35 minutes, Richie Hogan picked out Michael Fennelly charging through the middle and his goal opened a 1–7 to 0–4 lead nearing half-time. Tipp, realising they had a growing crisis and trouble in the middle of the field, put on Brendan Maher in the first half and at half-time made a further double substitution. They trailed at the interval 0–6 to 1–8.

In the 49th minute, Kilkenny scored a goal that looked to clinched the title, an exemplary finish worthy of winning an All-Ireland, sweeping the ball from defence to attack. Eddie Brennan gained possession and raced on, drawing the cover before releasing to Hogan, who took a touch on his stick and in one movement dispatched the ball into the far corner beyond Brendan Cummins. They were eight points up, 2–12 to 0–10.

A goal from Pa Bourke gave Tipp some hope and, by the 64th minute, they had trimmed the Kilkenny lead down to three points, 2–14 to 1–14. But they couldn't make a deeper incision. With the last point, Larkin made the game safe in injury-time.

Their eighth All-Ireland in 13 seasons under Cody was celebrated with a joy that spoke volumes. Kilkenny were back on top.

KILKENNY: D. Herity; P. Murphy, N. Hickey, J. Tyrrell; T. Walsh, B. Hogan, J.J. Delaney; M. Fennelly (1–0), M. Rice (0–1); E. Brennan (0–1), R. Power (0–2), H. Shefflin (0–7, 5fs); C. Fennelly (0–2), E. Larkin (0–2), R. Hogan (1–1); Subs: T.J. Reid (0–1) for E. Brennan (60 mins), J. Mulhall for R. Hogan (65).

TIPPERARY: B. Cummins; P. Stapleton, P. Curran, M. Cahill; J. O'Keeffe C. O'Mahony (0–1), Padraic Maher; G. Ryan (0–2), S. McGrath; S. Callanan, N. McGrath (0–3, 0–1 sideline), Patrick Maher; E. Kelly (0–8, 0–1 65, 7fs), J. O'Brien (0–1), L. Corbett; Subs: B. Maher for J. O'Keeffe (30 mins), B. Dunne (0–1) for S. McGrath (HT), P. Bourke (1–0) for S. Callanan (HT), D. Young for C. O'Mahony (58), J. O'Neill for J. O'Brien (66).

Referee: B. Gavin (Offaly)

Attendance: 81,214

97. Maroon Mirage

2012 LEINSTER FINAL (Croke Park, 8 July)
Galway 2–21 Kilkenny 2–11

---

*Not even the team itself would have predicted obliterating Kilkenny
in the first half. Because that's what it was, obliteration. It just shows you,
when you match their work-rate and physicality and intensity, face up
to them, it can be done.*
Former Galway hurler, Alan Kerins[1]

IT WAS THE day Galway probably should have had 'Supermen'
rather than 'Supermac's' emblazoned across their chests.

Brian Cody, ever mindful of the 2001 and 2005 All-Ireland
semi-final defeats to the same opposition, had seemed to suspect
another Galway special was afoot. A few days before the game, in
keeping with his respectful habit of talking up the opposition, he
warned that 'the last day against Offaly, they [Galway] produced
a whirlwind start, the game was over early on. People talk about
Kilkenny killing off teams, Galway killed off Offaly completely
in the early stages of that game.' But having heard the Kilkenny
manager make similar noises about so many teams in the past,
most hurling people were inclined to disregard his alarm about the
maroon-clad wolf approaching from the west.

Instead, there was a consensus that, following the blips of the
2010 All-Ireland and 2011 league final defeats, Kilkenny had
regained much of the momentum of the four-in-a-row years by
systematically putting Tipperary and Dublin back in their place.
Donal Óg Cusack, who had labelled them the 'Stepford Wives' of

the game in his autobiography, was now talking of Kilkenny as 'hurling's All Blacks'. Nicky English, citing their ruthless 2–21 to 0–9 crushing of Dublin on 23 June in the Leinster semi-final, felt Galway didn't have a prayer. In his *Irish Times* preview the day before the game, he wrote:

> Kilkenny are performing at a different level ... It's not Kilkenny's fault, but they're getting better and better, finding new quality players every year and of the other counties, only Tipperary are anywhere within reach.

Cusack and English based their assessments on what they had witnessed over the spring when Kilkenny had regained the league title by overrunning Cork 3–21 to 0–16 in the final. On 1 April, they had torn strips off Galway in the final group game, winning by 3–26 to 0–10 in Nowlan Park. Galway somehow recovered from that dismal day to defeat Dublin in a relegation play-off replay three weeks later. Something seemed to click within the Galway team about five minutes before half-time in Tullamore when they went from dicing with defensive collapse to win by 4–21 to 0–19, playing some exhibition hurling in the second half. Against that, argued their critics, they had conceded 7–27 against Westmeath and Offaly in the Leinster quarter and semi. What would Kilkenny do to this defence even if Galway's forwards, led by a noticeably slimmed down and toned Joe Canning, were shooting the lights out?

One dissenting voice, though, was former Clare selector Tony Considine who actually predicted a victory for the 11/2 outsiders. He had detected signs of 'wear and tear' in Kilkenny's rout of the Dubs. 'This is a great chance for Galway. It could be now or never – I think it's now,' he wrote in the *Examiner*. Considine had served alongside Ger Loughnane when he had unveiled his philosophy of 'demonic ferocity' to the hurling world in 1995. It was an approach replicated by Galway for the first half hour or so of this game when, bar a few wides, they went as close as any team in maroon to hurling perfection. 'Kilkenny didn't know what hit them. They had no shape, no pattern and no idea how to handle what Galway were throwing at them,' was Nicky English's summing up in his *Irish Times* column the day after the final. 'Not only did they win all the 50–50 balls, they were winning the 20–80 balls as well. Galway players were moving all over the place at huge pace and huge power.'

A splendid strike from Joe Canning in the third minute when he fetched a high ball and turned inside Jackie Tyrrell in one rapid movement set Galway on their way. Unrelenting but legitimate ferocity in the tackle shook the champions to the marrow. The Kilkenny defence and midfield struggled to cope with the speed of Galway's forwards and the relatively simple but very effective tactic of bringing Damien Hayes out around the middle third and isolating Canning, and the other forwards in their turn, one on one with the Kilkenny full-back line.

Ten of the Galway players had featured in the April Fools' Day massacre in Nowlan Park, yet here they were bouncing off the ground and almost inviting Kilkenny to hit them harder, to give them some sort of a game. Wing-back David Collins drifted up the field to score a point in the 19th minute that made it Galway 1–6, Kilkenny 0–0. 'They're not used to this, Marty,' remarked RTÉ's co-commentator Donal O'Grady to the main man, Marty Morrissey. A minute later, Henry Shefflin raised a flag from a free, but Kilkenny didn't score from play until the 31st minute when Richie Power angled over a point. By then, Galway had amassed 2–9, David Burke scoring a second goal and Cyril Donnellan chipping in with some precision points.

Brian Cody sent in his first sub, Aidan Fogarty, in the 23rd minute and reconfigured his midfield and defence, but it was a lost cause, even for Kilkenny, when they went in 2–12 to 0–4 behind. Donnellan scored the first point of the second half, while Kilkenny gained some sort of a foothold with a Richie Hogan goal in the 45th minute and a second from Shefflin four minutes later.

Between the goals, there were genuinely sublime individual points from David Burke and Canning that underlined Galway's class as well as power and self-possession on the day. Kilkenny reduced the deficit to eight points with five minutes left, but Galway were so well set up around midfield and defence, a calamity never threatened. They closed it out with late points from Cyril Donnellan and Joe Canning, both on the Man of the Match shortlist along with Johnny Coen, Iarla Tannian and David Burke, as Galway claimed a first Leinster title.

Given what's happened since, that gloomy July afternoon when Fergal Moore raised the Bob O'Keeffe Cup almost has the quality of a mirage for Galway supporters. The new management team of Anthony Cunningham, Tom Helebert and Mattie Kenny, appointed after overseeing Galway's 2011 All-Ireland under-21 victory, had masterminded the ambush to end all Galway ambushes. Five of the previous year's under-21s started the match and two more came on as subs – so apart from the victory, it looked as though Galway had finally cracked the challenge of bringing underage talent through to the big time.

However, they have been unable to rediscover the energy and collective purpose of that freakish but wonderful day. They went close for another half hour in that year's drawn All-Ireland final, but since then they have looked like a team who made one superhuman burst for glory in 2012 and are still recovering from all that it required.

GALWAY: J. Skehill; F. Moore, K. Hynes, J. Coen; D. Collins (0–1), T. Regan, N. Donoghue; I. Tannian, A. Smith; N. Burke (0–1), D. Burke (1–2), D. Hayes (0–1); J. Canning (1–10, 7fs), C. Cooney, C. Donnellan (0-6); Subs: J. Glynn for C. Cooney (53 mins), J. Regan for Tannian (57), T. Haran for N. Burke (61), J. Cooney for C. Donnellan (71).

KILKENNY: D. Herrity; P. Murphy, N. Hickey, J. Tyrrell; T. Walsh, B. Hogan, R Doyle; C. Buckley, P Hogan; H. Shefflin (1–8, 7fs), T.J. Reid, E. Larkin; C. Fennelly, R. Power (0–2), R. Hogan (1–0); Subs: A. Fogarty for C. Fennelly (23), M. Rice (0–1 for R. Hogan (27), M. Ruth for T.J. Reid (57).

Referee: James McGrath (Westmeath)

Attendance: 22,171

98. Cat o' Nine Tales

2012 ALL-IRELAND FINAL REPLAY (Croke Park, 30 September)
Kilkenny 3–22 Galway 3–11

I've played with great players before and great players now and without those team-mates I would not have any medals in my pocket. Today, we had a very good team performance, and that has always been the hallmark of this team.
Henry Shefflin[1]

A FTER A SPECTACULAR Leinster final, and a drawn All-Ireland final, Galway and Kilkenny returned a third day to settle their differences. In the first All-Ireland senior final replay since 1959, Henry Shefflin reached a unique pinnacle when he won a ninth All-Ireland medal on the field of play. Kilkenny broke new ground too, capturing a first MacCarthy Cup through the scenic route. It was their seventh final in succession, the previous year's sixth consecutive appearance already a record.

Asked what kept him going, Shefflin gave this response.

> I think it's very simple. It's because of the feeling I have now, and the feeling I had at the final whistle. That's what drives you on. I have been very fortunate and very privileged in my career to have so many of those days. I love playing the game, I love training and I love being involved with such a great team of fellas.[2]

Having played under Brian Cody from his first year managing Kilkenny in 1999, Shefflin has brought inspirational leadership to every match he's played. By the close of 2012, he had started all 62 championship matches in Cody's time in charge. During that time, he'd suffered two cruciate knee ligament injuries.

I've had those injuries but I could not stand here with nine All-Ireland medals and say it's all gone perfectly for me. You have to have the downs as well as the ups.[3]

Galway, without an All-Ireland win since 1988, might see the irony in that last remark. Their chequered history of championship matches with Kilkenny in the Cody era featured some bad beatings and three memorable triumphs: the All-Ireland semi-finals of 2001 and 2005, and the Leinster final of 2012. Beating Kilkenny twice in one championship season would be a unique claim but a tall order. They blew their best chance in the drawn match, although they needed Joe Canning to rescue them with a late, disputed free. In the replay, Galway did not hurl with the same fluency and yet remained in the match until a few vital breaks went against them in the second half, culminating in Cyril Donnellan's 49th-minute red card.

Kilkenny unearthed a new hero in Walter Walsh, a 21-year-old from the Tullogher-Rosbercon club near the Wexford border, who had shelved a promising rugby career to focus entirely on making the county hurling team. His first start was in the All-Ireland final and he hurled himself into legend with a Man of the Match performance, scoring 1–3.

He scored Kilkenny's second goal in the 58th minute and Colin Fennelly added a third four minutes after that. Even when Jonathan Glynn, a Galway substitute, fired in a goal in the 66th minute, Galway fans had already resigned themselves to another year of coming up short.

In the first half, goals kept Galway's challenge alive. They scored two in a minute, both from David Burke, shortly after the quarter-hour. But each goal brought a Kilkenny score in response, a point from T.J. Reid after the first, a goal from Richie Power answering the second. Ahead by three points, Galway were six down nearing half-time, before two late scores gave them some encouragement. Kilkenny led 1–11 to 2–4 at the interval.

What looked like a third Galway goal in the 44th minute, from Donnellan, was ruled out when the referee called back the play and awarded a free instead. Canning pointed, but a goal at that stage would have left Galway within two points of Kilkenny and would have lifted the team after a slow start to the second half. Canning landed a sideline to leave a goal between them and then had a shot off the butt of the upright which almost brought the sides level. Donnellan's dismissal came two minutes later, after he swung his hurl at J.J. Delaney near the sideline.

Kilkenny showed the greater level of improvement on the drawn game. Their backs had held their positions, unlike the first day when Galway's forwards' rotation destabilised their defence. Paul Murphy was Kilkenny's outstanding defender. At the other end, Shefflin conducted the Kilkenny attacking orchestra. Canning, influential in the drawn game when he scored a wonderful early goal, was less effective and played in deeper positions. Their midfield, in which Iarla Tannian was the drawn match's best player, also had a performance dip.

Kilkenny had earlier defeated Limerick in their All-Ireland quarter-final to set up another encounter with Tipperary. That match was possibly the most bizarre in their long history, Kilkenny winning 4–24 to 1–15, with the bewildering sight of Lar Corbett spending the day following Tommy Walsh, in an effort to avoid Jackie Tyrrell. Tyrrell was having none of it, and pursued Corbett all over the field, while Corbett tailgated Walsh, who was detailed to mark Pa Bourke. A four-man cavalcade ensued but to Kilkenny's advantage, with Corbett eliminated from the play. Tipperary's hurling morale was on the floor and pressure was put on Declan Ryan and his selectors to step down.

Galway defeated Cork in their All-Ireland semi-final by five points. For the final replay, there was concern over the fitness of their goalkeeper James Skehill. The decision to play him, following a test on his injured shoulder, looked ill-judged and he didn't last the full match. Their defence also found Kilkenny harder to manage in the replay, with Shefflin causing problems down the middle and Walter Walsh too much for Johnny Coen. Galway's first point from play did not come until the 39th minute, but they were still within four points of Kilkenny.

Donnellan's sending off ended their chances. For a 15-minute spell, Kilkenny outscored them 2–7 to 0–1, Walsh scoring a goal from a rebound and then Fennelly adding another.

Kilkenny headed home to the acclaim of their public with their 34th title, now four ahead of Cork and eight clear of Tipperary. They kept finding new worlds to conquer.

KILKENNY: D. Herrity; P. Murphy, J.J. Delaney, J. Tyrrell; T. Walsh, B. Hogan, K. Joyce (0–1, f); C. Buckley (0–1), M. Fennelly (0–1); E. Larkin (0–1), H. Shefflin (0–9, 0–2 65s, 5fs), T.J. Reid (0–1); W. Walsh (1–3), R. Hogan (0–3), R. Power (1–2); Subs: N. Hickey for J.J. Delaney (49–61 mins, blood), for K. Joyce (65), C. Fennelly (1–0) for W. Walsh (58), A. Fogarty for T.J. Reid (65).

GALWAY: J. Skehill; F. Moore, K. Hynes, J. Coen; D. Collins, T. Regan (0–1), N. Donoghue; I. Tannian, A. Smith (0–1); N. Burke, D. Burke (2–0), J. Canning (0–9, 0–1 65, 0–1 sideline, 5fs); J. Regan, C. Donnellan, D. Hayes; Subs: J. Cooney for N. Donoghue (28 mins), J. Glynn (1–0) for J. Regan (34), F. Flannery for J. Skehill (HT), C. Cooney for N. Burke (53), D. Glennon for A. Smith (64).

Referee: J. McGrath (Westmeath)

Attendance: 82,274

Shefflin stands apart

Henry Shefflin is the most successful hurler of all time, winning ten All-Irelands on the field of play. The leading championship scorer in history, he has received a record 11 All Stars and is the only player to have been named Hurler of the Year on three occasions.

99. Blue Heaven

2013 LEINSTER FINAL (Croke Park, 7 July)
Dublin 2–25 Galway 2–13

It's my dream to win a Leinster final. I think it's still on the cards even though we're in trouble at the moment. If the right players were picked, the right manager in place, I think we'd definitely go forward.
Conal Keaney[1]

A T THE VICTORY presentation for the 2013 Leinster final, Jimmy Gray, Dublin's goalkeeper in the 1961 All-Ireland final, proudly handed the Bob O'Keeffe Cup to Johnny McCaffrey. The moment aptly captured the day's historical connotations – the long stretch back to Dublin's last senior provincial title finally bridged. Dublin, a week after slaying Kilkenny in a replayed semi-final, were champions of Leinster and now, it seemed, a force to be reckoned with.

Defeating All-Ireland champions Kilkenny was a momentous achievement. The previous year's crushing loss to the same county had left deep scars and resurrected fresh doubts. From early in the year, Dublin had earmarked the match and by the time it came around, they were tipped to win in some quarters. But the side seemed to freeze.

The road from there led to Ennis and Cusack Park, familiar territory for Clarecastle-born Daly. They let a good lead slip and Clare put them out of the championship. Just as in 2010, following the defeat by Antrim, Daly and Dublin weren't sure if they had a future together. And so, it was drawing-board time yet again.

Having received the backing of the players, Daly returned for another shot at the Leinster championship, and the inevitable day against Kilkenny. Along the way, they lost one of their players, Tomás Brady, to football as well as their trainer Martin Kennedy.

The spring did not end well. They had a hiding from Tipperary in the National League semi-finals, having earlier won promotion out of the second tier to where they had been relegated the previous year. Signs of a bumper year remained well concealed when they escaped with a draw in Wexford and their win in the replay still left them preparing for Kilkenny with none of the bloated expectation of 2012.

They should have won the first day, losing a late lead, and most wrote off their chances of beating Kilkenny in a replay. But, with a goal from Danny Sutcliffe, they did just that and lowered Kilkenny's sails for the first time since 1942. The worry about the replay was that it fell only seven days after the first game and was their fifth match without a weekend off. In the Leinster final, they faced the team that had almost won the previous year's All-Ireland and that had taken Leinster after a spectacular exhibition of hurling against Kilkenny.

Fears among Dublin followers of their team suffering stage-fright or fatigue were quickly eased. By half-time, they led 1–12 to 0–7, the goal coming from a Paul Ryan strike in the 24th minute. Five minutes into the second half, he had another. After the tight and physical ordeal of two games in Portlaoise, one in Wexford Park and another in Donnycarney, Croke Park liberated Daly's team and they grabbed their historic opportunity.

Daly spoke of a good feeling in his bones ahead of the final.

We did a bit on Friday night, just a few pucks, and you could see that they were bulling for the road. It's a nice way to be, playing the games and feeling the excitement building. We've been building all the time, from a poor first night to today.[2]

His defeated counterpart, Anthony Cunningham, delivered a gracious tribute afterwards to the team that had replaced his as champions of Leinster, the first time since 1997 that Kilkenny had failed to win the province two years running.

> Let's be honest, the amount of work that has gone into hurling in Dublin means they deserve a day like this. It is reward for the inventiveness and investment that has gone into Dublin. We got a great crowd today and they deserve it. They are tremendous ambassadors for the game in Dublin. They have stuck at it through thick and thin.[3]

A Johnny McCaffrey point had Dublin leading 0–10 to 0–5 after 21 minutes, and the margin varied from there on, but was never any shorter. There were still anxious moments. Only five minutes from the end, Joe Canning went for goal and was denied by Gary Maguire's reflexes when Dublin led by six. Earlier in the second half, David Burke had also found the Dublin net. Peter Kelly's job of policing an ever-threatening Canning was crucial in maintaining order around the Dublin goal and would help him to an All Star later in the year. Conal Keaney had one of his finest days. Ryan scored 2–7, 2–3 from play. His 41st-minute goal helped Dublin to an 11–point lead.

Canning's goal in the 50th minute and another from Burke four minutes later reduced the lead to a manageable six, 2–17 to 2–11, but, from there, Dublin kicked for home, outscoring Galway 0–8 to 0–2.

Ryan was declared Man of the Match but Keaney was at the centre of everything. Eight years after stating that he wanted to win a Leinster senior hurling medal, and after six seasons in exile with the county footballers, his dream had been realised.

On Dublin charged to the All-Ireland semi-finals with hope in their hearts.

DUBLIN: G. Maguire; N. Corcoran, P. Kelly, P. Schutte; S. Hiney, L. Rushe, M. Carton (0–1); J. McCaffrey (0–2), J. Boland (0–2); C. Keaney (0–2), R. O'Dwyer (0–3), D. Sutcliffe (0–1); P. Ryan (2–7, 4fs), D. O'Callaghan (0–4), D. Treacy; Subs: C. McCormack (0–2) for D. Treacy (53 mins), O. Gough for P. Schutte (55), S. Durkin for J. McCaffrey (56), M. Schutte for D. O'Callaghan (60), S. Lambert (0–1) for R. O'Dwyer (67).

GALWAY: J. Skehill; J. Cooney, F. Moore, K. Hynes; J. Coen, S. Kavanagh, D. Collins; I. Tannian (0–1), J. Regan (0–1); D. Burke (1–0), C. Cooney (0–2), C. Donnellan; D. Glennon, J. Canning (1–7, 4fs), N. Burke; Subs: A. Smith for J. Regan (22 mins), D. Hayes for C. Donnellan (HT), A. Harte (0–1) for I. Tannian (HT), J. Glynn (0–1) for D. Glennon (45), A. Callanan for J. Cooney (63).

Referee: J. Ryan (Tipperary)

Attendance: 36,657

100. Champagne Hurling

2013 ALL-IRELAND FINAL REPLAY (Croke Park, 28 September)

Clare 5–16 Cork 3–16

If I had a dream last night that I was going to score 3–3, I'd have woken up saying, 'That's ridiculous.' I'd have been happy with one, like. But it really is the stuff of dreams, from back when you were six and you pick up a hurley.
Shane O'Donnell[1]

ONE OF THE greatest hurling championships of them all was won by outsiders who fashioned a new style of play without deserting the game's intrinsic skills. A few days after the final replay, *The Guardian* ran a short editorial that marvelled at the game's 'terrifying velocity'. It was one way of looking at Clare's short passing and constant movement, the essential elements in a game-plan hinging on supreme confidence and ease on the ball.

The style wasn't to everybody's liking. It was predicated on minding possession and making each ball count and demanded a high level of intuition and technique. Nor was it an instant success. Clare lost in Munster to Cork when their short game broke down and, at times, the hurling looked too baroque and over-elaborate. By September, it had been fine-tuned enough to win Clare a first All-Ireland since 1997.

To work that kind of game required a purity not synonymous with Clare hurling across the generations. But the prototype Clare hurler had evolved radically over the 16-year gap since the county's previous success. The modern archetype was more wristy and bold.

The underage supply lines in Clare placed greater stock on ball players. Mentors visited other counties and examined their juvenile structures, including Kilkenny's, and gradually the results began to materialise.

When Clare won their second senior All-Ireland in three years in 1997, and the All-Ireland minor title, there was a belief that they were destined for further success. But they struggled badly at underage grades and no obvious dividend accrued after their senior triumphs. The picture began to change in 2009 when they won their first Munster under-21 title and added the All-Ireland. The next year, the county's minors were desperately unlucky to lose the All-Ireland final to Kilkenny. These Clare hurlers were quick on their feet, cerebral and used to winning, but 2013 was deemed too soon for the bright young graduates to win an All-Ireland at senior level.

Kilkenny, having won the previous two All-Irelands, again began the year as favourites, with Clare available at 22/1.

However, in 2013, nothing followed expected lines, and the result was the most open and thrilling championship since the 1990s. In terms of quality, many rated it the greatest in living memory.

Kilkenny experienced an unusually short summer and, for the first time since 1951, they didn't make it to Croke Park. The back door beckoned after they lost in Portlaoise to Dublin in a replayed Leinster semi-final – Dublin's first win over Kilkenny in 71 years. Kilkenny dusted themselves down and overcame Tipperary in Nowlan Park in one of the season's highlights, a win-or-bust duel. They then needed extra-time to quell Waterford, but they went down to a resurgent Cork who had lost the Munster final to Limerick, the Treatymen's first provincial success since 1996.

The match between Cork and Dublin produced another classic from the year's impressive portfolio, before Cork squeezed through, The unique semi-final derby between Clare and Limerick went in favour of the Bannermen, who had ridden into Croke Park after a quarter-final defeat of Galway. What followed was the perfect coronation for a golden hurling year.

Clare bossed the drawn match but looked to have blown it when Pat Horgan scored a point in injury-time. With time gone over the two minutes displayed by the fourth official, Domhnall O'Donovan, the corner-back who had never previously scored, went up the field and took a pass and fired over off his left. Cork felt the additional 30 seconds allowed were unjustified. The drawn game created a furore over Anthony Nash's free-taking, his technique of lifting the ball forward several metres before striking, and the decision of his Clare counterpart Patrick Kelly on one occasion in the first half to rush out and block the missile with his body. Cork argued that the free should have been retaken; Clare claimed he should have been 20 metres away from the goal when striking. Confusion reigned.

The replay was set for three weeks later, for the first time on a Saturday, and it finished with the floodlights turned on as Clare produced the fireworks. Davy Fitzgerald made one critical switch in playing Shane O'Donnell, a 19-year-old from Ennis, instead of the towering Darach Honan who had been well marked by Shane O'Neill in the first match. O'Donnell scored three goals after just 19 minutes and finished with 3–3 from nine touches. His three-goal haul emulated Lar Corbett's in 2010, as he joined a select group of All-Ireland hat-trick men, the fourth in 50 years. He wasn't told he was starting until match day.

Clare managed to improve on their performance in the replay, and Cork were again chasing the game for long periods but a feature of the match was the Rebels' obstinacy. In spite of conceding much of the play, they repeatedly fought their way back. They made a rally when they were eight points down in the first half and outscored Clare 0–9 to 0–1, to go level 17 minutes into the second half at 1–16 to 3–10. But Clare were never led. Over the course of the two matches, they were only in arrears for 90 seconds.

Clare responded by drawing three points clear and, on the hour, a goal from Seamus Harnedy, in his first season and another of the year's finds, squared them again. Clare were undaunted. Conor McGrath raced through two minutes later and planted the ball in the top-left corner; they widened the margin to six points and looked to have done enough. Back came Cork with another goal, with normal time up, from the substitute Stephen Moylan. They were pressing for an equalising goal when Clare broke and the ball ran to Honan, who had been introduced late, and he scored the clinching fifth major.

The final, in two chapters, was a fitting epilogue to an exciting season. Pace and movement were the new hurling buzzwords and Tony Kelly, a young wizard from Ballyea, became Hurler of the Year. The game hadn't witnessed as many goals in an All-Ireland final since the 80-minute decider in 1972. The first All-Ireland outside the traditional counties for 16 years had been delivered in spectacular fashion.

CLARE: P. Kelly; D. O'Donovan, C. Dillon, D. McInerney; P. O'Connor, B. Bugler, C. Ryan; C. Galvin, P. Donnellan; J. Conlon (0–2), T. Kelly (0–3), Colin Ryan (0–7, 7fs); P. Collins, S. O'Donnell (3–3), C. McGrath (1–1); Subs: C. McInerney for C. Galvin (52 mins), N. O'Connell for P. Collins (59), D. Honan (1–0) for S. O'Donnell (66), S. Morey for T. Kelly (71).

CORK: A. Nash (1–0); B. Murphy, S. O'Neill, C. O'Sullivan; C. Joyce, S. McDonnell, W. Egan; L. McLoughlin (0–1), D. Kearney; S. Harnedy (1–2), C. McCarthy, P. Horgan (0–9, 7fs); L. O'Farrell, P. Cronin (0–1), C. Lehane (0–2); Subs: S. White for W. Egan (23 mins), S. Moylan (1–1) for L. O'Farrell (HT), T. Kenny for D. Kearney (39), C. Naughton for C. McCarthy (55), K. Murphy for S. McDonnell (67).

Referee: J. McGrath (Westmeath)

Attendance: 82,276

Nash rule

The Kanturk goalkeeper Anthony Nash unveiled a radical style of free-taking that brought a mix of admiration and alarm and eventually forced rule change. Nash's technique of carrying the ball several metres forward on the lift considerably steepened the task of defending 20-metre frees and penalties. Traditionally, players have gained a few metres, but Nash took it to another dimension. When defending players started to rush out to meet him, the GAA was compelled to revisit the rule, not least because of safety concerns. The 2014 season had already started when a new rule was introduced, stating that the ball needed to be struck from on or behind the 20-metre line.

Clare used larger goalkeeping hurls to defend a 20-metre free from Nash in the 2013 All-Ireland final replay and packed their goal. He still found a way through.

Epilogue

A FEW MONTHS AGO, an elderly man contacted a newspaper to discuss an interview it had published with one of the Wexford hurlers of the 1950s. Reading accounts of the time had reawakened a childhood fascination with that team, though the caller had no Wexford connections and did not come from a hurling stronghold. His parish, in west Limerick, had no hurling at all.

In that decade before television, when news of matches was conveyed by radio or the newspapers or word of mouth, tales of Wexford's gallantry had captured his imagination. Every Monday, his teacher would regale the classroom with the latest exploits of men who had sprung from nowhere to win All-Irelands. Eager to play, but lacking the necessary resources, local boys like him started chopping pieces of wood and a primitive form of hurling began.

Over the course of its history, hurling has tried to take foothold in unfamiliar territory, but tradition still beats the big drum. And so, after 2013, when Clare rose to the summit playing a new brand of hurling, it was Kilkenny who returned to win the most recent championship with an exceptional group of players and a desire befitting a county with no All-Irelands, let alone 34. One hundred and ten years after their first, Kilkenny's 35th All-Ireland confirmed their status as high kings of hurling.

Some counties have leaned on Kilkenny's wisdom and tried to learn from their structures, but a tradition like theirs is a slow build and is decades in the making. But hopefully, the hurling evangelists will continue to spread the gospel and bring the joy of the game to a wider playing audience.

When it comes to contenders for the top honours, the hurling map

of Ireland has barely changed since the 1880s. The last new addition
to the All- Ireland roll of honour was Offaly in 1981; before that, it
was Waterford in 1948 and before that again, it was Laois in 1915.
What are the chances of three new names being inscribed on the
Liam MacCarthy in the coming century? Can counties like Antrim,
Westmeath or Kildare find the wherewithal to break through? Can
Laois and Kerry add to their sole All-Ireland titles?

Yet there are now more people playing, or being given the
chance to play, than at any time in the game's history. It would
be fascinating to take a leap in time, to 100 years from now, and
see if hurling has broken free from its geographical shackles. The
challenge for the GAA is to broaden the landscape to the wider
population so that the young hurler in Armagh or Leitrim, who has
wrists as natural as his Kilkenny or Cork counterpart at 14, isn't
lost to the game as an adult.

The arrival of Sky as a player in the GAA's broadcasting market
has widened the game's reach, and this new audience come to the
party at a good time. The scoring levels in the drawn 2014 All-
Ireland final – 3–22 for Kilkenny, 1–28 for Tipp – would have won
every previous All-Ireland. The quality of play in that game, the
intensity of the exchanges, and the tactical variations reflected a
sport that is continually pushing out the frontiers.

And yet Kilkenny, in these modern and innovative times, still
found a way. A few days after their latest All-Ireland triumph, their
goalkeeper Eoin Murphy produced a photograph he'd kept from the
day Henry Shefflin visited his school with the MacCarthy Cup in
2000. Murphy is pictured in the classroom in his county jersey. The
first of Shefflin's medals inspired a boy who would be a team-mate
when he won his tenth.

It has been a pleasure journeying through time to write this book
and especially meeting and talking to the men who were part of some
of the great matches. To paraphrase Jack Lynch when speaking at
the graveside of Christy Ring, the story of hurling will be told as
long as the game is played – and that will be forever.

Endnotes

1. Easter Rising

1. Introduction to the *GAA Rule Book* (1888).
2. Kearns, Christy and Maeve, *The History of the GAA in Meelick-Eyrecourt-Clonfert 1884–2007* (2008), p. 3.
3. Conwell, John Joe, *Hearts of Oak: The Rise to Glory of Portumna GAA Club* (2008), p. 28.
4. *ibid.*, p. 27.
5. Ó Ceallaigh Seamus, *Story of the GAA* (1977), p. 45.
6. *ibid.*, p. 46.
7. *ibid.*, p. 67.
8. Fullam, Brendan, *Off the Field and On: Triumphs and Trials of Gaelic Games* (1999).
9. King, Seamus, 'Hurling and Southeast Galway' in *Galway GAA Annual* (1984), pp. 44–45.
10. Kearns, Christy and Maeve, *The History of the GAA in Meelick-Eyrecourt-Clonfert 1884–2007* (2008) p. 5.

2. Building a Dynasty

1. Horgan, Tim, *Cork's Hurling Story* (2010). p. 5.
2. *ibid.*, p. 5.
3. *ibid.*, p. 4.
4. Power, John P., *A Story of Champions* (1941) pp. 43–44.

3. The First Invincibles

1. Newspaper account, quoted in Fogarty, Philip (Canon), *Tipperary's GAA Story* (1960).
2. Smith, Raymond, *The Clash of the Ash* (1972) p. 160.
3. Mehigan, P.D. (Carbery), *Hurling: Ireland's National Game* (1944).
4. Fogarty, Philip (Canon), *Tipperary's GAA Story* (1960) p. 72.
5. *ibid.*
6. Ryan, Philip F., *The Tubberadora-Boherlahan Hurling Story* (1973), p. 22.
7. Leahy, Seamus, *Tipperary Association Yearbook* (1984).

4. Exiles in Excelsis

1. Doyle, Eamon, 'The Yellow Bellies and the Hurling Men of Cornwall', *History Ireland* (Spring 2003).

2. http://colclough-resource.blogspot.ie/2013/05/duelling-and-hurling.html.
3. Byrnes, Ollie, *Against the Wind* (1996), p. 15.
4. Ó Maolfabhail, Art, Camán: *Two Thousand Years of Hurling in Ireland* (1973).
5. *New York Gazette and Weekly Mercury* (4 June 1781).
6. Horgan, Tim, *Cork's Hurling Story* (2010), p. 20.
7. Mehigan, P.D. (Carbery) *Hurling: Ireland's National Game* (1941).
8. Power, John P., *A Story of Champions* (1941) pp. 17–18.

5. Expert Wielders of the Camán
1. O'Dwyer, Michael, *The History of Cricket in Kilkenny: The Forgotten Game* (2006), pp. 13–14.
2. O Duill, Antoin, *Famous Tullaroan* (1984).
3. *ibid.*

6. Tom Semple's Hurling Machine
1. Fogarty, Philip (Canon), *Tipperary's GAA Story* (1960).
2. *ibid.*, pp. 123–124.
3. Smith, Raymond, *The Clash of the Ash* (1972) p. 171.
4. *ibid.*, p. 171.

7. More Satisfaction Than a Thousand Years in America
1. Ryall, Tom, *Kilkenny: The GAA Story* (1984), pp. 26–27.
2. *ibid.*, pp. 26–27.
3. *ibid.*

8. Raging Fires, Dying Flames
1. O'Neill, Phil, *Twenty Years of the GAA* (1931), p. 14.
2. Smith, Raymond, *The Clash of the Ash: A Popular History of the National Game* (1972), p. 173.
3. Fogarty, Philip (Canon), *Tipperary's GAA Story* (1960), p. 151.
4. Cody, Joe, *The Stripy Men: Kilkenny's Hurling Story to 2008* (2009), pp. 20–21.

9. After the Goal Rush
1. O'Neill, Phil, *Twenty Years of the GAA* (1931), p. 26.
2. Fullam, Brendan, *Captains of the Ash* (2002) p. 191.
3. Smith, Raymond, *The Clash of the Ash: A Popular History of the National Game* (1972) p. 181.

10. The Toomevara Greyhounds
1. O'Neill Phil, *Twenty Years of the GAA* (1931), p. 65.
2. Smith, Raymond, *The Clash of the Ash: A Popular History of the National Game* (1972), p. 171.
3. O'Neill, Phil, *Twenty Years of the GAA* (1931), p. 76.
4. *ibid.*, p. 46.

11. To the Banner Born

1. *Freeman's Journal* (19 October 1914).
2. Byrnes, Ollie, *Against the Wind* (1996), p. 27.
3. MacIomaire, Tomás, 'Tip and Slashin': *Clare Association Yearbook* (2006).
4. GAA Museum (Laois/73).
5. Fullam, Brendan, *Giants of the Ash* (1992), p. 41.
6. MacIomaire, Tomás, 'Tip and Slashin': *Clare Association Yearbook* (2006).

12. Wild With Delight

1. Ó Maolfabhail, Art, *Two Thousand Years of Hurling in Ireland* (1973), p. 22.
2. O'Neill, Phil, *Twenty Years of the GAA* (1931), p. 107.
3. King, Seamus, *A History of Hurling* (1996), p. 64.
4. Hyland, Jackie, www.laoisgaa.ie.

13. 1916

1. O'Neill, Phil, *Twenty Years of the GAA* (1931).
2. Puirseal, Padraig, *The GAA in Its Time* (1982), p. 168.
3. Cronin, Mike, Murphy, William and Rouse, Paul (eds), *The Gaelic Athletic Association 1884–2009* (2009), p. 66.
4. Walsh, Jim, *James Nowlan: The Alderman and the GAA in His Time* (2013).
5. McElligott, Richard, '1916 and the Radicalisation of the GAA', *Éire Nua-Ireland* (Spring–Summer 2013), pp. 95–111.
6. Puirseal, Padraig, *The GAA in Its Time* (1982), p. 171.
7. Ryall, Tom, *Kilkenny: The GAA Story* (1984), p. 39.

14. Scaling the Summit

1. O'Neill, Phil, *Twenty Years of the GAA* (1931) p. 58.
2. Puirseal, Padraig, *The GAA in Its Time* (1982), p. 174.
3. de Burca, Marcus, *The GAA: A History* (1980). p. 112.

15. Blood and Bandages

1. Puirseal, Padraig, *The GAA in Its Time* (1982), p. 178.
2. Farrelly, Daniel, 'Competitors who choose to be red have higher testosterone levels', *Psychological Science* (University of Sunderland, May 2013).
3. Hill, Russell and Barton, Robert, 'Red enhances human performance in contests', *Nature* (University of Durham, May 2005).
4. de Burca, Marcus, *The GAA: A History* (1980), p. 115.

16. Hurricane Hurling

1. Ryall, Tom, *Kilkenny: The GAA Story* (1984) p. 41.
2. *The Irish Times* (10 September 1923).

17. Into the West

1. *Galway GAA Yearbook* (1965).

18. Changing of the Guard

1.   Nolan, William (ed.), *The Gaelic Athletic Association in Dublin 1884–2000* (2005), p. 142.
2.   Kenny, Thomas, *Tour of the Tipperary Hurling Team in America 1926* (1928).

19. Up the 'Dubs'

1.   Rouse, Dr Paul, 'How Dublin Saved Hurling: The 1880s and the Making of a Modern Game', Sport and the City Seminar (2010), www.dublinheritage.ie.
2.   Nolan, William (ed.), *The Gaelic Athletic Association in Dublin 1884–2000* (2005), pp. 169–170.
3.   *ibid.*, p. 143.
4.   Direct scores from sideline cuts – 'touch pucks' – were not allowed in hurling until 1931.
5.   Ó Ceallaigh, Seamus, *Story of the GAA* (1977), p. 116.

20. Rebel Halted

1.   Horgan, Tim, *Cork's Hurling Story* (2010), p. 33 (quoting P.D. Mehigan).
2.   Fullam, Brendan, *Giants of the Ash* (1991), p 187.
3.   Byrnes, Ollie, *Against the Wind* (1996), p. 37.
4.   King, Seamus, *A History of Hurling* (1998), p. 87.

21. 1931

1.   Pat'O, *The Irish Times* (2 November 1931).
2.   Puirseal, Padraig, *The GAA in Its Time* (1982), p. 286.
3.   Fullam, Brendan, *Captains of the Ash* (2002), p. 143.

22. Raging Tull

1.   Smith, Raymond, *Clash of the Ash* (1971), p. 321.
2.   *ibid.*
3.   Ryall, Tom, *Kilkenny: The GAA Story* (1984) p. 41.
4.   Cody, Joe, *The Stripy Men* (2009), p. 52.

23. Disgusting and Un-Gaelic Scenes

1.   *Camán* (12 August 1933).

24. Jubilee Jitters

1.   Fullam, Brendan, *Hurling Giants* (1994), p. 155.
2.   Power, John T., *A Story of Champions* (1941).

25. Grit and Élan

1.   Martin, Henry, *Mick Mackey: Hurling Legend in a Troubled County* (2011), p. 22.
2.   Puirseal, Padraig, *The GAA in its Time* (1982), p. 287.
3.   Fullam, Brendan, *Captains of the Ash* (2011).

26. The Ahane Colossus

1. Martin, Henry, *Mick Mackey: Hurling Legend in a Troubled County* (2011), p. 256.
2. *ibid.*, p. 85
3. Murphy, Seán (ed.), *The Life and Times of Jackie Power: Prince of Hurlers* (1996), p. 93
4. Keane, Colm, *Hurling's Top 20* (2002), p. 32.
5. Puirseal, Padraig, *The GAA in Its Time* (1982) p. 292.
6. Dorgan, Val, *Christy Ring* (1980), p. 50.

27. 'A Master Leathering'

1. Dick Walshe, interviewed by Dermot Crowe (December 2013).

28. Up the Déise

1. Ó Ceallaigh, Seamus, *The Story of the GAA* (1977), p. 16.
2. Keane, Colm, *Hurling's Top 20* (2002), p. 23.
3. Smith, David, *The Unconquerable Keane* (2010), p. 53.

29. Thunder and Lightning

1. Cronin, Jim, *Cork's Hurling Story* (2010), p. 69.
2. Shem Downey, quoted in *Kilkenny Voice* (2 May 2006).
3. Cody, Joe, *The Stripy Men* (2009), p. 71.
4. Cronin, Jim, *Cork's Hurling Story* (2010), p. 69.
5. MacNeice, Louis, *The Strings Are False* (1965).
6. McEvoy, Enda, *The Godfather of Modern Hurling: The Fr Tommy Meagher Story* (2012), p. 57.

30. Hell for Leather

1. Martin, Henry, *Mick Mackey: Hurling Legend in a Troubled County* (2011), p.55
2. Murphy, Seán (ed.), *The Life and Times of Jackie Power: The Prince of Hurlers* (1996), p. 134.
3. Martin, Henry, *Mick Mackey: Hurling Legend in a Troubled County* (2011), p. 54.
4. *ibid.* p. 55.
5. *ibid.* p. 67.

31. 'A First-Class Sporting Sensation'

1. Dick Walshe. interviewed by Dermot Crowe (December 2013).
2. McAnallen, Donal, Hassan, David and Hegarty, Roddy (eds), *The Evolution of the GAA* (2009), p. 135.
3. *ibid.*, p. 23

32. Solo Brothers

1. Quoted by Horgan, Tim, *Christy Ring: Hurling's Greatest* (2007), p. 63.
2. *ibid.*
3. *ibid.*, p. 91.

33. The Pride of Knocknagow

1. Smith, Raymond, *The Clash of the Ash* (1972).
2. John Maher profile, premierview.ie.
3. Martin, Henry, *Mick Mackey: Hurling Legend in a Troubled County* (2011), p. 85.
4. Ó hEithir, Breandán, *Over the Bar* (1984), pp. 76–77.
5. John Maher profile, premierview.ie.

34. Ring on Fire

1. Christy Ring, quoted in Hayes, Seamus, *The Fold* (Cork Diocesan magazine).
2. *ibid.*
3. Downey, Paddy, 'Here Comes the King' in Liam Ó Tuama (ed.), *The Spirit of the Glen* (1973).
4. Christy Ring quoted in Hayes, Seamus, *The Fold* (Cork Diocesan magazine).
5. Dorgan, Val, *Christy Ring* (1980), p. 41.

35. 'A Dazzling Sheen of Brilliancy'

1. Carey, Tim, *Croke Park: A History* (2004), p. 104.
2. Horgan, Tim, *Christy Ring: Hurling's Greatest* (2007), p. 83.
3. Ryall, Tom, *Kilkenny: The GAA Story* (1984), p. 66.
4. Horgan, Tim, *Christy Ring: Hurling's Greatest* (2007), p. 82.
5. *ibid.*

36. 'The Greatest Man in Ireland'

1. Fullam, Brendan, *Captains of the Ash* (2002), p. 106.
2. Smith, David, *The Unconquerable Keane* (2010), p. 116.
3. *ibid.*, p. 120.
4. *ibid.*, p. 132.
5. *ibid.*, p. 90.

37. The Heat Is On

1. Harrington, John, *Doyle: The Greatest Hurling Story Ever Told* (2011), p. 57.
2. Dorgan, Val, *Christy Ring* (1980), p. 69.
3. *ibid.*, p. 80.
4. Harrington, John, *Doyle: The Greatest Hurling Story Ever Told* (2011), p. 48.
5. *ibid.*, p. 49.

38. Anarchy in the GAA

1. Referee Willie O'Donoghue's match report to the Munster Council.
2. Dorgan, Val, *Christy Ring* (1980), pp. 82–83.
3. Harrington, John, *Doyle: The Greatest Hurling Story Ever Told* (2011), p. 71.
4. *ibid.*, p. 72

39. Tipp Titans
1. Harrington, John, *Doyle: The Greatest Hurling Story Ever Told* (2011), p. 95.
2. Ryall, Tom, *Kilkenny: The GAA Story* (1984), p. 68.

40. Ring the Merciless
1. Horgan, Tim, *Christy Ring: Hurling's Greatest* (2007), p. 121.
2. Puirseal, Padraig, *The GAA in its Time* (1982), p. 296.
3. Dorgan, Val, *Christy Ring* (1980), p. 84.

41. 1953
1. Ó hEithir, Breandán, *Over the Bar* (1984), p. 142.
2. Horgan, Tim, *Christy Ring: Hurling's Greatest* (2007), p. 158.
3. Harrington, John, *Doyle: The Greatest Hurling Story Ever Told* (2011), p.75.
4. Dorgan, Val, *Christy Ring* (1980), p. 73.
5. *ibid.*, p. 74.
6. Ó hEithir, Breandán, *Over the Bar* (1984), p. 141.

42. Alien Attack
1. Quoted in, Dorgan, Val, *Christy Ring* (1980), p. 164.

43. The Hurling Immortal
1. Ned Wheeler, interviewed by Dermot Crowe (2014).
2. 'Another hurling triumph for Cork and Ring', *Irish Independent* (6 September 1954).
3. Rackard, Billy, *No Hurling at the Dairy Door* (1996) p. 219.

44. The Great Awakening
1. Radio match broadcast RTÉ, moments after Nickey Rackard's goal (23 September 1956).
2. Byrne, Gus, *Wexford Wheelers Cycling Club* (July 1998).
3. *ibid.*

45. Closing Time
1. Rackard, Billy, *No Hurling at the Dairy Door* (1996), p. 254.
2. 'Good hurling final anticipated', *The Irish Times* (3 August 1957).
3. Furlong, Nicholas, *The Greatest Hurling Decade* (1993), p. 166.

46. White Magic
1. Pat Fanning, former GAA President and Waterford native.
2. 'Power's Memory Lane Lined with Tales of Great Battles', *Sunday Independent* (27 June 2004).

47. Dublin's Light Declines
1. Jimmy Gray, former Dublin goalkeeper, Leinster senior medal winner 1961.
2. Ó hEithir, Breandán, *Over the Bar* (1984), p. 196.
3. 'Rivalry that Encourages Myth', *Sunday Independent* (26 June 2005).

4. Harrington, John, *Doyle: The Greatest Hurling Story Ever Told* (2011), p. 177.
5. 'Rivalry that Encourages Myth', *Sunday Independent* (26 June 2005).

48. Brawn *and* Class

1. 'Strong Reliance on Youth and Speed', *The Irish Times* (1 September 1964).
2. 'Tipp No Longer the Roman Empire', *Sunday Independent* (28 May 2000).
3. *ibid.*
4. *ibid.*

49. Doyle's Eight

1. 'Sowing the Good Seed', *The Irish Times* (23 March 1965).
2. Fullam, Brendan, *Hurling Giants* (1994), p. 90.

50. Twelve Years a Slave

1. Fullam, Brendan, *Hurling Giants* (1994), p. 56.
2. *ibid.*

51. Sweet 16

1. Dick Walshe, interviewed by Dermot Crowe (December 2013).
2. 'More Enthusiasm Than Ever Before', *The Irish Times* (31 August 1967).
3. Fullam, Brendan, *Hurling Giants* (1994), p. 132.

52. Never Say Die

1. Vinnie Staples, report in the *Irish Independent* (2 September 1968).
2. Fullam, Brendan, *Hurling Giants* (1994), p. 214.
3. 'Captain, Dan Quigley, Typifies the Style and Power of Wexford Hurlers', *The Irish Times* (30 August 1968).
4. Duggan, Keith, *The Lifelong Season* (2002), p. 61.

53. Faithful Departed

1. Johnny Flaherty, *Sunday Independent* (29 May 2011).
2. Fullam, Brendan, *Giants of the Ash* (1992), p. 161.
3. Fullam, Brendan, *Legends of the Ash* (1997), p. 200.
4. 'Only Inexperience Stood Between Offaly and Success', *The Irish Times* (21 July 1969).

54. Drinks, Shoots, Leaves

1. Matt Aherne, interviewed by Dermot Crowe (May 2014).
2. *The Irish Times* (7 September 1970).
3. *ibid.*

55. A Winter's Tale

1. *The Nenagh Guardian* (25 December 1971).
2. Interviewed by Dermot Crowe (July 2014).
3. Damien Martin, interviewed by Dermot Crowe (July 2014).
4. *Tipperary Star* (December 1971).

56. Barefoot Chic

1.   Len Gaynor, interviewed by Dermot Crowe (June 2014).
2.   Keating, Michael and Keenan, Donal, *Babs, A Legend in Irish Sport* (1996).
3.   Len Gaynor, interviewed by Dermot Crowe (June 2014).
4.   *ibid.*

57. The Great Escape

1.   Mick Lanigan, interviewed by Dermot Crowe (December 2013).
2.   McCarthy, Justin and Shannon, Kieran, *Hooked: A Hurling Life* (2002), p. 82.
3.   *ibid.*, p. 85.
4.   McEvoy, Enda, *The Godfather of Modern Hurling* (2012), p. 150.

58. Rain Men

1.   Jackie Power, Limerick hurler, speaking shortly before the final (August 1973).
2.   Martin, Henry, *Unlimited Heartbreak* (2009) p. 39.

59. Perfect Ambush

1.   'The Man from Boolavogue Has Been Through it all Before' *The Irish Times* (3 September 1976).

60. Rebel Treble

1.   Horgan, Tim, *Christy Ring: Hurling's Greatest* (2007), p. 321.

61. No Surrender

1.   'Offaly a Monster Created by Kilkenny', *Sunday Independent* (11 July 1999).
2.   *Irish Independent* (14 July 1980).

62. Banished Misfortunes

1.   From Galway captain Joe Connolly's speech when he received the MacCarthy Cup.
2.   'Taking the Plunge for the Tribe', *Cork Examiner* (29 September 2012).
3.   Cody, Joe, *The Stripy Men* (2009), p. 146.
4.   Farrell, Cyril, *The Right to Win* (1994), p. 95.
5.   *ibid.*, p. 116.

63. Here Comes Johnny

1.   *Cork Examiner* (11 June 2005).
2.   Farrell, Cyril, *The Right to Win* (1994), p. 123.
3.   *Midland Tribune* (14 October 1981).

64. Centenary Classic

1.   Ger Cunningham, interviewed by Dermot Crowe (July 2014).
2.   Interviewed by Dermot Crowe (March 2014).
3.   Keating, Michael and Keenan, Donal, *Babs: A Legend in Irish Sport* (1996).

65. Thurles Tornado
1.   Farrell, Cyril, *The Right to Win* (1994), p. 55.
2.   *ibid.*, p. 60.
3.   Horgan, Tim, *Cork's Hurling Story* (2010), p. 259.
4.   *ibid.*, p. 260.
5.   Farrell, Cyril, *The Right to Win* (1994), p. 63.

66. Tipp, Tipp Hooray!
1.   'Rivalry that Encourages Myth', *Sunday Independent* (26 June 2005).
2.   *ibid.*, p. 299.
3.   *ibid.*, p. 300.
4.   *ibid.*, p. 300.
5.   *ibid.*, p. 301.

67. The Hunger Games
1.   *Irish Independent* (5 September 1987).
2.   Farrell, Cyril, *The Right to Win* (1994), p. 18.
3.   *Irish Independent* (5 September 1987).

68. Tale of the Unexpected
1.   McNaughton, Terence, *Sambo: All or Nothing* (1998), p. 66.
2.   Terence McNaughton, interviewed by Dermot Crowe (June 2014).
3.   *ibid.*
4.   *ibid.*

69. Winner Takes All
1.   Potts, Sean (ed.), *Voices from Croke Park* (2010).
2.   Leahy, Seamus, *The Tipp Revival: Return to Glory 1987–1994* (1995) p. 78.
3.   *ibid.*, p. 78,
4.   *ibid.*, p. 78,

70. A Rare Vintage
1.   Danny Morrissey, interviewed by Dermot Crowe (April 2014).
2.   Jack Nolan, interviewed by Dermot Crowe (April 2014).
3.   The attendance of 35,315 in Thurles for the 1996 All-Ireland under-21 final between Galway and Wexford is excluded as the football final was also on the same bill.
4.   Michael Duignan, interviewed by Dermot Crowe (April 2014).
5.   Duignan, Michael, *Life, Death & Hurling* (2011), p. 76.
6.   Danny Morrissey, interviewed by Dermot Crowe (April 2014).
7.   Michael Duignan, interviewed by Dermot Crowe (April 2014).
8.   Danny Morrissey, interviewed by Dermot Crowe (April 2014).
9.   *ibid.*
10.   *ibid.*
11.   Michael Duignan, interviewed by Dermot Crowe (April 2014).

71. Donkeys and Derbies
1.   Mark Foley, interviewed before the Munster final (July 1990).

2.   Michael Cleary, interviewed by Dermot Crowe (June 2014).
3.   Ger Fitzgerald, interviewed by Dermot Crowe (June 2014).

72. Rebel Heaven
1.   Farrell, Cyril, *The Right to Win* (1994), p. 123.
2.   Horgan, Tim, *Cork's Hurling Story* (2010), p. 280.

73. Through the Barricades
1.   'I Wish I Could Turn the Clock Back', *Sunday Independent* (6 January
      2002).
2.   Ger Cunningham, interviewed by Dermot Crowe (July 2014).
3.   Michael Cleary, interviewed by Dermot Crowe (July 2014).
4.   'I Wish I Could Turn the Clock Back', *Sunday Independent* (6 January
      2002).
5.   Michael Cleary, interviewed by Dermot Crowe (July 2014).
6.   'Keating Dilutes the Euphoria', *The Irish Times* (22 July 1991).

74. Fenian Flame
1.   'Walsh a Keeper of the Faith', *Irish Independent* (6 September 1993).
2.   'Rabbitte Regrets Missed Scoring Chances' *Irish Independent*
      (6 September 1993).

75. The Great Hurling Heist
1.   *The Irish Times* (5 September 1994).
2.   *Irish Independent* (11 April 1994).

76. Bye Bye Biddy
1.   'Torturous Journey Ends for Loughnane', *The Irish Times* (11 July 1995).
2.   Eamon Taaffe, interviewed by Dermot Crowe (March 2014).
3.   'Exorcising Old Ghosts the Main Motivation', *The Irish Times* (10 July 1995).
4.   *ibid.*
5.   Walsh, Denis, *The Revolution Years* (2005), p. 32.

77. Passion Play
1.   *Irish Independent* (8 August 2009).
2.   Stephen McNamara, interviewed by Dermot Crowe (March 2014).
3.   'The Staring Down of Defeat was Theme of Historic Victory', *The Irish
      Times* (4 September 1995).
4.   Eamon Taaffe, interviewed by Dermot Crowe (March 2014).
5.   'The Staring Down of Defeat was Theme of Historic Victory', *The Irish
      Times* (4 September 1995).

78. Border Crossing
1.   Liam Griffin, speaking at the homecoming in Wexford town after Wexford
      won the 1996 All-Ireland.
2.   Liam Griffin, interviewed by Dermot Crowe (June 2014).
3.   'Defeats Put in Dustbin of History', *The Irish Times* (15 July 1996).

79. Banner Nirvana
1. Ger Loughnane, speaking in July 1997.
2. Scally, John, *Raising the Banner* (2001), p.58.
3. 'Hurling Through Hatred', *Sunday Independent* (18 May 2003).

80. The Empire Strikes Back
1. The Cork manager, speaking after defeating Kilkenny in the 1999 All-Ireland final.
2. Interviewed by Dermot Crowe (May 2014).

81. Derry Heirs
1. 'McNaughton to Make History', *The Mirror* (6 July 2000).
2. Interviewed by Dermot Crowe (February 2014).

82. Stars and Stripes
1. 'DJ Hits all the Right Notes', *The Irish Times* (11 September 2000).

83. Déise Delirium
1. 'A Little More Action for Kings of Munster', *Sunday Independent* (11 August 2002).
2. 'Inconsistency is a Big, Big Bugbear', *The Irish Times* (11 June 2001).
3. 'A Little More Action for Kings of Munster', *Sunday Independent* (11 August 2002).
4. 'So Good They Didn't Want to Leave', *The Irish Times* (1 July 2002).
5. 'A Little More Action for Kings of Munster', *Sunday Independent* (11 August 2002).

84. Setanta's Tears
1. 'When the Going Gets Tough', *The Irish Times* (15 September 2003).
2. 'Cody is Happy to Enjoy the Moment', *The Irish Times* (16 September 2003).
3. 'Cork Haunted by What Might Have Been', *The Irish Times* (15 September 2003).

85. Camán, Lights, Action
1. Former secretary of the Games Administration Committee, now retired, speaking in February 2006, www.breakingnews.ie.
2. 'Wexford Get Lost in the Glare of Enthusiastic Cork', *The Irish Times* (1 March 2004).
3. Interviewed by Dermot Crowe (June 2014).
4. 'Lighting the Way in an All-Ireland Final', *The Irish Times* (27 September 2013).

86. Lucky Dipper
1. 'The Ecstasy of Getting it Right on the Big Day', *The Irish Times* (28 June 2004).
2. Interviewed by Dermot Crowe (May 2014).
3. *ibid.*

87. Style Makeover
1. Newtownshandrum manager, father of Jerry and Ben O'Connor.
2. 'Shining Light of Total Hurling', *Sunday Independent* (15 February 2004).
3. *ibid.*
4. Shannon, Kieran, *Every Single Ball: The Brian Corcoran Story* (date), p. 253.

88. All Guns Blazing
1. 'Preparation the Key for Hayes, Not Reparation', *The Irish Times* (22 August 2005).
2. 'Time Running Out for Canning's Medal Hopes', *Sunday Independent* (31 July 2005).

89. No Limits
1. 'I Think We Just Wanted it More', *The Irish Times* (4 September 2006).
2. *ibid.*

90. Spring in the Step
1. Shanahan, Dan, *My Autobiography* (2010), p. 175.

91. The Masterpiece
1. 'Force of Nature,' *Irish Independent* (8 September 2008).
2. Tiernan, Damien, *The Agony and the Ecstasy* (2010), p. 275.
3. Shanahan, Dan, *My Autobiography* (2010), p. 195.
4. *ibid.*, p. 231.

92. Primal Passions
1. Quoted in, Breheny, Martin, *Cody: The Autobiography* (2009).
2, *ibid.*, p. 153.

93. The Late, Late Show
1. 'Divided by Borders, United by the Game', *Sunday Independent* (6 September 2009).
2. *ibid.*
3. *ibid.*

94. Perfect Storm
1. 'I Think We Saw Today What This Team Can Do', *The Irish Times* (6 September 2010).
2. Corbett, Lar, *All in My Head* (2012) p. 170.
3. 'Cody Had No Worry Playing Shefflin', *The Irish Times* (7 September 2010).

95. Darlin' Dubs of May
1. 'Hard Work Through Lean Years Pays Off', Michael O'Grady, speaking to Friends of Dublin Hurling website (fodh.ie) (3 May 2011).
2. 'Hard Road Pays Off for Daly as Perseverance Drives Hurling's Nearly Men into the Fast Lane', *Sunday Independent* (7 July 2011).

3.   'Furious Tyrrell Slams Cats Slipping Standards', *Irish Independent*
      (4 May 2011).
4.   *ibid*.

96. Premier Downgrade
1.   'Cody Can't Hide his Joy After Most Satisfying Victory of All', *Irish
      Independent* (5 September 2011).
2,   Corbett, Lar, *All in My Head* (2012), p. 189.
3.   Interviewed by Dermot Crowe (May 2014).
4.   *ibid*.

97. Maroon Mirage
1.   *The Irish Times* (10 July 2012)

98. Cat o' Nine Tails
1.   'Henry Shefflin Pays Tribute to Kilkenny Team After Record Ninth All-
      Ireland Medal', rte.ie (1 October 2012).
2.   *ibid*.
3.   *ibid*.

99. Blue Heaven
1.   'Capital's Crisis Compounded', *Sunday Independent* (16 January 2005).
2.   'Victorious Daly Does his Best Impression of the Strong, Silent Type', *The
      Irish Times* (8 July 2013).
3.   *ibid*.

100. Champagne Hurling
1.   'Hat-Trick Hero Makes His Mark in Style', *The Irish Times* (30 September
      2013).

Bibliography

Byrnes, Ollie (1996), *Against the Wind* (Dublin: Mercier Press).

Carey, Tim (2004), *Croke Park: A History* (Cork: The Collins Press).

Cody, Joe (2009), *The Stripy Men: Kilkenny's Hurling Story to 2008* (MacÓda Publishing).

Conwell, John Joe (2008), *Hearts of Oak: The Rise to Glory of Portumna GAA Club*.

Courtney, Sean and Medcalf, David (2005), *Purple and Gold: A Photographic Record of Gaelic Games in Wexford*.

Cronin, Mike, Murphy, William and Rouse, Paul (eds) (2009), *The Gaelic Athletic Association 1884–2009* (Dublin: Irish Academic Press).

de Burca, Marcus (1980), *The GAA: A History* (Dublin: Gill & Macmillan).

Donegan, Des (ed.) (2009), *The Complete Handbook of Gaelic Games* (DBA Publications).

Dorgan, Val (1980), *Christy Ring* (Ward River Press).

Duggan, Keith (2002), *The Lifelong Season* (Dublin: TownHouse).

Duignan, Michael (2011), *Life, Death & Hurling* (ISP).

Farrell, Cyril (1994), *The Right to Win* (Dublin: Blackwater Press).

Fogarty, Philip (Canon) (1960), *Tipperary's GAA Story* (Tipperary: *The Tipperary Star*).

Fullam, Brendan (1991), *Giants of the Ash* (Dublin: Wolfhound Press).

Fullam, Brendan (1996), *Giants of the Ash* (Glory Press).

— (1994), *Hurling Giants* (Dublin: Wolfhound Press).

— (1999), *Off the Field and On: Triumphs and Trials of Gaelic Games* (Dublin: Wolfhound Press).

— (2009), *Lest We Forget: Gems of Gaelic Games and Those Who Made Them* (Cork: The Collins Press).

Harrington, John (2011), *Doyle: The Greatest Hurling Story Ever Told* (ISP).

Horgan, Tim (2007), *Christy Ring: Hurling's Greatest* (Cork: The Collins Press).

— (2010), *Cork's Hurling Story* (Cork: The Collins Press).

Keane, Colm (2002), *Hurling's Top 20* (Mainstream Publishing).

Kearns, Christy and Maeve (2008), *The History of the GAA in Meelick-Eyrecourt-Clonfert 1884–2007*.

Kenny, Thomas (1928), *Tour of the Tipperary Hurling Team in America* (London: G. Roberts).

King, Seamus (1996), *A History of Hurling* (Dublin: Gill & Macmillan).

Lawlor, Damian (2014), *Fields of Fire* (Dublin: Transworld Ireland).

Leahy, Seamus (1995), *The Tipp Revival: Return to Glory 1987–1994* (Dublin: Gill & Macmillan).

Lennon, Joe (2000), *A Comparative Analysis of the Playing Rules of Football and Hurling 1884–1999* (NRC).

Martin, Henry (2011), *Mick Mackey: Hurling Legend in a Troubled County* (Cork: The Collins Press).

McAnallen, Donal, Hassan David and Hegarty Roddy (eds) (2009), *The Evolution of the GAA* (Comhairle Uldah CLG).

McEvoy, Enda (2012), *The Godfather of Modern Hurling: The Fr Tommy Meagher Story* (Ballpoint Press).

McNaughton, Terence (1998), *Sambo: All or Nothing* (Dublin: Wolfhound Press)

Mehigan, P.D. (Carbery) (1940), *Hurling: Ireland's National Game* (Gaelic Publicity Services).

Murphy, Seán (ed.) (1996), *The Life and Times of Jackie Power: Prince of Hurlers* (Jackie Power Memorial Committee).

Nolan, William (ed.) (2005), *The Gaelic Athletic Association in Dublin 1884–2000* (Geography Publications).

O'Ceallaigh Seamus (1977), *Story of the GAA* (Gaelic Athletic Publications).

O'Connor, Christy (2005), *Last Man Standing* (Dublin: The O'Brien Press).

O Duill, Antoin (1984), *Famous Tullaroan*.

O'Dwyer, Michael (2006), *The History of Cricket in Kilkenny: The Forgotten Game* (O'Dwyer Books).

Ó hEithir, Breandán (1984), *Over the Bar* (Ward River Press)

O'Maolfabhail, Art (1973), *Camán: Two Thousand Years of Hurling in Ireland* (Dún Dealgan Press).

O'Neill, Phil (1931), *Twenty Years of the GAA* (*The Kilkenny Journal*).

O'Sullivan, Thomas F. (1916) *Story of the GAA*.

Potts, Sean (ed.) (2010), Voices from Croke Park (Mainstream Publishing).

Power, John P. (1941), *A Story of Champions* (Lee Press).

Puirseal, Padraig (1982), *The GAA in its Time* (the Purcell family).

Ryall, Tom (1984), *Kilkenny: The GAA Story* (Kilkenny People Printing Ltd).

Ryan, Philip F. (1973), *The Tubberadora-Boherlahan Hurling Story* (Tipperary: *The Tipperary Star*).

Smith, David (2010), *The Unconquerable Keane* (Original Writing Ltd).

Smith, Raymond (1972), *The Clash of the Ash* (Creative Press).

Sweeney, Eamonn (2002), *Munster Hurling Legends* (Dublin: The O'Brien Press).

Walsh, Denis (2005), *Hurling: The Revolution Years* (Dublin: Penguin Ireland)

Walsh, Jim (2013), *James Nowlan the Alderman and the GAA in His Time* (Kilkenny County Board).

Acknowledgements

The authors would like to acknowledge the people whose help made this venture possible. We are especially grateful to Hachette Books Ireland for taking on the book, and, in particular, we would like to thank our publisher Ciara Considine, and editorial and PR executive Joanna Smyth. They were the source of much encouragement and assistance along the way. A special word of thanks goes to Seamus O'Doherty for taking on the task of reading the work in progress. Like the best hurlers, his eye was always in.

There were many others who kindly gave of their time in interviews or helping in various ways such as sourcing old photographs, programmes and match reports. We would like to acknowledge the generous assistance of the following and offer an apology in advance to anyone we may have overlooked:

Dick Walshe, Shem Downey (RIP), Ann Downey, Mick Lanigan, Eddie Nolan, Paddy Burtchaell, Donal McAnallen, JJ Kennedy, Liam Griffin, Ned Wheeler, Tony Wall, Pat O'Connor, Len Gaynor, Sambo McNaughton, Michael Duignan, Danny Morrissey, Stephen McNamara, Eamon Taaffe, John O'Dwyer, Jimmy Gray, Milo Hennessy, Willie O'Connor, Michael Cleary, Ger Cunningham, Benny Dunne, George Cunningham, Damien Martin, Mick Minogue, Pat Daly, Damien Fitzhenry, Wayne Sherlock, Liam O'Donoghue, Pat Bracken, Nicholas Furlong, Pat Nolan, Grainne Doran, Des Brennan, Jim Walsh, Seán Ó Súilleabháin. The staff at the National Library in Dublin provided much appreciated assistance and advice